D1453111

This is the first comprehensive study in English of one of the most important bodies of verse in European literature. Seventeenth-century Spanish poetry represents the culmination of a rich Renaissance tradition, and Professor Terry sets out to make this accessible not only to Hispanists but to readers of English, French and Italian poetry, with which it had many points of contact. He deals both with the major poets – Góngora, Lope de Vega, Quevedo, Sor Juana Inés de la Cruz – and with the impressively large number of good minor poets, from the Argensolas to Bocángel and Soto de Rojas, whose work is still relatively little read. Drawing upon recent developments in literary criticism as well as paying close attention to individual poems, the book discusses a wide range of issues including the re-working of classical and Renaissance models, the importance of rhetoric, and the relationship between author, poem and reader.

SEVENTEENTH-CENTURY SPANISH POETRY

SEVENTEENTH-CENTURY SPANISH POETRY

The power of artifice

ARTHUR TERRY

Professor of Literature, University of Essex

CAMBRIDGE
UNIVERSITY PRESS

Published by the Press Syndicate of the University of Cambridge
The Pitt Building, Trumpington Street, Cambridge CB2 1RP
40 West 20th Street, New York, NY 10011-4211, USA
10 Stamford Road, Oakleigh, Melbourne 3166, Australia

First published 1993

Printed in Great Britain at the University Press, Cambridge

A catalogue record for this book is available from the British Library

Library of Congress cataloguing in publication data
Terry, Arthur.
Seventeenth-century Spanish poetry: the power of artifice /
Arthur Terry.
p.   cm.
Includes bibliographical references and index.
ISBN 0 521 44421 7 (hardback)
1. Spanish poetry – Classical period, 1500–1700 – History and
criticism.   1. Title
PQ6081.T47   1993
861'.309 – dc20   92-40121   CIP

ISBN 0 521 44421 7 hardback

For Molly

Contents

Preface

My first idea for a book on the lines of the present one came at the end of the 1960s. In 1967, I had completed what professed to be a critical anthology of sixteenth- and seventeenth-century Spanish poetry – now long since, alas, out of print – which aimed at presenting something of the range, as well as the quality, of the best verse of the period, along with a brief account of Renaissance poetics and its impact in Spain. Like most anthologies, mine had its limitations: the decision to print only complete poems meant excluding a number of important longer works, and one whole genre – the literary epic – had to be omitted altogether. The next step, therefore, seemed to be a book which would make good such omissions and at the same time allow more space for discussing actual poems. Two considerations, in particular, gave conviction to the project: one was the awareness that most university students of Spanish, because of the limited nature of academic courses, were seldom encouraged to go beyond the work of a few major poets and so could have little idea of the richness of the period as a whole; the other was the wish to provide readers of other poetry of the time – English, French, Italian – with an accessible and reasonably detailed account of the corresponding Spanish poetry – in other words, to bring Spanish poetry, for all its distinctiveness, a little closer to the general European context.

Though neither of these concerns has lost its urgency, the book which has finally emerged differs from my original conception in several ways. For one thing, it deals almost entirely with seventeenth-century poetry, even though, as my first chapter should make clear, the roots of that poetry go back through earlier Renaissance verse and, in some instances, to the late Middle Ages. To retrace those earlier stages in equal detail, however, would require a book to itself, though parts of my own discussion may help to suggest what such a book might be like. Moreover, the fact that for various reasons –

other commitments, other interests – my original project was post-poned until fairly recently has meant coming to terms with two whole decades of scholarship and criticism, often of a kind which could hardly have been foreseen in the 1960s. To begin with, there has been a striking increase in editions of individual poets: better editions of major poets like Herrera and Lope de Vega, as well as the first serious editions of many good minor poets whose work had previously been relatively inaccessible or vitiated by textual errors. And more crucially still, the work of certain British and American scholars – Terence Cave, Brian Vickers, Thomas Greene and Stephen Green-blatt, among others – has called into question many of the traditional commonplaces concerning Renaissance poetry and poetics in ways that can often enhance one's reading of the poems themselves.

One result of this, as I explain in my second chapter, has been a greater awareness of the function of rhetoric, not only as the means of constructing a poem, but as something which determines the whole nature of the relationship between author, poem and reader. Another has been the reassessment of key concepts such as imitation and decorum, whose implications go far beyond the narrow textbook definitions of the time in ways which, properly understood, can be seen as central to an entire culture.

All this may seem to lead to a paradox: Renaissance culture is not our own, and the more accurately one understands it, the more 'strange' it can come to seem. For a modern reader, this is both a source of difficulty and a challenge. Certain difficulties, as I argue at one point, can be explained, though they should never be explained away: though we can never see into the minds of seventeenth-century readers, we can at least develop what Rosemond Tuve calls a 'working contemporaneity' with the poems they read – not in order to reduce them to museum pieces, but as a way of recognizing the real sources of their strength. One way of evading the challenge, on the other hand, is to praise certain kinds of poem for their 'modernity' – a sure sign, more often than not, that we have assimilated them too easily. In other words, if we can pass from such poems to post-Romantic poems without experiencing some sort of shock, it almost certainly mean that we have been misreading them. Conversely, what we might come to value in poems of the period is precisely the sense of 'otherness', the fact that such fine poetry has been written on assumptions which actively question our own ideas about the nature of poetic writing. In this connection, it is worth recalling that the notion of cultural shock applies even more forcibly to the Renaissance itself. Thus the American scholar Thomas Greene contrasts our present way of assimilating other cultures with the 'shock of confrontation' experienced by early Renaissance writers when faced with the fragmentary yet compelling evidence of the classical world: 'Our easy contemporary way of acculturating the remote, appropriating the shards of all eras, costs us that shock of confrontation which might assist us to situate ourselves more knowingly in time, might help us uncover the vulnerabilities of our own specific historicity.'[1] And this, perhaps, is the essential point: to be able to 'situate ourselves more knowingly in time' is surely no bad aim, and if reading the poetry of the past with sympathy, but also with a due sense of distances as well as proximities, is one way of doing this, then it seems well worth the effort.

Whether the present book will make the effort any easier is another matter. Any study of this kind is bound to have its limitations, not all of which can be put down to reasons of space. Though I have tried hard to suggest the extraordinary range of seventeenth-century Spanish poetry – a range only equalled, it seems to me, by the English poetry of the time – I have not attempted to be encyclopedic: not every minor poet finds a place in my account, and I have done no more than hint at the vast penumbra of popular poetry which extends far beyond the more sophisticated poetry of the period and of which no serious poet could fail to be conscious. As in my earlier anthology, it seemed important to keep a balance between the major poets and the impressively large number of good minor ones, from the Argensolas to Bocángel and Soto de Rojas, whose work is still relatively little read. Thus, to a specialist eye, my chapters on the major poets may seem over-selective or, worse still, perfunctory; where writers like Góngora and Quevedo are concerned, one could nearly always have chosen different poems to discuss, or have said more about those one did choose. And much the same applies to the scholars and critics on whose work I have drawn throughout: these represent only a small proportion of those from whom I have learnt in one way or another over the years, but are quoted here both for the intelligence of their insights and as an indication of what, to my mind, are the most interesting developments in recent criticism.

My only justification is that such risks seemed worth taking in the attempt to produce a manageable and not overly specialized account of an outstanding body of verse which is still too little known outside the circle of Spanish readers and professional Hispanists. If, as Henry Gifford once remarked, European poetry is 'a single literature using a diversity of tongues',[2] it is surely time for the distinctive tones of seventeenth-century Spanish verse to be heard more clearly beyond their national limits – a possibility I have tried to keep firmly in mind in writing the present book.

Finally, I must express my gratitude to Professor Trevor Dadson for advice on some difficult problems of translation and to Professor Gareth Walters, who read the complete manuscript and made a number of valuable suggestions for improvement. (What errors and shortcomings remain, needless to say, are entirely my own.) My greatest debt, however, is to my wife, who has helped me in countless ways over the years, and to whom the book is dedicated as a small return for her patience and encouragement.

ARTHUR TERRY

Abbreviations

AEF	*Anuario de Estudios Filológicos*
BAE	*Biblioteca de Autores Españoles*
BH	*Bulletin Hispanique*
BHS	*Bulletin of Hispanic Studies*
CC	Clásicos castellanos
CCa	Clásicos Castalia
CSIC	Consejo Superior de Investigaciones Científicas
Fi	*Filología*
HR	*Hispanic Review*
JMRS	*Journal of Medieval and Renaissance Studies*
LH	Letras Hispánicas
MHRA	Modern Humanities Research Association
MLN	*Modern Language Notes*
MLR	*Modern Language Review*
MPh	*Modern Philology*
PMLA	*Publications of the Modern Language Association of America*
RF	*Romanische Forschungen*
RFE	*Revista de Filología Española*
RLC	*Revue de Littérature Comparée*
RoN	*Romance Notes*
SP	*Studies in Philology*

The inheritance

1

Most of the poems discussed in this book were written between 1580 and 1650. There is a good reason for this: quite simply, that the first half of the seventeenth century saw a concentration of poetic talent which is unique in the history of Spanish literature, though the roots of what was achieved lay firmly embedded in the previous century. Again, if one thinks in terms of individual writers, the matter of dates becomes clearer: of the three major poets of the period, Luis de Góngora (1561–1627) and Lope de Vega (1562–1635) both began their literary careers in 1580 or shortly after; Francisco de Quevedo, the youngest – born, by coincidence, in 1580 – lived on until 1645, by which time the poetic tradition itself seemed to be nearing exhaustion. Yet, even so, the situation is by no means clear-cut: the dramatic verse of Calderón (1600–81) triumphantly prolongs the dominant poetic mode well into the second half of the century and, later still, the work of the Mexican poet Sor Juana Inés de la Cruz (1648–95) shows that earlier seventeenth-century practice was still very much alive for anyone with sufficient skill and intelligence to learn from it.

It is at the beginning of the period, however, that one needs to make most qualifications. If 1580 is a useful working date – it also marks the appearance of Herrera's famous commentary on the work of Garcilaso de la Vega (1501?–36), the first great poet of the Spanish Renaissance – it in no sense interrupts the feeling of continuity which must have been as evident at the time as it is now. A modern reader, as I shall argue, may justifiably regard the last two decades of the sixteenth century as a transitional period, a phase of interesting cross-currents and innovations. For a young poet setting out to write at the time, however, the important thing, almost certainly, would have been his sense of coming to a flexible and well-established poetic tradition, one which, moreover, had the advantage of embodying several separate, though compatible, lines of force. At this stage, the most powerful of these was the type of Italianate verse established fifty years earlier by Garcilaso and still practised, with few variations, by Herrera himself and other poets of his generation. 'Italianate verse', in this context, means much more than the adoption of certain metres and forms – the sonnet, the ode, the elegy, the eclogue; it brings with it a commitment to the imagery and attitudes of what is generally termed 'the Petrarchan tradition', a mode of writing which goes back beyond Petrarch himself to the conventions of medieval courtly poetry and which is further refined in the sixteenth century by contact with Renaissance neo-Platonism. In its more sophisticated forms, such verse is also able to assimilate certain classical Latin poets, notably Virgil and Horace, and to take account of more recent Italian writers like Sannazaro, Bembo and Della Casa.

Yet one of the strengths of this kind of poetry – and certainly one of the reasons for its success in sixteenth-century Spain – is that it overlaps to a considerable extent with the much older love poetry of the fifteenth-century *cancioneros* or songbooks. It has often been noted, for example, that one of the books of poems most frequently reprinted in the sixteenth century was the *Cancionero general* of Hernando del Castillo (1511), an extensive anthology of fifteenth-century verse, both lyrical and didactic, which continued to form part of the basic literary culture of poets and their readers until well after 1600. This fact was immensely more important for the development of Spanish poetry than any initial opposition to Italianate verse. However committed they may have seemed to the new kind of writing, there were few important poets of the sixteenth and seventeenth centuries who did not make use on occasion of the more traditional metres or *versos castellanos*, and many continued to alternate between the two with no sense of inconsistency.

Forty-four years after the death of Garcilaso, the *Anotaciones* of Fernando de Herrera (1534–97) present him as the first classic of Spanish Renaissance poetry: 'classic', that is to say, in the sense that he deserves to be imitated in the same spirit as Petrarch or Virgil. Yet Herrera's vast commentary is more than just the tribute of one poet to the master of his own generation; his admiration is occasionally tempered by criticism, both of Garcilaso and of Petrarch himself:

not every thought and consideration of Love and of those other matters which concern poetry occurred to the minds of Petrarch, Bembo and the ancients. For the argument of Love is so diverse and abundant, and of such volume in itself, that no wit can embrace it entirely; rather is occasion left for their successors to achieve that which it seems impossible they should have left untouched.[1]

Herrera in 1580, therefore, is able to acclaim a body of poetry whose achievement justifies the kind of detailed attention to be found in his own commentary, and at the same time to foresee the possibility of future development. If, as Christopher Ricks has said, 'great poetry is created from the tension between what has been done and what is to be done',[2] the real lesson of the *Anotaciones* is that Garcilaso, precisely because of his greatness, demands to be treated as a living model – in other words, as a poet whose strengths and occasional weaknesses can be equally instructive to later poets.

Herrera insists more than any other sixteenth-century Spanish poet on the purity of poetic diction and, as we shall see, both the strengths and limitations of his own poetry are entirely consistent with his theoretical views. Moreover, his criteria exclude altogether one of the most vital influences on sixteenth-century poetry, the popular lyric and its narrative counterpart, the traditional ballad. Like the more sophisticated poetry of the *cancioneros*, a large body of popular verse was available to sixteenth-century poets in the form of anthologies like the *Cancionero de romances* (Antwerp, c. 1547–9) and through the settings of composers like Juan Vásquez and Luis Milán. The question of literary status is important here: though the finest of the traditional ballads, or *romances viejos*, were composed well before 1500, their prestige, as against their popularity, remained a little uncertain until the early sixteenth century, partly because of their relative metrical freedom. Menéndez Pidal, the greatest authority on the Spanish ballad, places the period of their greatest popularity between 1515 and 1580, that is to say, at a time when the composition of new *romances viejos* had virtually ceased. The crucial factor, however, is that the conditions for oral performance remained constant; as Pidal himself explains, 'the greatest poets of the nation carried in their memories the ancient ballad creations, transmitted by oral tradition, not learnt by reading printed collections'.[3] And the proof of this comes in the second half of the sixteenth century, with the appearance of the *romance nuevo* or *romance artístico*, the conscious imitation of the traditional ballad, which was to achieve a new kind of artistic success after 1580 in the work of Góngora and Lope de Vega.

As for the status of the popular lyric, or *poesía de tipo tradicional*, this is much less in doubt than that of the ballad. In the last quarter of the fifteenth century, it formed an essential part of the revival of court music under Ferdinand and Isabella and was taken up on a large scale by the dramatists of the early sixteenth century: Encina, Lucas Fernández and, above all, Gil Vicente. The basic patterns of such poetry go back to the early Middle Ages and remained alive until well into the seventeenth century. Though individual poems vary, their essential nucleus is the short opening stanza known as the *villancico*, which is glossed in a number of stanzas, each with a refrain or *estribillo* which refers back to the original *villancico*. Thus the opening sequence of a poem by Juan del Encina (1468–1529?) runs:

> No te tardes que me muero,   (*villancico*)
> carcelero,
> no te tardes que me muero.
>
> Apresura tu venida   (*glosa*)
> porque no pierda la vida,
> que la fe no está perdida.
>
> Carcelero,   (*estribillo*)
> no te tardes que me muero...

Do not be long, I am dying, gaoler; do not be long, I am dying. Come quickly, that I may not lose my life, for I have not lost faith. Gaoler, do not be long, I am dying...

The musical possibilities of such verse were not lost on later poets; the *villancico*, like the short metres of the *cancionero* lyrics, continues to flourish long after Italianate poetry has become the dominant mode. Again, one is struck by the number of poets in the later part of the sixteenth century – Cervantes is a good example – who move freely between one kind of writing and another. Nevertheless, what is distinctive about a great deal of seventeenth-century poetry is something rather different: namely, the ability to combine both the popular and the sophisticated in a single poem, to create complex verse while preserving the lightness of tone one associates with the *villancico* and the ballad.

All that has been said so far relates in the first place to secular verse. When one turns to sixteenth-century religious poetry, it is harder to know what would have been likely to claim the attention of a poet writing in the 1580s. Compared with the seventeenth century, one cannot fail to notice how relatively few secular poets before 1600 also wrote religious verse. The two great religious poets of the sixteenth century, Fray Luis de León (1527–91) and San Juan de la Cruz (1542–91), were both members of religious orders. Neither, to be sure, was unaware of developments in secular poetry. In the present context, though, such matters may seem irrelevant, since neither poet's work was published in his own lifetime. Yet Luis de León's poetry was not entirely unknown to his contemporaries, and that of San Juan represents, though admittedly at a far higher level, a poetic tendency one meets throughout the sixteenth century and which has its origin in the medieval practice of composing religious verse on the basis of existing secular poems.

This technique can be seen at its simplest in the poem by Santa Teresa de Jesús (1515–82) beginning 'Véante mis ojos, / dulce Jesús bueno' (Let my eyes behold you, good sweet Jesus), which is a spiritualized version of an older love poem: 'Véante mis ojos / y muérame yo luego' (Let my eyes behold you and may I then die). Such *a lo divino* poems or *contrafacta*, to use the term suggested by Bruce Wardropper, were mostly intended to be sung to popular tunes, the only exceptions being those based on the work of Italianate poets, like the sacred versions of Boscán and Garcilaso by Sebastián de Córdoba (1575), which are thought to have influenced San Juan himself. It would be a mistake to overrate such poetry: though certain examples remain fresh and memorable, most of it is mediocre and at worst parasitic. At the same time, it would be equally wrong to ignore the existence of a familiar type of devotional poetry which must have helped to prepare many people's minds for more serious verse and which was clearly read and absorbed by some of the finest poets of the next century.

II

These, roughly, are the various strands which go to make up the tradition of Spanish poetry as it might have appeared towards the end of the sixteenth century – the types of poetry which could be taken for granted, and which seemed to hold the most vigorous possibilities for the future. Yet can one be certain that this is how it looked to a contemporary? Here we are faced with a problem which has already been touched on in connection with Luis de León and San Juan de la Cruz: namely, that no sixteenth- or seventeenth-century reader could have known more than a fraction of the range of poetry which is available to a modern reader.[4] What this meant for contemporary readers is hard to gauge, but it should at least prevent us from regarding Golden Age poetry as a unified body of work of which every single poet would be wholly aware. It is more helpful, in fact, to think of poets working in a number of centres, often geographically remote from one another, and only occasionally, as in Andalusia, forming a wider pattern. Given such fragmentation, in a country over four times the size of England, the degree of unity which undoubtedly existed may seem remarkable. By 1580, certainly, the sense of a strong and fertile tradition may well have been sufficient to ensure continuity and, if the most significant developments of the next half-century were registered slowly and unevenly, one may feel that the variety and distinctiveness of the poetry which resulted could hardly have been achieved in different circumstances.

If we regard seventeenth-century poetry as the final stage in a process which begins with Garcilaso and with the revaluation of certain kinds of popular poetry, one obvious question arises, namely, to what extent can its eventual decline be associated with the fortunes of Spain itself? There is no clear answer to this. Several recent historians, notably J. H. Elliott, have gone so far as to question the concept of 'decline' itself, or rather to limit the area in which such a concept could have a valid meaning. On this view, it would be wrong to make too much of the differences, however real, between Habsburg Spain and the rest of Europe. As Elliott himself observes:

At the end of the sixteenth century there was no particular reason to believe that the future development of the Peninsula would diverge so markedly from that of other parts of Western Europe as it was later to do. Habsburg Spain had, after all, set the pace for the rest of Europe in the elaboration of new techniques of administration to cope with the problems of governing a world-wide Empire. The Spain of Philip II would seem to have had as good a chance as the France of Henry III of making the transition to the modern centralized State.[5]

The fact remains, then, that at least until the 1640s, Spain still appeared a great power in the eyes of the rest of the world. This means that, however far back one traces the sense of national crisis – to, for example, the reactions to the defeat of the Armada (1588) or to the economic warnings of late sixteenth-century social analysts – there was always a feeling that the solutions of the reign of Philip II, based on military achievement and religious unity, could still be made to work. When the reverse is felt to be the case, the result is not a desire for radical change, but a sense of frustration and disillusionment which finds its way into much of the writing of the time.

If one asks what kind of a society it was in which such writing took shape, the answers are even less easy to come by, and any generalizations at all may seem out of place. Nevertheless, there are several features which suggest, if not the quality of that society, at least the kind of public for whom literature held some interest. One of these – the frequent geographical isolation of one group of writers from another – has already been mentioned, and it is a question to which we shall have to return in considering the relationship between poets and their audiences. Another is the growing importance of Madrid, especially after the turn of the century: a late capital, by European standards, but one which for that reason attracted both men and wealth in increasing quantities at precisely the period we are concerned with.[6]

More important, perhaps, in the long run, the balance of Castilian society was changing. One major factor here is Philip III's decision to admit the higher aristocracy to the centre of government; the fact that so many of the nobility of the time were encouraged to neglect or abandon their estates can only have added to the difficulties of the already depopulated rural areas. Industry and commerce suffered similar neglect, a process which also deeply affected the nature of the middle classes. By 1600, except in seaports like Barcelona, Valencia and Seville, the old merchant class had virtually ceased to exist: the great commercial centres of the north – Burgos, Medina del Campo, Valladolid – had lost their prosperity to Madrid, and most towns in the interior suffered a similar eclipse. The new middle class, on the other hand, relied for its wealth, not on trade or industry, but on investment and speculation. Moreover, this new and economically unproductive bourgeoisie was a poor breeding ground for writers; as far as one can tell, no important poet born after 1600 comes from this kind of background, though quite a number of the previous generation, including Cervantes and Lope de Vega, had their origins in the older type of middle class. And, though it would be rash to accuse an entire social class of indifference to literature (these same people must have comprised a large proportion of seventeenth-century theatre audiences), it is likely that its main contribution was to provide the reality on which a great deal of seventeenth-century satirical writing is based.

To know something about the society in which a poet lives is hardly enough to explain why he writes the kind of poems he does, or why certain circumstances should be more favourable than others for the writing of poetry. At the same time, if more general speculations concerning the relations between literature and society raise too many imponderables, it is important to recognize that there *were* certain features of seventeenth-century society which affected the actual writing of poetry, though not necessarily its quality.

The important question here is the relationship between poet and audience. One aspect of this has already been mentioned in passing: the fact that no single reader at the time could have known more than a small proportion of the poetry which is accessible to a modern reader. The conclusion, therefore, seems inescapable: though the work of certain older writers was freely available – the poems of Boscán and Garcilaso de la Vega (1543) and the *Cancionero general* (1511), both reprinted many times in the course of the sixteenth century, are obvious examples – a poet's readers were more often than not personal acquaintances – friends, other poets, and occasionally enemies, all of whom could be assumed to possess a certain literary education. This is perhaps hardly surprising in a society with a high rate of illiteracy. It would be a mistake, even so, to equate illiteracy with lack of culture; one of the refreshing things about Habsburg Spain, as about Tudor England, is the persistence of a strong and lively oral tradition on which serious poets were prepared to draw. Yet the fact remains that, as far as sophisticated poetry was concerned, audiences, however discriminating, were small, and a poet's reputation often depended more on praise at second- or third-hand than on close acquaintance with his actual poems.

In this world of limited audiences, two features stand out: the growth of patronage and the vogue of literary academies. Neither of these institutions is exclusively Spanish, nor are they confined to the seventeenth century, though their increasing importance bears at least some relation to changes which were taking place in society around 1600.

Of the two, patronage is the more difficult for a modern reader to regard sympathetically, partly because of the degree of flattery it entails. There is no denying the amount of trivial and sycophantic versifying such a system encouraged, and it can be disturbing to find a poet of the stature of Góngora addressing the unscrupulous and incompetent Duke of Lerma as a paragon of virtue. On the other hand, if we are to keep such activities in proportion, there are several things we should bear in mind. One is the practical importance for a poet of having a 'place' which would enable him to continue to write and which would occasionally give him access to the kind of library he could hardly hope to accumulate for himself. Again, in more general terms, there is no doubt that patronage, whatever its moral implications, was a natural phenomenon in an age when social values were strongly hierarchical. From this point of view, the relationship between patron and writer appears as a possibly trivial expression of something more important, a view of the world in which deference to one's superiors and the honours which ensued were a direct reflection of the belief in a universal order. Understandably, the quality of the patronage varied, from the mainly formal to the almost intimate. Though in Spain there is no equivalent to the kind of emotional relationship which existed between Tasso and the Este family or between Donne and Magdalen Herbert, the extraordinary epithalamium which Góngora wrote for an unknown aristocratic couple (see p. 76) has a depth of feeling which would be out of place in a purely formal composition, while Lope de Vega's complicity in the sexual affairs of the Duke of Sessa goes a long way beyond the requirements of a conventional master–secretary relationship.

After 1600, the most sought-after patrons tended to be those at the centre of political life: favourites and advisers like Lerma and Olivares who, whatever their shortcomings as administrators, were for the most part men of taste and learning, on friendly terms with many of the writers of the time. Even at this stage, however, not everything is centred on Madrid; though towns like Toledo, Salamanca and Valencia lose something of the cultural status they had in the sixteenth century, the economic prosperity of the south, and particularly of Seville, created an atmosphere of cultural opulence from which writers and artists continued to benefit well into the seventeenth century. In these circumstances, patronage was more localized and less dependent on the political eminence of the patron; as far back as the 1570s, Fernando de Herrera had been a member of the group of writers and painters which met at the house of the Count of Gelves, whose wife, Doña Leonor de Milán, was the chief inspiration for his love poems. At the turn of the century, the

characteristic figures are men like Juan de Arguijo (1567–1623) –
business magnate, founder of a literary academy and one of the most
accomplished minor poets of the period – and the Count of Niebla,
later Duke of Medina Sidonia, the patron of Carrillo and Espinosa
and dedicatee of Góngora's *Fábula de Polifemo y Galatea* (1613).

Already one can begin to see how patronage and the phenomenon
of literary academies worked together. More than one member of the
higher aristocracy took part in the Madrid academies of the time, the
most famous of which were founded shortly after 1600, and the
pattern is repeated, usually on a smaller scale, in several parts of the
south. Remembering the example of Herrera, it is tempting to
associate the growth of literary academies with the increasing interest
in poetic theory towards the end of the sixteenth century, and also
possibly with the rise of the drama. The history of the more important
academies is well documented; in most cases their activities followed
a similar pattern: the reading and discussion of original work,
debates on poetic theory, tributes to visiting authors and the
organization of verse competitions.[7] In a situation where opportunities for publishing were limited, the existence of such meeting
places for poets and other writers was clearly valuable, though the
extent to which the academies actually encouraged good writing is
harder to judge. The presence of a Cervantes or a Lope de Vega
(both of whom are known to have attended sessions of academies in
Madrid) must have made a difference; too often, however, such
details as were recorded suggest that a great deal of time was spent on
pedantries and uncritical praise. The fashion, at all events, was in
decline by the 1630s; yet while it lasted, it supplied at least one kind
of cohesion at a time of intense, if scattered, poetic activity.

III

These, then are some of the material factors which concern the
writing of poetry in Spain in the seventeenth and late sixteenth
centuries. Beyond them, as in other Western European countries, lies
a whole range of knowledge and attitudes which contribute to the
mental climate of the period, but whose effect on poetry is much
harder to estimate. In describing the tensions of Spanish political life
under the Habsburgs, J. H. Elliott speaks of 'the continuing interplay
between the ambitions and commitments of a European-minded

dynasty and the responses and resistances of a relatively inflexible and still largely medieval society'.[8] Inflexibility may well have been one of the weaknesses which distinguished Spain from other countries in the seventeenth century; the persistence of medieval attitudes, on the other hand, is such a basic feature of the Renaissance period as a whole that one could hardly expect Spain to be an exception. The fact that fifteenth-century forms and concepts survive in the poetry of the following century is only one aspect of the process by which the Middle Ages were absorbed by the Renaissance. This is not to underrate the achievement of the Renaissance, but rather to set it in the kind of perspective which has been created in more recent times. As Peter Burke has remarked: 'In 1860, Jacob Burckhardt saw the Renaissance as essentially modern: a modern culture created by a modern society. In the 1970s it does not look modern any more. This change is due in part to more than a century of research on continuities between the Middle Ages and the Renaissance, but much more to the change in our conception of the modern.'[9] This need not prevent one from feeling that certain seventeenth-century poets – Quevedo, for example – can speak at times in what seems a distinctly 'modern' voice, though even here one has to be careful not to oversimplify. What it does mean is that, however much actual poetic techniques may change, the majority of Golden Age writers continue to accept a body of ideas, on subjects from kingship to the nature of sexual love, which is still basically medieval.

From a literary point of view, the continuing existence of a coherent body of ideas concerning the nature of man and his place in the universe – ideas which, moreover, could be conveyed by means of easily comprehensible analogies – was both a source of confidence and an unfailing reservoir of poetic imagery. Yet, even if the body of accepted ideas remains fairly constant, it is possible for its actual status to be challenged and revalued. Something like this happens, in fact, in the second half of the sixteenth century, as a result of the Counter-Reformation, some of whose doctrines have important implications for the arts in general.

These doctrines were embodied in the decrees of the Council of Trent (1545–63): their overall effect was to elevate the function of art by enlisting it in the service of Catholicism, while at the same time denying its exclusively aesthetic appeal. The consequences of this for the visual arts were immense, particularly in Spain and Italy. For a long time it was assumed that the effect on secular literature was equally direct: that, for example, a very deliberate attempt was made to 'christianize' both prose and verse and to drive unsuitable books out of circulation by means of censorship. This view has recently been challenged, with great cogency, by Peter Russell, who points out how little importance was given to censorship by the members of the Council, and how restricted were the types of books actually prohibited.[10] Similarly, it would be wrong to suppose that the vogue for *a lo divino* poetry already mentioned was part of a conscious effort to replace secular poems for moral reasons. As John Crosbie has made clear, the moralists of the time never refer to such poetry, and many of the writers of religious *villancicos* seem to have been more concerned with taking over secular tunes than with the systematic re-wording of a particular poem.[11] Moreover, the fact that a work like Sebastián de Córdoba's *a lo divino* version of Boscán and Garcilaso (1575) is clearly meant to be read in conjunction with the original poems suggests that for many such writers the interest of the genre lay, not so much in its moral possibilities, as in the scope it offered for parody and other types of verbal ingenuity.

What is more important here, in short, is the existence of a kind of wit which relies on the disparity between religious language and the secular context on which it builds. The latter need not be an actual poem: it is enough that there should be a reference to familiar experience or to commonplace objects. The kind of homely imagery this entails is a regular feature of popular preaching, in the Counter-Reformation period as at other times; poetic form merely sharpens the parallels and makes it possible to deploy them at greater length. Thus José de Valdivielso (1562?–1638), one of the outstanding religious poets of the early seventeenth century, compares Christ on the Cross to a swimmer:

> Como nadador
> los heridos brazos abre,
> por sacar a nado el hombre
> que dicen que iba a anegarse.

Like a swimmer he opens his wounded arms to bring man, whom they say was drowning, to shore.

Clearly, there is nothing sophisticated about this: the basic simile is arresting, as it is meant to be – so much so that the 'witty' explanation which follows seems flat by comparison. (Notice, however, the effect of 'dicen' (they say) in establishing an easy relationship between poet and audience.) Yet the technique is identical with that used by Lope de Vega in a much finer poem:

> Pastor que con tus silbos amorosos
> me despertaste del profundo sueño;
> tú, que hiciste cayado de ese leño
> en que tiendes los brazos poderosos...

Shepherd, who with your fond whistling awoke me from deep sleep; you, who made a crook out of that piece of wood on which you stretch your powerful arms...

Such homely images appear constantly in late sixteenth-century devotional writing, and often give rise to a type of extended metaphor calculated to appeal to popular taste. Some of the most ingenious examples appear in the poems of Alonso de Ledesma (1562–1633), whose *Conceptos espirituales* (1600) and later collections were widely read in the seventeenth century. Ledesma is often thought of wrongly as an *a lo divino* poet; his usual technique, rather, is to take a homely comparison and to work it out in minute detail. So in one of his poems, Christ appears as a visitor to a university which is in need of reform:

> El reformador de escuelas
> entró víspera de Pascua,
> a fin de poner en orden
> la universidad humana...

The reformer of schools arrived on Christmas Eve to set in order the human university...

and the basic metaphor is developed through various kinds of academic terminology for over 200 lines. The didactic purpose of such a poem is obvious; nevertheless, the fact that Ledesma's *Juegos de Noche Buena moralizados* (Christmas Eve Games Moralized; 1611) was placed on the Index in 1667 suggests that such verses may have been read more for their facile ingenuity than for their moral lesson. What is certain, however, is that the poems of Ledesma were read by other, greater poets and that both homely imagery and ingeniously extended metaphor account for some of the most striking effects in seventeenth-century verse.

Both these tendencies owe something to the mood of late sixteenth-century popular religion, though their roots go back to the medieval doctrine of 'prefiguration'. This habit of seeing images and events of the Gospels as symbolically anticipated in those of the Old Testament – of associating the tree in the Garden of Eden with the Cross, or of drawing parallels between Noah and Christ – is inevitably committed to the production of ingenious conceits. Speaking of Christ, Luis de León, for example, writes: 'At other times, He is called "house of wine", as in the Song of Songs [i.e. Solomon 2.4]...as if one were to say the store and treasure house of all joys',[12] and the reference is taken up again by Pedro de Espinosa (1578–1650) in the second of his two 'Psalmos':

> El generoso vino, alegremente,
> de tu botillería
> robó mis ojos de la luz del día.

The generous wine from your wine-shop happily robbed my eyes of the light of day.

The force of such images depends on centuries of biblical exegesis, and also on the capacity of a contemporary reader to grasp spontaneously a type of connection which may now seem strained or merely pedantic. What has been lost, of course, is a habit of mind to which everything is potentially religious and most things in practice are symbolic. In Spain, as in other European countries, this spirit persisted into the second half of the seventeenth century and even, in some instances, later. And, while it lasts, it helps to account for the ease with which the same writers are able to use both secular and religious imagery in their poems.

If one looks for specific influences of the Counter-Reformation mentality on poetry, one is likely to find them, not in the effect of actual dogma, but in the language of popular spirituality, and in the type of meditation encouraged by religious manuals of the time. Here the outstanding example is one of the crucial documents of the Counter-Reformation, the *Spiritual Exercises* (1548) of St Ignatius Loyola, the founder of the Jesuit Order. This also builds on medieval practice; yet what is important is not so much the presence of traditional habits of prayer, as the way these are worked into a systematic technique for meditation. In the Ignatian scheme, the meditator prepares for his exercise in two 'preludes', and in the first of these, he attempts to visualize the subject of his meditation – either an episode from the life of Christ or some more general theme. This preliminary process is known as the 'composition of place'. In the meditation itself, the three powers of the soul – memory, understanding and will – are applied to the subject which has already been evoked; in the final stage, the exercise of the will involves a decision to act on the basis of the understanding, and the meditation ends with a 'colloquy' addressed to Christ on the Cross. The words of the text suggest the tone to be adopted: 'The colloquy is properly made by speaking as one friend speaks to another, or as a servant to his master; at one time asking for some favour, or at another blaming oneself for some evil committed, now informing him of one's affairs and seeking counsel in them.'

In the present context, what is important is that two features of the technique – the insistence on mental images and the final colloquy – can be applied equally well to the composition of a poem. Often the colloquy occupies the whole poem, as in the following sonnet by Bartolomé Leonardo de Argensola (1562–1631) on the Agony in the Garden:

> ¿Qué estrategema hacéis, guerrero mío?
> Mas antes, ¿qué inefable sacramento?
> ¡Que os bañe en sangre sólo el pensamiento
> de que se llega el plazo al desafío!
>
> Derramad de vuestra alma otro rocío
> que aduerma o arme al flaco sentimiento;
> mas vos queréis que vuestro sufrimiento
> no cobre más esfuerzo por cobrar más brío.
>
> Que no es temor el que os abrió las venas
> y las distila por los poros rojos,
> que antes él los espíritus retira,
>
> sino como se os viene ante los ojos
> mi culpa, ardéis de generosa ira,
> y en esta lucha aumento vuestras penas.

What stratagem are you performing, o my warrior? Or rather, what unutterable sacrament? That the mere thought that the time of challenge is approaching should bathe you in blood! Scatter from your soul a different dew which will soothe or arm weak feelings; but you do not wish your suffering to receive more strength in order to increase your courage. For it is not fear which has opened your veins and which distils them through red pores, since fear, on the contrary, withdraws the spirits, but since my guilt appears before your eyes, you burn with generous anger, and in this struggle I increase your torment.

Here, the crucial question is what the image of Christ praying in the Garden of Gethsemane can mean to the sinner at the moment of writing, and it is the effort to heighten the sense of immediacy which accounts for the tone and many of the details of the poem. 'Image' suggests visualization; yet for the purpose of contemplation a single visual detail is enough: the phrase from Luke 22.44 which compares Christ's sweat to 'great drops of blood falling to the ground'. Much of the poem consists of an attempt to tease out an explanation for this one disturbing image, rather in the manner of a preacher expounding a text. At the same time, the opening lines, by insisting on terms like 'estratagema' and 'inefable sacramento', suggest that true understanding may be beyond the powers of the human intelligence. Thus the explanation which accompanies the first expression of wonder ('¡Que os bañe... al desafío!') is clearly inadequate: ordinary mortals would be likely to feel fear at the thought of execution, but not Christ. Yet in a sense, this reading is too reductive: Christ's agony, after all, is a genuine one, so that the speaker's imagination may well entertain the thought of momentary weakness. This, in fact, is the reading of the situation which is continued into the second quatrain: Christ *has* the power to overcome his own weakness (if this is what it is), but the fact that he does not choose to do so has its own explanation: 'but you do not wish your suffering to receive more strength in order to increase your (human) courage'. This has the effect of denying the speaker's own explanation at the beginning of the quatrain ('Derramad de vuestra alma otro rocío...'); by this stage we are aware that the poem's own stratagem is to embody possible misreadings of the situation by way of imitating the movements of the reflecting and all too fallible mind. Significantly, the explanation on which the poem finally comes to rest is one which directly involves the sinner himself. The idea of fear is now dismissed (it cannot be fear, since, according to Renaissance medicine, fear withdraws both heat and blood from the surface of the body); the emotion which causes Christ's suffering is 'generous anger' – anger at the speaker's sins, but 'generous' (with a hint of 'noble') since Christ will die to save sinners – and since the sinner persists in his nature, Christ's agony is increased accordingly.

Thus the poem, by entertaining a number of occasionally conflicting interpretations, arrives at a 'solution' which involves both a confession of guilt on the part of the speaker and – by implication, at least – a desire for penitence. The movements and countermovements of the speaker's logic are in themselves a dramatization of this effort to reach understanding; yet what gives a special urgency to the drama is the abrupt tone of the opening which, as in definitions of the colloquy, immediately establishes the tone of intimacy which knits together the ensuing speculations. Just as the latter revolve around the single detail of the blood-like sweat, so the initial quatrain achieves still greater concentration by dwelling on the possibilities of the Christ/warrior metaphor. Every keyword in the constellation – 'estratagema', 'sacramento' (both sacrament and military oath) and 'desafío' (challenge) – plays its part in the whole. The fact that 'estratagema' actually precedes the basic metaphor ('guerrero mío') adds to the arresting quality of the opening. If Christ is a 'warrior' who 'does battle' for sinners ('mío' suggests both intimacy and the recognition that Christ is acting on behalf of the speaker), his present action can legitimately be seen as a 'stratagem'. A moment later, however, 'stratagem' is 'corrected' to 'sacrament', thus introducing a directly religious meaning, while still maintaining the military metaphor. So by a skilful series of transitions, the religious dimension of the subject is extended without losing the more human associations of the 'general-on-the-eve-of-battle'. Both 'plazo' (time limit) and 'desafío' fit into this pattern; at this point, the human analogy makes the divine example more vivid and apparently more comprehensible. But only apparently; and in the end this particular line of metaphor is rejected. The emotional state suggested at the end of the second quatrain – '[cobrar] más esfuerzo por cobrar más brío' – would be entirely appropriate to a human leader, yet it has no part in the 'new' interpretation of Christ's suffering. The poem, after all, is about the Agony in the Garden, and only indirectly about the Crucifixion. What matters is the reason for Christ's suffering *now* – not the approaching 'challenge' of the fourth line, but the 'struggle' of the ending – and it is to this that the rest of the poem is dedicated as it works towards the final note of self-reproach.

A poem like this represents a type of meditative verse which becomes increasingly common towards the end of the sixteenth century and is particularly prominent in the work of Lope de Vega and Quevedo. Its effect, moreover, is not confined to religious poetry; where the Italianate tradition is concerned, both the existence of a strong current of popular religious poetry and the type of devotional practice encouraged by the Counter-Reformation influence the development of the shorter poem, and particularly that of the sonnet, while the use of colloquial diction and dramatic emphasis tend to counterbalance the fluent commonplace of the average Petrarchan lyric. The process, moreover, is mutual, as one sees from the number of poets who write both secular and religious verse. Generally speaking, this is neither a matter of compartmentalizing one's work nor of rejecting one kind of poem in favour of another; the truth is that the religious poetry of the period shares a considerable area of sensibility and expression with the poetry of secular love, and that this common ground increases after 1600 with the popularity of certain types of poetic conceit.

                                    IV

Such possibilities for interplay depend, of course, on a close awareness of the central tradition of sixteenth-century love poetry which, although it is associated above all with Italianate verse, derives partly from the *cancionero* poetry of the previous century. This poetry in its turn goes back to the work of the Provençal troubadours, and presents a peculiarly concentrated version of what has come to be known as 'courtly love'.[13]

By the date of the *Cancionero de Baena* (c. 1445) – the first important collection of courtly love poetry in Castile – the subject-matter of the Provençal tradition has been partially transferred to Castilian, and the characteristic stress on artistry and verse technique is firmly established. One says 'partially' since, as R. O. Jones has pointed out, *cancionero* poetry involves both a narrowing and an intensification of the courtly love tradition.[14] This narrowing is a matter partly of poetic language and partly of verse form. The great majority of *cancionero* lyrics consist of three octosyllabic quatrains, or *redondillas*, with certain obligatory repetitions of rhyme. Thus a typical example from the *Cancionero general* of 1511 runs as follows:

> Bien fue bien de mi ventura
> con tales penas penarme
> amores que quieren darme
> por su gloria mi tristura.
> Y fue tanto bien ser vuestro
> que no sé cuál me consuele
> no meresceros que duele
> o merescer lo que muestro.
> Assí que por mi ventura
> comiençan en acabarme
> amores que quieren darme
> por su gloria mi tristura.   (129r; Quirós)

It was surely a blessing [literally: 'good'] of my fortune for me to endure such suffering: love which would give me my sadness for its own glory. And to be yours was so great a good that I do not know which of the two things should console me: not to deserve you, which is painful, or to deserve what I show [i.e. in my appearance]. Thus for my fortune it begins to end [i.e. kill] me: love which would give me my sadness for my own glory.

Here, as in most poems of this kind, the conscious limitations of the poetic form entail a corresponding strictness of vocabulary, a tendency to move between a small number of abstractions. Within the circular pattern created by the verse movement, there is a parallel technique of dwelling on the same words by means of variation and paradox. On the other hand, the intensification which Jones and other critics have noted is not simply a matter of the concentration enforced by a particular set of verbal conventions. It has often been pointed out, for instance, how such poetry as a whole tends to centre on extreme, and often neurotic, situations. Thus, in many *cancionero* poems, the lover's suffering becomes a desire for death which, paradoxically, is his one hope of life, the 'morir para no morir' (dying so as not to die) which was to be taken up in a mystical sense by Santa Teresa de Jesús in the next century. This condition of emotional instability seems deliberately invited; as Pedro Salinas puts it: 'Life is lived in a state of emotional imbalance, held in check by the poet's will, which endorses it and cultivates it as a theme.'[15]

The difficulty for a modern critic is to know how much to read into the abstractions. In the poem just quoted, for example, what exactly is the nature of the suffering ('penas'), and in what sense could it be described as a 'good'? Or again, is love 'glorying' in the lover's sadness, or is the sadness part of the lover's 'glory'? Moreover, the possibility that the reference to possession ('ser vuestro') may be a euphemism (but how are we to know?) suggests a kind of ambiguity which frequently occurs in such poems. As Keith Whinnom has shown, terms like 'gloria' and 'voluntad' (will) often have an obvious sexual connotation; thus, as he rightly argues, it is absurd to regard *cancionero* poetry as consistently platonic: sometimes it is, sometimes it clearly isn't, and in between there are a great many poems where sexual innuendo is possible, though difficult to prove.[16] Seen in these terms, *cancionero* verse begins to look much more like the Provençal poetry from which it ultimately derives: a poetry, that is to say, in which sexual desire, however much it may be repressed or concealed beneath euphemisms, seldom renounces the hope of consummation.

The vocabulary and most of the attitudes of *cancionero* poetry pass almost unchanged into the sixteenth century; what alters is not so much the basic concept of love as the way in which this is presented. This is partly a matter of literary form: though the poetry of Petrarch and his Spanish imitators still depends on medieval attitudes to love, the prevalence of the sonnet and the longer types of poem – the ode, the elegy, the eclogue – makes for a kind of spaciousness which is lacking in the older type of verse. This is not simply a matter of length, but also of rhythms: even in the relatively brief compass of a sonnet, the possibilities of organizing both sound and sense are much more varied than in the fifteenth-century *canción* and, even though the traditional abstractions persist, they can be more closely defined within the more elaborate context. Moreover, apart from the differences of form, there is a whole range of fresh poetic material which, although it in no way denies the existing concept of love, is so distinctive in its effects that one is tempted to speak of a new sensibility. Petrarch himself not only provides Renaissance love poetry with its most characteristic paradoxes – fire/ice, night/day, storm/calm and so on;[17] he also develops very skilfully the kind of symbolic landscape common in medieval poetry, but notably absent from the *cancionero* lyric. More important still, none of these effects is incidental; everything – imagery, verse structure and situation – is directed to one end: the poetic rendering of an individual passion, not in its factual details, but as a centre of conflicting emotions which have more to do with introspection than with the exploration of a genuinely mutual relationship. What Petrarch sets out to record are his own feelings – of regret, longing, absence, melancholy – still filtered through the traditional abstractions, yet organized in terms of a poetic self which is present throughout the poems.[18]

It was the particular components of this style which made Petrarch the supreme model for vernacular eloquence in the sixteenth century, though in his lesser imitators the eloquence often became the sole intention of the poem. Both the high status of Petrarch and the dangers implied in such an evaluation emerge from one of the decisive documents of the Italian Renaissance, the *Prose dell volgar lingua* of Bembo, published in 1525. By stating that the chief aim of vernacular writers should be to imitate the achievement of classical Greek and Latin literature and by setting up Petrarch as the chief model for the new kind of fine writing, Bembo was in effect sanctioning a more drastic separation of poetry and experience than one finds in Petrarch himself. As F. T. Prince has remarked:

Both the weakness and the strength of the new aesthetic ideals are indicated when we point out that they were above all literary. They made possible the creation of great literary epics, the *Gerusalemme Liberata* or *Paradise Lost*, by poets of exceptional power; but they encouraged minor talents to treat literature as a self-justified activity, with the rules and assumptions of an elaborate game, and this could not but lead to an impoverishment of poetry in particular.[19]

Already, the seeds of this impoverishment are present in Petrarch himself, in the growing insistence with which his poetry separates body from soul. In practice, this amounts to a major shift in the nature of courtly love poetry; this division is noticeably absent from the poems of the troubadours and – if one takes the hints we have just seen – only questionably present in the *cancionero* lyric. In the sixteenth century, the body–soul dualism is compounded, often with great subtlety, by the increasing use of philosophical concepts derived from Renaissance-Platonism. The subtlety here comes from the attempt to distinguish between different degrees of sensuous experience and from the more sophisticated vocabulary which this provides for the analysis of the lover's feelings. Moreover, these now form part of a much wider range of reference, since love itself is seen as the creative principle which lies behind the harmony of the universe. As Bembo puts it in Book Two of *Gli Asolani*: 'This vast and beautiful fabric of the world itself, which we perceive more completely with the mind than with the eyes, and in which all things are contained, if it were not full of Love, which holds it bound in its discordant bonds, would not endure nor would ever have existed for long.'

Nevertheless, it is in terms of human experience that the ideal of Platonic love, as described by Castiglione and Bembo, can be seen to lack a serious moral dimension. To regard sexual relationships as one stage in an easy ascent to the divine does little justice to the complexities of actual living. Moreover, as A. A. Parker has argued, it offers no sense of evil as a continuing threat to human integrity: 'In so far as Neoplatonism considered this at all, it was only as concupiscence, which it tended to present as a potential aberration that an intelligent man would either never fall into or would quickly surmount.'[20] Sixteenth-century attitudes to love, to be sure, are not always as superficial as this: certain poems of Francisco de Aldana (1537–78) show how much power can be gained from a serious awareness of the paradoxes of sexual love,[21] while at the theoretical level, the *Dialoghi d'amore* of Leone Ebreo (1535) convey a very genuine sense of the ways in which both mind and body can suffer from the recognition of human limitations.[22]

Hardly surprisingly, it is Christian values which provide the most searching critique of neo-Platonic love. What is interesting, in the context of the late sixteenth century, is that they are able to do so precisely because of their ability to make use of Platonic ideas for their own purposes. In Luis de León and other Counter-Reformation theologians, as Parker has observed, 'Platonic doctrine finds its proper fulfilment in divine love without being led astray by the moral illusion of a spiritualized human love'. He goes on:

It was in this way that the religious literature of the Counter-Reformation brought the ideal of perfect love down from the clouds, while at the same time retaining the vision of the ideal: the union of the soul with God. It counteracted the prevailing idealistic humanism by placing the ideal where it properly belonged, in the realm of the spiritual, and by laying stress on the real world, on the reality of human nature, and on social obligations and moral duties.[23]

The results of this new equilibrium can be seen, not only in the religious writing of the time – for example, in the prose works of Luis de León himself – but also in secular literature, in the complex ironies of *Don Quixote* and in the vast spectrum of the seventeenth-century drama. One symptom of this, as we shall discover, is that after 1600 it becomes increasingly difficult to point to a single dominant type of love poetry: by that stage, the conventional Petrarchan lyric has run its course and, though both Petrarchan and neo-Platonic elements persist, the subject-matter of love tends to be drawn more and more deeply into general considerations of human nature or, alternatively, to become the basis of a more public type of court poetry.

V

Before this occurs, however, the Petrarchan tradition reaches a new kind of synthesis in Fernando de Herrera, a poet whose work has often been seen as a bridge between the two centuries. In one obvious sense this is true: both the criteria expressed in the *Anotaciones* to Garcilaso and the linguistic sophistication of his own poems made a deep impression on many poets of the next generation, including

Lope de Vega and Góngora. Whether the actual view of love conveyed in both poems and commentary had a comparable impact is less certain: both its complexity and its intensely personal, and at times obsessive, nature would have been difficult, if not impossible, to imitate. To begin with, Herrera's love poems – especially in the greatly expanded edition of 1619 – suggest a deliberate attempt to produce a *canzoniere* in the Petrarchan manner. They are all concerned with a single woman – Doña Leonor de Milán, the wife of Herrera's patron, the Count of Gelves – and the volume of poems he published in 1582 (the only one to appear in his lifetime) was probably intended as a tribute to her memory. These facts may suggest a fairly standard courtly relationship; yet in practice Herrera rejects most of the social implications of such a situation in order to present his feelings in their purest terms. As Oreste Macrí has pointed out, Herrera is in some ways closer to Petrarch than to Garcilaso: in his mature love poems, he not only avoids the characteristic smoothness of the Italianate manner, but also returns to the more sombre and abstract qualities of the *cancionero* poets and of Petrarch himself.[24] Herrera's peculiar contribution to the tradition, therefore, involves a reassessment of the entire course of courtly love from Petrarch onwards. And to this end, he draws not only on neo-Platonic doctrine as expressed by Castiglione and Leone Ebreo but also on the vast range of humanistic erudition displayed in the *Anotaciones*.

At the centre of this enterprise lies his own poetry. If we ask how theory and practice work together, there is one particular passage in the *Anotaciones* which enables us to glimpse an answer. At one point in his discussion of Garcilaso's Eighth Sonnet, Herrera quotes two stanzas of his own (Estancias II, 17–32):

> Cuando en vos pienso, en alta fantasia
> me arrebato, y ausente me presento,
> y crece, contemplandoos, mi alegria
> donde vuestra belleza represento;
> las partes con que siente la alma mia
> enlazada en mortal ayuntamiento,
> y recibe en figuras conocidas
> al sentido las cosas ofrecidas;

> Aunque en honda tiniebla sepultado,
> y estó en grave silencio y escondido,
> casi en perpetua vela del cuidado

se me adormecen; y en el bien crecido
desta memoria con amor formado
se vencen, y alli todo suspendido
el espiritu os halla, y tanto veo,
cuanto pide el Amor y mi deseo.

When I think of you, I am carried away in lofty fancy and, absent, am present, and, contemplating you, my happiness grows where I imagine your beauty; those parts with which my soul feels, bound by a mortal yoke; and it receives in familiar images those things which are offered to the senses. Although I am buried in deep darkness and in solemn, hidden silence, as if keeping perpetual vigil over my love, they [i.e. the things offered to the senses] fall asleep and in the increased good of this memory formed by love they are overcome, and there the spirit, totally suspended, finds you and I see all that Love and my desire ask for.

Herrera is describing the process by which the image of the beloved becomes internalized, so that the lover's desire is as content as if she were present; the second stanza completes the description of the way in which subsidiary things – the 'things which are offered to the senses' – lose their force by contrast with the central experience of love. It is the 'memory formed by love' which becomes the new object, and in the commentary which precedes the quotation Herrera explains how sight, the most acute of the bodily senses, transmits the image of beauty to the 'common sense', and how it passes first from this to the imagination and thence to the memory. In both the poem and the commentary, then, Herrera is describing, not the sources or the motivation of love, but the way it functions in terms of Renaissance psychology. This may seem no more than another textbook demonstration; yet in the poem itself, the lines which Herrera quotes are preceded by a very different passage which begins:

Abrázame las venas este fuego;
las junturas y entrañas abrasadas
siento, y neruios arder y correr luego
las llamas por los vesos dilatadas...

This fire sets my veins alight; I feel my joints and inner organs burn, and my nerves catch fire, and then the flames running along my bones...

Again, the sensuous vividness of these lines can be justified by neo-Platonic theory. In an earlier passage from the same commentary, Herrera describes the effects of 'love at first sight': 'thus the lover dissolves, breaks up, and turns to liquid when he sees a beautiful woman, as if his whole being were about to pass into her' (*Anotaciones*, 312–13). What the poem itself is describing, therefore, is the way in which the vision of beauty literally 'takes over' the body of the lover. In the commentary, Herrera goes on to point out how the same experience can occur in the absence of the woman once the original vision has been fed into the memory. In the context of the poem, however, the effect of such a passage is to create a discrepancy which Herrera at times seems to admit. In the revised version of the second stanza published in the 1619 edition, the lines on memory read: 'el dulce bien perdido / d'esta memoria en puro amor formado' (the sweet lost good of this memory formed in pure love). The argument now is that the woman, although 'lost' in a literal sense, is still present in the lover's imagination, and that this is all his desire can ask for. Desire, in other words, has adjusted its demands to the process of spiritualization, so that the idea of 'loss' has become irrelevant.

But is this really so? If it were, the attitude of the woman would hardly matter: the lover would be satisfied with the static, internal image of her beauty. Yet the poem as a whole emphasizes the relentless nature of suffering: the flame of beauty which the lover desires – the same flame which runs through his body in the lines quoted – can only be quenched by tears, and this is a self-renewing process. The lover willingly embraces his suffering, which exists precisely because of the continuing indifference of the woman, and this operates directly on his senses. Thus soul and body are in constant tension; despite the neo-Platonic overtones, there is a strong sense of stoicism and of ennoblement through suffering which recalls the poetry of the *cancioneros*. The same abstractions – desire, will, good and evil – are continually present; what Herrera does is to elaborate them in terms of Renaissance psychology by relating them to natural causes. On the one hand, therefore, he draws out the Platonic implications of Petrarchan poetry by insisting on the permanence of the inner vision; on the other, he emphasizes the visceral effects of passion, as in the lines above.

What happens in the end is that the old abstractions are subsumed under new ones – Virtue, Beauty, Honour – in the attempt to create a higher unity. As terms of praise addressed to the woman, Virtue (in the sense of 'strength', 'power') and Beauty are given their full weight of neo-Platonic meaning. Honour (and its cognate, 'glory') can refer to both lover and beloved; in the former instance, it is associated with pride in constancy and, by extension, in suffering. And suffering, in this context, comes, not from the inability to achieve an ideal spiritual relationship, but from the tensions inherent in the relationship as it is experienced. What links all these abstractions, of course, is the idea of nobility. For Herrera, the conventional Petrarchan paradoxes are charged with notions of cosmic grandeur; throughout the poems, for instance, the woman is referred to by names which are synonymous with light ('Luz', 'Lumbre', 'Estrella'). If this recalls Petrarch's own play with the name 'Laura', it also reminds one of the neo-Platonic belief in love as the generative force in nature itself. Yet, if this seems to place the woman at an impossible distance, it also helps to define the nature of the lover's own task. What is really distinctive about Herrera, in fact, is the poetic status he confers on the whole relationship. Though the neo-Platonic ideal is continually in view, there is no question of an easy Platonic ascent; the obstacles which Herrera sets himself are continually renewed – without this, there would be no 'heroism' – and the tension between spirit and senses is maintained.[25]

VI

No other sixteenth-century love poetry is as complex or as ambitious as this. Despite the confidence with which Herrera expounds neo-Platonic ideas, the poems themselves are full of doubts and indecisions which the contemplation of an ideal love can do nothing to relieve. From an aesthetic point of view, the best poems often seem to thrive on such inconsistencies, on what Herrera himself describes as states of mental confusion. And, significantly, it is his poetic language, rather than his exhaustive investigation of the nature of love, which seems to have left the greater impression on his younger contemporaries. As a model for this kind of writing one can point to the stanza from the 'Oda a San Fernando' which describes the river god:

> Cubrio el sagrado Betis de florida
> purpura i blandas esmeraldas llena
> i tiernas perlas la ribera ondosa,
> i al cielo alçò la barba revestida
> de verde musgo; i removio en l'arena
> el movible cristal de la sombrosa
> gruta, i la faz onrosa,

de juncos, cañas i coral ornada,
tendio los cuernos umidos, creciendo
l'abundosa corriente dilatada,
su imperio enel Océano estendiendo;
qu'al cerco de la tierra en vario lustre
de sobervia corona haze ilustre.

Sacred Betis [i.e. the River Guadalquivir] covered the wave-lapped riverbanks laden with flowering purple, soft emeralds and tender pearls, and raised his green, moss-covered beard to the sky; and stirred in the sand the moving crystal of the shady grotto, and the revered countenance, adorned with reeds, rushes and coral, stretched out its moist horns, swelling with the spreading, abundant current, extending its empire to the Ocean, which adorns earth's circle with the changing brilliance of its splendid crown.

The fact that in these lines Herrera is re-casting a kind of set-piece familiar in classical Latin poetry makes his intentions still clearer: the 'fine writing' suggests a deliberate attempt to improve on a model and, in doing so, to extend the resources of his own poetic language.[26] This precise combination of brilliant colouring and pictorial imagery scarcely exists in sixteenth-century poetry before Herrera; for the next few decades, on the other hand, one finds it constantly, and most especially in the series of Andalusian poets which runs from Juan de Arguijo to Soto de Rojas. In the early poems of Espinosa and in other poets of the Antequera group (Luis Martín de la Plaza, Agustín de Tejada) the manner becomes a whole descriptive style; in a more ambitious poet like Góngora, on the other hand, it is absorbed into a much wider vision in which the relations between man and the natural world are re-created through a dense texture of verbal artifice.

It would be wrong, however, to restrict Herrera's influence to the treatment of a single kind of subject-matter; for many seventeenth-century poets his real importance lay in the authority with which he came to establish a particular kind of vocabulary which could be used in a variety of contexts. 'Vocabulary' here is to be taken in its widest sense: not simply individual words, but grammatical constructions, turns of syntax and networks of imagery. The contemporary term for this vocabulary is *culteranismo*: the deliberate use of 'palabras cultas' (cultivated words), often in conjunction with a strongly Latinized syntax. The term itself only began to circulate after Herrera's death; there is no doubt, however, that Herrera, as most contemporary poets recognized, was the real innovator. Even at the level of single words, Herrera's contribution to the *culto* lexicon is impressive: colour words like 'cerúleo' (cerulean), 'pálido' (pale) and 'púrpura' (purple) in association with 'nieve' (snow); 'cristal' (crystal) = 'río' (river), 'luces' (lights) = 'ojos' (eyes), 'error' = 'confusión', 'número' (number) = 'cadencia' (cadence); 'esplendor' (splendour), 'fulminar', 'errante', 'insano', 'terso' (smooth) and many others. Not all these words and associations originate with Herrera; what matters here is not so much novelty as the effect of selection and concentration. As Macrí remarks, it was Herrera who, as far as posterity was concerned, had 'selected, analysed, illustrated and increased the living resources of the tradition'.[27] And this, ultimately, is the justification of the *Anotaciones*: a celebration, but also a critique, of the poems of Garcilaso in terms of the possibilities they still represent for poets of a later generation.

VII

Herrera, clearly, is an exceptional writer in several ways: his full effect is not felt until some years after his death in 1598, and discussion of his work almost inevitably leads one away from his actual love poems to the kind of theoretical issues I shall be concerned with in the next chapter. If, on the other hand, one wants to know what kind of literary options were open to the majority of Spanish poets in the 1580s, there are certain minor writers of the time who help to provide an answer, among them – though a major writer in other respects – Miguel de Cervantes (1547–1616).[28]

If there are certain characteristics which make it possible to think of the 1580s as a transitional period, particularly when one sets them against the early work of the major poets of the next generation, Lope de Vega and Góngora, the one established writer who saw both these changes and their aftermath was Cervantes, whose admiration for Garcilaso remained undiminished throughout his writing career and who nevertheless, towards the end of his life, was one of the first to praise the major poems of Góngora. One difficulty in approaching his own verse is that, both in his lifetime and for long afterwards, his fame as a novelist tended for obvious reasons to eclipse his minor, but genuine, poetic talent. Another is that, apart from his one book-length poem, the *Viaje del Parnaso* (Voyage to Parnassus; 1614), he published no collection of verse, and most of his shorter poems and songs are contained in plays and works of fiction. Moreover, these difficulties, such as they are, have been compounded by Cervantes's apparently modest opinion of his own gifts:

> Yo, que siempre trabajo y me desvelo
> por parecer que tengo de poeta
> la gracia que no quiso darme el cielo.

I, who always labour and sit up late so as to appear to have the grace as a poet which Heaven was unwilling to give me.

These lines from the *Viaje del Parnaso* should not, however, be taken literally; in their context, they are ironical, if not openly burlesque, and the poem as a whole presents a writer who is perfectly confident of his own merits. What is clear from the *Viaje* is that, although Cervantes is prepared to recognize the major poets of the time, he is also concerned to assert his own poetic integrity in the face of mere fashionable novelty. From this and the evidence of his own poems, it seems fair to deduce that Cervantes's tastes in poetry were formed early and that they remained remarkably constant. Gerardo Diego's claim that he is in spirit a poet of the 1560s is obviously an exaggeration, though not without its point.[29] The crucial years for his poetry, in fact, were probably those immediately following his return to Spain in 1580 after his five years' captivity in Algiers; though several poems, including the verse epistle to Mateo Vázquez, Secretary to Philip II, are earlier than this, it is clear that he studied Herrera's *Anotaciones* (1580), and the long roll-call of poets in the 'Canto de Calíope' (Song of Calliope) section of *La Galatea* (1585) suggests that he had deliberately brought himself up to date on the younger writers who had begun to emerge during his absence.

The evidence for most of this comes in the seventy poems included in *La Galatea*, Cervantes's first work of fiction. The fact that this is a pastoral novel imposes certain restrictions on the nature of the poetry it presents: almost all the poems are concerned with love, and most of them are made to reflect the situations of the fictional characters. Within these limitations, the variety of poems is surprisingly great; though their quality varies a good deal, they range over most kinds of Italianate verse and include a number written in traditional metres. The most obvious influences are Garcilaso and, to a lesser extent, Herrera and Camões.[30] Several peculiar features stand out, however: one is Cervantes's knowledge of the poetry of Luis de León, whom he imitates in the ode beginning '¡O alma venturosa…!' (O fortunate soul);[31] another is that he is the only writer of the period to use the *arte mayor* stanza – eight twelve-syllable lines, rhyming abbaacca – associated with the fifteenth-century poet Juan de Mena.[32]

Nevertheless, the listing of influences, as is often the case, tells one little about the quality of the poems, and still less about the effect they make in the context. In the first place, this is because, whatever their intrinsic merits, they play an important functional role in the book as a whole. This is partly a matter of structure: more than any other pastoral novel, *La Galatea* relies for its strength on the alternating rhythm of prose and verse in which each kind of writing sustains the other. And this leads to a second, and more important, point: the fact that, since the poems themselves are part of the fiction, both their occasions and the attitudes they embody are determined by the characters themselves. Thus, as a vehicle for analysing the nature of love, the pastoral novel has one obvious advantage over the Petrarchan sonnet-cycle: it can play off a number of divergent voices against one another and, by doing so, invite a constant questioning of both theory and experience. In connection with this, one should also bear in mind the basic claim of the pastoral convention to present the experience of love in a uniquely pure state; as Timbrio remarks in a crucial passage of *La Galatea*: 'At this very moment it has dawned on me that the powers and wisdom of Love reach to the four corners of the earth, and that where it is most refined and purified, is in the hearts of shepherds' (II, 74).

This comes immediately after the debate between Lenio and Tirsi in which each half is brought to a climax in a corresponding poem. From a theoretical point of view, this debate is the centre of the novel: Lenio attacks love in terms of the suffering and destruction it causes; Tirsi (who is a thinly disguised version of the poet Francisco de Figueroa) accuses him of confusing love with desire and goes on to praise the institution of Christian marriage and the virtue of suffering in a worthy cause. Several things emerge from this episode. One, which I have already referred to in general terms, is the complementary nature of the prose and verse: in itself, neither of the two poems concerned rises above decent mediocrity, yet each is given a greater weight of meaning by the prose discourse which leads up to it, just as the latter needs the poem in order to reach a convincing climax. Another, which concerns the whole debate about Platonic love, is Tirsi's allusion to Christian values, a theme only embryonically present in *La Galatea*, but which takes on increasing importance in the rest of Cervantes's work.[33] And finally, in view of the events which follow, there is the implied gap between theory and experience. Tirsi's victory in the debate may seem – and may be meant to seem – too easy; Lenio, certainly, is not convinced by his arguments, though when, later in the novel, he finds himself in love for the first time, he openly admits their truth. Theory, in other words, must be tested by experience before it can be accepted, though at the same time there is a strong suggestion that the illogicality of life finally escapes any attempt at rationalization. Thus, in the course of the book, both the abstractions of the poems and the theorizing passages of the prose are judged in terms of human passions which, because they are presented dramatically, are more 'real' than either.

Such considerations, it may be felt, make these poems a special case. To some extent this is true: yet the reason for introducing them here is not to make any special claims for Cervantes as a poet, but to show how much poetic territory he shares with other writers of his generation. What he makes of this common ground – the fact that as a potentially great novelist he is able to link his poetic resources to a more general exploration of the pastoral convention – is another matter, though one which has its own bearing on the conception of love which underlies so much sixteenth-century poetry. The common ground does not end here, however, though again there are interesting differences between Cervantes and the other two poets I have mentioned. Like Espinel, he is a master of the short song-like poem in the popular tradition, as can be seen from the examples which occur in his later novels and plays. These, however, like the *Viaje del Parnaso*, fall outside the period we are immediately concerned with.[34] If, on the other hand, one looks among the earlier poems for an equivalent of the 'middle range' of verse one finds in both Espinel and Barahona de Soto, there is only a single obvious example: the Epistle to Mateo Vázquez, apparently written during Cervantes's captivity in Algiers (1575–80), part of which at least is likely to be authentic.[35]

There are two other poems, however, both written just before the turn of the century, which fall somewhere in this area, though there is nothing else quite comparable to them at the time. Both are satirical sonnets, and each in its way represents a reaction against the patriotic feelings which had centred a few years earlier around the defeat of the Armada, and to which Cervantes himself had contributed. The first refers to the sacking of Cadiz in 1596 by the

Earl of Essex, when the Spanish troops from Seville arrived only after the enemy had departed. The tercets, like the rest of the poem, make their point with economy and wit:

> Bramó el becerro, y púsoles en sarta;
> tronó la tierra, oscurecióse el cielo,
> amenazando una total ruina;
>   y al cabo, en Cádiz, com mesura harta,
> ido ya el conde sin ningún recelo,
> triunfando entró el gran duque de Medina.

The calf roared and threw them into confusion; the earth thundered and the sky grew dark, threatening total ruin; and finally, with much dignity, now that the Count had left, without the slightest fear, the great Duke of Medina entered Cadiz in triumph.

The second poem – strictly speaking a *soneto con estrambote*, i.e. with an additional tercet – dates from 1598, and is altogether more complex in its technique. The occasion, once again, is a contemporary event: the erection of a catafalque, or imitation tomb, in the Cathedral of Seville, in connection with the funeral ceremonies of Philip II:[36]

> Voto a Dios que me espanta esta grandeza
> y que diera un doblón por describilla;
> porque ¿a quién no sorprende y maravilla
> esta máquina insigne, esta riqueza?
>   Por Jesucristo vivo, cada pieza
> vale más de un millón, y que es mancilla
> que esto no dure un siglo, ¡oh gran Sevilla,
> Roma triunfante en ánimo y nobleza!
>   Apostaré que el ánima del muerto
> por gozar este sitio hoy ha dejado
> la gloria donde vive eternamente.
>   Esto oyó un valentón, y dijo: 'Es cierto
> cuanto dice voacé, señor soldado.
> Y el que dijere lo contrario, miente'.
>   Y luego, incontinente,
> caló el chapeo, requirió la espada,
> miró al soslayo, fuese, y no hubo nada.

By God, this grand thing terrifies me; I'd give a doubloon to be able to describe it. For who is not amazed and dumbfounded by this illustrious construction, this display of riches? By the living Christ, each part is worth over a million, and it's a shame this can't last for a century, O great Seville, O Rome triumphant in spirit and nobility! I'll bet that today the dead man's soul has left the glory in which it dwells eternally in order to enjoy this place. A swashbuckler heard this, and said: 'All you say, sir soldier, is true, and whoever says the contrary is lying.' And then, straight away, he rammed on his hat, checked his sword, looked sideways, went, and there was nothing left.

The rhetoric of the poem – the constant deflation of 'noble' terms and the timing of the last three lines – is flawless. Yet, as Luis Cernuda has claimed, its real originality lies in its anticipation of the dramatic monologue technique, in the skill with which Cervantes mimics the quite distinct accents of the two voices: the military oaths of the soldier and the Sevillian speech of the *valentón*.[37] And, as in a true dramatic monologue, the judgement of the poet himself is conveyed obliquely, though no less certainly, through the way in which the speakers are made to 'place' themselves. All that the poet's own voice needs to do, in fact, is to pick out the series of empty gestures which concludes the poem; the real evaluation has already taken place, and the quality of the soldier's wonder has brought out, as no direct statement could, the hollowness of an entire ethos.

Another way of indicating Cervantes's originality is to say that we have to wait for Quevedo in order to find satirical poetry as pointed and as verbally inventive as this within the compass of the sonnet. Nevertheless, the comparison holds only up to a point: Quevedo's technique is more self-consciously 'witty' and his humour altogether more harsh. Even on this small scale, Cervantes, one is inclined to say, demonstrates the instinctive sense of character and the evenness of judgement which are continually present in his fiction. Whatever the truth of this, it is no longer possible, as it was until quite recently, to dismiss Cervantes as a mediocre poet. Both the range of his verse, and its occasional excellences, are the work of a writer who, for all his apparent 'backwardness', has a clear sense of what it is possible to write at a given time, and of the way in which poetry itself may take its place at the centre of a much vaster literary enterprise.

The work of Cervantes by no means exhausts the different kinds of poem which were being written in the closing years of the sixteenth century. What it does show is the existence of a strong tradition within which even minor poets could be expected to produce distinctive work. By the 1580s, new possibilities are beginning to emerge: the status of Garcilaso remains as high as ever, but the type of poetry he represents is coming to be regarded with a more critical eye, and its preoccupations combined with others which are partly thematic and partly linguistic. Like other poets of the period,

Cervantes shows the persistence of traditional modes alongside the dominant Italianate tradition, and he is known to have shared in the revival of the ballad – the beginning of the *romance nuevo* or *romance artístico* – which leaps to importance in the 1580s with the early poems of Góngora and Lope de Vega.

One kind of poem is not represented at all; this is the literary epic, whose growing popularity, from the *Araucana* (1569–90) of Ercilla onwards, will be discussed in a later chapter. Already in Barahona de Soto, however, one can sense a new interest in a different kind of long poem, that is to say, the mythological fable. Unlike the epic, this has no special justification in Renaissance poetic theory. Its popularity with poets can partly be explained by the opportunities it gave for extended narrative and descriptive set-pieces and partly by sixteenth-century interest in the *Metamorphoses* of Ovid, which for many centuries had provided the standard versions of classical myths. As the result of medieval commentaries and of handbooks like Boccaccio's *De genealogia deorum* (1472), Renaissance readers were familiar with the allegorical interpretations of classical myth which deeply influenced the painting and sculpture of the time and which found their way into the more popular medium of the emblem books. In Spain, earlier sixteenth-century poets occasionally attempted the mythological poem, in both Italianate and traditional metres, though the most outstanding examples come early in the seventeenth century, in the work of poets like Carrillo, Góngora and Villa-mediana. By this stage, important changes in technique and sensibility have taken place which, though they are still clearly related to the kind of tendencies we have just seen, both extend and concentrate them in ways which could hardly have been predicted in the 1580s. These will be largely, though not entirely, the work of the major poets of the next two generations, Góngora, Lope de Vega and Quevedo. But in order to understand both the differences and the continuity we need to know something of the prevailing literary conceptions which governed the writing of poetry, and of the ways in which theory and practice were related.

2

Theory and practice

I

Rules, as C. H. Sisson has observed, 'always deceive the pedantic, because they get taken for wilful instructions when they are in fact the laws of the material'.[1] The material of Renaissance poetry is of course language, or rather language filtered through a mass of preconceptions which differ considerably from those of a modern reader and which often seem remote from poetry itself. This is easier to understand once one realizes that all Renaissance theory and practice rests on a philosophical basis – more precisely, on a view of reality and of the nature of the universe – which has more in common with medieval views on man's place in the Divine Order than with the theories of a Descartes or a Newton. The key term here is analogy: broadly speaking, the Renaissance still retains the idea of a hierarchical cosmos in which the universal and the particular are inextricably bound together by a complex network of analogies or 'correspondences'. This operates at all levels: earthly things are in some sense a reflection of heavenly things; the body politic can be compared in detail to the workings of the human body; or to use a favourite concept of neo-Platonism, the relation between earth and heaven is that of a 'microcosm' to a 'macrocosm' – a 'little world' dependent on a greater – and all things on earth can be seen as imperfect copies of eternal archetypes. There is something very impressive, not to say awe-inspiring, about this vision of a harmonious universe in which everything – men, creatures and natural phenomena – is bound together in natural sympathy. Yet, as Michel Foucault points out in his brilliant account of the seventeenth-century intellectual revolution,[2] the system of knowledge it entails is extremely precarious: a mixture of inaccurate observation, rational ingenuity and sheer fantasy. It is this mixture which is finally challenged in the seventeenth century: by Bacon when he speaks of 'putting nature to the question', in other words, by scientific experiment, and by Descartes when he insists on the differences between things, rather than on their similarities. Nevertheless, it is the older view of reality which underlies Renaissance opinions on the purpose of poetry, just as it determines some of its basic literary conceptions like imitation and the theory of styles, and colours the whole nature of its poetic imagery.

We can never, of course, hope to see into the mind of a Renaissance poet; at the same time, it is important to recognize that the conception of reality I have just outlined involves certain assumptions about the workings of the mind itself, and that these can affect the actual nature of verbal expression. Failure to grasp this has often led modern critics to judge Renaissance poetry in terms of distinctions which would have had little or no meaning at the time. As Rosemond Tuve puts it:

The very divisions and oppositions accepted in modern writing, and nuclear to the controversial stand taken on these matters, are foreign to a writer used to thinking in terms of Renaissance psychological theory. Renaissance writers do not oppose 'an experience' and 'a thought', or 'emotions' and 'ideas', nor separate 'logic' from 'association', nor divide 'imagination' from 'logic' in composition; nor do they identify 'reason' with 'intellect', nor see the implications we see in 'rational' or 'expository'.[3]

The detailed implications of this should become clear in what follows; the important point here is the one made by Tuve herself at an earlier stage in her argument: namely, that by applying the kinds of distinctions which are common in post-Romantic criticism, 'we would make it impossible for a Renaissance writer to describe how he thought a poem was written'.[4]

II

Sixteenth-century poetic theory is an international phenomenon which springs partly from Renaissance humanism and partly from the spread of the Italianate tradition itself. In Spain, the most interesting discussions of the nature of poetry do not appear until the last quarter of the sixteenth century. Nevertheless, sixteenth-century poetry and poetic theory are so closely interdependent that any poem written in the Italianate manner is a concrete embodiment of the theory which lies behind it, and even a slight working knowledge of this can affect one's whole understanding of the poetry.

Renaissance theory as a distinctive body of argument begins early in the sixteenth century with the first translations of Horace's *Ars poetica*, followed closely by the earliest commentaries on Aristotle's *Poetics* (Robortello, 1548; Maggi, 1559). This combination of Horace and Aristotle is at the root of most sixteenth-century thinking about poetry; to a great extent, the entire critical movement in the years around 1550 is concerned with the reinterpretation of Horatian precepts in the light of Aristotle. There was never at any point a clear break with the past: Horace's views on poetry, unlike those of Aristotle, had been familiar in the Middle Ages; a number of the pre-Aristotelian commentaries, like that of Landino (1482; reprinted 1555), remained in circulation, and through them a large amount of Ciceronian doctrine passed into the body of Renaissance ideas. Much of the Platonism of the earlier theorists came by way of Cicero, Horace and Quintilian, who were also partly responsible for transmitting the concept of poetic imitation to the sixteenth century. Thus by the mid-1550s most of the commonplaces one find in Scaliger, Minturno, Castelvetro and a large number of minor commentators were already current, and from that time onwards it becomes increasingly difficult to trace original sources for many of the ideas in common use.

In so far as it is possible to separate the converging strands of classical theory, it is Horace who provides the sixteenth century with its most popular definition of the purpose of poetry: *prodesse et dilectare* – to give both profit and pleasure. Aristotle's *Poetics*, though mainly concerned with drama, contains the most influential version of the theory of poetic imitation, while the explanation of metaphor proposed in the Third Book of the *Rhetoric* – closely reflected in the corresponding passage of Herrera's *Anotaciones* – becomes an important ingredient in seventeenth-century discussions of poetic wit. The influence of Plato is more difficult to define, partly because there is no central Platonic text which could count as an Art of Poetry. Nevertheless, there are three aspects of Plato's views on poetry which preoccupy sixteenth-century theorists. One is the notion of *furor poeticus*: the idea that the poet speaks in a state of divine frenzy or inspiration which overrules all considerations of art. Another, which follows from Plato's theory of archetypes, is that poetic imitation can scarcely be taken seriously, since the poet can only imitate appearances, never reality itself. The third is Plato's notorious wish to banish poets as a threat to the moral foundations of the state – an attitude never openly endorsed by sixteenth-century theorists, but which perhaps explains why so much of their work takes the form of a defence of poetry against this and other possible attacks.

It is difficult to generalize about the mass of theoretical writing which derives from these various classical authorities: no two Renaissance theorists coincide exactly, though the degree of unity is greater than one might expect in an area which seems fraught with potential conflict. This is partly a matter of the way in which the authorities themselves were treated; as Bernard Weinberg has argued: 'The theorists ignored or discarded the systematic nature of each separate tradition [i.e. Plato, Aristotle and Horace], seeking in all simultaneously what each had to say about a given topic.'[5] The result was a roughly unified theory of poetry, centring on the relations between art and nature, and deriving its terms of analysis from the existing rhetorical tradition. This debt to rhetoric has a number of consequences. On the one hand, it makes for awareness of the effect a poem or a particular figure of speech may be expected to have on a reader. On the other, it runs the risk of judging a poem by non-poetic criteria and of reducing poetry to a branch of argument. As Weinberg remarks: 'Much of the strife over the proper bases for judging poems might be described in terms of the resistance to the establishment of a truly poetic approach.'[6] This helps to explain why in the sixteenth and seventeenth centuries there are so few examples of what we would nowadays call 'practical criticism'; instead of discussing a poem as an artistic whole, there is a constant tendency to separate content (*res*) from form (*verba*) and to refer each to different sets of critical concepts.

For any Renaissance poet, the short answer to the question 'what is poetry for?', as we have seen, lay in Horace's phrase *prodesse et dilectare*: poetry should give both profit and pleasure, or, as C. H. Sisson paraphrases it, 'the poet should not only give pleasure but say something sensible'.[7] In most Renaissance contexts, however, the distinction is sharper than this, and consequently less easy for a modern reader to accept, since it seems to imply that poetry 'teaches' – that it has an openly didactic purpose, in which pleasure will merely act as the bait. Yet, more often than not, the didactic aim of Renaissance poetry works more subtly than this. As Rosemond Tuve makes clear, pleasure and profit are not in competition with one another: 'Sixteenth- and seventeenth-century poets did not feel themselves faced with the grim alternative of teaching or delighting; they tried to be as thoroughgoingly witty or as deep-reaching as it was in them to be, on the understanding that intelligent men delight to be taught.'[8]

This refusal to make distinctions which are taken for granted by modern readers affects not only the aims of poetry in general but also the purpose of the individual poem and the nature of its structure and language. Thus, where a modern critic will often point to the way in which a poem has been shaped by the writer's experience, a Renaissance critic will speak of a poem's 'cause', meaning both the subject of the poem and the poet's intention in writing it. The subject will impose certain conditions on the poet – the pastoral and the love elegy, for example, have their own differing conventions of vocabulary and diction – but it is these conditions which call forth the artistic skill with which the poet embodies his intention in a work of art. Thus poetry claims to express truth, though not in the form of ideas which can be detached or paraphrased. Conversely, the criterion of 'pleasure' insists that the truth which a poem contains shall be conveyed as part of an artistically satisfying whole, and in this both concepts and feeling have their place. Or, to put it another way, the reader is more likely to be convinced of a poem's truthfulness if he finds pleasure in the relation between words and subject.

The question of the poet's 'truthfulness' involves one of the basic concepts of Renaissance theory, that of imitation. Though the term is constantly redefined in the course of the sixteenth century, it is used for the most part in three different, though related, senses: (i) imitation of older authors, classical or vernacular, as a means of evolving one's own way of writing; (ii) the Aristotelian concept of drama as the 'imitation of an action'; and (iii) the idea that the writer or the artist 'imitates' nature. Renaissance non-dramatic verse is concerned with the first and third senses, and both need some explanation.

Imitation, in its broadest sense, involves the whole question of Renaissance attitudes to the past; more precisely, to those classical Latin and Greek texts which had survived what came to be known as the 'Middle Ages'. Petrarch, once again, is the crucial figure: the first humanist to experience both the authority and the cultural remoteness of ancient literature, and the first to express the new kind of historical perspective this entails. Thus, as Thomas M. Greene explains: 'to be a humanist after Petrarch was not simply to be an archaeologist but to feel an imitative/emulative pressure from a lost source'.[9] The whole nature of Petrarch's encounter with classical texts is determined by his sense both of rupture and continuity. As against what Greene calls the 'diachronic innocence' of the Middle Ages, Petrarch and his successors attempt to bridge what they feel to be a cultural gap by mediating the 'otherness' of the classics through their own 'modern' sensibility. The important point here is that such a sensibility cannot be taken for granted, but is something which can only emerge in the course of dialogue with older texts. This means that in those writers, like Petrarch himself, who respond most intensely to the challenge of classical authority, imitation becomes a means to self-knowledge, a way of defining one's own literary identity in the course of alluding to existing models. Allusion, in fact, is the central procedure of most Renaissance writing; as Terence Cave has observed, the writer in this context is always a re-writer, concerned with the 'dismemberment and reconstruction of what has already been written'.[10] This is a very different matter from conventional notions of 'sources' and 'influences' – terms which scarcely suggest the strenuousness which such re-writing can involve.

Where Spain is concerned, attitudes to classical writers are hard to gauge: theoretical discussion only begins to gather weight in the 1570s, by which time the initial shock of discovery has died away, and the existence of a vernacular 'classic' – Garcilaso – has removed some of the emphasis from the imitation of Latin models. The much-quoted statement of Sánchez de las Brozas (El Brocense) – 'I consider no one a good poet who does not imitate the excellent ancients' – is disappointingly vague, and slightly later writers like López Pinciano (El Pinciano) and Luis Alfonso de Carballo do little more than warn against the dangers of plagiarism. Herrera, as we have seen, is more interesting, in so far as he no longer holds the classical writers to be infallible: 'I do not consider the authority of Garcilaso so great, nor – always excepting Virgil – that of the ancients in general, that it should be revered in such a way as to prevent us from understanding and judging their works...'[11] More strikingly, in view of his debt to Petrarch as a poet, Herrera attacks those who adhere too strictly to his own master. The Italians, he claims, have not confined themselves to imitating Petrarch, and the 'argument of love' is by no means exhausted.

The question of intertextuality – the presence within a given work of elements from earlier works – will recur frequently in the course of this book. At this stage, however, we need to turn to the other meaning of 'imitation' I have referred to: the sense in which the writer or artist may be said to 'imitate' nature. Here we must put out of our minds any Romantic idea of nature as emotionally charged landscape; what writers from Horace onwards mean by 'nature' is sometimes the whole of external reality, at other times what is conventionally regarded as 'natural', whether in terms of human behaviour or of the workings of the universe itself. On the surface, therefore, there is a basic opposition between nature and art, since nature is by definition 'artless' and art 'unnatural'. As we shall see in a moment, this antithesis is not as clear-cut as it might seem: a good deal of Renaissance writing is concerned with the possibility of mediating between the two concepts, in other words, of finding 'art' in nature and 'naturalness' in art.

The main question at issue, clearly, is one of verisimilitude, of the possibility of creating by artificial means the impression of reality and truth. The danger, which Renaissance theorists do not always avoid, is of failing to distinguish sufficiently between the poem itself and its object in nature, and consequently of misunderstanding the part played by specific poetic means in determining the reader's response.

Again, it is not necessary to think of the poet as someone who imposes order on a chaotic nature. Nature, it is often claimed by Renaissance writers, is never chaotic: however inscrutable it may seem to human understanding, it is still the source of all forms, including the form in which the poet expresses the substance of his poem. Thus, when Renaissance theorists speak of the poet as 'improving on' nature, the sense is usually one of co-operating with nature to reveal truths which are already implied, though possibly overlooked. And at times the principle of imitation can be made to suggest that the poet behaves in a way like nature itself: both can be regarded as craftsmen engaged in producing an artefact, an idea which is brought out very strongly in Garcilaso's Third Eclogue:

> Cerca del Tajo en soledad amena,
> de verdes sauces hay una espesura,
> toda de hiedra revestida y llena,
> que por el tronco va hasta el altura,
> y así la teje arriba y encadena,
> que el sol no halla paso a la verdura;

el agua baña el prado con sonido
alegrando la vista y el oído   (lines 57–64)[12]

Near the Tagus, in pleasant solitude, there is a thicket of green willows, all clothed and covered in ivy, which climbs the whole way up the trunk, and so weaves and enchains it above that the sun cannot penetrate the greenness: the water bathes the meadow in sound, delighting sight and hearing.

All the views I have just mentioned are commonplace in the sixteenth century; the difficulty, as with textual imitation, is that the balance between the basic terms – art and nature – is continually shifting: so much so, that it would be misleading to speak of a generally agreed pattern. Thus in Edward Tyler's survey of the art/nature dichotomy in English Renaissance literature, nature appears as *both* the principle of perfection and the principle of imperfection, with corresponding consequences for art:

When Art is viewed eulogistically – as the product of man's 'erected wit', of a faculty not entirely impaired by the Fall, of a faculty capable of rational creativity – then Nature usually signifies the unformed, the inchoate, the imperfect, or even the corrupt...When, on the other hand, Art is viewed pejoratively – as mere imitation, falsification, reprehensible counterfeit, or even perversion – then Nature signifies the original, the unspoiled, the transcendent, or even the perfect.[13]

The same kind of ambivalence can be seen at work in another of the basic notions of Renaissance theory: the idea of decorum, the demand that style should be appropriate to the subject. As has often been noted, decorum is the guiding principle from which most other sixteenth-century critical terms take their bearings. It is, of course, precisely the kind of literary principle one would expect to find in a hierarchically organized society which believes that everything in the universe has its divinely appointed place. In practice, it is responsible for many kinds of critical decision, from choice of genre to the use of individual words and images. Moreover, it is decorum which qualifies the didactic theory of poetry as the Renaissance understood it, so that writing a poem will not be merely a question of conveying ideas in a pleasurable way, but of rendering them in a proper aesthetic form.

So much is taken for granted by sixteenth-century theorists, in Spain and elsewhere. Yet what strikes a modern reader is the lack of any firm intellectual ground for such a notion; as Derek Attridge has pointed out in a brilliant essay on the Elizabethan theorist George Puttenham:

Decorum is clearly by far the most important rule in the poet's handbook – without it he might as well not begin to write. Yet what emerges with striking clarity from Puttenham's text is that *there is no such rule, and there could not possibly be one.* Decorum is precisely that aspect of the poet's art that is not reducible to rule. And human activity that is not reducible to rule is usually called 'natural'.[14]

Thus decorum, paradoxically, may seem to be a way of controlling nature by 'natural' means – a case of nature itself providing the principle by which it may be 'corrected'. Yet this is not strictly true: the 'naturalness' of decorum, far from corresponding to some unchanging order of things, is a social construct, a necessary illusion by which art can be integrated into a particular kind of community. As Attridge puts it: 'Although the naturalness of decorum is determined by a minority culture, it must be *believed* to be identical with nature itself.'[15] Or, to change his terms slightly, if poetry is a learned, and therefore exclusive, art, it is also a 'natural' one, not because it is a part of common human nature, but because its governing principle – decorum – is what is held to come 'naturally' to its practitioners and their audience.

Decorum, however problematical in its implications, is also responsible for the Renaissance theory of styles,[16] a connection made clear in a statement from Carballo's *Cisne de Apolo* (Swan of Apollo; 1602):

Decorum is a decency and consideration which must be applied to the entire work and to each part of it, to the characters, objects and words... Decorum is kept by considering the material which is to be employed, whether it is humble and common, like things for laughter and jest, or whether it is middling as in the ordinary dealings of folk of the mean estate, or whether it is a lofty matter, such as heroic deeds or elevated concepts and thoughts or holy and divine matters, and to what extent the humble, mean or high style is appropriate. (p. 163)

This division into three styles – the low or 'base', the 'mean' and the high or 'elevated' – applied, with some variations, to individual types of writing or genres. Thus the epic, as the highest form of non-dramatic verse known to antiquity, demands the high style (a notion which helps to account for the sixteenth-century revival of literary epic); the mean, or middle, style includes the more serious kinds of lyric poetry, while the base style is suited to satire, light verse and poetry dealing with humble people and situations. Sixteenth-century theory goes further than this, in fact, and a work like Herrera's *Anotaciones* gives detailed definitions of the main types of Italianate poem – the sonnet, the eclogue, the ode and the elegy – together with observations on the kind of imagery and vocabulary appropriate to each.

Like the idea of decorum itself, the division of styles is clearly more than just a literary artifice, and the terms it involves – high, mean and low – once again suggest the structure of a hierarchical society. This general division, however, does not aim at placing every poem in one of three boxes. Broadly speaking, a poem is taken as belonging to one or other of the three styles, but in practice it may contain a mixture of styles without necessarily offending against decorum. Thus homely or prosaic images, which suggest the base style, may be justified in a serious lyric, provided they do not conflict with the poet's intention. (A desire to convey the insignificance of something will be more decorously expressed by a trivial image than by a more weighty one.) Similarly, poems which seem deliberately to play off one style against another – a tendency which increases after 1600 – generally observe decorum in their individual images. As we shall see, a semi-burlesque poem like Góngora's *Fábula de Píramo y Tisbe* (1618) involves more than a simple juxtaposition of the elevated and the base styles; its technique, in fact, assumes a detailed awareness on the part of its readers of what is appropriate to either style and, though it presses certain types of contrast to their limit, these lose much of their force unless they are related to the principle of decorum.

All the aspects of Renaissance theory so far mentioned come together in the functioning of poetic imagery. In any sixteenth-century poem which belongs to the Italianate tradition, the nature of the images is determined by the poet's intention and by his understanding of the concept of imitation. Because poetry is more concerned with the universal than with the particular, images and epithets are used, more often than not, to direct the reader's mind towards the value of what is being described, rather than to its precise physical appearance. Thus Aldana introduces one of the most remarkable descriptions in sixteenth-century poetry ('Carta para Arias Montano', lines 352–432) with the words 'Quiero el lugar pintar' (I want to paint the place) and goes on to imagine a walk by the seashore in the company of the friend to whom the poem is addressed:

Bajaremos allá de cuando en cuando,
altas y ponderadas maravillas
en recíproco amor juntos tratando...
Verás mil retorcidas caracoles,
mil bucios estriados, con señales
y pintas de lustrosos arreboles:
los unos del color de los corales,
los otros de la luz que el sol represa
en los pintados arcos celestiales,
de varia operación, de varia empresa,
despidiendo de sí como centellas,
en rica mezcla de oro y de turquesa...

(lines 373–5; 382–90)

We shall go down there now and again, discoursing in mutual love of lofty, well-considered marvels... You will see a thousand twisted shells, a thousand ridged whelks, with the shades and markings of glowing red clouds: some the colour of coral, others of the light which the sun imprisons in the painted rainbows, various in function and enterprise, emitting as it were sparks, in a rich mixture of gold and turquoise...

Much of the power of this passage comes from the precise observation of the natural scene; yet what ultimately matters is the way in which the individual objects are evaluated by phrases like 'altas y ponderadas maravillas' (lofty, well-considered marvels) ... 'de varia operación, de varia empresa' (various in function and enterprise), so that even a factual detail like '*retorcidas* caracoles' (twisted shells) is made to convey the beholder's amazement at the riches and variety of creation. This is why an image must always be considered in its poetic context; what in itself may seem a straightforward piece of description will often take on an evaluative function when seen as part of a whole poem.

There are two possible sources of confusion in speaking of Renaissance imagery: one is the Horatian tag *ut pictura poesis* – 'poetry should be like painting' – which is often quoted by the theorists; the other is the unsatisfactory nature of the term 'image' itself when applied to writing.

The latter problem arises from a common misunderstanding of the nature of 'mental imagery', compounded by certain false analogies with the visual arts. As P. N. Furbank has argued:

People still tend to think of mental images as having an actual optical reality, as if 'seeing' things in the head were fundamentally not different from seeing them in the world outside. They believe that mental pictures are presented to them and that they contemplate them. In fact...one does not contemplate mental images. A mental image is no less and no more than what you put there...You can never stand back and scrutinize a mental image, since you are fully occupied in creating it – it represents your consciousness in action. If you imagine St Paul's Cathedral to yourself, you cannot *count* the columns of the portico, to see how many there are, for it is entirely up to you how many you put there...[17]

In the case of a painting, the mental imagery of the spectator is controlled by the particular image which the artist has created on the canvas – an image which exists only in terms of the actual medium. An 'image' in a poem, on the other hand, has no such connection with the medium of poetry: however specific it may appear, any visualization takes place entirely within the reader's mind, a fact which appears to undermine any notion of the poet as 'copying reality'.

Yet, if we take the *ut pictura poesis* formula literally, it may seem that Renaissance theorists are praising poetic imagery for precisely this reason, in other words, for its ability to 'decorate' literal meaning by adding pictorial ornament in the same way as a painter will embellish his theme by the use of pigment. This, if it were true, might suggest a view of poetic imagery in which the image itself would be valued mainly for its capacity of producing an accurate mental picture – something, that is to say, which could exist separately from the actual language of the poem. However, as we have just seen, the notion that one can produce an 'accurate mental picture' by verbal means is inherently false, a fact which might appear to invalidate the whole Renaissance approach to poetic imagery. Nevertheless, this does not happen in practice, since the formula is never adhered to as strictly as this. Though both poets and theorists are fond of quoting certain classical anecdotes which stress the power of painting to deceive the eye, they are also aware that painting, like poetry, is ultimately concerned with essences and universals. Thus, if they describe poetry as a 'speaking picture' and painting as 'silent poetry',[18] it is not because they confuse the two media, but because they recognize an underlying similarity of intention, an ordering of particulars which speaks to the intellect through the senses. Just as sixteenth- and seventeenth-century writers praise a picture for being 'lifelike', so they will value a poetic image for the power with which it affects the reader.[19] Individuality may contribute to this power – there is nothing in Renaissance theory to suggest that an image should be vague rather than specific – though, as in the example from Aldana, the precision of a particular image will only take on its full force when it is related to the wider, more conceptual, meaning of the poem.

Inevitably, a poetry which deals with concepts rather than with emotional states will accept all the help which logic and rhetoric can give it, and will not feel plain statement to be 'unpoetic'. On the other hand, it will not exclude the expression of emotional power, since it recognizes that emotions play a central part in human action.[20] As a consequence, the functioning of imagery in Renaissance poetry, like that of metaphor, is never felt to conflict with the use of non-figurative language, since both can serve equally well to convey universal significances. Nevertheless, it would be wrong to regard metaphor simply as a particular kind of image: if 'image' implies 'picture' or 'representation', a metaphor, since it involves a comparison, cannot present an 'image' in this sense, for the simple reason that no one can visualize two things at once. Granting this distinction, as Renaissance theory invariably does, metaphor is usually justified on three grounds: it adds variety; it is 'necessary' because sometimes there are no words for naming things; and it makes for intellectual richness by widening the area of meaning. As usual in Renaissance theory, all three qualities involve either the reader's pleasure or his judgement: if a metaphor sharpens the meaning of a poem or states a just affinity between different objects, then it is to be praised; if it is far-fetched or confused – in other words, if it is neither clear nor truthful – it has failed in its purpose. Sixteenth-century critics do not deny that a metaphor may appeal to the senses; this is part of the force of metaphor. Where they differ from modern critics is in not looking to metaphor for a more *accurate* rendering of a sense impression.

Rosemond Tuve makes the point clear when she contrasts 'the modern habit of emphasizing the nature of *that to which* the comparison is made' with the sixteenth-century stress on 'the nature of the affinity seen'.[21] The truth of this becomes obvious once one refers to Aristotle's classification of metaphor in the *Poetics*: 'Metaphor consists in the assigning to a thing the name of something else; and this may take place from genus to species, or from species to genus, or from species to species or proportionally' (*Poetics*, 21), and in Rhetoric III, 7 he adds: 'Of the four kinds of metaphor, the most popular are those based on proportion' (i.e. A is to B as C is to D). All four types of metaphor, in other words, are concerned, not with the actual terms of the relationship, but with the nature of the relationship itself and the means by which it is produced. In the proportional type, one relationship exists between A and B and another between C and D, and the appropriateness of the metaphor depends on the similarity of the relationships. (In the example given by Aristotle – 'as the shield is to Ares, so the goblet is to Dionysus' – there is no suggestion that the shield resembles the goblet in any way.)[22]

By modern standards, Aristotle's account of metaphor has serious limitations. For one thing, by restricting the metaphorical process to the transference of names, it fails to allow for the extent to which metaphorical meaning may be bound up with the sentence as a whole.[23] This in turn reflects an absolute distinction between plain and metaphorical speech. As Terence Hawkes has observed:

Beyond this view of metaphor there may be discerned two fundamental ideas about the nature of language and its relationship to the 'real' world; first that language and reality, words and the objective world to which they refer, are quite separate entities; and second, that the *manner* in which something is said does not significantly condition or alter *what* is said.[24]

Thus, though Aristotle does not deny that metaphor may have a didactic function – it may, after all, suggest new ideas – its purpose, nevertheless, is essentially decorative; as he himself declares at one point in the *Rhetoric*, an excess of metaphor will make 'ordinary' language 'too much like poetry'.

This decorative theory of metaphor persists into the Renaissance, along with the distinction between plain and metaphorical speech. Eventually, however, it finds itself in conflict with another of the notions current in the late sixteenth century – the doctrine of universal analogy. This goes back ultimately to Plato's theory of archetypes; in its Christian version, familiar to the Middle Ages, it conceives the world as 'God's book' – a vast and complex system of relationships which man must learn to 'read' correctly. As mentioned earlier, this single controlling metaphor implies a network of 'correspondences' which can only be grasped in terms of other metaphors. In the seventeenth century, as we shall see, this notion of 'correspondences' becomes a key factor in discussions of poetic wit. For the moment, however, it is enough to recognize that, on this view, the relationships which the poet establishes through metaphor are already present in the divinely created universe. Thus the poet does not so much invent metaphors as discover them; it is the poet who, through his gift for seizing on analogies which already exist, can see more deeply into the divine plan than other men. And it follows that metaphors conceived in this way will no longer be seen as decorative, but as revealing truths which cannot be expressed in any other way.[25]

III

Any brief summary of Renaissance poetics runs the risk of making them seem more consistent than they actually were. As I have tried to explain, the whole way in which most Renaissance theorists approached the classical authorities tended to produce an appearance of unity, even where more systematic exploration would have revealed serious discrepancies. Since most late sixteenth-century Spanish theory is neo-Aristotelian, my account has, if anything followed the same direction. Nevertheless, not every theorist of the time follows this pattern exactly, the most notable exception being Herrera.

Because of the way they are organized, the *Anotaciones* do not offer the steady line of argument one would expect from a genuine poetic treatise. Like most sixteenth-century theorists, Herrera is thoroughly eclectic: his discussion of metaphor, for instance, draws heavily on Cicero and Aristotle, and elsewhere he is prepared to incorporate passages from a writer like Scaliger whose general approach to poetry is quite at odds with his own.[26] Nevertheless, when he comes to examine the aims and nature of poetry, Herrera puts forward a point of view which is both consistent and, by implication at least, critical of the conventional didactic theory. As one might expect from his poetic practice, Herrera's theoretical opinions are basically neo-Platonic: they centre on the notion of poetic inspiration and interpret imitation in the Platonic sense, that is to say, as the imitation of an idea in the poet's mind rather than of any 'real' object.

At one point in his discourse on elegy, Herrera appears to reject the usual *prodesse et dilectare* formula by placing the emphasis entirely on the production of aesthetic pleasure: 'The aim of the poet is to speak through his composition [*compuestamente*] in such a way as to cause wonder [*admirar*], and he strives only to speak admirably [*admirablemente*].'[27] Here, the words 'admirar' and 'admirablemente' carry the whole weight of Latin *admiratio*, with its overtones of 'astonishment', 'wonder' and 'awe' – a type of pleasure which does not necessarily exclude instruction, but which in the present context is linked to the ways in which rhythm and diction may 'enrich' the subject-matter of the poem.[28] Throughout the discourse, in fact, Herrera insists on what he calls the 'ornament of elocution', a phrase which inevitably recalls the conventional sixteenth-century division between subject-matter (*res*) and language (*verba*). Yet, as Andreina Bianchini has argued, there is a sense in which he goes beyond this limitation of traditional rhetoric:

> The interesting aspect of this problem in Herrera's theory is that he manages to transcend the distinction by devoting himself wholly to *verba*, which become, in consequence, their own *res*... As one reads through Herrera's many annotations to Garcilaso's poetry it becomes increasingly clear that the artistic manipulation of a poetic language according to wholly aesthetic criteria becomes the *res* of poetry for this Sevillian. And while the question of poetic truth and verisimilitude were typically Aristotelian topics, Herrera offers no direct discussion of these in the *Anotaciones*. Poetic truth for Herrera is implicitly an aesthetic truth emerging from the *verba* rather than the *res*.[29]

This surely helps to explain some of the attitudes to poetic language we saw in the previous chapter: the defence of neologisms, the rejection of unsophisticated language and above all the latitude with which Herrera regards existing models. At the same time, one may wonder whether subject-matter in the conventional sense is quite so secondary to Herrera as this seems to suggest. Elsewhere in the discourse on elegy, he specifically emphasizes the power of rhythm and diction to enhance the emotional content – the *conceptos amorosos* – of the poem, and we may also recall the statement quoted earlier (p. 40) to the effect that the great poets of the past, for all their achievement, have still left certain things unsaid.

Love, for Herrera, is so clearly the central subject of lyric poetry that he might well have argued that his concern for verbal refinement was an intrinsic part of the neo-Platonic search for beauty in which love is the prime instrument. Whatever the truth of this, his defence of poetic inspiration and his insistence on verbal discipline are not as incompatible as they might seem. If one appears to offer a prospect of unlimited creativity, the other ensures that the poet will be fully responsible for the quality of his creations, and both together emphasize the potentialities of language itself. As for his apparent rejection of the didactic theory, it is perhaps truer to say that he does not so much reject it as re-define the nature of 'profit'. Thus whenever he refers to the possible effect of a poem on the reader, Herrera speaks, not in terms of conveying truths, but of engaging his mind and sensibility. In the discourse on metaphor, for example, he remarks on the pleasure which is caused by transferring words from another context:

And among other reasons, this should occur, either because it is a demonstration and triumph of wit [*ingenio*] to go beyond those things which lie at one's feet and to employ those which are distant and brought from afar; or because the thoughts and speculations of the hearer are borne elsewhere, although he neither errs nor strays from the path; and because the entire transference [*traslación*], if it is based on reason, approaches and touches the very senses, and principally that of sight, which is the most acute sense of all...because they [i.e. metaphors] set things which we could neither see nor behold as it were in the presence of the soul.[30]

In the context of late sixteenth-century theory, the shift which this implies is a crucial one. Metaphor is no longer seen as poetic ornament, but as a guiding power; though language is sometimes inadequate to the needs of expression, by means of metaphor one can persuade the reader to think of connections which are not directly stated. Just as Herrera's own poetic language points the way to *culteranismo*, or the conscious Latinizing of diction and style, so a statement like this already provides some of the arguments which were later used to justify the complexities of *conceptismo*.[31]

If, as Bianchini claims, the *Anotaciones* represent the 'hidden theoretical side...of Spanish baroque poetry',[32] it would nevertheless be a mistake to assume that Herrera was completely conscious of the implications of his theories. The independence of mind with which he confronts important issues like imitation and the functions of metaphor and epithet has no parallel among other Spanish theorists of the time,[33] and it is possible that the digressive nature of his commentary may have allowed him to say certain things more forcefully than he might have done within the more conventional form of a poetic treatise. Yet, however much his own poetry may have influenced later writers, it shows little trace of 'wit' in the seventeenth-century sense and remains firmly attached to neo-Platonic values. Once again, one is made aware of Herrera's importance as a transitional figure. Though most of the arguments later used in defence of *conceptista*, or 'conceited', writing had been current since the 1550s, the new manner only crystallized when such arguments came to be used as the conscious basis of poetic technique.

Herrera only indirectly anticipates this moment: yet with the *Anotaciones*, and occasionally in his own practice,[34] the movement towards a different type of writing is becoming increasingly clear.

IV

This different type of writing is often referred to as 'Baroque', in order to distinguish it from earlier 'Renaissance' literature. The chief justification for such a distinction lies in the nature of the works themselves: where Spanish poetry is concerned, it is impossible to imagine that the major poems of Góngora or the love sonnets of Quevedo could have been written fifty years earlier, and similar examples can be found in other European literatures of the time. The difficulties begin, however, as soon as one starts to consider the kind of qualities which the word 'Baroque' has been made to imply and the ways in which it has been used as a means of linking works which are often radically different from one another.

Part of these difficulties comes from the fact that the present use of the term 'Baroque' derives from art history, where it is made to describe certain differences between Renaissance art and later developments in the sixteenth and seventeenth centuries. The literary use of the term begins by observing certain parallels between seventeenth-century writing and contemporary Baroque art. Such analogies are usually structural or thematic: changes in the internal patterning of the sonnet are held to reflect new kinds of structure in painting or architecture; similarly, certain key symbols common to literature and the other arts – the hour-glass, ruins and gardens, life as a bubble or as the water of a fountain – are said to represent a distinctive 'Baroque sensibility'. Yet, however ingenious such comparisons may be, they are often less illuminating than one might hope, mainly because they tend to overlook crucial differences between the various media concerned. Thus unity and multiplicity – a favourite contrast in discussions of the Baroque – mean very different things, according to whether one is speaking of poetry or architecture; alternatively, the use of painting terms and elaborate colour effects in a poem can only be referred to the 'picture' created in the reader's imagination, not to an actual arrangement of pigments on a canvas. What ultimately undermines such attempted analogies is the absence of fixed points of reference, a point well made by Peter Russell:

The label 'baroque' often tends to blur rather than to elucidate a critical statement since there is as yet no agreed definition of baroque art itself and no general agreement about the meaning of the term when applied to literature. Its use may distract the reader's attention from what is important in strictly literary terms about the work under discussion.[35]

Despite the problems it raises, however, we seem to need some such term to suggest what happened to both literature and the other arts after the Renaissance, and it can sometimes be positively helpful to talk about a 'Baroque period', using the term in a neutral, historical sense to indicate a particular cultural phase, common to most of Western Europe and parts of South America, which spans the end of the sixteenth century and most of the seventeenth. As for literature itself, it seems clear by now that there is no single 'Baroque style', but rather a multiplicity of styles which share a certain family likeness. As René Wellek has observed:

Periods and movements 'exist' in the sense that they can be discerned in reality, can be described and analysed. It would, however, be foolish to expect a single noun or adjective to convey unimpeded and still clearly realized a dozen different connotations.[36]

In practice, what we tend to find is a number of features – both themes and stylistic devices – none of which is unprecedented, but which are brought together in new ways and with emphases which vary from one poet to another. From a theoretical point of view, the body of ideas on the nature of poetry described earlier in this chapter remains unchallenged in the seventeenth century, at least where Spain is concerned, though new inferences are drawn from it, and these are reflected in stylistic developments which are often thought of as 'Baroque'. The most striking of these are the twin tendencies known to more recent criticism as *culteranismo* and *conceptismo*, both of which have their roots in Renaissance theory and practice, but which assume a quite unprecedented importance in the early seventeenth century.[37]

Culteranismo, as usually understood, represents a conscious attempt to enrich the language of poetry by assimilating it more closely to Latin, thus removing it as far as possible from ordinary discourse. The intention is already clear in the fifteenth-century poet Juan de Mena (1411–56), many of whose neologisms, or words coined from Latin models, are taken up later by Herrera and Góngora. In Góngora himself, the wish to rival the literary status of Latin is quite explicit:

As for honour, I believe that this poetry [i.e. the *Soledades*] has honoured me in two ways: if it is understood by the learned, it will give me authority, since they cannot fail to respect the fact that, in consequence of my labours, our language has achieved the perfection and elevation of Latin. (Letter of 30 September 1615)[38]

The signs of this are evident in almost every line of Góngora's major poems: words like *canoro* (canorous), *lascivo* (playful, wanton), *prolijo* (lengthy), *impedido* (obstructed) not only elevate the tone of the verse but help to create its characteristic weight and movement.

The effect on syntax is even more striking: Góngora's sinuous verse periods systematically extend the possibilities of hyperbaton – the displacement of normal word-order – beyond the limits of sixteenth-century practice. The results are not only complicated, but often highly expressive. Many of the best examples occur in the *Polifemo* and the *Soledades*, though there is a good instance in one of the sonnets composed in 1611 for the *túmulo* or catafalque erected in Córdoba for the dead Queen Margaret of Austria:

> Máquina funeral, que desta vida
> nos decís la mudanza, estando queda;
> pira, no de aromática arboleda,
> sí a más gloriosa fénix constrüida;
>   bajel en cuya gavia esclarecida
> estrellas, hijas de otra mejor Leda,
> serenan la Fortuna, de su rueda
> la volubilidad reconocida,
>   farol luciente sois, que solicita
> la razón, entre escollos naufragante,
> al puerto; y a pesar de lo luciente,
>   oscura concha de una Margarita,
> que, rubí en caridad, en fe diamante,
> renace en nuevo Sol en nuevo Oriente.

Funereal structure who, unmoving, tell us of the mutability of this life; pyre, not of aromatic wood, though erected, indeed, for a more glorious Phoenix; vessel on whose illustrious topsail stars, the children of another, better, Leda [i.e. the Virgin Mary], subdue the well-known capriciousness of Fortune's wheel; you are a shining lantern which guides reason, running on rocks, to harbour; and despite your brilliance, the dark shell of a pearl [*margarita*: also the name of the Queen] who, a ruby in charity, in faith a diamond, is reborn in a new Sun, a new Orient.

Though the poem owes a lot of its force to the skilful handling of metaphor and paradox, syntax plays an important part in underlining the sense, particularly by stressing certain key images. The whole poem, in fact, consists of a single fourteen-line sentence which is brilliantly played off against the sonnet form. Thus, in the first eight lines, the three nouns in apposition – 'Máquina [structure]...pira [pyre]...bajel [vessel]' – are clearly marked off from their accompanying clauses by their position at the beginning of a line, and the delayed appearance of the only main verb – 'farol luciente *sois*' (you are a shining lantern) – is emphasized by the slight pause after the second quatrain. One can observe other similar devices, for example, the effect of the parallel constructions in the last two lines which triumphantly close off the more irregular movement which precedes them, or the way in which Góngora develops a whole series of conjunctions of the 'si...no' type ('A, if not B'; 'despite X, Y') in order to control his interlocking images. The important point, however, is that the creation of such a diction represents a deliberate attempt to invent a distinctive poetic language which will take over some of the functions of the 'high' style from the epic.[39]

The *culto* style also brings with it an intensification of classical allusions and a preference for a particular kind of metaphor. Góngora's classical allusions are seldom difficult in themselves – most, if not all, of them could be traced to the *Metamorphoses* of Ovid – but they are harder to grasp when they form the basis of a metaphor. Thus in the sonnet just quoted, we are not only expected to recognize a reference to Castor and Pollux, but also to be capable of making the leap from 'bajel' (vessel), which is itself a metaphor, to the idea of divine protection.[40] By using metaphor in this way, Góngora is enlarging the possibilities of Renaissance practice, rather than denying the theory which lies behind it. Very often in the course of his work he will build a new metaphor on the basis of another, more conventional, comparison. One of his most frequent devices consists of turning a commonplace simile into a metaphor. So, in 'Angélica y Medoro' (1602), a ballad based on a famous episode from the *Orlando Furioso* of Ariosto, Angélica is described as 'una ciega con dos soles' (a blind woman with two suns) (line 68): her eyes, that is to say, are not *like* two suns, they *are* two suns. Góngora's originality lies not only in creating this kind of metaphor, but in using it to construct a system in which many different kinds of object can be referred to in terms of one common attribute. Thus the single word *cristal* (crystal) may refer to water, tears or the limbs of a woman; *oro* (gold) can denote anything which is golden, and any more specific qualities are conveyed by epithets: *oro líquido* 'honey'. The effect of this technique, in Dámaso Alonso's phrase, is to create 'a kind of ennobling simplification of the world',[41] which forms part of the central purpose of the *Soledades*, and can be seen on a smaller scale in 'Angélica y Medoro'. Again, Góngora is taking one of the basic concepts of Renaissance theory to its logical conclusion: if the particular attributes of objects are suppressed or evaded, one is left with a network of images which are related, with unusual directness, to the world of universals.

Until recently, as I have explained, it was usual to regard *culteranismo* and *conceptismo* as opposing phenomena, with Góngora and Quevedo as their respective exponents. The evidence of the poetry itself, however, contradicts this: Góngora's *culto* poems would be much less effective without the firm structure of ingenious metaphors which underlies them, and the quarrel between Góngora and Quevedo, personal animosity apart, is really over the question of *culto* vocabulary and the attitude to language which this involves.[42] This also suggests the general relationship between *conceptismo* and *culteranismo*: contrary to the older view, these are not a pair of opposing tendencies, but, more often than not, a particular way of using metaphor (*conceptismo*), and a distinctive kind of poetic language (*culteranismo*) which may be combined with the basic metaphorical technique.

Conceptismo is not peculiar to Spanish poetry, but is part of a general European tendency which includes the English metaphysical poets, as well as a number of seventeenth-century French and Italian writers. It takes its name from the *concepto* (usually translated as 'conceit') which is its most striking stylistic device.[43] Though many definitions of the conceit are given by the theorists of the time, its essential nature lies in establishing an intellectual relationship between two dissimilar terms. This, of course, is one of the normal functions of metaphor, and the majority of seventeenth-century conceits are examples of the figure known in traditional rhetoric as *catachresis*, or 'violent metaphor'. Both the appeal to the intellect and the effect of surprise are important: conceits are often praised for the wit which the poet displays in finding an unexpected relationship between remote objects. To quote Helen Gardner:

A conceit is a comparison whose ingenuity is more striking than its justness, or, at least, is more immediately striking. All comparisons discover likeness in things unlike: a comparison becomes a conceit when we are made to concede likeness while being strongly aware of unlikeness.[44]

Thus the difference between conceit and ordinary metaphor is only one of degree, and both have the same justification in Renaissance theory. Just as in other kinds of figurative language particulars are continually referred to universals, so the idea of the conceit suggests a universe in which the terms it links are already, in a sense, connected. As the seventeenth-century Italian theorist Emmanuele Tesauro put it: 'Whatever the world has of wit either is God or is from God, so that the poet can only express relationships which already exist in creation.'[45] Not all conceits measure up to this ideal, and many were never intended to. A successful conceit, however, will invariably extend the reader's perceptions by making him aware for the first time of a genuine, though surprising, relationship.[46]

The best way to grasp the nature of a poetic conceit is to see how it functions within the context of an entire poem. Take, for example, the following sonnet by Quevedo, entitled 'Afectos varios de su corazón fluctuando en las ondas de los cabellos de Lisi' (Various feelings of his heart, fluctuating in the waves of Lisi's hair):

> En crespa tempestad del oro undoso,
> nada golfos de luz ardiente y pura
> mi corazón, sediento de hermosura,
> si el cabello deslazas generoso.
>
> Leandro, en mar de fuego proceloso,
> su amor ostenta, su vivir apura;
> Ícaro, en senda de oro mal segura,
> arde sus alas por morir glorioso.
>
> Con pretensión de fénix, encendidas
> sus esperanzas, que difuntas lloro,
> intenta que su muerte engendre vidas.
>
> Avaro y rico y pobre, en el tesoro,
> el castigo y la hambre imita a Midas,
> Tántalo en fugitiva fuente de oro.

In an angry [also 'curling'] storm of waving gold, my heart, thirsting for beauty, swims through gulfs of pure, burning light if you unbind your generous hair. Leander, in a stormy sea of fire, displays his love, refines his life; Icarus, on an insecure path of gold, burns his wings to die a glorious death. Attempting to be a phoenix, its hopes on fire – whose death I mourn – it [i.e. my heart] endeavours to make its death engender lives. Miserly and rich and poor, in its treasure, its punishment and its hunger it resembles Midas, [and it resembles] Tantalus in a fleeting fountain of gold.

The opening of the poem (lines 1–8) is based on the idea that love is a source of danger to the lover. The conceits of the first four lines attempt to show this in a particularly vivid way, among other things by making possible the simultaneous perception of the twin sources of danger (water and sun), which are both expanded by the references to Leander and Icarus. As A. A. Parker remarks in his fine analysis of this poem, the point of these conceits is that the woman's hair is all these things at once.[47] The idea of suffering through love can be related to the courtly love tradition; in Quevedo's poem, the conventional idea is expressed in a number of conceits deployed in a firm rhetorical structure.[48]

The next three lines (9–11) define the nature of the speaker's suffering. The final tercet takes up the central idea – that the reason knows what the heart's punishment will be – and presents it through the examples of Midas and Tantalus. Leander and Icarus illustrate the theme of danger; Midas and Tantalus refer to another, closely related, aspect of courtly love: the state of 'having and not having' – a slight shift of emphasis from one part of a convention to another, but no essential difference.

However, if we look more closely at the first tercet (lines 9–11), we find that it is not really enough to say that the speaker is defining the nature of his suffering (though he is doing just that); it is also a question of the way in which the definition is presented. To begin with, there is a carefully maintained distinction between reason and passion: 'encendidas/ sus esperanzas, que difuntas lloro' (its hopes on fire, whose death I mourn). Again, the poem as a whole deals with the eternity – in other words, with the spiritual aspect – of human love, so that the contrast between the spirit and the senses involves the opposition between the eternal and the temporal: 'The heart acts as if love were eternal; the reason knows that it is not.' It is this basic opposition – in itself, one of the great paradoxes of traditional metaphysics – which is projected on to the image of the phoenix. The terms of the conceit are 'heart' and 'phoenix'; what links them is the idea of burning. The action implied ('its hopes on fire') selects from the two terms only those properties which are relevant to the comparison: that is to say, the essential process is one of abstraction. The contrast here is not between 'phoenix' and 'heart', but between the heart's belief that it will be reborn and the reason's knowledge that it will die. The whole tendency of the poem, in fact, is to maintain the distinction between reason and passion, and the conclusion suggested by the last three lines is that, although he may acknowledge reason to be in the right, the lover will continue to act as his passion demands. Thus the final effect lies in holding together terms which are usually regarded as irreconcilable: in the phoenix reference, the juxtaposition of eternal and temporal qualities is surprising, as any conceit must be, yet at the same time is justified by the paradoxical nature of amorous discourse.

This should make us reflect on the nature of the speaker himself, on the fact that the 'I' of the poem is a 'rhetorical self', a fiction deliberately constructed in order to produce a particular kind of effect on the reader. It would be a mistake, therefore, to read such a poem as an attempt to re-create the personal experience of a private individual, in other words, to re-direct its emotional force from the reader to some image of the author which exists outside the poem. Rhetorical skill, it should be stressed, does not preclude genuine feeling; it simply ensures that such feeling is generated within the poem itself, where it is reinforced by specific techniques of persuasion. Thus from the reader's point of view, a poem like this works in terms of recognition and expectation: the units of sense are manoeuvred in such a way that the reader both assents to what he is being told and comes to expect further developments which will present him with other possibilities of recognition – always, of course, within the poem's own chosen terms.

Quevedo's poems, as I shall later argue, do not always fit easily into seventeenth-century theories of wit, the most striking of which are considerably later than the poetry they are concerned to justify. Nevertheless, it is interesting that early seventeenth-century discussions of poetic language should tend more and more towards the defence of difficulty. As we have seen, both Herrera and Góngora speak of the need to stretch the reader's powers of comprehension, and it is significant that both poets refer to the *ingenio*, or wit, as the means by which remote connections are perceived. Moreover, *ingenio* is also the power which produces conceits, and therefore itself suggests the intellectual character of the process. In seventeenth-century theory, the *ingenio* comes to be regarded not only as the main instrument of poetic choice, but as the metaphysical core of poetic style. One important consequence of this is the way in which the conventional sixteenth-century distinctions between genres become submerged in the general principle of the conceit. As Mazzeo points out, Praz and other critics are mistaken in attributing the popularity of the conceit to an extension of the sixteenth-century taste for epigram and emblem:

Indeed, this theory of the conceit was implicitly rejected by the seventeenth-century theorists of the conceit in whose works the emblem and the *impresa*... are treated as individual types involved in the analysis of conceit or metaphor. They were fully aware that any theory of the conceit had to be a theory of metaphor or analogy, not a theory of genres.[49]

The boldest and most elaborate attempt to justify the conceit along these lines was made by Baltasar Gracián (1601–58), in his *Agudeza y arte de ingenio* (Wit and the Art of the Mind; 1646),[50] and both the attempt itself and the difficulties into which it leads him bear directly on the limitations of Renaissance theory. In the first place, it is important to recognize that Gracián is not merely offering a theory of the conceit, but a treatise on the nature and functioning of wit. His central term, *agudeza* (literally, 'acuity'), refers both to wit itself and to the mental power which is capable of grasping or producing it. The immediate consequence of this emphasis is to extend the discussion beyond the range of *conceptismo* proper; if *conceptismo*, more often than not, implies the use of conceits, *agudeza* points to a mental attitude which is not essentially tied to conceits, however much it may resort to these as a means of expressing itself. Secondly, it is clear that Gracián uses the term *concepto* in more than one sense: as well as 'conceit', it can mean both 'concept' and the 'act of conception'.[51] These usages suggest the intellectual nature of Gracián's inquiry; at the same time, he insists that the nature of wit is quite different from philosophical speculation, and that its operation must be grasped in terms of traditional rhetoric. This brings us back to the role of the *ingenio*. As Parker has pointed out, 'mind' is hardly an adequate translation of this highly complex term; if, as I have said, the *ingenio* is the means by which remote connections are perceived, it is also true that its powers are not to be confused with those of reason itself. As Parker goes on to argue, Gracián's use of the term seems to imply the kind of distinction between reason and intellect which is to be found in the medieval Platonic tradition:

The highest type of knowledge is that of intellect (*intellectus*), which synthesizes and harmonizes. This is an activity of the mind superior to reason. The intellect denies the oppositions of reason; the latter affirms that A cannot be its opposite, Z, but intellect can deny the separateness of A and Z because it apprehends God as the being in which opposites coincide, as the *coincidentia oppositorum*. This apprehension cannot be stated logically, because that is the language of reason; intellect uses language to *suggest* meaning rather than to state it, and employs analogies and symbols.[52]

Gracián's own vocabulary does not always distinguish as sharply as this between intellect and understanding – his best-known definition of the *concepto* is 'an act of the understanding which expresses the correspondence which exists between objects'[53] – yet it is clear that he regards the *ingenio* as combining both intellectual and imaginative functions. Unlike reason, wit is concerned to establish beauty as well as truth; thus Gracián's whole enterprise becomes an exercise in aesthetics for which there is no parallel in sixteenth-century theory.

At the same time, though he is careful to separate the art of the *ingenio* from the study of rhetoric, Gracián does not so much reject traditional rhetoric as build on it for his own purposes. Like the sixteenth-century theorists, he is interested in the relationship between the terms of a comparison, rather than in the terms themselves, and it is clear from many of his examples that the aesthetic pleasure to be derived from a witty comparison has for him something of the beauty of a mathematical proof.

In sixteenth-century theory – though not necessarily in practice – this kind of relationship is usually fairly simple, and most Arts of Rhetoric before 1600 give instructions to aspiring writers for the composition of 'similitudes' or extended metaphors, based on either the Ciceronian types or the Aristotelian categories.[54] Aristotle lists ten such categories or 'predicaments': substance, quantity, quality, relation, manner of doing, manner of suffering, when, where, *situs* (place) and *habitus* (condition). These, or their Ciceronian equivalents, are to be found in any conventional sixteenth-century logic, where they are put forward as a conveniently practical method of constructing an argument. When applied to poetry, they serve in a similar way to invent images; an object need only be contemplated under one or other of these aspects for a number of images to suggest themselves, and from these a competent poet may make his choice. In Gracián, the relation between subject and representation becomes more complex, but the influence of the categories can still be seen in one of the key passages of the *Agudeza*:

The subject on which one meditates and ponders...is like a kind of centre from which the power of reflection traces lines of thought and subtlety to the entities which surround it, that is to say, to the adjuncts which encircle it, such as its causes, effects, attributes, qualities, contingencies, circumstances of time, place, manner, etc., and any other corresponding term.[55]

Here Gracián is describing what he calls *agudeza de proporción* (Wit of Proportion); he goes on to explain how the subject may be compared with its adjuncts, and these with one another, in order to discover some 'conformity' which may then be expressed: 'So this first type of wit consists in a certain necessary and pleasing correspondence which the terms display between themselves or with the subject.'

As T. E. May has pointed out, Gracián's approach to different types of conceit is generally made through some such consideration of the subject and its adjuncts, and where there are no adjuncts, but only a second term, the relationship is again analysed along lines familiar to any Renaissance student of logic. Difficulties arise, however, once one begins to investigate the nature of the 'correspondence'. As May goes on to say:

> Gracián does not explain his term *correspondencia*, as used in his definition, but its actual use appears to rest ultimately, if not on the doctrine itself, certainly on the attitude that formerly produced in metaphysics the doctrine of the analogy of being. The intellectualist tendencies of Gracián's treatment of the conceit, and indeed of his whole aesthetic, are thus the product of the search for a metaphysical heart in the style he practised.[56]

Yet a 'metaphysical heart' implies metaphysical reality, and this is something which the *ingenio*, once it is severed from philosophical understanding, is unable to deal with.

At the root of these difficulties is Gracián's wish to prove that wit is a unique kind of mental act and that, by extension, the conceit is different in kind from all other types of figurative language. In order to appear to do this, he has to regard metaphor chiefly as verbal ornament and to overlook the strong intellectual bias which it has in Renaissance theory. For Gracián, metaphor and other tropes belong exclusively to rhetoric, while the *ingenio*, as we have seen, involves a special kind of mental process, which is distinct from both rhetoric and dialectic. Again, this view of the *ingenio* is made to include a number of functions which cannot be treated as purely intellectual: the conceit which is produced by the *ingenio* is held to convey both beauty and truth. In the end, therefore, the *ingenio*, whatever its relation to the understanding, is made to seem a kind of creative intellect combining both logical and aesthetic functions. What Gracián wishes to retain – and this is why his analyses are often so illuminating – is the sense in which the conceit functions as an experience; his difficulty here is that traditional theory is of no help to him in explaining how experience may be identified with thought.

The result is that, in some of his most central arguments, he seems to be moving away from Renaissance theory towards a more modern conception of knowledge in which aesthetic intuition can become part of the process of meaning.

The value of poetic theory lies ultimately, of course, in the poems which it helps to produce. If Gracián deserves the credit for expanding Renaissance theory up to, and beyond, its furthest point of logical consistency, it was left to Góngora, Quevedo and their contemporaries to carry Renaissance practice to its greatest pitch of refinement, and to pursue the possibilities of a language which is neither static nor merely decorative, but infinitely flexible and at times profound. At this period, as at any other, practice frequently outstrips theory. In the sixteenth century, this is hardly surprising: the attempt to construct a coherent poetics on the basis of classical models which themselves offered no detailed account of lyric poetry made it difficult to separate poetic theory from rhetoric and, consequently, to define the true status of poetic language. Herrera to some extent counteracts this tendency by concentrating his attention on questions of poetic form – on *verba*, rather than *res* – and his defence of erudition and verbal refinement provides a crucial example for the best poetry of the next generation. In the seventeenth century, the situation changes: though traditional theory still has its adherents (an Aristotelian like Cascales can still attack the *Soledades* for offending against decorum), the persistent concern with the nature of wit, and the need to supply actual illustrations, brings one much closer to the nerve of poetic creation and to the idea of poetry as a unique type of discourse. At the same time, one may wonder whether even a writer as intelligent as Gracián was capable of experiencing the full achievement of Góngora's major poems,[57] and at least one of Góngora's contemporary readers expresses his approval of the *Soledades* by saying that, like nature itself, they go beyond the existing rules of art: 'for even nature, in order to beautify herself still more, at times produces things, such as monsters, which are contrary to her specific intention'.[58]

It would of course be wrong to expect any theory to 'explain' every poem it is intended to match. As Mazzeo has said:

This is not the function of a poetic or a theory of poetry…Rather, it formulates conceptually a concrete body of literature already in exis-tence…What a poetic can do…is make explicit the cultural presuppositions which may underlie a particular body of literature, a style or a genre.[59]

These cultural presuppositions, as we have seen, may involve a whole way of looking at the world, and this, in turn, may often reach into the smallest details of poetic language. This is why knowledge of the theory and the experience of reading individual poems must be made to complement one another: overconcentration on theory may make us forget what the work of a particular poet actually sounds and feels like; failure to recognize the assumptions which govern the writing of the poems, on the other hand, may lead to serious misunderstanding. The best one can do, therefore, is to aim at what Rosemond Tuve has called a 'working contemporaneity' with older poetry,[60] a compromise which at least reduces the risk of false interpretations. As I have tried to suggest, even a little knowledge of Renaissance literary theory and the use it makes of traditional rhetoric can sharpen one's understanding of the poetry and help to explain some of its most striking qualities. Whatever else it demonstrates, the theory should remind us of the profound seriousness with which the best poets of the period worked, something which will become evident, I hope, in the course of the following chapters.

3

Luis de Góngora: the poetry of transformation

I

The earliest poems of Luis de Góngora (1561–1627) date from 1580, the year of Herrera's *Anotaciones* to Garcilaso. This might suggest a straightforward   progression – Garcilaso–Herrera–Góngora – with Góngora himself as the culmination of a central tradition. The facts, however, are less simple than this: the work which Góngora was to produce in the course of the next forty years not only prolonged existing genres and created new ones, but often flowed over generic boundaries in ways that contemporary theory found it difficult to explain. Again, though Góngora is in no sense a more sophisticated poet than Garcilaso, the dense verbal elaboration which extends far beyond his major poems makes quite unprecedented demands on the intellect and the imagination of his readers.

There is one different kind of consideration which marks Góngora off from his major contemporaries: the fact that his individual poems can be dated with reasonable accuracy, thanks to the so-called Chacón manuscript, prepared with the poet's own assistance, and first published in 1921.[1] The existence of such information is, of course, immensely valuable: to read the poems in chronological order is to become aware of the type of intertextual relationships which classification by theme or genre tends to suppress. The obvious disadvantage, on the other hand, is that it encourages critics to treat certain poems as biographical evidence, or, alternatively, to construct a partly fictitious 'life' into which the poems themselves can be conveniently slotted.

Góngora's life, fortunately, is well documented from other sources. He was born in Córdoba, of noble parentage – Robert Jammes calls him 'un *hidalgo* déclassé', a member of the minor aristocracy with decided middle-class tendencies – and attended the University of

Salamanca from 1576–80, gaining a reputation as poet and card player. His uncle Don Francisco, a prebendary (*racionero*) of Córdoba Cathedral, renounced his post in favour of Góngora, who took deacon's orders in 1586. Contemporary references suggest that he took his duties lightly, though later he was entrusted with a number of business missions on behalf of his Chapter and travelled widely inside Spain. In 1617, after several earlier contacts with the court, he moved to Madrid, where he was granted a royal chaplaincy and was ordained priest. His hopes of advancement, however, came to very little: of his two principal patrons, the Duque de Lerma fell from power in 1618 and Don Rodrigo de Calderón, Marqués de Sieteiglesias, was executed in 1621. After suffering various hardships in Madrid – described very movingly in his letters – he returned to Córdoba less than a year before his death, his memory by now impaired by a stroke. (In his last years he had begun to prepare his poems for publication, but died before the project was completed.)

Inevitably, the poems themselves reflect this trajectory at many points; what often remains uncertain, however, is the nature of the reflection: do Góngora's court poems represent a disappointingly conformist side to his otherwise independent nature, as Jammes claims, or did he see them as a way of converting his patrons to his own vision of things? Or, if one speaks of 'vision', what kind of weight should one give to the contemporary references in the *Soledades*, or to the 'seriousness' which often appears to intrude in his so-called 'burlesque' poems? Such questions, clearly, can only be answered, if at all, in terms of individual poems, and even here, given the scope of Góngora's work, there is a danger of seizing on details whose claims to priority are by no means self-evident.

Looking at Góngora's early poems, however, there are several features that strike one, some of which may suggest a way into the complexities of the later work. The first is the absolute assurance with which he handles existing poetic forms: the Herrera-type ode, as in his 1588 poem on the Armada (Millé, 385), and more especially the sonnet. Of the twenty-six love sonnets which date from 1582–85, a good number contain echoes of Italian poets – Petrarch, Sannazaro, Groto, Bernardo and Torquato Tasso – as well as the expected reminiscences of Garcilaso. Given the conventions of such poetry, there is no need to assume any deep personal involvement; like other poets of the time, Góngora is mainly concerned to produce a convincing work of art by the skilful deployment of rhetoric. More to the point, since these poems are often thought of as apprentice work, is the extent to which Góngora's supposed imitation of his sources often amounts to a genuine re-writing.[2] And one poem in particular stretches the possibilities of the conventional love sonnet in a way which already suggests Góngora's dissatisfaction with the limitations of genre:

> No destrozada nave en roca dura
> tocó la playa más arrepentida,
> ni pajarillo de la red tendida
> voló más temeroso a la espesura;
>   bella ninfa la planta mal segura
> no tan alborotada ni afligida
> hurtó de verde prado, que escondida
> víbora regalaba en su verdura,
>   como yo, Amor, la condición airada,
> las rubias trenzas y la vista bella
> huyendo voy, con pie ya desatado,
>   de mi enemiga en vano celebrada.
> Adios, ninfa crüel; quedaos con ella,
> dura roca, red de oro, alegre prado.   (Millé, 239)

No ship wrecked on hard rock ever reached shore more repentantly, nor bird ever flew more fearfully from the stretched net to the thicket; no lovely nymph tore her uncertain foot with such alarm or affliction from the green meadow which harboured a hidden snake in its grass, as I, o Love, now flee on loosened foot the angry state, the fair tresses and the beautiful gaze of my enemy, celebrated in vain. Farewell, cruel nymph; remain with her, hard rock, net of gold, happy meadow.

Is this a love sonnet or a moral (or even burlesque) sonnet? The question is hardly important, except for an editor who feels constrained to place it in one or other of these categories. What is clear, on the other hand, is the sense of parody which emerges in the latter part of the poem and which compels us to revise our reading of the quatrains. The three comparisons – the ship in a storm, the bird caught in a net, the girl who treads on a snake – are Petrarchan commonplaces, associated with the trials of the lover. Each corresponds to a different element – the fourth, fire, is implicit in the later reference to love – though the net or snare, again in keeping with Petrarchan convention, is firmly identified with the woman's hair. The reversal occurs in the first tercet, where the speaker deliberately renounces the 'prison of love' – the source both of joy and anguish for the Petrarchan lover – along with the other symbols of the woman's indifference. The final effect of the poem, however, is more subtle than this: 'en vano celebrada' (celebrated in vain) suggests the futility of the speaker's earlier attempts at the Petrarchan mode; at the same time, one might say, the parody, by preserving the aesthetic effect of its conventional imagery, does not so much reject the mode itself as open it up to new possibilities.

The second feature involves a different kind of possibility, that of making aesthetically satisfying poems out of existing popular forms. It is here that Góngora differs most sharply from Garcilaso and Herrera, whose most important work remains strictly within the Italianate tradition. Góngora, on the other hand, shows an as-tonishing ability to assimilate both themes and techniques from the most diverse sources – folksong, traditional ballads, popular satirical verse – which is evident in some of his earliest poems. Though he seems at first to have kept the hendecasyllabic, or eleven-syllable, line for 'serious' purposes – his first satirical sonnet dates from 1588 – the opening of 'Ándeme yo caliente' (1581) already shows his charac-teristic lightness of touch in shorter metres:

> *Ándeme yo caliente*
> *y ríase la gente.*
> Traten otros del gobierno
> del mundo y sus monarquías,
> mientras gobiernan mis días
> mantequillas y pan tierno,
> y las mañanas de invierno
> naranjada y aguardiente,
> *y ríase la gente...*   (Millé, 96)

As long as I am comfortable, let people laugh. Let others deal with the government of the world and its kingdoms as long as my days are ruled by butter and fresh bread, and on winter mornings orangeade and brandy, *and let people laugh...*

Technically, this poem is a *letrilla*, a variant of the *villancico* (see above, p. 4), in which each of a series of strophes leads back into the original *estribillo*, or refrain. (In Góngora's own later practice, the *estribillo* varies from a single word or phrase to eighteen lines.) As it progresses, the extravagance of the contrasts, as well as certain verbal allusions, turn it into something approaching a parody of the Horatian *Beatus ille*, a poem much imitated by sixteenth-century writers from Garcilaso onwards. What binds together an otherwise fairly disparate series of stanzas is the good-humoured scepticism of the *persona* who speaks – a nonchalance which refuses to be taken in by the pretentiousness of others, whether statesmen or romantic lovers. It would be too much to see such accomplished light verse as an example of Góngora's 'philosophy', though there is nothing here which conflicts with the much more complex vision of the 'simple life' he was later to present in the First *Soledad*. What is of more immediate importance for Góngora's poetic development is the speed with which he can move from a stanza like the one I have quoted to the simple lyricism of 'yo [busque] conchas y caracoles / entre la menuda arena, / escuchando a Filomena / sobre el chopo de la fuente' (let me seek for shells and snails in the fine sand, listening to the nightingale in the poplar by the spring) and then to the delighted mockery of the great lovers of antiquity, Hero and Leander and Pyramus and Thisbe – subjects he will return to in later poems.

In other *letrillas* of the time, like 'Que pida a un galán Minguilla' (That Minguilla should ask a suitor) – a poem which notably extends the range of satire in the direction of everyday life – the economy of the double refrain makes for a more pointed kind of wit:

> Que oiga Menga una canción
> con piedad y atención,
> > *bien puede ser*;
> mas que no sea más piadosa
> a dos escudos en prosa,
> > *no puede ser...*   (Millé, 95)

That Menga should listen to a song with compassionate attention, *it may well be*; but that she should not show more compassion for two *escudos* [i.e. coins] in prose, *it cannot be*.

Such wit, which depends more on word play than on actual conceits, is a basic feature of Góngora's early parodies and plays a crucial part in his treatment of the ballad form. Where the *letrilla* is virtually Góngora's own invention, the traditional ballad, as I have already explained (see above, pp. 3–4), was currently being transformed into the so-called *romance nuevo* or *romance artístico* by other writers. Though the earliest *romances nuevos* are little more than conscious re-workings of historical themes, the 'new ballads' of Góngora and his great contemporary Lope de Vega are genuine re-creations, rather than pastiches, and both the pastoral ballads and the *romances moriscos*, their two most popular inventions, show a distinctly Renaissance sensibility in their treatment of sexual love. This, in turn, suggests something else: despite their dependence on a previous mode, what

strikes one immediately about the new ballads is the aesthetic
distance which separates them from the old. One symptom of this is
the fact that they are normally composed in quatrains (occasionally
with refrain): originally a concession to their musical settings, but
eventually a sign that they are conceived in purely literary terms, as
poems intended to be read or recited rather than sung. This tendency
can already be seen in Góngora's early *romances*, for example in
'Servía en Orán al Rey' (In Oran there was serving the King),
which dates from 1581. A poem like this still moves like a traditional
ballad (not every quatrain is a complete sentence), but it is clear that
the possibility of regular pauses lends itself to more calculated literary
effects, like the contrasting phrases of lines 21–4. At this point, a
Spanish knight, in bed with his Moorish mistress, is surprised by a
sudden call to arms:

> Espuelas de honor le pican
> y freno de amor le para;
> no salir es cobardía,
> ingratitud es dejalla.   (Millé, 23)

Spurs of honour prick him and reins of love hold him back; not to go forth
is cowardice, it is ingratitude to leave her.

Here also, the presence of sophisticated metaphors ('Espuelas de
honor...freno de amor') suggests the cross-fertilization of styles
which leads to Góngora's most complex poems in the ballad form,
Angélica y Medoro (1602) and the semi-burlesque *Fábula de Píramo y
Tisbe* (1618). Even at this early stage, however, one can see how such
techniques not only create aesthetic distance but help to avoid a
potential stylistic clash between the simplicity of the traditional
ballad and the much more deliberate rhetoric of the Renaissance
lyric.[3] Yet here again, as in the case of the early sonnets, Góngora's
critical sense leads him to question the kind of poem he has helped to
create. As usual, he is quick to seize on anything which threatens to
become a convention; thus where the *romances moriscos* (including his
own) tend to dwell on the hero's splendid accoutrements, Góngora
provides the parodic equivalent:

> No lleva por la marlota
> bordada cifra, ni empresa
> en el campo de la adarga,
> ni en la banderilla letra;
> porque el moro es idïota

> y no ha tenido poeta
> de los sastres de su tiempo
> cuyas plumas son tijeras. (Millé, 21)

He has no embroidered figure on his robe, or device on the face of his shield, or motto on his banner; because the Moor is an idiot and has found no poet among the tailors of his age, whose pens are shears.

Though he parodies other kinds of ballad, notably the chivalresque, Góngora concentrates his main efforts on the two most popular types. Here the question of rivalry comes into play: where Lope de Vega uses both the *romance morisco* and the pastoral ballad for disguised autobiography, Góngora for the most part distances himself from such personal intrusions. It would be wrong, however, to see such a reaction as purely negative; behind the immediate circumstances of composition one can detect what Bruce Wardropper calls his 'peculiar complexity': the sense that 'his whole body of poems lies at the centre of the struggle between the popular and the *culto* traditions of Spanish poetry'.[4] The full implications of this can only be seen in Góngora's major poems; at this early stage, his main concern seems to have been to find new ways of combining different – and often dissonant – kinds of poetic material in an aesthetic whole. Though the question of aesthetic intention hardly arises in his earliest parodies, a poem like the one I have just quoted, which dates from 1586, already goes beyond simple travesty by the obvious device of alternating 'serious' and 'burlesque' stanzas. Thus this particular poem, as Jammes has pointed out, contains both model and parody;[5] though the effect is still relatively crude, the juxtaposition of 'poetic' and 'anti-poetic' elements already suggests ways in which the latter might be used for a serious poetic purpose. The process is taken a stage further when Góngora begins to handle potentially tragic material, as in the first of the two Hero and Leander ballads (1589; Millé, 27), where the dominant tone of sarcasm is occasionally replaced by what seems like genuine compassion. And, as we shall see, it is this growing awareness of the tragicomic possibilities of the burlesque which eventually leads to the most puzzling of Góngora's masterpieces, the *Píramo y Tisbe* of 1618.

Almost half of Góngora's *romances* date from the first twenty years of his career. By the turn of the century, he is writing two clearly distinguishable kinds of ballad: those which can be roughly classed as burlesque or satirical and those with more serious artistic pretensions – though often witty and humorous – which culminate in the

splendid *Angélica y Medoro* (Millé, 48) of 1602. The latter kind covers
an enormous range, from an early poem like 'Hermana Marica'
(Sister Marica; Millé, 4) – one of the few Spanish poems in which
everyday reality is seen through the eyes of a child – to Góngora's
own variations on the *romance morisco* and the pastoral ballad: the
romance de cautivos, or prisoner's ballad, the *romance de piratas*, or pirate
ballad, the *romance venatorio* and the *romance piscatorio* (on hunting and
fishing motifs) and the *romance de aldea* (on village themes). Such
classification, inevitably, does little to suggest either the genuine
differences or the family likenesses which exist between the various
types of poem, still less the interest of such poems for Góngora's later
work. Thus a fuller study would show how the *romances de cautivos* are
more restrained, and consequently more realistic, than the *romances
moriscos*; how the ballads based on hunting imagery are more
idealized and aristocratic than the much more original *romances
piscatorios*, where marine imagery enters Góngora's poetry for the first
time, or how the *romance de aldea* replaces conventional pastoral
artifice by a more sympathetic, though no less artificial, rendering of
country life. The finest example of the latter is 'Ánsares de Menga'
(Menga's geese), a late poem (1620) which I shall discuss in the final
section (see p. 91); nevertheless, the theme itself is crucial for the
Soledades, in which, moreover, hunting and fishing are central
activities, and where, in the Second *Soledad*, the marine setting is
essential to the progress of the poem.

   Such thematic parallels, though interesting in themselves, need to
be set against Góngora's maturing skill as a writer and the increasing
complexity of his reactions to existing poetry. Both of these are very
evident in *Angélica y Medoro*, his ballad based on an episode from
Canto XIX of Ariosto's *Orlando Furioso*. In the *Furioso*, Angelica, the
Princess of Cathay, discovers the body of the Saracen, Medoro, who
has been left for dead after an attack by the Christians. Angelica takes
him to a shepherd's hut, where she restores him to health: they fall in
love and marry, thus exposing themselves to the fury of the jealous
Orlando. (In Cantos CCII–XXIV, Orlando, in his madness, literally
destroys the pastoral landscape which has been the setting for their
love.) Góngora's poem retells this story – though it excludes the
marriage ceremony – in the space of 136 lines. Yet, despite the many
deliberate echoes of Ariosto, the result could hardly be described an
as 'imitation'. This is not simply a matter of condensation and the
tighter poetic logic this entails: Góngora does not so much 'imitate'

Ariosto as re-write him, replacing his text with a radically different one, which implicitly questions the whole nature of pastoral. Hence what E. M. Wilson has called the 'calculated ambiguity' of the poem:[6] the sense that Góngora is drawing on deeper sources which Ariosto himself fails to exploit, and at the same time producing a version of the story which will preclude any further imitation. Moreover, as Robert Ball has shown,[7] the poem contains a veiled attack on Lope de Vega's diffuse and conventional treatment of the theme in *La Hermosura de Angélica* (The Beauty of Angelica; 1602, though written considerably earlier). Thus where both Ariosto and Lope rely on 'pictorial' effects, long speeches and frequent authorial intervention, Góngora presents his characters in dumb show, without comment, and any potentially visual effects are dissolved in the play of verbal ingenuity.

This in itself creates the impression of an intensely *written* poem. Stylistically, *Angélica y Medoro* builds, with astonishing verve, on the kind of witty paradoxes – now often amounting to true conceits – which one finds in the earlier poems. Thus the two lovers are described as 'un mal vivo con dos almas, / y una ciega con dos soles' (lines 67–8; a man scarcely alive with two souls and a woman blind with two suns [i.e. eyes]). Or again, when Angelica yields to Medoro, they become 'Segunda envidia de Marte, / primera dicha de Adonis' (lines 79–80; Mars's second envy, Adonis's first delight). (Angelica is compared to Venus, who was 'Adonis's first delight'. Adonis was Mars's first object of envy, so that Medoro may be regarded as the second.) Such word play, however, is not merely decorative: in the idyllic part of the poem, the parallels and antitheses create a sense of balance which is notably absent from the closing lines. And this last example suggests the myth of Venus and Adonis (with the absent Orlando as Mars) which for Góngora, though not for Ariosto, underpins the whole story. Once one grasps this, other details of the poem fall into position: the fact that the lovers' names are deferred until this mythological identification takes place; the image of Medoro's blood soaking the ground from which flowers spring – a possible allusion to the ancient accounts of the dying Adonis. In the idyllic section of the poem, one could argue, the direction of the myth is reversed, and the joy of the lovers, in contrast to Ariosto, is made to seem more than human. At the same time, if this adds to the perfection of the idyll, it also underlines its precariousness. So much is implied in the controlling metaphor of the poem: love as a more benign form of war. In the *Furioso* itself, the pastoral setting is a refuge from the destructiveness of real warfare, a parenthesis or space in which love can assert its claims, however much it may be threatened from outside. All this is true of Góngora's own poem: where he goes further, however, is in suggesting that the text itself is precarious, that the pastoral conventions he takes up and transforms are no more than literary fictions, and that the 'nature' on which they are made to depend is merely a verbal illusion. The closing lines are crucial here:

> Cuevas do el silencio apenas
> deja que sombras las moren
> profanan con sus abrazos
> a pesar de sus horrores.
> Choza, pues, tálamo y lecho,
> cortesanos labradores,
> aires, campos, fuentes, vegas,
> cuevas, troncos, aves, flores,
> fresnos, chopos, montes, valles,
> contestes de estos amores,
> el cielo os guarde, si puede,
> de las locuras del Conde. (lines 125–36)

Caves in which silence scarcely allows shadows to dwell, they profane with their embraces, despite the gloom. Hut, then, bed and marriage bed, courtly labourers, breezes, fields, springs, meadows, caves, tree trunks, birds, flowers, ash trees, poplars, hills, valleys, fellow-witnesses of these loves: may Heaven preserve you, if it can, from the mad deeds of the Count [i.e. Orlando].

In the first stanza, which describes the end of the idyll, the pastoral imagery disappears, along with the characteristic parallelisms. More important, where Ariosto's mention of the cave brings in a casual, and non-tragic, reference to Dido and Aeneas, Góngora suppresses the reference to Book IV of the *Aeneid*, but emphasizes the sombre tones with which Virgil himself anticipates the fate of his lovers. Thus, far from representing a climax of sensual fulfilment, as is usually claimed, the darkening tone of these lines prepares us for one of Góngora's most extraordinary rhetorical effects. With the exception of 'vegas' (meadows; a final allusion to Lope?), the bare list of nouns recapitulates the essential items of the pastoral idyll. In the context, the effect is to reduce all of these to mere words. It is as if Góngora, like Prospero at the end of *The Tempest*, had deliberately broken his spell, in this instance by subjecting his own poem to a final self-criticism. Thus both creation and analysis are contained within a single poem; as Robert Ball puts it: '[In *Angélica y Medoro*] Góngora lays a twofold claim to superiority: first the text promotes its own positive status by reflecting critically on the texts of others and improving on them, then it turns to reflect on itself as "other" and subjects itself to critical revision, by demystifying the very means just employed to achieve the desired effect.'[8] In thematic terms, the precariousness of the idyll, as Góngora must have been aware, if anything adds to its beauty. What is even more striking, however, is his persistent questioning of the ways in which language creates meaning, and of the kind of meanings it creates – something which already points the way towards his major poems.

II

With the benefit of hindsight, it is easy to see the various ways in which Góngora's poems of the early 1600s converge on the *Polifemo* and the *Soledades* – a fact which should not blind one to their merit as individual poems. Sometimes the connection is a relatively simple one: Góngora's friendship with the Marqués de Ayamonte, whose estate at Lepe, near the mouth of the Guadalquivir, he visited in the spring of 1607, gave rise to a number of poems which already sketch out what was to become the marine landscape of the Second *Soledad*. Again, from a stylistic point of view, the complex syntax of the ode on the surrender of Larache (1611; Millé, 396) marks the kind of advance without which the writing of the major poems would scarcely have been possible. And in the splendid tercets of 1609, '¡Malhaya el que en señores idolatra...' (Woe to him who worships the great), with their echoes of the Third Satire of Juvenal, Góngora's disenchantment with the life of the Court is contrasted with what is already becoming one of his central themes:

> ¡Oh Soledad, de la quietud divina
> dulce prenda, aunque muda, ciudadana
> del campo, y de sus Ecos convecina!
> Sabrosas treguas de la vida urbana,
> paz del entendimiento, que lambica
> tanto en discursos la ambición humana. (Millé, 395)[9]

O Solitude, sweet though silent token of divine quiet, citizen of the country and neighbour to its echoes! Pleasant truce to city life, peace of the mind which so ornaments men's ambitions with fine speeches.

If this last poem displays the irrepressible vigour of Góngora's art, there are others which show, in altogether more subtle ways, the workings of a poetic imagination which is rarely content to remain within the limits of conventional forms. Thus 'En los pinares de Júcar' (1603), though technically a ballad with refrain, manages to convey the impression of popular song modes in language of great sophistication:

> En los pinares de Júcar
> vi bailar unas serranas,
> al son del agua en las piedras
> y al son del viento en las ramas.
> Una entre los blancos dedos
> hiriendo negras pizarras,
> instrumento de marfil
> que las musas le invidiaran... (Millé, 52)

In the pinewoods of Júcar I saw some country girls dancing to the sound of water on stones, to the sound of the wind in the branches... One striking together pieces of black slate between her fingers, instruments of ivory which the Muses might envy...

This image of country girls singing and dancing appears, greatly elaborated, in the First *Soledad*, and in both instances the treatment is essentially the same. Despite Góngora's insistence that these are real girls, not classical nymphs, the poem is in no sense a simple celebration of folklore; as in the later poem, 'nature' is contemplated through the eyes of 'culture':[10] something originally 'seen' has been transformed into a verbal structure which creates its own, consciously artificial, kind of beauty.

One other outstanding poem of this period, '¡Qué de invidiosos montes levantados...' (What envious lofty mountains) helps us to take the full measure of Góngora's powers in the years leading up to his major poems. Here, the connection with the later work is more oblique, though none the less genuine. If nothing else, it shows how Góngora – as in *Angélica y Medoro*, though by very different means – is prepared to put his art at risk; at the same time, however – and such is the nature of the risk – it enables one to see more clearly the kind of erotic strength most readers feel in both the *Polifemo* and the *Soledades*, however hard it may be to define. Though the poem has sometimes been described as an epithalamium, this seems wrong: although it ends by celebrating a marriage, the emotional trajectory which leads up to this is both too intense and too *risqué* for the kind of public homage the genre normally demands. Though there is no reason to suppose that the poem is autobiographical – there is no 'story' that we know of behind it – it opens in the manner of a Petrarchan lyric: the speaker is separated by an immense distance from the woman he loves, though he can still be with her in thought. Very quickly, however, the tone changes: the woman in question is married, and she is imagined as making love with her husband. What we are reading, it emerges, is a poem of sexual jealousy in which thought, now personified and directly addressed by the speaker, is sent on a mission of voyeuristic revenge. This creates a complex situation in which thought is imagined as arriving (in the future) at the marriage bed. But now comes the turning-point of the poem: thought (still in the speaker's imagination) arrives too late; the lovemaking is already over and the couple are now sleeping:

> Desnuda el brazo, el pecho descubierta,
>   entre templada nieve
> evaporar contempla un fuego helado,
> y al esposo, en figura casi muerta,
>   que el silencio le bebe
> del sueño con sudor solicitado.   (Millé, 388)

Her arm naked, her breast uncovered, behold [it is 'thought' which is being addressed] a frozen fire evaporate among temperate snow, and see the husband, how the silence of sleep, sought by his labours, consumes him, almost in the image of death.

Immediately after this, the speaker introduces a counterforce into the poem: the god Cupid, who will watch over the couple's sleep. The seemingly free flight of thought – like that of Icarus to which it is implicitly compared[11] – has failed, and the poem can now end with the conventional hymeneal wish ('Sleep, noble lovers') and a final *envoi* in which thought is ordered to conclude both the scene and the poem:

> Canción, di al pensamiento
>   que corra la cortina,
> y vuelva al desdichado que camina.

Song, tell thought to draw the curtain and to return to the unhappy wanderer.

The wanderer figure inevitably recalls the protagonist of the *Soledades* – another unsuccessful lover in exile; in the poem itself, however, the failure, first of love and then of jealousy, leads to a reconciliation: the solitary lover accepts his exclusion and seeks for mercy in the hostile landscape of the opening. Thus the emotional track of the poem is made clear: by courting the dangers of prurience, the speaker, as in so many of Góngora's poems, shows how it is possible to arrive at a sadder and wiser attitude. And much the same could be said of the poem itself, which, for all its hints of Petrarch and Tasso, both transgresses the sexual limits of the Petrarchan lyric and then, with exquisite tact, restores the privacy which it had set out to violate.

Most of the poems I have referred to so far differ so radically from their apparent sources that 'imitation' seems altogether too facile a term to describe the process of poetic creation. Góngora's most ambitious attempt at 're-writing', however, comes in his first major poem, the *Polifemo*, or *Fábula de Polifemo y Galatea* (Millé, 416), composed in 1612–13. Once again, the question of genre is crucial: in re-telling the story of Acis, Galatea and the cyclops Polyphemus from Book XIII of Ovid's *Metamorphoses*, Góngora is deliberately choosing a central subject of the Renaissance mythological fable, both Spanish and Italian. His own originality is both stylistic and thematic: in the Dedication, he refers to his Muse as 'culta sí, aunque bucólica, Talía' (Thalia, a rude yet cultured Muse), thus signalling his intention of writing a pastoral poem in a consciously 'elevated' style. In the poem itself, as we shall see, both the notion of 'pastoral' and the normal connotations of the 'high' style undergo drastic revision; as for theme, Góngora's innovations are equally radical: where Ovid has Galatea tell her own story in retrospect, he uses an impersonal present-tense narrative which gives a quite different weighting to the three protagonists, largely suppressing the rustic clumsiness of Polyphemus and greatly expanding the central encounter between Acis and Galatea. All this places Góngora's poem at several removes from earlier Spanish attempts at the subject, including its immediate predecessor, the very beautiful, though much more literal, 'Fábula de Acis y Galatea' (1611) of Luis Carrillo y Sotomayor (see p. 144). At the same time, as Antonio Vilanova has shown,[12] it is an intensely intertextual piece of work, full of echoes – conscious or unconscious – of earlier Renaissance poems, as if part of Góngora's intention were to create a final synthesis of the existing poetic vocabulary.

Though the *Polifemo* is generally acknowledged to be one of Góngora's masterpieces, critics have differed notoriously over the general sense of the poem. For some, notably Dámaso Alonso, the temptation to see it in terms of 'Baroque contrast' seems irresistible; yet to polarize the two extremes of 'beauty' (Galatea) and 'monstrosity' (Polyphemus), as Alonso does, is surely overschematic – Polyphemus is as much a scorned lover as a 'monster', and it is his awareness of Galatea's beauty which accounts for his pathos. Again, though Góngora seems to minimize the details of Acis's death, Jammes's claim that the poem represents the 'triumph of love over death' seems doubtful, given the presence of images of death and destruction in the early part of the poem.[13] Nor can one take very seriously the suggestion that Acis and Galatea behave with the innocent simplicity of animals; at their first meeting, Góngora is at pains to suggest their mutual courtesy, just as he shows Acis to be capable of the deceptions of a sophisticated lover. (The fact that Acis and Galatea never speak may have more to do with the 'writerly' nature of the poem – something we have already seen in *Angélica y Medoro* – than with any supposed lack of articulacy.)

What, then, can one usefully say about the poem at this level? First, there is the question of the setting: Góngora's imaginary Sicily, despite its resemblance to classical pastoral, is not a re-creation of the Golden Age – in Ovid, the myths belong to the Age of Iron, which represents fallen man; thus there is nothing in the poem to suggest that men were *better* under such conditions, and the various historical anachronisms make it clear that Góngora's imagination is working in two worlds at once. Secondly, as Michael Woods has pointed out, since none of the protagonists in the poem is strictly human, one should be careful not to leap to conclusions about 'Góngora's view of man's place in the world'.[14] And thirdly – pursuing the parallel with *Angélica y Medoro* – it seems clear that Góngora not only has a predilection for scenes of awakening love, but that he sees love as beautiful, fragile and potentially disruptive, as something whose 'ideal space' – the 'space' of the text – is always subject to violation from outside. In the *Polifemo*, of course, the violator is Polyphemus himself; as in Ovid, though without his insistence on the actual process of transformation, he crushes Acis with a rock from which the latter emerges in the form of a river:

> Corriente plata al fin sus blancos huesos,
> lamiendo flores y argentando arenas,
> a Doris llega, que, con llanto pío,
> yerno lo saludó, lo aclamó río.   (lines 501–4)

Finally, his white bones [turned to] running silver, lapping flowers and silvering the sands, he reaches Doris [i.e. the mother of Galatea], who, with pitiful lamentation, greeted him as a son-in-law, acclaimed him as a river.

In Ovid, Acis is changed into a river god; Góngora, by contrast, ends his poem on a mixed note of celebration and lamentation – again, one might think, a characteristically muted acknowledgement of what Parker calls the 'sorrow of existence'.[15]

Nevertheless, to place this degree of human weight on what is essentially a triumph of artistic re-creation may already be running the kind of risk I have just indicated. At this point one needs to turn to the actual language of the poem, by way of correcting a possible overinsistence on 'theme'. One way of making both the transition and the connection is to note how in Góngora what for Ovid is theme – metamorphosis – becomes internalized as metaphor. Thus change, experienced now as a principle of composition, becomes part of the rhetorical functioning of the poem. Take, for instance, the passage which describes Acis's first glimpse of the sleeping Galatea:

> ...llegó Acis; y, de ambas luces bellas
> dulce Occidente viendo al sueño blando,
> su boca dio, y sus ojos cuanto pudo,
> al sonoro cristal, al cristal mudo.   (lines 189–92)

Acis arrived; and, seeing the sweet setting of her twin suns in gentle sleep, he gave his mouth, and his eyes as best he could, to the sounding crystal [i.e. the stream] and the silent [i.e. Galatea's body].

Until recently, there was a tendency to read such a passage mainly for its sensuous effect, as a series of visual images filtered through the complexities of Góngora's *culto* style. Yet, as critics like Rivers and Parker have shown, the *Polifemo* is essentially a 'witty' poem, in Gracián's sense of the word (see above, p. 60), a poem which is generated through a series of *conceptos* whose mutual relationships form a large part of the poetic structure. So, in this particular example, the original metaphor (eyes as lights or suns) gives rise to a second one in which sleep becomes the 'west' ('Occidente') which hides the sun, a connection reinforced by the balancing adjectives ('dulce – blando'). The participle 'viendo' links this clause to the next by way of cause and effect: Acis is thirsty and drinks from the stream, and at the same time attempts to 'drink in' the beauty of the sleeping Galatea. In the original, however, there is no equivalent to the verb 'drink': Acis's simultaneous actions are joined by the relatively weak verb 'dio' (gave), which shifts the emphasis on to the nouns, 'boca' (mouth) and 'ojos' (eyes). This in turn adds to the symmetry of the rhyming couplet, since the placing of these nouns is reflected in the closing antithesis ('sonoro cristal...cristal mudo'). Though such concentration of language is peculiar to Góngora, there is nothing here which could not be explained in terms of traditional rhetoric. Yet if rhetoric is designed to create a particular effect on the reader, the effect of a passage like this is oddly elusive – most conspicuously so in the last two lines. I have already referred to Góngora's habit of referring to different objects in terms of a single attribute (see above, p. 55), and to Dámaso Alonso's claim that, by doing so, he is creating 'a kind of ennobling simplification of the world'. This now needs some qualification. As I argued earlier, to suppress the particular attributes inevitably leads one to think in terms of universals, as Renaissance theory invariably recommends; nevertheless, to suppose that, by linking 'body' and 'stream' by the same word ('cristales'), Góngora is trying to make us see 'the unity of creation' is surely excessive, insofar as it allows metaphor powers which are denied to ordinary language.[16]

At this point we can come back to the question of 'sensuousness'. Though, as I have already explained, traditional rhetoric never denies that a poem may appeal to the senses – the strongly erotic atmosphere of the *Polifemo* is one of the poem's triumphs – critics often refer to a passage like the one I have quoted as if it were the verbal equivalent of a painting by Titian or Rubens. Yet by now it should be clear that both metaphor and periphrasis work *against* visualization; any possible 'picture' – even a mental one – is disintegrated, one might say, in the kind of verbal play induced by the images themselves; what count, on the other hand, are the symmetries and relationships which the reader is compelled to work through from stanza to stanza, and which, in contrast to the *Soledades*, are controlled by the actual stanza form. To say this is to insist, once again, that the *Polifemo* is a poem of *ingenio*, the work of a poet whose imagination, paradoxically, seems to work most naturally within the intricate terms of verbal wit. Through wit, the 'elevated' style which Góngora promises in his Dedication is tempered by humour and ingenuity while retaining its essential seriousness; as for pastoral, the image of a Sicily teeming with fertility yet enslaved by love of Galatea is unlike anything in earlier versions of the mythological fable – like much else in the *Polifemo*, both an independent achievement and an anticipation of Góngora's next major poem, the *Soledades*.

Góngora appears to have been working on both the *Polifemo* and the First *Soledad* in late 1612 and early 1613. (Most of the Second *Soledad* probably dates from 1614.) According to contemporary accounts, Góngora intended to write four *Soledades*, though there is no direct evidence for this, and opinions as to the possible scheme are divided.[17] As it is, he is generally assumed to have stopped short just before the end of the Second, the last forty-three lines of which were added at a later date.[18] The poem as we have it amounts to just over 2,000 lines – a formidable achievement in itself, given the unvarying complexity of the writing. Running through it is a story of a kind, though this is hardly important enough for one to regard it as a narrative poem. In the First *Soledad*, a lovesick young nobleman is shipwrecked on the shore of an unknown land, where he makes his way through the countryside, encounters various inhabitants and attends a rustic wedding; in the Second, he stays for a time with a fisherman and his family and finally witnesses an aristocratic hawking party. This fairly casual narrative suggests the episodic nature of the poem as a whole – a fact which needs to be taken into account in considering its possible 'unity'. There are parallels here with other kinds of writing: with the Byzantine novel, or with a work like the *Arcadia* of Sannazaro, where poems are framed by an intermittent prose narrative. This suggests the characteristic rhythm of the *Soledades*: the way in which each new moment in the poem expands into a kind of set-piece – either a speech or a description – which interrupts the progress of the central figure. Thus from one point of view, the *Soledades* comprise both an anthology of Renaissance poetic forms and a series of classical imitations (Horace, Catullus, Virgil), with a constant undercurrent of Ovid – the poet always closest to Góngora's own imagination.

The originality of such a synthesis points to another, more problematic, aspect of the poem: its apparent refusal to adhere to a single genre. Jáuregui, for instance, writing in 1624, complains that the poem 'lacks a subject', in other words, that it deals neither with the central themes of lyric (love) nor with that of epic (war). Even allowing for a greater range of legitimate poetic material, it is clear that the *Soledades* draw on several genres at once – epic, pastoral and lyric – without settling definitively for one or the other. (Even pastoral, which is sometimes taken to be the dominant mode of the poem, is subjected to drastic revision, as we shall see, and the Second *Soledad* seems to move away quite deliberately from the 'pastoral' world of the First.) What is particularly striking is that Góngora himself appears to acknowledge such indeterminacy in his Dedication to the poem:

> Pasos de un peregrino son errante
> cuantos me dictó versos dulce Musa:
>   en soledad confusa
> perdidos unos, otros inspirados   (lines 1–4)

Whatever verses the sweet Muse dictated to me are the footsteps of a wandering pilgrim: the ones inspired, the others lost in confused solitude.

The *peregrino errante* is of course the protagonist of the poem we are about to read, whose 'verses' or metrical 'feet' are identified with the actual 'footsteps' of the wanderer. Thus the poem itself becomes the 'soledad confusa' where the poet has received his inspiration, and through which both pilgrim and reader must travel. The play of meaning, however, does not stop there: as Maurice Molho has pointed out, there is a submerged allusion here to the overall form of the poem: each of the two *Soledades* is composed as a single huge stanza (a fact generally obscured in modern editions), in the free combination of rhymes and line-lengths known as a *silva*. As Molho observes, the word *silva* in Latin means 'forest' (compare Spanish and Italian *selva*), so that, he claims, the *silva* of the poetic form can be equated with the *soledad* of the poem itself.[19] Molho forces his argument here, I think, since the literal setting of the poem is scarcely a 'forest'. Nevertheless, his essential point remains: the verse form, as anyone who has persisted with the poem will confirm, is an exact reflection of the freely structured (and possibly open-ended) content.

Before looking more closely at this content, there are several things one should notice about the *peregrino* himself. Firstly, as I have already suggested, he is the one link which binds the poem together, what John Beverley has called 'a *story* passing through a succession of moments of experience'.[20] Secondly, he is a *peregrino de amor* – a 'pilgrim of love' – a figure for whom there are many precedents in Renaissance literature, from Petrarch to late sixteenth-century romance fiction.[21] (In the *Soledades*, this central figure, who is never named, is a courtly lover, driven to exile by the indifference of the woman he loves, and of whom he is reminded at several points in the poem.) Thirdly, and more importantly, he provides the poem with a point of view. Just what this entails is hard to define: in a sense, he is the reader's representative in the poem – many of the poem's earliest readers would have been aristocrats, like the *peregrino* himself – though it would be wrong to assume that he represents the poet's own stance. He is also a reminder of a world which exists outside the immediate setting of the poem, of a city-based mentality whose present, historical concerns occasionally break into the texture of the poem. This works in two ways: through his wonder at what he sees, we are persuaded of the value of what he is experiencing; at the same time, his perceptions are limited: there are certain types of experience from which he is excluded, notably the kind of wise *desengaño*, or lack of illusion, which is predicted for the newly-married peasant couple at the end of the First *Soledad*. And finally, as Paul Julian Smith has pointed out, there is something curiously unvirile about the *peregrino*, who is defined in terms of beauty rather than of his capacity to act – something which is brought out strongly by contrast with the 'manly' activities of the fisherman's daughters in the Second *Soledad*.[22]

What, then, is Góngora trying to show us through the pilgrim's experience? Though a number of themes appear in the course of the *Soledades*, any attempt to reduce these to a single controlling theme only diminishes the poem. (To see the poem as 'anti-commercial pastoral',[23] for instance, assumes that Góngora is projecting his own views through the mouth of the 'politic old man' in the First *Soledad*, something which is by no means certain.) As one might expect in what seems a consciously impersonal poem, Góngora's own moral position, if he has one, is very difficult to judge. Nevertheless, certain individual themes stand out – the place of love in itself and in relation to society, the traditional *alabanza de aldea*, or praise of rustic life, the 'complexity of the simple' – though invariably transformed by the force of Góngora's verbal imagination.[24] One way of seeing how Góngora combines these themes is to consider the use he makes of what at first glance may seem to be the basic contrast of the poem: the town–country opposition. This contrast seems to be implied in the actual title; in seventeenth-century usage, *soledad* means not only 'solitude', but more generally 'country' as against 'city', a point made by contemporary commentators.[25] It appears more obviously in the imitation of *Beatus ille* which occurs early in the First *Soledad* (lines 94–135) – 'tus umbrales ignora / la adulación, Sirena / de

Reales Palacios' (Adulation, the Siren of Royal Palaces, does not know your thresholds) – and in the same speech, the *peregrino* contrasts the natural simplicity of the goatherds's huts with the complex structures of 'modern artifice'. Even at this early stage, however, there is no sense that artifice as such is to be condemned – the poem itself, after all, is a supreme example of artifice – and the main thrust of the attack is directed against the vices of the Court. This does not necessarily mean that the country dwellers are to be taken as representatives of natural goodness; as the poem develops, it becomes clear that they too are involved in a world of artifice in which they display their dominion over nature. 'Nature', as I have already suggested (see above, p. 42), can mean many things in Renaissance writing; here, it is neither an example of order nor an underlying source of value. Above all, as Michael Woods has pointed out, there is no question of confronting artifice with nature in an abstract sense – 'nature' in the *Soledades* is not the opposite of 'art' – and what matters is the interaction of a specific community and its milieu.[26] Here, for instance, are some lines which come just before the climax of the First *Soledad*. After describing the dancing on the eve of the village wedding-feast, the poem goes on:

> Vence la noche al fin, y triunfa mudo
> el silencio, aunque breve, del rüido:
>   sólo gime ofendido
> el sagrado laurel del hierro agudo;
> deja de su esplendor, deja desnudo
> de su frondosa pompa al verde aliso
>   el golpe no remiso
>   del villano membrudo;
>   el que resistir pudo
> al animoso Austro, al Euro ronco,
> chopo gallardo – cuyo liso tronco
> papel fue de pastores, aunque rudo –
> a revelar secretos va a la aldea,
> que impide Amor que aun otro chopo lea.
> Estos árboles, pues, ve la mañana
> mentir florestas, y emular viales
> cuantos muró de líquidos cristales
>   agricultura urbana.   (lines 687–704)

Night finally wins, and dumb silence triumphs, if only briefly, over the noise: only the sacred laurel moans, offended by the sharp axe; the relentless strokes of the sturdy peasant strip the green alder of its splendour, of its leafy pomp; the graceful poplar, which could resist the brisk South wind and the hoarse Southwester – whose smooth trunk had served the shepherds as rough parchment – now goes to the village to reveal the secrets which Love forbids even other trees to read. Thus the morning sees these trees form mock groves and imitate those avenues which urbane agriculture walls in with liquid crystal.

Here, far from living in simple pastoral harmony with nature, the country people are actually desecrating nature in the interests of artifice. The trees are wounded and stripped – it is the 'pomp' of natural beauty which is made to seem vain, not that of artifice – and in the end they are used to construct another piece of artifice: the imitation forest which forms part of the wedding decorations. The crucial phrase here is 'agricultura urbana': 'urbane architecture', but also 'urban architecture', in that it reminds one of the values of the city. This is characteristic of the entire poem: more than once the country people are praised, not because they live in beautiful surroundings, but because they dominate those surroundings with intelligence and skill – with artifice, in fact – and nevertheless remain free from the moral risks of life at court.

The ultimate artifice, as I have said, is clearly the poem itself, the complex structure of words in whose shaping the reader is made to collaborate. As in the *Polifemo*, metaphor and conceit are the main instruments of transformation. What is remarkable about the *Soledades*, however, is not just the sense in which Góngora reconstitutes the natural world through the medium of language, but also the fact that, at various points in the poem, nature itself is made to share in the process of verbalization. The idea of the world as a text is, of course, a very old one,[27] yet it is hard to think of another seventeenth-century poem in which the metaphor is given such concrete force. In an earlier passage which he eventually discarded, Góngora refers to the river which flows through the landscape as a 'twisting discourse' ('torcido discurso') – a more literal version of Cicero's *flumen orationis* or 'river of speech' – whose 'sentences' are interrupted by 'parentheses' of islands:

> en brazos divididos caudalosos
> de islas, que paréntesis frondosos
> al período son de su corriente.

Divided into abundant branches of islands, which are leafy parentheses in the main period of its course.

And in the 'agricultura urbana' passage, there is a curious persistence about the references to the lovers' names inscribed on the trees. There, not only do the trees serve as writing materials ('parchment'); they are also possible 'readers' of the secret messages written on them. What is being suggested, in other words, is the idea of a world which both writes and reads itself. And so one experiences a kind of mirror effect, in that the book – the poem – now *reflects* nature and, in so doing, helps it to complete itself by adding this extra dimension.[28] Or as Andrés Sánchez Robayna puts it: 'The book is nature thinking itself, seeing itself... to write [according to the *Soledades*] is to remake the text of the world.'[29]

Yet nature in the *Soledades*, as Paul Julian Smith has argued, is in a sense 'denaturalized':[30] it is no longer a touchstone for permanent values, as in the conventional pastoral; it is celebrated, but also at times subverted, with the result that any account of the poem's subject-matter risks becoming over-rigid. If Góngora's contemporaries, as we have seen, had difficulty in assigning it to a particular genre, this is only part of a more general indeterminacy. In terms of rhetoric and its supposed effects on the reader, it is as if the reader here were being not so much persuaded as questioned; as we make our way through the text, we are made to follow out its constantly shifting perspectives, actively taking part in the production of meaning, rather than simply assenting to something we already know, and never settling into a final sense of order.

III

Both the *Polifemo* and the *Soledades* belong to Góngora's most productive period, the years spent in Córdoba between 1610 and 1617.[31] In April, 1617, however, he took up residence in Madrid, where he was to remain until 1626, less than a year before his death. Though he was granted a royal chaplaincy – not a very lucrative post – his hopes of advancement at Court, as we have seen, came to very little, and his attempts to keep up appearances under financial stress eventually reduced him to poverty. Góngora's initial intention of turning his poetic gifts to profit is spectacularly evident in the unfinished *Panegírico al Duque de Lerma* (1617; Millé, 420), a poem of seventy-nine octaves, whose account of the public life of the royal favourite breaks off in the year 1609. In the hands of most other poets, the attempt to write a heroic poem on a fairly unheroic political figure would have been a disaster; as it is, Góngora's celebration of Lerma, though finely wrought, ultimately fails through the unremitting 'nobility' of the writing. Nevertheless, it is an interesting failure insofar as it reflects Góngora's ideal vision, rather than the reality, of Court life, and his genuine taste for the visual splendour of Court occasions is balanced by a sense of their evanescence, as in the passage describing the aftermath of a royal baptism:

> Prolija prevención en breve hora
> se disolvió, y el lúcido topacio,
> que occidental balcón fue del aurora,
> ángulo quedó apenas de palacio.
> De cuantos la edad mármores devora,
> igual restituyendo al aire espacio
> que ámbito a la tierra, mudo ejemplo
> al desengaño le fabrica templo.   (lines 521–8)

The lengthy preparations were dissolved in one short hour, and the gleaming topaz [i.e. the hall where the ceremony had taken place], which had been the western balcony of dawn [i.e. where the bright lights had shone through the night], became scarcely a corner of the Palace. A silent example of all those marbles which time devours, restoring space to the air and their site to earth, it raises a temple to disillusionment.

What Góngora was still capable of doing with a more congenial subject is clear from his last major poem, the *Fábula de Píramo y Tisbe* (Millé, 74) of 1618. As well as being his most ambitious attempt at the ballad form, this is also his most radical recasting of an Ovidian fable. Once again, the relationship between style and subject-matter is decisive. Salazar Mardones, who devoted a whole volume of commentary to the poem (*Ilustración y Defensa de la Fábula de Píramo y Tisbe*, 1636), refers to Góngora as 'the first inventor of this heroicomic kind of poem, a mixture of the burlesque and the serious', which, though true in a general sense, leaves open the question of the effect he is trying to produce. The nearest precedent, as one might expect, is in Góngora's own parodies of existing models, in particular his two ballads on the Hero and Leander theme (1589 and 1610; Millé, 27 and 64) and his earlier, unfinished poem on the subject of Pyramus and Thisbe itself (1604; Millé, 55).[32] All these, however, are relatively small-scale poems, of no great complexity; what is immediately striking about the *Píramo y Tisbe*, on the other hand, is both its length and the fact that it continues to build on the style which had been used for serious purposes in the *Polifemo* and the *Soledades*. The question of style, in fact, is raised in the opening stanzas:

> La ciudad de Babilonia
>
> ...
>
> digno sujeto será
> de las orejas del vulgo;
> popular aplauso quiero,
> perdónenme sus tribunos.   (lines 1 and 13–16)

The city of Babylon [and its two lovers] ... will be a fit subject for the ears of the crowd; I want the applause of the common people, may their tribunes forgive me.

There is an obvious irony in these lines, coming as they do at the beginning of one of Góngora's most difficult poems; nevertheless, the pretence that he is writing for a popular audience helps to justify the presence of the 'base' style, while at the same time, because it *is* a pretence, it enables Góngora to parody this style when the occasion demands.[33] Moreover, the allusion to Babylon, commonly identified with Babel, the traditional site of verbal confusion, can be taken as a challenge to Góngora's critics, as if he were saying: 'You have accused me of creating a new Babel; here, then, is another Babel for you to decipher.'[34] At the least, then, the poem may be seen as an unrepentant affirmation of a way of writing which had come under attack; at the same time, Góngora's remorselessly witty parody of his own *culto* vocabulary and diction goes further than anything his critics could have anticipated, as if impatience with a style which lent itself to parody by others had led to a new kind of flexibility. At times, as in earlier poems, this is achieved by the use of 'non-poetic' vocabulary – in this instance, by the introduction of legal or culinary terms;[35] elsewhere, potentially 'serious' effects are avoided by hyberbole or bathos, as in the description of Thisbe:

> De plata bruñida era
> proporcionado cañuto
> el órgano de la voz,
> la cerbatana del gusto.   (lines 65–8)

The organ of her voice, the conduit of her taste [i.e. her throat] was a well-shaped pipe of polished silver.

Or later, of Thisbe's limbs:

¿ebúrneos diré o divinos?
divinos digo y ebúrneos.   (lines 407–8)

Shall I say ivory or divine? I say divine *and* ivory.

This last example points to the extraordinary degree of authorial intervention in the poem, as if Góngora continually wished to draw attention to the artificiality of what he is doing, that is to say, to the actual rhetorical fashioning of the poem. In this, of course, Góngora is playing a very deliberate game with his readers: by blurring the limits between the 'high' and the 'base' styles to a greater extent than any of his contemporaries, he is creating a kind of dissonance which can only be grasped by reference to the rules themselves. Or, as C. S. Lewis has said of English Metaphysical poetry: 'It uses discords on the assumption that your taste is sufficiently educated to recognize them. If the immemorial standard of decorum were not in your mind before you began reading, there would be no "point", no "wit": only clownish insipidity.'[36]

Much of the effect of the *Píramo y Tisbe* depends, in fact, on what Lewis calls a 'calculated breach of decorum', on knowing exactly how Góngora is stretching the limits of what is conventionally permissible. In the long run, however, it is impossible to isolate such stylistic considerations from the actual subject-matter of the poem. The two lovers, after all, are a rhetorical construction which itself deconstructs earlier versions of the theme. Here, confusion of styles is directly related to the mixture of genres. In Ovid himself, as Barry Ife has pointed out, there is a curious ambivalence, insofar as the point of view he adopts works against the tragic potentialities of the story.[37] In Góngora's version, on the other hand, as Salazar Mardones already sensed, there is a 'seriousness' which goes beyond mere burlesque, and which Ovid does not allow for. One sign of this is that its comic dimension, though evident throughout, is seriously undermined; as Ife rightly argues, the comedy seems deliberately to avoid any firm basis: 'each strand [of the poem's texture] surface[s] successively as norm and deviation: one moment it is the norm from which its neighbours deviate, the next it is the deviation from its neighbouring norm'.[38] If, then, the comedy is unstable, where does the seriousness lie? Mainly, I would argue, in the way the poem ultimately denies us both the consolation of laughter and the distancing effect of tragedy. The poem ends, predictably, with the lovers' deaths – unnecessary and in a sense ridiculous deaths, though deaths none the less. At an obvious level of meaning, what is finally tragicomic – what cannot be fully absorbed either as tragedy or comedy – is human idealism itself as exemplified by the two lovers. Yet in terms of the whole poem and its rhetorical procedures, it is as if, in order to show this, Góngora had had to break through his own comic mode – a strategy which may remind us of the ending of *Angélica y Medoro*, not least because of the way in which it appears to question the nature of poetic creation itself.

According to Salazar Mardones, the *Píramo y Tisbe* was the poem 'which [Góngora] took most trouble over and of which he thought most highly'. Whatever the truth of this, it is clearly the work of a poet at the height of his powers – one, moreover, whose astonishing ability to synthesize his own earlier achievements seems matched by a strong desire to move on from them in unexpected directions. Though none of the poems of his final years is conceived on this kind of scale, his skill in the minor forms which had been cultivated from the beginning of his career remains undiminished. Thus the *letrilla* 'Ánsares de Menga', which dates from 1620, is the finest of the series of rustic poems which had begun with 'En los pinares de Júcar' (see above, p. 76). As so often, the success of the poem depends on a skilful fusion of style and matter; in this instance, a 'humble' subject – a peasant girl and her geese beside a stream – and the sophisticated verbal texture which uncondescendingly reinforces the beauty of what is being described:

> *Ánsares de Menga*
> *al arroyo van:*
> *ellos visten nieve,*
> *él corre cristal.*
> El arroyo espera
> las hermosas aves
> que cisnes süaves
> son de su ribera;
> cuya Venus era
> hija de Pascual.
>   *Ellos visten nieve,*
>   *él corre cristal.*   (Millé, 187)

Menga's geese go to the stream; they are clothed in snow, it [i.e. the stream] *runs crystal.* The stream waits for the lovely birds which are the gentle swans of its bank, whose Venus was Pascual's daughter. *They are clothed in snow, it runs crystal.*

It is hard to reconcile the delicacy of this and other late poems with the harsh realities of Góngora's life at Court as described in his correspondence.[39] Nevertheless, the wit which continues to flicker through the letters, even at their worst moments of depression, bursts out with full force in the splendid sonnet to the new favourite, Olivares, which begins:

> En la capilla estoy y condenado
> a partir sin remedio de esta vida;
> siento la causa aun más que la partida,
> por hambre expulso com sitïado...   (Millé, 376)

I am in the chapel [i.e. like a criminal on the eve of his execution, but also referring to the fact that Góngora was a chaplain] and irremediably condemned to depart from this life [i.e. both 'to die' and 'to leave behind Court life']; I regret the cause even more than the departing, driven out by hunger like one besieged.

And in his two final moral sonnets: 'En este occidental, en este, oh Licio, / climatérico lustro de tu vida...' (In this declining, this climacteric season, o Licio, of your life; Millé, 373) and 'Menos solicitó veloz saeta...' (Millé, 374), written in 1623 within ten days of one another, whatever disillusionment Góngora may have felt in the last few years of his life is embodied in verses of implacable precision:

> Menos solicitó veloz saeta
> destinada señal, que mordió aguda;
> agonal carro por la arena muda
> no coronó con más silencio meta,
>   que presurosa corre, que secreta
> a su fin nuestra edad. A quien lo duda,
> fiera que sea de razón desnuda,
> cada sol repetido es un cometa.
>   ¿Confiésalo Cartago, y tú lo ignoras?
> Peligro corres, Licio, si porfías
> en seguir sombras y abrazar engaños.
>   Mal te perdonarán a ti las horas;
> las horas que limando están los días,
> los días que royendo están los años.

Less swiftly did the arrow seek its destined mark, which it sharply bit; the chariot in the dumb arena at the Roman games did not round the pillar more silently than, quickly and secretly, our life runs to its close. For him who doubts it, even a brute deprived of reason, each repeated sun is a comet. Does Carthage confess this, and you ignore it? You are taking a risk, Licio, if you persist in chasing shadows and embracing deceptions. You will scarcely be pardoned by the hours; the hours which are filing down the days, the days which are gnawing at the years.

'Licio' here is Góngora himself – distanced by the classical pseudonym he had used in some of his earliest writing. Again, one may think of possible precedents: there is a natural progression from the earlier funeral sonnets, like the one I discussed in the previous chapter (see above, p. 54) or the fine epitaph for El Greco (1614; Millé, 332), to a poem like this one. Yet nowhere else does Góngora come as close to what one critic calls the 'architectural solidity' of Latin.[40] This is not just a matter of images, but also of diction – the suppression of articles in the first quatrain ('veloz saeta / destinada señal... agonal carro... meta') – and of the concentrated rhetorical structure in which the central question – '¿Confiésalo Cartago, y tú lo ignoras?' – acts as the crucial link between the opening statements and the final admonition. This structure, clearly, is dramatic: the question itself, which relates an individual fate to that of vast empires, introduces a note of uncertainty which is intensified in the terrifying chain effect of the closing lines. Again, one is struck by Góngora's extraordinary powers of compression: just as the question sums up the whole poetry of ruins, so the eleventh line ('en seguir sombras y abrazar engaños') hints at the Baroque obsession with false appearances and the destructive force of time. As for the uncertainty, this comes from the sense that any possible resolution could only take place outside the poem; in the poem itself, there is no guarantee that the 'wise' voice of the speaker will prevail over his 'lesser' self, whose resistance is necessary to the force of the argument. Such force, as R. D. Calcraft has argued, ultimately relies for its effect on a Christian sense of order, though Góngora is nowhere as explicit as this.[41] It would be wrong, of course, to read such a poem as expressing some kind of personal conflict on the part of the poet: what matters is the effect on the reader, who may be expected to heed the admonition which, as part of the poem's strategy, the speaker addresses to himself. Nevertheless, this reluctance to force things to a premature conclusion seems characteristic of a poet who, while commanding greater verbal resources than most of his contemporaries, never ceased to question the basic assumptions of his art or to pursue that art to its ultimate consequences.

4
Lope de Vega: re-writing a life

I

The careers of Góngora and Lope de Vega (1562–1635) run in a kind of counterpoint, often amounting to open rivalry. Certain differences immediately stand out: where Góngora is almost exclusively a poet, Lope is also the leading dramatist of his generation, as well as the author of several works of prose fiction; unlike Góngora, whose collected poems were never published in his lifetime, Lope is a professional writer, whose volumes of verse appear at frequent intervals from 1602 onwards.[1] Other differences take the form of polarities: mass literature – the theatre – versus minority literature, Castilian (often equated with 'Spanish') versus Andalusian, and, more tentatively, the confessional as against the reticent. Not all of these contrasts, as we shall see, are absolute – much of Lope's poetic activity, for example, was aimed at the same minority audience as Góngora's – yet, taken together, they at least suggest the lines of force which were to dominate Spanish poetry in the first decades of the seventeenth century.

What is debatable here is the term 'confessional' – a word often used to describe Lope's seemingly inexhaustible ability to turn the events of a turbulent life more or less directly into verse. From a literary point of view, such events – two marriages, interspersed with a number of extra-marital relationships; a series of spiritual crises, both before and after his entering the priesthood – seem inseparable from his extraordinary energy as a writer. And there are moments, certainly, when 'confessional' seems the right word, whether he is evoking the memory of his dead son, Carlos Félix,[2] or the blindness and insanity of his last mistress, Marta de Nevares:

> Aquella que, gallarda, se prendía
> y de tan ricas galas se preciaba,

94

que a la Aurora de espejo le servía,
y en la luz de sus ojos se tocaba,
curiosa, los vestidos deshacía,
y otras veces, estúpida, imitaba,
el cuerpo en hielo, en éxtasis la mente,
un bello mármol de escultor valiente.

(*Amarilis* [1635], lines 505–12; C, p. 438)

That woman who dressed so elegantly and prided herself on such rich finery, who served as a mirror for Dawn, who arranged her hair in the light of her eyes, would eagerly destroy her clothes, or else, in stupor – her body frozen, her mind beyond itself – would resemble the fine statue of a bold sculptor.

The correspondence between life and poetry, however, is seldom as exact as this, and biographical criticism has often done Lope a disservice by attempting to draw the links too tight, thus emphasizing the man at the expense of the conscious artist. Yet Lope's art itself, it could be argued, seems positively to invite such an approach; as Mary Gaylord Randel, one of his most discerning critics, says of the *Rimas*: 'these verses disconcert us because they do not stand alone either in art or life'.[3] Any attempt to find firmer ground, as we shall see, involves not only the question of the relations between reality and fiction, but also, at a deeper level, the nature of the poetic 'I' which speaks through Lope's more personal verse. Most of the evidence here comes from the *Rimas* of 1602, by which time Lope has begun to theorize about his poetic intentions. Something of what it entails, however, can already be seen in the *romances artísticos*, or 'new ballads', which he and Góngora did so much to popularize in the 1580s. As we saw in the previous chapter, Góngora was quick to parody the type of ballad which he himself had helped to establish. This involves both self-parody and parody of others: his own ballad which begins 'Ensíllenme el asno rucio' (Saddle me the grey ass; Millé, 10) is an almost line-by-line travesty of Lope's 'Ensíllenme el potro rucio' (Saddle me the grey colt; C, p. 142), one of the most popular examples of the *romance morisco*. One reason for such an attack, as Orozco Díaz suggests,[4] may have been resentment at the appropriation of Moorish, or properly Andalusian, material on the part of a Castilian writer; another, given Góngora's preference for impersonality, may well have been the autobiographical connections of this and similar poems. As many of Lope's contemporaries recognized, these *romances moriscos* and the slightly later pastoral ballads are related at many points to an actual love affair. The facts are well established: sometime in 1587, Elena Osorio, the daughter of an actor-manager with whom Lope had had professional dealings, left Lope for a richer lover, Perrenot de Granvela; as a result of his libellous attacks on her family, Lope was arrested, tried and eventually banished from Castile for eight years.[5] This episode not only underlies the early ballads but also an important group of sonnets in the *Rimas*, and re-surfaces under more mature scrutiny in Lope's final masterpiece, the prose dialogue *La Dorotea* (1632). In the ballads, there is no doubt that Lope is re-enacting his own emotions both before and after the break; what is interesting is that he does this through a series of 'masks' or *personae* – Zaide/ Gazul and others in the Moorish ballads, Belardo/Fabio in the pastoral – which give him considerable scope for role-playing. This ludic element is essential to both sets of poems: rather than writing from a fixed 'self', Lope is able to call on a range of feelings – anger, self-pity, resignation, fantasies of reconciliation – which, though often self-contradictory, make up what Trueblood calls a 'constellation of emotions'[6] which he will revert to time and again in his later work. And, more often than not, as we shall see in a moment, this means 're-inventing' the facts in order to create a new kind of literary fable.

The most sophisticated example of this occurs in the ballad which begins 'Hortelano era Belardo / de las huertas de Valencia' (Belardo was a farmer on the farms of Valencia; C, pp. 186–91). Belardo is Lope's favourite 'mask', not only in the pastoral ballads, but also in his early theatre (*Belardo furioso*; the Madness of Belardo, c. 1588) and in some of his later eclogues. In this particular poem, he has changed his employment under duress – the reference to Valencia suggests Lope's own exile at the time – and is looking back on his recent past with something like detachment. In the early part of the poem, Belardo is sowing what amounts to a 'garden of love': the characteristic catalogue of plants –

> El trébol para las niñas
> pone al lado de la huerta,
> porque la fruta de amor
> de las tres hojas aprenda.

Clover for young girls he plants at the side of the garden, so that the fruit of love may learn from the three leaves.

– is less a cornucopia than a reminder of their sexual properties.[7] This deliberately created erotic atmosphere prepares one for the rest of the poem, which hinges on the figure of the scarecrow, first described, then directly addressed in the closing lines. Belardo has dressed the scarecrow in his own court clothes – here the slight pastoral fiction breaks down completely – thus making it into a grotesque simulacrum of his past. And in his final mocking address he relates it directly to his 'tragedy':

> ¡Oh ricos despojos
> de mi edad primera
> y trofeos vivos
> de esperanzas muertas!
> ¡Qué bien parecéis
> de dentro y de fuera,
> sobre que habéis dado
> fin a mi tragedia!...

O rich spoils of my early youth and living trophies of dead hopes! How fine you look, inside and out, having brought my tragedy to an end!

What follows, in conclusion, is an account of the double relationship which underlies these exclamations; Belardo's fine clothes once enabled him to seduce a girl and then to marry her – Lope's own first marriage, to Isabel de Urbina, dates from 1588 – and the news of this had angered his former mistress:

> Supo mi delito
> aquella morena
> que reinaba en Troya
> cuando fue mi reina.
> Hizo de mis cosas
> una grande hoguera,
> tomando venganza
> en plumas y letras.

That dark-haired girl who reigned in Troy when she was my queen [Elena Osorio = Helen of Troy] heard of my crime. She made a great bonfire of my things, taking her vengeance in pen and ink.

There are two things to notice here. One is the way in which Lope/Belardo splits his 'self' into an 'I' and an 'other' through the device of the scarecrow (the speaker's former 'I') which is then addressed by an 'other' who is also the 'I' of the present. Thus, as Carreño points out,[8] the scarecrow becomes a 'carnivalesque' version of the self, an object of self-parody through which an idyllic past is ironically transformed. The second has to do with another kind of transformation, with the way Lope re-writes his own 'story' in the latter part of the poem. The mention of Troy, as the translation indicates, is a scarcely disguised reference to Elena Osorio; in reality, however, the one who took vengeance 'in pen and ink' was Lope himself, not Elena – a clear inversion of the roles of victim and aggressor. Moreover, by placing the account of his marriage before the reaction of the other woman, Lope/Belardo suppresses the fact of his displacement by a rival lover – a move which, once again, works to his own advantage. Such departures from the truth, needless to say, have no effect on the success or otherwise of the poem; what they *do* show, on the other hand, is the extent to which Lope is already touching, however, unconsciously, on the kind of relations between art and experience which emerge more explicitly in his later work.

The apparent spontaneousness of such poems points not only to Lope's extraordinary inventiveness – a virtue which often degenerates into mere fluency – but also to his instinctive feeling for all types of popular poetry. This is almost impossible to illustrate in isolation: his versions of *poesía de tipo tradicional* (see above, p. 4) occur mostly in his plays, and many of the best examples are virtually untranslatable. One sign of their authenticity is that it is often hard to tell whether Lope has composed a new poem or merely taken over an existing original, as he does in the case of the famous *seguidilla* from *El caballero de Olmedo* (The Knight of Olmedo):

> Que de noche le mataron
> al caballero,
> la gala de Medina,
> la flor de Olmedo.[9]

For they killed him in the dark, the knight, the pride of Medina, the flower of Olmedo.

What is certain, however, is Lope's amazing ability to create a mood by the simplest of means, often within the compass of two or three lines:

> Río de Sevilla,
> ¡cuán bien pareces
> con galeras blancas
> y remos verdes!

River of Seville, how fine you look, with white ships and green oars!

or, more economically still:

> Caminito toledano,
> ¡quién te tuviera ya andado![10]

Little road to Toledo, oh to have got to the end!

Yet against Lope's sureness of instinct in re-creating forms of popular art, one must set his constant ambition to write as a 'serious' poet – that is to say, within the accepted modes and conventions of Italianate verse. Thus his pastoral novel, *La Arcadia* (1598), like the *Galatea* of Cervantes (see above, p. 29), includes a considerable number of poems – sonnets, odes, eclogues – which, taken collectively, read like a conscious attempt to appropriate as much as possible of the existing Petrarchan tradition. Four years later, Lope published his first independent volume of verse, the *Rimas* (1602), often known as the *Rimas humanas* (Human [i.e. secular] Rhymes).[11] By this time, as we shall see, Lope has worked out something like a consistent poetics; what it is more important to notice at this stage, however, is the way in which the opening sonnet – a deliberately introductory poem – reflects, at times problematically, on the entire enterprise:

> Versos de amor, conceptos esparcidos,
> engendrados del alma en mis cuidados;
> partos de mis sentidos abrasados,
> con más dolor que libertad nacidos;
>   expósitos al mundo, en que, perdidos,
> tan rotos anduvistes y trocados,
> que sólo donde fuistes engendrados
> fuérades por la sangre conocidos;
>   pues que le hurtáis el laberinto a Creta,
> a Dédalo los altos pensamientos,
> la furia al mar, las llamas al abismo,
>   si aquel áspid hermoso no os aceta,
> dejad la tierra, entretened los vientos:
> descansaréis en vuestro centro mismo.   (B, p. 23)

Verses of love, scattered conceits, fathered by my soul upon my cares, offspring of my burning senses, born with more pain than liberty; abandoned to the world, where, lost, you wandered so ragged and changed that only where you were begotten would you be recognized by your blood; since you steal the labyrinth from Crete, from Daedalus your lofty thoughts, your anger from the sea, your flames from the abyss, if that fair asp does not accept you, leave the earth, entertain the clouds: [there] you will rest in your own centre.

What immediately strikes one here is the potential contrast of the opening line, and the way this is developed in the rest of the poem.

'Versos de amor' (Verses of love) leads to 'partos de mis sentidos abrasados' (offspring of my burning senses) – verses, in other words, as the direct product of emotion. Against this, however, there are 'conceptos esparcidos' (scattered conceits), echoed by the 'altos pensamientos' (lofty thoughts) of Daedalus, the inventor of the Cretan labyrinth. (The labyrinth, here and elsewhere in these poems, is a frequent symbol of the confusions of love.)[12] *Conceptos*, whether thought of as 'concepts' or 'conceits', entail the shaping of experience by the intellect, together with a possible dilution of that experience. Once again, therefore, there is an unresolved discrepancy between life and art, a de-centring of experience which is compounded by the reference to the woman ('aquel áspid hermoso'; that fair asp). In the kind of Petrarchan lyric which Lope is clearly imitating, the 'centre' is almost invariably the beloved in terms of whom the speaker seeks to define himself;[13] here, however, the poems are said to find their 'centre', not in any mortal creature, but in the winds – traditionally, a symbol of freedom and mutability, though also of fame. Thus the expected position of the woman has been subtly shifted: if she is no longer the 'centre' of the poems, then the poems themselves, if they survive, may become *her* 'centre'.

This might seem overingenious if it were not for the series of biological metaphors ('engendrados... partos... expósitos... sangre'; fathered... offspring... abandoned... blood) which control the opening quatrains. Literally, the poems are 'abandoned' because they have circulated in barely recognizable versions. Yet the anxiety to establish their paternity hints at a deeper question which must affect any poetry based on the imitation of existing models and especially that which, like the *Rimas*, involves an attempt at self-definition, namely: to whom do such verses belong? Just now I referred to Lope's early attempts at the Petrarchan mode as an act of 'appropriation'. In practice, this means that Petrarch (and by implication his sixteenth-century imitators) acts both as model and antagonist, the creator of a 'space' which must be filled (or usurped) by one's own inventions. Thus, at a relatively superficial level, a sonnet like 'Era la víspera alegre del día...' (It was the happy eve of the day; B, p. 24) reads like a conscious attempt to deviate from a chosen Petrarchan motif:[14] to write one's own, different, poem on an established theme and, in doing so, to absorb the original poem into one's own poetic system. As Mary Randel has shown, however, the question of 'belonging' goes much deeper than this, and concerns not only the source of the poems' actual words, but also the authority of the 'voice' which is speaking through them. As she points out, there is a curious paradox here, in that Lope's apparently most personal statements rely more often than not on 'borrowed' words; as she puts it herself: 'imitation and intimacy do not alternate, see-saw fashion ...they are inseparable: the most intensely confessional verses tend also to be the most profoundly imitative'.[15] In terms of the speaker of the poems, this means of course that the 'I' must construct itself through the words of others. The kind of biographical criticism to which I referred earlier has no difficulty in identifying this subject with the Lope of real life. The sonnets themselves, however, suggest a more fragmentary poetic self – one which, despite appearances, never becomes fully present. How far Lope was conscious of this, it is difficult to tell, though, as in his later work, there are poems in which the feeling of loss of identity seems more than merely conventional.[16] Although there is no place here for the 'masks' of the early ballads, there are times when the sense of veiling and unveiling is almost as strong; the ludic elements, in other words, persist, together with the display of self-contradiction, as if this now had become an essential part of the experience of love. This means, in turn, that such authority as the poet has is continually under threat, both from the difficulty of establishing a sufficient identity – the problem of making others' words one's own – and from the sense that appropriation, in life as in art, is never easily achieved.

The kind of tensions this involves can be seen at work in one of Lope's finest love sonnets, the last of a group of three written over a period of something like ten years:

> Suelta mi manso, mayoral extraño,
> pues otro tienes de tu igual decoro;
> deja la prenda que en el alma adoro,
> perdida por tu bien y por mi daño.
>   Ponle su esquila de labrado estaño,
> y no le engañen tus collares de oro;
> toma en albricias este blanco toro,
> que a las primeras hierbas cumple un año.
>   Si pides señas, tiene el vellocino
> pardo encrespado, y los ojuelos tiene
> como durmiendo en regalado sueño.
>   Si piensas que no soy su dueño, Alcino,
> suelta, y verásle si a mi choza viene:
> que aun tienen sal las manos de su dueño.   (B, p. 135)

Set free my gentle sheep [literally 'bellwether', i.e. leader of a flock], strange head shepherd, since you have another of your own kind; release the prize which in my soul I adore, lost to your advantage and to my hurt. Put on its bell of wrought tin and do not deceive it with your gold collars; take in exchange this white bull which will be a year old this spring. If you want markings, it has dark curly fleece and little eyes which seem to sleep in pleasant slumber. If you think I am not its master, Alcino, let it go and you will see if it comes to my hut, for its master's hands still have salt [for it].

All three sonnets, it is clear, refer to the Elena Osorio affair, in other words, to the emotional situation which lies behind the early ballads. Again, what is interesting is the re-shaping of the experience itself, this time through the medium of the pastoral convention.[17] Taken as a group, the poems read like variations on a theme, in which the constituent figures – speaker, woman and rival – are made to appear each time in a different relationship. The first sonnet, addressed to a friend, is vituperative and more sexually explicit than the others:

> ... aquel me hurtaron ya, Vireno hermano;
> ya retoza otro dueño y le provoca;
> toda la noche vela y duerme el día.
>   Ya come blanca sal en otra mano;
> ya come ajena mano con la boca
> de cuya lengua se abrasó la mía.   (C, p. 280)[18]

Now they have stolen that one from me, brother Vireno; now it provokes and plays with another master; it stays up all night and sleeps by day. Now it eats white salt from another hand; now it eats another's hand with the mouth whose tongue set my own on fire.

In the second, as Lázaro points out, there is no reference to 'stealing': the stress falls, a little overrhetorically, on the error of the 'sheep' which has foolishly, though voluntarily, left its owner, who now begs it to return: 'Aquí está vuestra vega, monte y selva, / yo soy vuestro pastor y vos mi dueño...' (Here is your plain, your hills and woods, I am your shepherd and you my master). The pun on 'vega' (plain, pasture) seems more than just casual: as Randel emphasizes, the mountainous landscape of the early part of the poem has strong sexual overtones, and Lope's use of his own name here can be construed as a deliberate attempt to appropriate both the *manso*/ woman and the pastoral scene itself.

The third sonnet – 'Suelta mi manso...' – re-shapes the situation in yet another way, by moving it still further in the direction of 'literature'. Here, for the first time, it is the rival who is addressed. A few hints of the real-life situation remain: 'de tu igual decoro' (of your own kind) and the detail of the gold collars refer to differences of social rank, just as one senses the presence of a woman behind the description of the first tercet. Yet here, for the most part, the pastoral fiction is more skilfully sustained than in the other two poems.[19] Lope's specific use of this convention, with its potentially blasphemous echoes of the parable of the Good Shepherd, not only allows him to simplify the original situation but also to manipulate it in the interests of aesthetic harmony. At the same time, the kind of control this entails verges once again on appropriation. The idea of harmony, after all, lies at the centre of the pastoral convention itself: within the convention, the sheep, however allegorized, is the property of the shepherd, and any disruption of this bond amounts to an offence against nature itself. Thus the imagined reconciliation will also be a restoration of nature – the implicit meaning from which the poem derives much of its power. In terms of the situation itself, of course, this is pure fantasy; yet beneath this deliberate re-writing of experience there lies a more crucial kind of re-making, in which Lope is laying claim, not only to a particular woman, but also to a whole way of thinking about love in which the ultimate issue is his own poetic *persona*.

The *Rimas* are often referred to as a *canzoniere* in the Petrarchan sense, in which Lope moves through a number of relationships in the manner of a *peregrino de amor* or 'pilgrim of love'. The overall design of the collection, however, scarcely bears out the idea of a progression: the love poems tend to group themselves around certain key images (ruins, labyrinths, the *manso* figure), rather than in a deliberate sequence. What is more, over a third of the two hundred sonnets belong to what are by now the recognized sub-genres of their kind: the classical, the mythological, the biblical, the funereal and so on. Though a good deal of attention has been directed, understandably, to the more problematical love sonnets, the best of the remaining poems have qualities which should not be overlooked, and which in some cases look forward to the preoccupations of Lope's later work. This is especially true of the sonnets on biblical themes, like the fine poem on the death of Absalom, 'Suspenso estaba Absalón entre las ramas...' (Absalom was hanging in the branches; B, p. 84),[20] or the justly famous 'Al triunfo de Judit' (On the Triumph of Judith):

Cuelga sangriento de la cama al suelo
el hombro diestro del feroz tirano,
que opuesto al muro de Betulia en vano,
despidió contra sí rayos al cielo.
    Revuelto con el ansia el rojo velo
del pabellón a la siniestra mano,
descubre el espectáculo inhumano
del tronco horrible, convertido en hielo.
    Vertido Baco, el fuerte arnés afea
los vasos y la mesa derribada,
duermen las guardas, que tan mal emplea;
    y sobre la muralla coronada
del pueblo de Israel, la casta hebrea
con la cabeza resplandece armada.   (B, p. 78)[21]

There hangs bleeding from the bed to the ground the right shoulder of the
fierce tyrant who, vainly besieging the wall of Bethulia, sent thunderbolts
against heaven to his own cost. Disarrayed in his agony, the red curtain of
the tent reveals, on the left, the cruel spectacle of the dreadful trunk, now
turned to ice. Spilt Bacchus [i.e. wine] stains his strong armour, the cups and
the overturned table; the guards sleep whom he employs to little purpose;
and on the wall crowned by the people of Israel, the chaste Hebrew woman
shines forth, armed with the head.

Several cultural currents converge in a poem like this: Counter-
Reformation spirituality, with its insistence on the exemplary nature
of religious art; the Renaissance tradition of the 'triumph', deriving
from the *Trionfi* of Petrarch;[22] and the so-called 'Parnassian' style,
associated especially with Lope's friend the Sevillian poet Juan de
Arguijo (see p. 128) – a consciously 'pictorial' kind of writing which
seems to aim at a verbal equivalent of painting or sculpture. Yet, as
we saw earlier (see above, p. 52), parallels between poetry and the
visual arts need to be treated with caution; as Erdman points out in
his own analysis of this poem, there is no need to appeal to any
pictorial source for a final clarification of the sonnet, which is entirely
consistent within its own terms. Certain details, to be sure, seem
designed to create a mental picture in the reader – 'el hombro
diestro' (the right shoulder) and 'a la siniestra mano' (on the left)
have the effect of stage directions – just as the various objects referred
to in the description of Holofernes's tent seem deliberately 'placed'.
Nevertheless, to insist too much on this 'visual' aspect can distract
one from the way the poem works as a whole. This depends partly on
the various threads which bind the poem together, and partly on the

culminating effect of the last three lines. In the first place, Lope is clearly familiar with the tradition of biblical interpretation which sees Holofernes as a symbol of pride and Judith as a figure of the Church Militant. Secondly, the sense of 'triumph', clearly stated in the title and reinforced by the 'military' vocabulary, thrusts the poem, so to speak, towards the final apotheosis of Judith. Moreover, the two apparently distinct visual moments are both described in the same unremitting present tense: 'Cuelga sangriento...resplandece' (There hangs bleeding...shines forth). The effect of this, surely, is to blur the distinction by superimposing one scene on the other. What Lope has done, in other words, is to select the one 'frozen moment' – Erdman's phrase – which implies both past and future: the immediate aftermath of the killing, which looks back to the murder itself and already contains within it the climax, i.e. the public triumph.

II

A poem like this might well have gone into Lope's next major collection of verse, the *Rimas sacras* (Sacred Rhymes) of 1614. Though this contains a good deal of fairly mechanical writing, it also includes some of the finest religious poems in the language – poems which are in every way equal to the spiritual crisis they reflect. The sources of this crisis are difficult to locate: in the years preceding the publication of these poems, Lope is clearly drawing nearer to the Church – after joining several lay orders, he finally became a priest in 1614 – and a series of personal losses – the deaths of his son (1612) and second wife (1613) – may have contributed to his increasing sense of guilt at past transgressions. This first emerges in the *Soliloquios* of 1612, a group of four verse soliloquies, later expanded to seven and published anonymously, with prose commentaries, in 1626. The full title of the 1612 edition suggests the general tenor of the poems: *Cuatro soliloquios de Lope de Vega Carpio; llanto y lágrimas que hizo arrodillado delante de un crucifijo pidiendo a Dios perdón de sus pecados, después de haber recibido el hábito de la Tercera Orden de Penitencia del seráfico Francisco* (Four Soliloquies of Lope de Vega Carpio; the Weeping and Tears He Shed while Kneeling before a Crucifix Asking God's Forgiveness for his Sins, after having Received the Habit of the Third Order of the Seraphic Francis). Though the *Soliloquios* are more loosely structured than the much finer meditations of the *Rimas sacras*, the prose commentaries point directly to the preoccupations of the latter: 'But alas, Lord, now I recall how long I took to free myself from the shroud of habits that wound me in'; or again, speaking of the torments of recollection: 'As, if the sea were to dry up, such strange monsters would be seen, so, Lord, I see my evil actions [*torpezas*] in the sands of my past years.'

This note of self-reproach appears repeatedly in the more personal poems of the *Rimas sacras*. At the same time, though this is clearly something new in his work, it would be wrong to pass over the more public, not to say traditional, side of Lope's religious verse. It has often been pointed out how easily the secular and the divine interpenetrate in his work. As we shall see in a moment, the influence of Petrarch by no means disappears in the sonnets of spiritual crisis, just as Lope's immense skill in re-creating popular poetry reappears no less impressively in the religious *villancicos* of the prose romance *Los pastores de Belén* (The Shepherds of Bethlehem; 1612). Again, as I explained in the first chapter (see above, p. 13), Lope is fully conversant with the tradition of *conceptismo sacro* or religious conceit which is a central feature of so-called *a lo divino* poetry, a type of ingenuity which he often turns to good account, as in the sonnet quoted on p. 13, but which can also lead him into tasteless trivializing.[23]

Taken as a whole, the *Rimas sacras*, even at their least successful, provide a valuable index to Lope's complex and deeply emotional spiritual attitudes. If one looks for a unifying principle, this is surely to be found in his constant references to a 'new life' – in other words, to his urgent desire for spiritual rebirth. Thus in a very real sense, the best of the *Rimas sacras* represent the most radical of all Lope's attempts to re-write his own life, first by transposing his whole conception of love to a divine plane, and secondly, by subjecting his poetic self – the 'I' of the poems – to the kind of questioning we have already seen in his secular love poetry.

Once again, the opening sonnet sets the tone for the rest:

> Cuando me paro a contemplar mi estado,
> y a ver los pasos por donde he venido,
> me espanto de que un hombre tan perdido
> a conocer su error haya llegado.
> Cuando miro los años que he pasado,
> la divina razón puesta en olvido,
> conozco que piedad del cielo ha sido
> no haberme en tanto mal precipitado.

> Entré por laberinto tan extraño,
> fiando al débil hilo de la vida
> el tarde conocido desengaño;
>   mas de tu luz mi escuridad vencida,
> el monstro muerto de mi ciego engaño,
> vuelve a la patria la razón perdida.   (B, p. 316)

When I pause to consider my state and to survey the path I have travelled, I am amazed that a man so lost should have come to recognize his error. When I behold the years I have spent in ignorance of divine reason, I realize that it has been an act of mercy on Heaven's part that I have not plunged into such evil. I entered on so strange a labyrinth, entrusting to the weak thread of life the disenchantment so long deferred, that, my darkness [now] vanquished by your light, the monster of my blind deception dead, lost reason returns to its home.

It is instructive to compare this with the introductory sonnet of the *Rimas*, published twelve years earlier (see above, p. 99). Once again, the image of the Cretan labyrinth appears, now greatly expanded and translated into openly allegorical terms. Moreover, the later poem continues to move in the same area of intertextuality as the earlier one: its first line is a direct quotation from Garcilaso's much-imitated Sonnet 1, which in turn echoes Petrarch's Sonnet 298: 'Quand'io mi volgo indietro a mirar gli anni...' (When I turn back to gaze at the years). Thus imitation, for a second time, though in a very different connection, acts both as homage and appropriation: by taking over what in both instances is a strictly secular context and by writing his own, religious, poem within it, Lope is both acknowledging the weight of a tradition and deviating from it to his own ends. The relation between the poems, however, goes further than this: by taking over Garcilaso's metaphor of the journey – his own second line, again, is virtually a quotation – and by fusing it with that of the labyrinth, Lope insists on the idea of a progress through confusion towards a final spiritual encounter. As Carreño rightly points out,[24] it is this dynamic juxtaposition of past and present which enables Lope to focus on the question of individual identity; the speaker's detachment in comparing 'what he is now' with 'what he was then' becomes a means of constructing the 'self' which he now wants to present to God.

Yet, as Lope is the first to acknowledge, the kind of resolution this implies is fraught with paradox. The sonnet which I referred to in the first chapter – 'Pastor que con tus silbos amorosos...' (Shepherd who with your fond whistling... ; see above, p. 13) – ends with a sudden twist:

> ...Oye, pastor, pues por amores mueres,
> no te espante el rigor de mis pecados,
> pues tan amigo de amores eres.
>   Espera, pues, y escucha mis cuidados;
> ¿pero cómo te digo que me esperes,
> si estás para esperar los pies clavados?   (B, p. 323)

Listen, shepherd, since you die for love, do not let the gravity of my sins alarm you, since you are such a friend to the helpless. Wait, then, and listen to my cares; but why should I tell you to wait if your feet are nailed [i.e. to the Cross] to make you wait?

The urgency with which the speaker addresses Christ on the Cross – 'Oye... Espera... escucha' (Hear... wait... listen) – is interrupted in the last two lines by a traditional, though nonetheless effective, religious conceit. This final paradox is enforced by the rhetorical strategy of the poem as a whole: not only has Christ never ceased to hear the speaker – he literally cannot turn away – but it is the speaker himself, in the 'profundo sueño' (deep sleep) of the first stanza, who fails to 'listen' to Christ – a reversal just as potent as the one which ends the poem.

The kind of humility this entails – the sense that Christ has already allowed for anything the speaker might conceive of – is familiar to English readers through the poetry of George Herbert. And, as in Herbert, the 'self' of the speaker creates certain problems which hardly arise in the context of secular love poetry. Such poetry, as I have tried to show, more often than not depends on a 'rhetorical self' whose stability or otherwise does not need to go beyond the limits of the individual poem. In religious poetry, on the other hand, the very idea of a 'soul', in the Christian sense, seems to presuppose, not a 'rhetorical self', but what one might call a 'central self', a core of identity which remains unchanged, whatever the circumstances. Moreover, there is the fact that many religious poems, like those I am discussing, are directly addressed to God, in other words to a deity who cannot by any stretch of the imagination be confined within the boundaries of a poem.

One further example may suggest what is involved here:

> ¿Qué tengo yo que mi amistad procuras?
> ¿Qué interés se te sigue, Jesús mío,
> que a mi puerta cubierto de rocío

pasas las noches del invierno escuras?
  ¡Oh cuánto fueron mis entrañas duras,
pues no te abrí! ¡Qué extraño desvarío,
si de mi ingratitud el hielo frío
secó las llagas de tus plantas puras!
  ¡Cuántas veces el Ángel me decía:
'Alma, asómate agora a la ventana,
verás con cuánto amor llamar porfía'!
  ¡Y cuántas, hermosura soberana,
'Mañana le abriremos', respondía,
para lo mismo responder mañana!   (B, pp. 324–5)

What do I have that you seek my friendship? What does it profit you, my Jesus, to spend the dark winter nights at my door, covered in dew? Oh, how hard my heart was that I did not open to you! What strange madness that the cold ice of my ingratitude dried up the wounds of your pure feet! How many times did the angel say to me: 'Soul, come now to the window, you will see with what love he persists in knocking!' And how many times, o sovereign beauty, I would reply: 'We shall open to him tomorrow', [only] to reply the same the next day.

The urgency of this poem is surely of a different kind from that of the previous one. The reason for this is that it seems much closer to the kind of meditative tradition I discussed in the first chapter (see above, p. 14). There I explained how the notion of a colloquy addressed to Christ may account for the type of colloquial abruptness one finds in Donne or Herbert: 'Batter my heart, three-personed God...', or 'I have considered it and find / there is no dealing with Thy mighty Passion...'. So here, the conversational thrust of the opening quatrain releases a steadily mounting current of self-reproach, conveyed through a series of striking sense images. Most of these are traditional, if not strictly biblical, and there are other, more direct, echoes of the Bible in the course of the poem: the Psalmist's cry, 'What is man, that Thou art mindful of him' (Psalms 8.4); the Book of Job, which asks why God should set his heart on man and 'try him every moment' (Job 7.18); and finally the words of Christ himself: 'Behold I stand at the door and knock' (Rev. 3.20). Moreover, in the repeated references to 'tomorrow', it is possible to hear the famous words of St Augustine: 'How long, how long, this "tomorrow and tomorrow"? Why not now? Why not finish this very hour with my wickedness?' (*Confessions*, Book VIII, ch. 12, 28–9).

What knits all these allusions together and makes them live within a single context is, of course, the voice of the speaker. And here one can think with some confidence of the speaker as Lope himself, or at least as a Lope who exists within the limits of the poem. Where in the love poems the self tends to fragment under the pressure of self-contradiction, here, faced with the omniscience of God, the need to establish such a 'presence' becomes otiose. Though we can read the poem as a personal confession, the terms in which it is expressed are so traditional, and so general in their application, that anyone else, we feel, might make use of it in an equivalent spiritual situation. Clearly, a good deal of skill has gone into the writing of the poem; yet it is significant, surely, that the one conceit – 'de mi ingratitud el hielo frío / secó las llagas de tus plantas puras' (the cold ice of my ingratitude dried up the wounds of your pure feet) – represents a kind of religious wit much older than the so-called 'metaphysical' conceit. And though this particular conceit – like that of Christ's feet nailed to the Cross in the previous poem – is strikingly simple, it points to something which seems true of many seventeenth-century religious poems: the fact that their metaphors are often more complex than those of secular poems, precisely because they can build on a much longer tradition of meditation on familiar symbols.

III

The kind of consciousness at work in the *Rimas sacras* extends to many of Lope's later poems, where the spirit of disenchantment and self-criticism reaches something like a final maturity. Before we come to these, however, we should reflect for a moment on Lope's actual conception of poetry, since it is this, more than anything else, which defines his relationship to other poets of the time.

If the *Rimas* of 1602 represent a more deliberate kind of art than the early ballads, this is partly because Lope has begun to think seriously about the nature of the particular verse forms he has inherited. Thus, in the two dedicatory essays addressed to Arguijo, he both defends the ballad as a specifically Spanish genre and elaborates on the qualities of the Italianate sonnet: 'since this type of poem must consist of *conceptos*, which are images of things, the better the things, the better they will be; and since words are imitations of *conceptos*, as Aristotle claims, the more sonorous the words, the more sublime the poems will be'. And just before this, he refers to commonplaces, such as familiar mythological allusions, as the 'plainsong [*canto llano*] on which are founded various *conceptos*'. Here again, one sees the advantages of a term which covers both 'concept' and 'conceit' (see above, p. 56): for Lope, *concepto* means something on the lines of Gracián's 'acute and sententious saying' (*dicho agudo y sentencioso*), in other words, a well-turned thought which is both paradoxical and just. Such *conceptos* often, though not always, involve metaphor; when they do, as one can see from his own practice, they tend to create contrasts which can then be explored by means of rhetorical figures – a technique which is well suited to the divided mentality of the love poems. And, whether metaphorical or not, what is crucial to Lope's understanding of the *concepto* is that it has to do with content, not words,[25] that is to say, with the substance of a poem rather than with verbal complexity for its own sake.

This should suggest the kind of weight which lies behind the phrase which introduces the *Rimas*: 'Versos de amor, conceptos esparcidos' (Verses of love, scattered *conceptos*). What is particularly striking, however, is that Lope thinks of the *concepto* as specifically Spanish: in a later critical statement, he argues that Italianate metres are superior to the traditional ones, but praises the *cancionero* poets of the fifteenth century for their skilful use of *conceptos*, which can still serve as a model for later poets.[26]

This sense that he is following a predominantly Spanish, not to say Castilian, mode comes out very strongly in Lope's contributions to the controversy which followed the appearance of Góngora's major poems – the *Polifemo* and the First *Soledad* – in 1613. The details and ramifications of this spectacular literary dispute, which lasted for over ten years, are too complicated to go into here.[27] Personal animosity apart, however, the overall result for Lope was that it caused him to sharpen the focus of his own poetics, and also to respond in various ways to what he clearly saw as a threat to his own poetic authority. For much of the time, Lope's attitude to Góngora is ambiguous, and often devious: even behind his harshest strictures, one can detect a concealed admiration for his rival, as well as anger at the fact that this admiration is not reciprocated. Nevertheless, Lope's literary quarrel with Góngora centres on several fundamental points: (1) 'difficulty' is justified in poetry, but only when it concerns substance, not words; (2) *culteranismo* – a term he never applies to Góngora himself – was not invented by Góngora, but is something to which he has 'succumbed', thereby denying his own splendid poetic talents; (3) the great master of *culto* diction is Herrera, whose lines beginning 'Cubrió el sagrado Betis...' (quoted above, p. 26) Lope praises as the supreme example of what it is possible to do in Spanish without resorting to 'Latinizing'; (4) though Lope shares Herrera's belief in the centrality of metaphor, he objects to Góngora's technique of building one metaphor on another ('metáforas de metáforas'), with the implication that such language merely conceals the absence of content; finally, (5) Lope invariably defends what he regards as 'Castilian clarity' – his models among contemporary poets are the Argensolas and Esquilache (see pp. 135 and 140) – and suggests that there is something 'un-Spanish' about Góngora's writing.

In the context of the debate itself, such distinctions often appear less clear-cut: for the most part, the level of generality precludes direct quotation from the poems concerned, and Lope often evades responsibility by claiming to refer to Góngora's imitators, rather than to Góngora himself. More importantly, there are times when Lope seems unsure of his own stance: apart from his occasional attempts to imitate Góngora (see p. 113), his fear that the 'new poetry' might come to supplant his own seems to have led him to reconsider certain aspects of his aesthetics in ways that profoundly affect the poems of his final decade. And it is precisely in these years that he allows his admiration for Góngora to come into the open. Thus in the Academy scene (IV, 2) from his last masterpiece, *La Dorotea*, he takes the opportunity once again to assert the value of clarity and verbal moderation; yet at the climax of the scene, just before the parody of a bad *culto* poem, one of the characters praises not only Góngora's own achievement, but that of the best of his followers:

Some great wits, by speaking and writing, praying and teaching, adorn and clothe the Castilian tongue with new phrases and figures of speech which embellish and enamel it with admirable propriety, and these – and most of all one I could mention [i.e. Góngora] – should be greatly reverenced as masters. For they have honoured, increased, illustrated and enriched it with beautiful and uncommon terms, whose richness, increase and beauty are recognized by the applause of all who understand such matters.

Such a concession could hardly be imagined ten years previously: in the meantime, Lope, though still conscious of the distance which separates him from the innovations of Góngora, has come to appreciate the attempt at renewal these represent, and which he himself, as we shall see, has begun to emulate in his own terms.

IV

Lope's attempt to rival Góngora on poetic grounds lies behind the series of long mythological poems which date from relatively late in his career. The most important of these are the First Part of *La Filomena* (Philomel; 1621) – the Second Part is a thinly disguised literary polemic – *Andrómeda* (1621) and *La Circe* (Circe; 1624).[28] These were not, of course, Lope's first attempts at the long poem, though compared with an earlier poem like *Las lágrimas de Angélica* (The Tears of Angelica; see above, p. 73), they are less diffuse and more skilled in their narrative technique. Though none of them can stand comparison with the *Polifemo* – they are less concerned with verbal artifice than with the telling of a story – there are times when Lope, as in the Polyphemus canto of *La Circe*, seems to be writing with one eye on Góngora's text, and occasionally the writing itself reflects both the vocabulary and the syntax of its model.[29] It would be wrong, however, to insist on the comparison with Góngora; though Lope still has a tendency to overexpand the original fable – the *Andrómeda*, in particular, is spoiled by the addition of superfluous characters – all three poems show a vigorous command of narrative, as in the description of an incident at sea from *La Circe*:

> Cual suele el irlandés perro animoso,
> dividiendo las ondas que no bebe,
> formar en ellas círculo espumoso,
> mansas cristal y removidas nieve,
> se arroja al agua el joven temeroso,
> y en el cabello y ropa les embebe;
> aborda, danle un cabo, y en la popa
> sacude, antes de hablar, cabeza y ropa.
>
> (B, p. 975, lines 969–76)

As the brave Irish hound, cleaving the waves which do not drown him, forms in them a foaming circle – like crystal when they are calm, like snow when stirred – the bold youth plunges into the water and absorbs the waves in hair and clothes; he comes alongside the ship, they throw him a rope, and on the stern-deck he shakes both head and clothes before speaking.

As one might expect with Lope, the subject-matter of these poems is not entirely unconnected with his own more intimate concerns. In *La Circe*, the account of Circe's temptations reads at times like a transposition of personal conflict, just as Ulysses's resistance to these takes on a distinctly neo-Platonic cast – a tendency which will become increasingly familiar in Lope's later work. This interest in neo-Platonic solutions first emerges in what seems like another deliberate effort to rival Góngora: the attempt to create an intellectually difficult kind of poetry as a corrective to the verbal difficulty of Góngora's major poems. This accounts for the curious sonnet which begins:

> La calidad elementar resiste
> mi amor, que a la virtud celeste aspira,
> y en las mentes angélicas se mira,
> donde la idea del calor consiste...   (B, p. 193)

My love, which aspires to heavenly virtue, resists the elemental heat, and mirrors itself in the angelic minds where the idea of heat resides.

As Dámaso Alonso has shown, the whole poem is paraphrased from the Florentine neo-Platonist Pico della Mirandola (1463–94).[30] It first appears in Lope's play *La dama boba* (The Stupid Lady; 1613), is reprinted in *La Filomena* (1621), and is published for the third time, with a prose commentary, in *La Circe* (1624). The interesting thing, as Trueblood points out,[31] is that in the meantime what almost certainly began as an academic exercise has taken on personal significance for its author. As Lope himself put it in 1624: 'The purpose of this sonnet...was to depict a man who, after having followed his passions for some years, having opened the eyes of his understanding, stripped himself of them and concentrating on the contemplation of divine love, found himself entirely free of his inclinations' (B, p. 1312). The exemplary quality Lope now finds in the sonnet may reflect a poetic attempt to justify his scandalous relationship with Marta de Nevares (see p. 94), whose tragic final years cast a shadow over much of his later poetry. Here, as elsewhere, it is difficult to draw the line between the personal and the literary: though much of the evidence of Lope's changing attitude to love comes from the poems directly inspired by this relationship and incorporated in *La Dorotea*, there is also, as we shall see, a literary dimension to this attitude which expresses Lope's growing dissatisfaction with the conventions of Petrarchan love in the light of his deepening moral experience. Ultimately, what counts most for Lope at this stage is the chance of accommodating the desire for spiritual rebirth to his growing awareness of mortality. Thus, as Trueblood rightly argues: 'One cannot separate [Lope's] Neoplatonic aspirations from his relationship with Marta; they clearly answer a vital need. In the end, however, the Neoplatonic impulse transcends the context of his love for her and informs a more purely individual outlook, offering a way of reconciling himself to the transience of the world and to his own transience within it.'[32]

Though the full significance of *La Dorotea* goes far beyond the present context, there are several aspects of it which bear directly on Lope's poetics. At its most personal level, as I have already explained, it represents the final ironic re-working of the Elena Osorio situation, first dealt with in the ballads and later in the *Rimas*. The nature of the irony appears most clearly in the treatment of Fernando, the young poet who is in love with the heroine. Fernando's wooing of Dorotea is carried on in strictly Petrarchan terms; yet, as the whole course of the action demonstrates, such conventions can only falsify real experience by forcing it into artificial patterns. At this distance, Lope can write about the situation with detachment and understanding; where Fernando and the other characters are trapped in a world of self-interest and mistrust, the allusions to a higher, neo-Platonic order in the last act point to an ideal which, however unattainable, is seldom far from these later works.

The same kind of distancing can be seen in several of the poems included in *La Dorotea*, notably the ballad 'A mis soledades voy' (To my solitude I go) and the four *barquillas* or 'boat ballads' inserted at the last moment as a final tribute to Marta de Nevares. In the context, only the first of these poems is directly ascribed to Lope himself, yet throughout there is a sense that Fernando is incapable of grasping the deeper meaning of the poems which are given to him. 'A mis soledades voy', which occurs early in the dialogue, moves restlessly between the private and the social:

> A mis soledades voy,
> de mis soledades vengo,
> porque para andar conmigo
> me bastan mis pensamientos.
> No sé qué tiene el aldea
> donde vivo y donde muero,
> que con venir de mí mismo,
> no puedo venir más lejos…   (C, pp. 404–5)

I go to my solitude, I come from my solitude, since my thoughts are sufficient company for me. I do not know what there is about the village where I live and die, but, on coming from myself, I cannot come from further away.

Lope's *soledades*, clearly, are more subjective than Góngora's: they represent a desire for withdrawal – a movement towards the integration of the self – and a sense of isolation from the world in which one is compelled to live. The notion of 'aldea' (village) is equally ambiguous: a mental 'village' which at the end of the poem becomes a kind of Horatian retreat, but also a symbol of the public world against which the self attempts to define itself. And to this one can add the two meanings of 'understanding' (*entendimiento*) which are referred to in the course of the poem: the worldly *savoir-faire* which is discounted – 'No me precio de entendido' (I don't pride myself on my intelligence) – and the spiritual understanding which knows that 'un hombre que todo es alma / está cautivo en su cuerpo' (a man who is wholly soul is a captive in his body). These shifting meanings are dramatized in the swerves by which the private voice is displaced by the voice of social satire –

> En dos edades vivimos
> los propios y los ajenos:
> la de plata los estraños,
> y la de cobre los nuestros.[33]

We live in two ages, we [Spaniards] and others: an age of silver for foreigners and one of copper for ourselves.

– only to re-assert itself in the closing lines:

> Con esta envidia que digo,
> y lo que paso en silencio,
> a mis soledades voy,
> de mis soledades vengo.

With this envy I speak of and what I pass over in silence, I go to my solitude, I come from my solitude.

The 'envy' here is for the simple life divorced from worldly concerns – something which the speaker knows he has not yet attained. Yet envy, as he confesses just before this, is an ugly emotion – 'Fea pintan a la envidia' (They depict envy as an ugly woman) – a force which works against the integrity of his *soledades*. The final movement, however, returns us to the beginning; as Trueblood points out, 'lo que paso en silencio' can mean 'what I suffer in silence' and 'what I keep to myself': 'On the one hand, indignation and humiliation; on the other, something even less specific than the "pensamientos" [thoughts] of the opening, thoughts unmentioned and beyond expressing.'[34]

In this poem, Lope is still some way from the mood of neo-Platonic harmony which dominates the last act of *La Dorotea*. Yet beneath the hints of moral stagnation and the anger at social intrusion, there lies a sense of unexplored possibilities – hidden dimensions of the self – which the rest of the dialogue will attempt to reveal. The crucial factor here is the death of Marta de Nevares in April, 1632, by which time *La Dorotea* was virtually complete. The four *barquillas* which Lope added to the third act register the full force of his loss in terms which recall a whole literary tradition – Horace, Sannazaro and Garcilaso. For once, Lope's 'borrowed voices' seem less an appropriation than a means of imposing coherence on feelings otherwise too intense to be put into language. And in the third of them, 'Pobre barquilla mía' (My poor little boat), he uses the imagery of shipwreck to express his new sense of disenchantment:

> Pobre barquilla mía,
> entre peñascos rota,
> sin velas desvelada,
> y entre las olas sola:
>   ¿Adónde vas perdida?
> ¿Adónde, dí, te engolfas?
> Que no hay deseos cuerdos
> con esperanzas locas...   (C, p. 413)

My poor little boat, broken amongst the rocks, unsleeping without sails and alone amid the waves: lost, where are you going, where, tell me, are you heading for, since there are no sane desires with mad hopes?

The 'boat' here is a metaphor of the self: as in 'A mis soledades voy', there is an obvious difference between the social self which utters a series of general complaints against the world and the private self whose grief unexpectedly intrudes towards the end of the poem. By this stage, the images of risk and uncertainty have given way to an earlier scene of pastoral simplicity, now shattered by death:

> Esposo me llamaba,
> yo la llamaba esposa,
> parándose de envidia
> la celestial antorcha.
>   Sin pleito, sin disgusto,
> la muerte nos divorcia:
> ¡Ay de la pobre barca
> que en lágrimas se ahoga!

She called me husband, I called her wife, while the torch of heaven [i.e. the sun] stood still with envy. With no law-suit, no disagreement, death divorces us: also as for the poor boat which is drowned in tears!

In this closing part of the poem, the dead woman is directly addressed: she is the lost 'dueño de mi barca' (mistress of my boat), imagined now in an unmistakably neo-Platonic afterlife, as the speaker begs her to intercede for him and bring about their reunion. But these lines, which echo the ending of Garcilaso's First Eclogue, are not quite the end of the poem, which at this point returns to the more aphoristic manner of the opening:

> Mas ¡ay, que no me escuchas!
> Pero la vida es corta:
> viviendo, todo falta;
> muriendo, todo sobra.

But alas! you do not hear me... But life is short: while one lives, everything is lacking; when one is dead, everything is superfluous.

Though these lines appear to deny the gentle vision which precedes them, in reality they preserve the woman's now supernatural beauty while drawing a clear dividing line between this world and the next. And the final paradox, as Trueblood's gloss makes clear, is both a summary of all that *soledades* has come to mean and a beautifully terse expression of Lope's experience of *desengaño*: 'In this life nothing is stable; all eventually fails one, fades, falls away. [These are all possible translations of "falta".] In the next, as the first line of the final quatrain confirms, one is no longer aware of such distressing conditions.'[35]

This is not the place to pursue the final mutations of such an attitude in the closing stages of *La Dorotea*. One other thing should be stressed, however: the pleasure which Lope clearly takes in his own mastery, not only in showing up his characters' limitations, but also in arranging the sudden shifts between the comic and the serious which determine so much of the action. In all this, there is a strong ludic element – something we have seen in his earliest poems, and which re-emerges quite spectacularly in the last volume of poems published in his lifetime, the *Rimas humanas y divinas del licenciado Tomé de Burguillos* (Rhymes, Human and Divine, of the Licentiate Tomé de Burguillos; 1634). The mock-solemn title is beautifully judged:[36] Tomé de Burguillos is a *persona* first used by Lope as far back as 1620, an impoverished law student whose love for the washerwoman Juana is now commemorated in a series of splendid burlesque sonnets. In terms of the parody, Juana is Burguillos's Petrarchan 'muse', while, by an astute pun on the supposed author's name, the Petrarchan 'laurel' – both the beloved herself and the traditional reward of the poet – becomes a humble garland of thyme (*tomillo*). Thus Burguillos, one might argue, is Lope's most radical piece of role-playing: both an object of ridicule and a device through which he can speak with diminished responsibility. As with most play, however, there is a serious side; in his preface, Lope, while maintaining the fiction that these are not his own poems, points to the 'Platonic truth' which discriminating readers will find beneath their 'Aristophanic' [i.e. burlesque] exterior. What Burguillos has produced, in effect, is an anti-*canzoniere* – Carreño calls it a 'great anti-poem'[37] – which ultimately calls into question the entire range of Petrarchan topoi to which Lope himself had once subscribed. Thus parody becomes self-parody, as in the sonnet entitled 'Cánsase el poeta de la dilatación de su esperanza' (The Poet Tires of the Deferment of His Hope):

> ¡Tanto mañana, y nunca ser mañana!
> Amor se ha vuelto cuervo, o se me antoja.
> ¿En qué región el sol su carro aloja
> desta imposible aurora tramontana?
>
> Sígueme inútil la esperanza vana,
> como nave zorrera o mula coja;
> porque no me tratara Barbarroja
> de la manera que me tratas, Juana.
>
> Juntos Amor y yo buscando vamos,
> esta mañana. ¡Oh dulces desvaríos!
> Siempre mañana, y nunca mañanamos.
>
> Pues si vencer no puedo tus desvíos,
> sáquente cuervos destos verdes ramos
> los ojos. Pero no, ¡que son los míos!   (B, p. 1379)

So many tomorrows, and tomorrow never comes! Love has turned into a crow, or so it seems to me. In what region of this impossible dawn behind the mountains does the sun keep its chariot? Vain hope uselessly pursues me, like a clumsy ship or a lame mule; for Barbarossa himself would not treat me the way you treat me, Juana. Love and I go seeking together this morning. Oh, sweet madness! Always tomorrow, and we never reach tomorrow. Well, if I cannot conquer your indifference, may the crows on these green branches peck out your eyes. But no: they are mine!

Here, the Petrarchan details crowd in, sometimes in a grotesquely distorted form: the birds of spring become the crow who cries *cras, cras* ('tomorrow' in Latin); the allegorical ship is now difficult to manoeuvre, like the lame mule that goes with it. Alternatively, the few Petrarchan phrases which remain intact – 'esperanza vana' (vain hope), 'dulces desvaríos' (sweet madness), the image of the rising sun – are derided by the curse which is first uttered, then retracted in a well-worn conceit. Both the economy of the diction and the moral satire of these poems owe something to Quevedo, a poet whose traces can be increasingly seen in Lope's later work. More importantly, the intensely intertextual nature of the writing illustrates once again Lope's extraordinary capacity for re-making his own art. Hence the paradoxical nature of the poems: on the one hand, Lope's deliberate degradation of the Petrarchan code suggests an awareness that the language of lyric poetry itself has reached a point of crisis; on the other, his attempt to resolve this situation – as we shall see, not unlike that of Quevedo himself – lies not in destroying the tradition as such, but in using it to invent a new kind of poetry which, in retrospect, forms the last, wonderfully creative, variant of that tradition.[38]

If one detects a feeling of serenity in Lope's final poems, this is not because of any respite from personal crisis: the eclogue *Amarilis* (1633), from which I quoted at the beginning of the chapter (see above, p. 94) and the even later eclogue – *Filis* (1635) – on the elopement of his daughter Antonia Clara both convey a sense of loss which can barely be contained within the conventional forms. Yet in the slightly earlier *Égloga a Claudio* – strictly speaking, the last of a remarkable series of verse epistles – he addresses a lifelong friend in what seems like a series of final reflections on his life and work. Above all, it is the poem of a man who is preparing himself for death at the end of a long and active life:

> Pues, Claudio, así se muda cuanto vive.
> No sé si soy aquél; mas he llegado
> a no tener cuidado
> que más conmigo prive
> que prevenirme a mi fatal destino;
> que nunca le temió quien le previno...
>
> (C, p. 505, lines 73–8)

For, Claudio, everything that lives changes. I do not know if I am that man [I was]; but I have come to have no more intimate care than that which warns me of my inevitable destiny; for no one feared it who was prepared for it...

At the same time, Lope's wish to withdraw from the world does not preclude anxiety about the value of his literary achievement: the catalogue of his own works seems partly an attempt to exorcize his fears of competition from the 'new way of writing' (*esta manera de escribir tan nueva*), and once again he re-asserts what for him is the right relationship between art and nature: 'así con sus preceptos y rigores / cultiva el arte naturales flores' (thus with its rules and strictness art cultivates natural flowers).[39] All this, however, is bound in with more general reflections on life itself: on the pleasures, but also the fallibility, of memory in old age and, in the verses I have quoted, on the inescapable workings of mutability. The note of disenchantment on which the poem ends – 'Fuera esperanzas, si he tenido alguna; / que ya no he menester de la fortuna' (Hopes begone, if ever I have had any; for I no longer have any need of fortune) – is close to the spirit of *La Dorotea*; yet in this more intimate context, the sense of mutability which lies at the heart of *desengaño* centres ultimately on the idea of the self. In the lines just quoted, Lope wonders if he is still the same person who went through the youthful experiences he is now recalling; and at the beginning of the poem he has described himself as 'un loco que...intenta desatarse de sí mismo' (a madman who is attempting to cut loose from himself). No reader of Lope's work could fail to recognize his delight in the world of sense – a delight made all the more real by the knowledge that its objects cannot last. And so with the self: if the 'self' of the poems has continually to be reconstructed, this is partly because no experience – least of all one's experience of self – is immutably fixed. As I have tried to show, the apparently strong ego which tries to set its mark on the words of other poets is not without its anxieties. In these final poems, the same anxieties continue to surface, however unconsciously. Hence, in Trueblood's fine phrase, 'Lope finds it hard to regain a sense of the continuity of the self as against its fluidity.'[40] Yet without such fluidity, one may feel, it is difficult to imagine the extraordinary talent for self-renewal which asserts itself at almost every stage of his poetry.

5

Between two centuries: from Medrano to Valdivielso

The poetry of Góngora and Lope de Vega takes shape in an atmosphere of intense literary activity which, though difficult to reconstruct, impinges at many points on their own writing careers. The most obvious sign of this is the number of talented minor poets writing about the year 1600, a fact registered in the numerous verse anthologies of the time, such as the *Romancero general* (1600–5) and the *Flores* of Espinosa (1605). Thus, although none of the poets I shall be concerned with in this chapter could be described as 'major' – several, like Medrano, Carrillo, Arguijo and Rioja, died young or ceased to write poetry at a relatively early age – each adds a distinctive note to the poetry of the time and, in doing so, indicates some of the possibilities which lay open to Spanish poetry in the years preceding the appearance of Góngora's major poems.

Since over half the poets I shall be considering are Andalusian – the majority connected with Seville itself – this raises the possibility of an Andalusian 'school', a notion still current in certain histories of literature. However, the idea of a 'school', with its suggestion of a master and disciples, seriously distorts the kind of relations which actually existed among the poets of the time and does little justice to the variety of poems they produced. Again, despite their mutual admiration for Herrera – above all as an example of artistic integrity – their work often diverges very noticeably from Herrera's own practice or at the very least transposes his peculiar kind of verbal refinement to a different context. What links these poets together, in fact, is something more pervasive: the cultural opulence of the Andalusian middle classes based on the commercial prosperity of late sixteenth-century Seville. And above all, it was the combination of humanist teachers and scholars – Juan de Mal Lara (1524?–71),

Argote de Molina (1548–98), Francisco de Medina (1544–1615) –
and certain artistically inclined local aristocrats like Herrera's own
patron, the Conde de Gelves, and, later, the Conde de Niebla, which
created the conditions under which the Andalusian poets of the turn
of the century were able to write, and which, directly or indirectly,
encouraged something like a new 'classicism' to which Herrera's own
work is only peripheral.

The outstanding example here is the one-time Jesuit Francisco de
Medrano (1570–1607), most of whose poems were written in Seville
in the last five years of his life. Medrano's skill as an imitator of
Horace has tended to overshadow the achievement of his original
poems. Though they represent only a small part of his work, the
moral sonnets, like the one which begins '¿Qué ansias, Flavio, son
éstas? ¿Qué montones / de fatigas me envisten desiguales?' (What
worries, Flavio, are these? What heaps of different troubles assail
me?; DA, p. 218),[1] have a Latin *gravitas* which recalls the Argensolas
and occasionally reads like an anticipation of Quevedo. His love
sonnets, on the other hand, though for the most part they follow a
recognizable Petrarchan pattern, are capable of handling a sexual
relationship with the kind of freshness one also finds in Aldana (see
above, p. 21):

> No sé cómo, ni quándo, ni qué cosa
> sentí, que me llenava de dulçura:
> sé que llegó a mis braços la 'ermosura,
> de gozarse comigo cudiciosa.
>
> Sé que llegó, si bien, con temerosa
> vista, resistí apenas su figura:
> luego pasmé, como el que en noche escura,
> perdido el tino, el pie mover no osa.
>
> Siguió un gran gozo a aqueste pasmo, o sueño
> – no sé quándo, ni cómo. ni qué a sido –
> que lo sensible todo puso en calma.
>
> Ignorallo es saber; que es bien pequeño
> el que puede abarcar solo el sentido,
> y éste pudo caber en sola l'alma.   (DA, p. 254)

I do not know how, nor when, nor what I felt, which filled me with
sweetness: I know that beauty came to my arms, desiring to take pleasure
with me. I know that she came, even if, with fearful sight, I scarcely resisted
her shape: then I was scared, like one who on a dark night, having lost his
way, dares not take a step. A great delight followed this fright, or dream –
I do not know when, nor how, nor what it was – which set all my senses at

rest. Not to know this is to know; for it is a small good which sense alone can encompass, and this could only be contained in the soul.

What is remarkable here is not so much the skill with which the speaker negotiates his way between the negative and the positive, as the kind of vocabulary he employs in the process. As Dámaso Alonso has pointed out,[2] much of this derives from the common stock of mystical writing; though the poem clearly describes the sexual act and its aftermath, it is as though the language of human love appropriated by a religious writer like San Juan de la Cruz had been restored to its original context while preserving some of its spiritual overtones. Part of the dreamlike quality of the poem comes no doubt from the fact that the woman is referred to in the abstract as 'beauty'; at the same time, there is no sense of a neo-Platonic progression: it is the sexual experience itself which generates the almost inexpressible feeling of wonder, and the final contrast between the senses and the soul merely enlarges the nature of the original experience without denying its source.

The almost colloquial ease of such a poem may owe something to Medrano's experiments in translating the poems of Horace, himself a master of the conversational tone and a powerful influence on the sixteenth-century Spanish lyric from Garcilaso onwards. Medrano, in fact, is almost the last, and certainly the most brilliant, of a long line of translators which includes Luis de León (1527–91), one of the greatest poets of an earlier generation, and a number of minor Sevillian poets included by Herrera in the *Anotaciones*. Yet despite the astonishing accuracy of many of his versions of the Odes, to describe Medrano as a 'translator' does less than justice to the extraordinary achievement of these poems. To speak of 'originality' in connection with translations may seem something of a paradox: nevertheless, Medrano's re-workings of Horace differ in two important respects from earlier renderings, and both point to the creative resourcefulness which distinguishes him from other translators. The first is formal: the decision to abandon the *lira*-type stanza which for Luis de León had seemed the closest equivalent of the Horatian strophe,[3] and above all to attempt to re-create the effect of Horace's short last lines. Thus the ending of Ode I, xxii ('Integer vitae scelerisque purus...'; The man of upright life, free of guilt) in Medrano's version reads:

> ...que en cuanto el çielo vueltas multiplica,
> para que el sol al mundo luz envíe,

amaré a Flora, la que dulçe ríe,
la que dulce platica. (DA, p. 226)

For as long as the heavens increase their revolutions, so that the sun may send light to the world, I shall love Flora, she who laughs sweetly, she who sweetly converses.

This catches perfectly both the echo effect and the actual rhythm of the Latin – 'Dulce ridentem Lalagen amabo, / Dulce loquentem' (I shall still love sweetly smiling, sweetly chattering Lalage) – and the whole poem, like others, reproduces with extraordinary fidelity what Dámaso Alonso calls the 'rhythm of thought' of the original.[4]

The second difference has to do with the way Medrano reshapes his originals. Roughly speaking, where previous translators usually attempt a word-for-word version, Medrano frequently cuts out whole passages or will occasionally combine parts of two separate odes in the same poem. There is nothing arbitrary about this: Medrano systematically omits or simplifies anything a seventeenth-century reader might regard as 'dead matter' – allusions to pagan gods or to specific Roman customs – or, alternatively, replaces the original references by contemporary ones. Thus in one poem (Ode XII; DA, p. 233), he refers to the wealth of the Incas: '¿Quién trocará, prudente, / por cuanto el Inga atesoró, el cabello / de Amarili?' (What wise man would exchange Amaryllis's hair for all the Inca's treasure?), and in another (Ode x; DA, p. 223), the sea monsters and cliffs of Epirus are similarly transposed to the New World: '...quien con ojos enxutos / vio los escollos yertos? ¿la Bermuda? / y los caimanes brutos?' (Who could see with dry eyes the stiff rocks, Bermuda and the terrible alligators?). Medrano's most brilliant transpositions, however, occur when the Horatian concept of leisure (*otium*) is applied to his own circle of friends in Seville. His imitation of Ode I, ix ('Vides ut alta stet nive candidum / Soracte...'; You see how clearly Soracte stands out with its white mantle of snow) is addressed to one of these. At one point in the poem, Horace's 'four-year-old Sabine wine jar' (*quadrimum Sabina*) is replaced by a more familiar vintage, and the single detail is expanded to take in other winter comforts: '...¡y el Alicante / qué tal es! Come bien, que están süaves / las batatas, y bebe alegremente:...' (And what is the Alicante like? Eat up, the potatoes are soft, and drink merrily). The last three stanzas are wonderfully deft:

> Ahora da lugar la noche escura
> y larga al instrumento bientemplado,
> y al requiebro aplazado
> ocasión da segura.
>
> Baja a la puerta (de su madre en vano
> guardada) con pie sordo la donzella,
> y por debajo de ella
> te dexa asir la mano.
>
> 'Suelte', risueña, 'que esperar no puedo',
> dize, y turbada, '¡Suelte, no me ofenda!':
> quitarle as tú la prenda
> de el malrebelde dedo.   (DA, p. 200)

Now the long dark night makes way for the well-tuned instrument and gives a sure opportunity for postponed wooing. The girl comes down on silent feet to the doorway (watched in vain by her mother), and beneath it allows you to take her hand. 'Let go', smiling, 'I can't stay', she says, and, embarrassed, 'Let go, don't offend me!': you must remove the ring from her scarcely rebellious finger.

Again, one is struck by the skill with which Medrano uses short lines, and by the way in which he re-creates the sinuous movement of the original by allowing the sense to run on over the line breaks. Most of this, to be sure, is 'imitation', rather than 'translation': Horace's reference to meeting girls in the open spaces of Rome is replaced by a more domestic situation, and the beautifully placed snatches of direct speech are again Medrano's invention. Yet the last line is a perfect rendering of Horace's *digito male pertinaci* ('from a scarcely resisting finger')[5] and the whole poem remains astonishingly faithful to what Medrano conceives to be the spirit of Horace.

This last qualification is necessary, since, as Dámaso Alonso points out, there is an obvious difference between Horace's characteristic cynicism and what he calls Medrano's 'essential honesty'.[6] This raises the question of what Medrano is actually doing in his versions of Horace. The desire to improve on the work of previous translators, though probably real enough, is only part of the answer. On the other hand, to think of him as deliberately creating a 'persona' for himself by projecting his own preoccupations on to the work of another poet would be an exaggeration: however much he departs from his original, the example of Horace is always uppermost in his mind, and the quality of his best sonnets, like the one I quoted earlier, suggests a strong independent talent which has no need of obvious models to make itself felt. What seems certain, however, is the conscious 'classicism' of Medrano's enterprise: not only the wish to make an outstanding classical poet speak directly to a contemporary sensibility, but also the kind of refinement this might bring to the language of Spanish poetry itself.[7] What is more, such 'classicism' is not simply a literary matter, but something which Medrano seems to have seen as an essential quality of life. Hence the confidence with which he moves between direct translation and improvisation in the Horatian manner, as in the splendid ending of Ode xxxiii – possibly his finest poem, and one which, more than any other, seems to offer a glimpse of the kind of poet he might have become:

> Tú assí como rogando
> lo mandas, mas oculta fuerça tiene,
> fuerça de ley, aquel tu imperio blando.
> ¿Podrélo resistir? ¿Barquero viene,
> toldado el barco y fresco? Mueve, mueve
> los remos a compás, y apriesa, lenta-
> mente, vamos do, armada
> de paz, ya espera fácil, ya contenta
> la mesa, coronada
> de flores, y de frutas, y de nieve:
>
> y de amistad sabrosa,
> sazón de todo. ¿Y Iulio tuvo en preçio
> de un breve cetro la ambición medrosa?
> ¿Y era varón? ¡Oh deslumbrado! ¡Oh necio!
> Suena la lyra, Anfriso; y tú, Nerea,
> dame agua; bose el búcaro; bebamos;
> por los pechos se vierta:
> todo es salud. ¡Oh, assí vivir podamos!
> La ventana esté abierta,
> por si bullere un soplo de marea.   (DA, pp. 323–4)[8]

Thus you command, as though requesting, but that gentle authority of yours has a hidden power, the power of law. Can I resist it? Is that a boatman coming, his craft fresh and screened from the sun? Move, move the oars in time and quickly, slowly, let us go where, armed with peace, now in ease and contentment, the table awaits us, crowned with flowers, fruits and ice: and with pleasant friendship, which seasons everything. And Julius valued the fearful ambition of a tiny sceptre? And he was a man? O blind one! O fool! Strike the lyre, Anfriso; and you, Nerea, give me water; let the jar overflow; let us drink; let it pour down our chests; it is all health. O, if we could live like this! Let the window be open, should a sea breeze be blowing.

Medrano's friend Juan de Arguijo (1567–1623) offers a quite different version of 'classicism', based on the re-interpretation of ancient Greek and Roman motifs in sonnet form. Arguijo himself is very much a product of the time: a Sevillian magnate whose fortune enabled him to become one of the most brilliant literary patrons of his generation, but whose financial extravagance finally reduced him to a state of semi-seclusion which virtually put an end to his career as a poet. As his most recent editor, Stanko B. Vranich, suggests, Arguijo's classical training at the hands of the Jesuits, and the stimulus this gave to his poetic talents, may have unconsciously served as a compensation for his ineptitude in business and administrative matters.[9] Whatever the truth of this, there seems no doubt that the sophisticated assurance of his writing owes a great deal to the example of Herrera and his circle, and in particular, as we shall see, to the good judgement of one of its most outstanding members, Francisco de Medina.[10]

Compared with Medrano, Arguijo is a miniaturist: a poet whose best work, with few exceptions, relies on the deployment of small-scale effects within the conventional framework of the sonnet, and on the exclusion of all but the most general autobiographical references. Within their self-imposed limits, however, the best of Arguijo's poems create images of monumental clarity and dramatic power, reinforced by firm rhetorical structures and a skilful use of paradox. Their unmistakable 'Latin' feeling comes partly from this epigrammatical quality and partly from Arguijo's decision to ignore earlier Renaissance versions of his themes and to go back to their original classical sources. Something of this can be seen in his sonnet on Narcissus, which derives directly from Ovid's account of the myth in Book III of the *Metamorphoses*:

> Crece el insano ardor, crece el engaño
> del que en las aguas vio su imagen bella;
> i él, sola causa en su mortal querella,
> busca el remedio i acrecienta el daño.
>   Buelve a verse en la fuente ¡caso estraño!:
> del'agua sale el fuego; mas en ella
> templarlo piensa, i la enemiga estrella
> sus ojos cierra al fácil desengaño.
>   Fallecieron las fuerzas i el sentido
> al ciego amante amado; que a su suerte
> la costosa beldad cayó rendida.
>   I aora, en flor purpúrea convertido,

l'agua, que fue principio de su muerte,
haze que cresca, i prueva a darle vida.   (v, p. 149)

The mad love increases, the deception of him who saw his fair image in the waters increases; and he, sole cause in his mortal conflict, seeks a remedy and aggravates his hurt. Again he looks in the spring and sees – strange case! – that from it fire issues; but in it [i.e. the spring] he attempts to cool the fire, and the hostile star closes his eyes to simple disenchantment. Strength and senses failed the blind, beloved lover; for his fatal beauty fell victim to its fate. And now, changed into a bright flower, the water which was the cause of his death makes him grow and tries to give him life.

In a poem like this, every line seems carefully worked over, in terms both of sense and sound; the contrasts, already present in the Ovidian original, fall neatly into place and the concluding twist is achieved by means of a simple, though convincing paradox. Taken separately, these may seem negative virtues; together, they create an effect of studied elegance which is sometimes referred to as 'Parnassian': a combination of verbal artifice and the conscious re-creation of a scene whose vividness is left to make its own effect. As with Lope de Vega's sonnet on Judith and Holofernes (see above, p. 103), there is a tendency to select the particular 'frozen moment' which encapsulates an entire episode. Again, though his effects are generally less complex than Lope's, Arguijo shows a similar skill in choosing a point of view. Thus in the second of the three Orpheus sonnets (v, p. 219), the subject himself is made to speak, and in a poem on the Roman hero Horatius (v, p. 67), the energy of the description is underlined by the intervention of a first-person narrator: 'Con prodigioso ejemplo de osadía / un hombre miro en el romano puente... / Oigo del roto puente el son fragoso... / y al mismo punto escucho del gozoso / pueblo las voces...' (With a prodigious example of daring, I see a man on the Roman bridge... I hear the splintering sound of the broken bridge... and at that very moment I hear the cries of the delighted crowd). At other times, the speaker's intervention takes on a moral quality, as in the implied praise of Ulysses for resisting the sirens (v, pp. 154–5), or alternatively, as in one of the several references to Orpheus, the situation of the mythical subject is compared to that of the poet himself:

> ...Si del concento la admirable fuerça
> domestica los fieros animales,
> i enfrena la corriente de los ríos:

¿Qué nueva pena en mi pesar s'esfuerça,
pues con lo que descrecen otros males
se van acrecentando más los míos?   (v, p. 233)

If the marvellous power of music tames wild animals and holds back the
current of rivers: what new pain strives in my grief, that my own woes are
increased by what lessens those of others?

The actualization of myth or history involves the construction of a
poetic 'self' which eventually comes to displace the original subject-
matter altogether. As Antonio Prieto has argued, Arguijo's attempt
to recuperate the classical past in the form of moral *exempla* leads to
the more intense kind of self-scrutiny one finds in certain of his later
poems, like the one which begins: 'Pues ya del desengaño la luz
pura...' (Since now the pure light of disenchantment; V, p. 325).[11]
Thus although the first-person, even in the less 'classical' poems, is
never obtrusive, there is a natural progression from the 'I' as moral
focus for apparently objective material to the 'I' which rehearses its
own situation as an end in itself. Yet however finely phrased,
Arguijo's reflections on loss, or on the need to overcome passivity by
virtuous action, engage only obliquely with the circumstances of his
own life, and his final silence, whatever it owes to personal adversity,
suggests the exhaustion of a whole poetic mode.

Arguijo, unlike his younger contemporary Francisco de Rioja
(1583–1659), remained in Seville to the end of his life, quite
unaffected by the new literary atmosphere of the court of Philip III.
Rioja's career, on the other hand, clearly divides into two parts: his
youth in Seville, where he studied theology and the classics and
became a close friend of Gaspar de Guzmán (the future Conde
Duque de Olivares), and his life in Madrid as personal adviser to
Olivares when the latter came to power in 1621. It seems likely that
most, if not all, of Rioja's poems were written before this;[12] as a body
of work, they are clearly related to the atmosphere of Sevillian
humanism which grew up around Herrera, and take their place
between what Chiappini calls 'the break-up of the Petrarchan
cosmos and Góngora's "reconstruction" of a new reality'.[13] To call
Rioja a 'transitional' poet, however, though true in one sense, hardly
allows for the intelligence with which he absorbs the example of
Herrera and at the same time distances himself from it. Thus in his
Preface to the 1619 edition of Herrera's own poems, he praises the
strength and elegance of the older poet's verse, but goes on:

they are not lacking in sentiments [*afectos*], as some say, rather do they contain many, and generous, ones which, however, are concealed and lost to sight among the poetic ornaments, as happens with those who raise their style above customary humility. The more subtle and delicate the affective motions of the spirit, the more they should be expressed in simple and apt words, so that they are evident to the eyes and strike the spirit with their liveliness: in short, they should offer themselves to us and not have to be sought for among the words.[14]

Though elsewhere Rioja's praise of Herrera may seem excessive – 'the first to lend art and grandeur to the language of our poetry' – and though his own debt to his predecessor is very clear, this tactful critique of excessive ornament points to other differences which help to define the nature of his own verse. Some of these are obvious enough: unlike Herrera, Rioja does not attempt to construct a *canzoniere* – his love poems for the most part are fairly stereotyped – and he seems to regard Herrera's neo-Platonic aspirations as an evasion of reality, a way of blunting one's reactions to the world of phenomena. As Chiappini points out, there is a basic difference of poetics here: in rejecting the neo-Platonic ideal of pure expression, Rioja comes much closer to the Aristotelian–Horatian notion of a poetry which teaches through examples of clarity and beauty.

In practice, this insistence on the experience of living in the world means a concentration on the finer moments of existence which we have already seen in Medrano:

> Pues, ¡cuál parece el búcaro sangriento
> de flores esparzido
> i el cristal veneciano
> a quien l'agua de elada
> la tersa frente le dexó empañada!
> (Silva VI, 'Al verano' [To Summer], lines 53–7; LB, p. 195)

For, what a sight is the blood-red jar filled with flowers and the Venetian glass whose smooth surface the ice-cold water has misted!

As with Medrano, what taken out of its context can seem merely hedonistic, more often than not has serious moral implications. Though Rioja often refers to the external world, any suggestion of a 'landscape' is generalized and absorbed into the underlying tone of moral reflection. Thus the sea, as in Horace, becomes a metaphor for life itself, a source both of attraction and repulsion, as in the sonnet (XIX) addressed to Olivares on the lost city of Salmedina:

> Este ambicioso mar, que en leño alado
> sulcas oi, pesadumbre peregrina
> de fundación en otra edad divina,
> a entre soberbias olas sepultado... (LB, p. 166)

This ambitious sea, which today you plough in a winged ship, has buried beneath its proud waves the strange bulk of a city in former ages divine.

Such natural references, however, go beyond the merely conventional; for Rioja, nature and human life run in parallel, as mutually reinforcing sources of similarity and difference. As Chiappini puts it, nature always 'means something' in these poems,[15] whether as theatre for human endeavour or as fellow victim of the ravages of time. It is this last aspect which accounts for the sensitivity, as well as the iconic quality, of his *silvas* on flowers. Here, what might have been no more than a series of routine reflections on mutability is transformed by Rioja's sensual delight in the individual characterization of each plant. The result is a poetic language which moves easily between the symbolic meaning of the flower and the sense of its uniqueness as a particular manifestation of beauty. And often, as in the fine poem on the *arrebolera*, or Marvel of Peru – a flower which opens only at night – the combination of beauty and fragility becomes a consolation for the brevity of human life itself:

> I tú, admirable i vaga,
> dulce onor i cuidado de la noche,
> si la llama i color el sol apaga,
> ¿cuál mayor dicha tuya
> que el tiempo de tu edad tan veloz huya?:
> no es más el luengo curso de los años
> que un espacioso número de daños.
> Si vives breves oras,
> ¡ô, cuántas glorias tienes!...
> (Silva VII, 'A la arrebolera', lines 37–45; LB, p. 203)

And you, splendid and uncertain, sweet honour and beloved of night, if the sun extinguishes both flame and colour, what greater happiness could you have than that the time of your span should pass so quickly? The long succession of years is merely a drawn-out series of ills. If you live brief hours, o, what glories you possess!

The poem, which began with a bare comment on the flower's brief lifespan – '¡Tan poco se desvía / de tu nacer la muerte arrebatada!'

(How little divides your birth from sudden death!) – ends with a reflection which reassesses that brevity in terms of moral value:

> ...i passa en ocio i paz aventurada
> de tu vivir el tiempo oscuro i breve,
> esperando aquel último desmayo
> a quien tu luz i púrpura se deve.
>
> (lines 58–61; LB, p. 204)

And spend in leisure and fortunate peace your life's brief, obscure span, awaiting that final swoon to which your light and colour are subject.

As the last line hints, brevity and beauty are now interdependent: despite its imminent end, the flower's beauty, like that of a human life, may enjoy its plenitude, just as, one might argue, it is preserved in the poem itself.

Rioja's sense of mutability and the measured stoicism of his moral sonnets are reflected in two other poems which for a long time were thought to be his work: the *canción* 'A las ruinas de Itálica' (On the Ruins of Italica) and the 'Epístola moral a Fabio' (Moral Epistle to Fabio). The first of these – an ode of just over 100 lines – is now known to have been composed by the antiquarian and local historian Rodrigo Caro (1573–1647). Its theme – the ruins of the Roman city of Italica on the outskirts of Seville – is something of a topic among the Sevillian poets of the time; the great virtue of Caro's poem, however, lies in its ability to combine conventional moral reflection with the imaginative re-creation of past magnificence:

> Este llano fue plaza, allí fue templo:
> de todo apenas quedan las señales.
> Del gimnasio y las termas regaladas
> leves vuelan cenizas desdichadas.
> Las torres que desprecio al aire fueron
> a su gran pesadumbre se rindieron.
>   Este despedazado anfiteatro,
> impio honor de los dioses, cuya afrenta
> publica el amarillo jaramago,
> ya reducido a trágico teatro,
> ¡oh fábula del tiempo! representa
> cuánta fue su grandeza, y es su estrago.   (lines 12–23)

This flat space was a forum, over there stood a temple: of all this there hardly remains a trace. From the gymnasium and the luxurious heated baths sad ashes float lightly. The towers which defied the wind collapsed beneath their own weight. This crumbling amphitheatre, unholy tribute to the gods, whose disgrace the yellow charlock makes public, now reduced to a tragic theatre – o fable of time! – shows how vast was its grandeur and is now its ruin.

Despite obvious flaws – monotony of movement, stereotyped epithets, and an occasional forcing of the emotion – the poem is skilfully constructed, and in passages like the one I have just quoted, there is a genuine sense of awe at a spectacle which appears to speak to the present in a language which can now scarcely be deciphered.[16]

The 'Epístola moral a Fabio', an altogether more ambitious poem, is the work of an otherwise unknown Sevillian poet, Fernández de Andrada (1575?–1648?), a professional soldier and friend of Rioja's, one of whose poems is dedicated to him. That a relatively obscure poet should be capable of composing over 200 lines of impeccable *terza rima* is in itself an indication of the high level of craftsmanship expected – and often achieved – in the Sevillian circles of the time. Nevertheless, Andrada's poem, probably written between 1610 and 1612, belongs to a much wider tradition, that of the Horatian verse epistle, a form previously cultivated by Garcilaso, Aldana and other sixteenth-century poets and more recently, as we shall shortly see, by the Argensolas. Stylistically, the poem is remarkably direct and free from rhetorical devices; it moves easily through the commonplaces of the Stoic tradition, with an occasional heightening of imagery, as in the final address to death:

> ... Sin la templanza ¿viste tú perfeta
> alguna cosa? ¡Oh muerte!, ven callada,
> como sueles venir en la saeta;
>   no en la tonante máquina preñada
> de fuego y de rumor; que no es mi puerta
> de doblados metales fabricada...   (lines 181–6)

Without moderation, did you ever see anything perfect? O death! Come silently, as you are wont to come in the arrow; not in the thundering engine pregnant with fire and noise; for my door is not made of thick metal.

As Dámaso Alonso argues in his fine study of the 'Epístola',[17] the actual writing of the poem conveys a whole life style: roughly speaking, the moderate, semi-Christianized version of Stoicism which forms the ground bass to so much of the moral poetry of the period, and which is present here in its most restrained and dignified form. What is absent, on the other hand, is the kind of impassioned self-scrutiny one finds earlier in Aldana; though the limpidity of the writing is a remarkable achievement in itself, the poem as a whole shows signs of what Luis Cernuda calls a 'vital fatigue',[18] a resistance to metaphysical inquiry which suggests that this particular strain of 'classicism' is nearing exhaustion.

II

One classical mode which for the most part escapes the Andalusian poets of the turn of the century is verse satire, whose most notable exponents at the time are the two Aragonese poets, Lupercio and Bartolomé Leonardo de Argensola (1559–1613; 1562–1631). Though both brothers are aware of their Aragonese identity, there is no sense in which they help to form an 'Aragonese school'; both spent a considerable part of their lives in Madrid and Naples, partly as royal secretaries and official chroniclers, and both belonged to literary academies where they came to know Lope de Vega and other writers of the time. Moreover, despite Lupercio's relatively early death, the Argensolas' verse has a similar range, though there are some interesting differences, as we shall see. What marks them off most sharply, however, from their contemporaries is their relative indifference to the changing poetic climate; where the 'classicism' of poets like Medrano and Rioja edges towards greater syntactical complexity and the conscious deployment of *cultismos*, the Argensolas settle early on for a version of classical standards which builds on the achievement of earlier Renaissance poetry and remains virtually unchanged to the end of their writing careers.

For Lupercio, this means a lifelong allegiance to the Horace of the satires and the *Ars poetica* – rather than to the Horace of the Odes – which coincides with his belief in the moral nature of poetry: 'True and legitimate poetry...opened the way for moral philosophy to introduce its precepts into the world.' Thus the Horatian praise of *aurea mediocritas* – the 'golden mean' – recurs time and again, though with constantly varying imagery, as in the sonnet which begins:

> Dentro quiero vivir de mi fortuna
> y huir los grandes nombres que derrama
> con estatuas y títulos la Fama
> por el cóncavo cerco de la luna...   (B, p. 50)[19]

I wish to live within my fortune and to flee the great names which Fame strews with statues and titles around the concave circle of the moon.

This eventually turns into a love poem, though, as usually happens in Lupercio, any potential eroticism is avoided, either by recourse to neo-Platonism or by the kind of ironic distancing one finds in Horace himself. Often, to be sure, it is the oblique approach to the love theme, and the originality of perspective this entails, which makes for the success of the poem:

> Llevó tras sí los pámpanos otubre,
> y con las grandes lluvias, insolente,
> no sufre Ibero márgenes ni puente,
> mas antes los vecinos campos cubre.
>   Moncayo, como suele, ya descubre
> coronada de nieve la alta frente,
> y el sol apenas vemos en Oriente
> cuando la opaca tierra nos lo encubre.
>   Sienten el mar y selvas ya la saña
> del aquilón, y encierra su bramido
> gente en el puerto y gente en la cabaña.
>   Y Fabio, en el umbral de Tais tendido,
> con vergonzosas lágrimas lo baña,
> debiéndolas al tiempo que ha perdido.   (B, p. 109)

October carried off the vine shoots and, insolent with the great rains, the Ebro suffers neither banks nor bridge, but covers instead the surrounding fields. Moncayo, as is its custom, now displays its lofty brow crowned with snow, and scarcely do we see the sun in the east than the dark earth hides it from sight. The sea and the forests now feel the north wind's anger and its roaring keeps people in harbour and in their huts. And Fabio, stretched out on Thais's doorstep, bathes it in shameful tears, which he owes to the time he has lost.

Here, though winter is clearly a metaphor for old age, it is the panoramic sweep of the winter scene itself, with its specific top-ography,[20] which carries the weight of the poem and almost overshadows the final epigram. The same image of the lover braving the elements at his mistress's door – itself taken from Horace[21] – recurs in the self-mocking sonnet which begins 'Si quiere Amor que siga sus antojos...' (If Love wants me to follow its whims), where the caricature of the Petrarchan lover is turned against the speaker himself:

> ...la flaca luz renueve de mis ojos,
> restituya a mi frente su cabello,
> a mis labios la rosa y primer vello,
> que ya pendiente y yerto es dos manojos.   (B, p. 68)

Renew the weak light of my eyes, restore the hair to my brow, [restore] to my lips the rosiness and the down of youth, which now hangs stiff like two tufts of grass.

This familiar style reappears on a much larger scale in Lupercio's verse letters, where the satirical intention and the deliberate air of improvisation draw on a whole range of imagery which is denied to the more 'serious' poetry of the time. The objects of his satire, like that of his brother Bartolomé, are for the most part contemporary versions of classical themes: the corruption of court life, the rapaciousness of doctors and lawyers, the dangers of travel, the predatory nature of women. Yet what saves the poems from monotony is their constant inventiveness, as when Lupercio complains, with paradoxical eloquence, of his inability to construct verses:

> Como niño que corta con tijera
> en un papel doblado, sin aviso
> de lo que ha de sacar ni lo que espera,
> que cuando lo desdobla, de improviso
> halla con proporción una figura,
> que ni así la esperaba ni la quiso...   (B, p. 70)

Like a child who cuts a folded paper with scissors, not knowing what the result will be or what he expects, for when he unfolds it, he suddenly finds a well-formed shape which he did not imagine thus or intend.

With the Argensolas, satire, and the 'low' style which goes with it, become a central poetic mode which lasts well into the eighteenth century. Again, the 'classical' basis of such poetry is clear, not least in the new range of Latin poets – not only Horace, but Martial,[22] Juvenal and Persius – who are admitted to the canon. For Bartolomé, the traditional justification of satire – it is useful to the state, insofar as it attacks types rather than individuals – is linked to a concept of the 'low' style which dismisses any sense of inferiority:

> Este que llama el vulgo estilo llano
> encubre tantas fuerzas, que quien osa
> tal vez acometerle, suda en vano.   (B, II, p. 72)

This style that common people call 'base' contains such powers that he who dares to attempt it casually labours in vain.

Its 'difficult facility', as he goes on to call it, depends partly on keeping a balance between the rules – always to be treated flexibly – and what in another poem (B, II, p. 87) he terms the 'living voice'.

Thus in describing two kinds of imitation – the 'laconic' and the 'eloquent' – he argues for a combination of both: the power of the former may be diminished by over-compression, just as the latter's tendency to overexpand needs to be kept in place by a pointed diction. In practice, his belief in the power of simple words as against mere ingenuity accounts for the astonishing directness of many of the images thrown up in the course of his verse letters:

> Tropel de litigantes atraviesa,
> con varias quejas, varios ademanes,
> sus causas publicando en voz expresa,
>   entre mil estropeados capitanes,
> que ruegan y amenazan, todo junto,
> cuando nos encarecen sus afanes;
>   los vivanderos gritan, y en un punto
> cruzan entre los coches los entierros,
> sin que a dolor ni horror mueva el difunto.   (B, I, p. 115)

A bunch of litigants goes past, with various complaints and various gestures, publishing their causes in loud voices, among a thousand disabled captains who beg and threaten together as they expound their troubles to us; victuallers cry, and in an instant funerals pass between the carriages, though the dead person moves no one to grief or to horror.

Or again, describing a Madrid deserted by the absence of the court in Valladolid:

> Parecerán las gentes que han quedado
> por esas calles huérfanas y solas
> carpas en el estanque desaguado,
>   que echadas fuera las amigas olas,
> entre el junco, también desierto, azotan
> la medio enjuta arena con las colas.   (B, I, p. 145)

The people who have stayed behind in these lonely, orphaned streets will seem like carp in an emptied lake which, cut off from the friendly waves, among the reeds – likewise deserted – thrash the half-dry sand with their tails.

Thus far the poetry of the Argensolas shares common ground. Once one turns to other areas of their work, however, certain differences begin to appear, both in poetic temperament and in their relative degree of commitment to particular types of poem. Thus Bartolomé's religious verse (see above, p. 15), to which I shall return in the next section, reaches much greater depths than that of his brother. Again, where Lupercio's love poetry is either Platonizing or ironical, that of Bartolomé contains a fair amount of good-humoured sensuality and, though it has its own kind of irony, tends to engage much more directly with actual relationships:

> Por verte, Inés, ¿qué avaras celosías
> no asaltaré? ¿Qué puertas, qué canceles,
> aunque los arme de candados fieles
> tu madre y de arcabuces las espías?
>   Pero el seguirte en las mañanas frías
> de abril, cuando mostrarte al campo sueles,
> bien que con los jazmines y claveles
> de tu rostro a la Aurora desafías,
>   eso no, amiga, no; que aunque en los prados
> plácido iguala el mes las yerbas secas,
> porque igualmente les aviva el seno,
>   con las risueñas auras, que en jaquecas
> sordas convierte el húmedo sereno,
> hace los cementerios corcovados.   (B, I, p. 182)

In order to see you, Inés, what jealous shutters shall I not besiege? What doors, what gates, though your mother arm them with strong locks and spies with muskets? But to follow you on cold April mornings, when it is your custom to reveal yourself to the countryside, even though you challenge the dawn with the jasmines and carnations of your face, not that, my dear, no; for although in the meadows the gentle month levels the dry grasses, since it equally revives their hearts, with the smiling breezes which the damp dew converts into dull headaches, it makes the cemeteries hunchbacked [i.e. with graves].

Here, both the unforced conversational tone and the quiet wit of the closing lines seem to look ahead to the Lope of the Tomé de Burguillos poems (see above, p. 118). Nevertheless, it would be wrong to think of Bartolomé mainly as a creator of small-scale effects, however finely calculated. The strongest evidence for this occurs in a type of poem – the funeral elegy – not attempted by his brother: more specifically, in the two poems on the deaths of the Conde de Gelves (1610) and Queen Margaret of Austria (1611).[23] In the first of these, the attempt at consolation leads to a vision of change in what is seemingly most permanent:

> Quizá los verdes golfos, donde hoy vemos
> mover las esperanzas de los reyes
> globos de espuma entre ambiciosos remos,
>   culto recibirán y agrestes leyes;
> verán lucir las premiadoras hoces,
> y en su labor sudar los tardos bueyes.   (B, II, p. 59)

Perhaps the green gulfs where today we see the hopes of kings create bubbles of foam between ambitious oars will receive cultivation and rustic laws; they will see the beneficent sickles gleam and the slow oxen sweat at their labour.

And in the second, the spectacle of a world in mourning ends with the image of a final cataclysm whose cosmic sweep it would be difficult to parallel in any other poet of this generation:

> Los montes envejecen, las ciudades
> yacen, y de soberbias monarquías
> ven dudosos vestigios las edades.
>   Y un día llegará, tras luengos días,
> en que esta magnitud mortal, cansada,
> sienta las postrimeras agonías.   (B, II, p. 49)

Mountains grow old, cities lie fallen, and the years see the doubtful remains of proud monarchies. And a day will come, after long days, when, wearied, this mortal colossus will feel its final agony.

Though both the Argensolas, as I have suggested, remained virtually indifferent to contemporary literary polemics, their poetry, like that of their friend the Prince of Esquilache,[24] was used by Lope de Vega as an example of correctness and clarity in the course of his attacks on *culteranismo* (see above, pp. 111–12). By 1634, however, when their poetry was published for the first time, there are signs that it was already considered outmoded. One obvious reason for this, of course, is the triumph of Góngora, though to take the full measure of what has happened between, we need to look at other less spectacular, though significant, changes which were taking place in the poetic climate of the early 1600s.

One of these, which I have already mentioned in passing (see above, p. 22), is the emergence of a new type of courtier poet, of which the outstanding examples are the Conde de Salinas (1564–1630) and, in a slightly later generation, Villamediana and Antonio Hurtado de Mendoza. Salinas, one of the most splendid aristocrats of the time, had inherited a Portuguese connection through his father, the Prince of Eboli, and in 1616 himself became Viceroy and Captain-General of Portugal. This Portuguese link is crucial for his poetry: as Luis Rosales has made clear,[25] it is Salinas who is largely responsible for re-creating the tradition of love poetry which derives from Garcilaso and his most talented disciple, the Portuguese poet Luis de Camões.[26] 'Re-creation' here is not so much a question of imitation as of what Rosales calls an 'attitude to life': an emotional purity whose reticence and melancholy owe something to the older *cancionero* poetry which for both Camões and Salinas is still a living model. This affinity is also stylistic: if Salinas seems in some ways an archaizing poet, this is partly because of his open hostility to more contemporary models – 'aquel lenguaje crespo e intrincado, / oscuro y con cuidado oscurecido' (that tortuous and intricate language, obscure and deliberately obscured) – and partly because of the ease with which he deploys an older kind of wit:[27]

> Yo no llamo míos
> mis ojos ausentes;
> ojos son de puentes
> por do pasan ríos.
> Y en la ligereza
> de aguas pasajeras,
> como las riberas
> miro mi firmeza. (D, pp. 123–4)[28]

I do not call mine my absent eyes; they are the arches of bridges through which rivers flow. And in the lightness of passing waters, like the river banks, I behold my constancy.

At times, Salinas's wit assumes an anti-literary stance, as in Sonnet XVII, where he claims to have erased what he has written, since it interferes with the sight of the woman he loves:

> Pues no es razón que pierda yo de vista,
> por ver tinta, papel y consonantes,
> rato ninguno en que pudiera veros. (D, p. 53)

For it is not right that I should overlook, in order to see ink, paper and rhymes, a single opportunity of seeing you.

This in itself, of course, is a rhetorical strategem, roughly equivalent to Sir Philip Sidney's 'Fool, look in thy heart and write';[29] at the same time, it points to the gap between writing and experience – between feeling and the expression of feeling – which Salinas returns to time and again in his other poems, and notably in his sense that silence may be more expressive than words. And characteristically, in one of his finest sonnets (L), it is the distance between the speaker and the woman he addresses which guarantees the truth, and also the unrepeatability, of his love:

> Ardo en amor y por amores muero;
> ¡ved qué extraño dolor y desconcierto!
> Tiéneme muerto amor y, estando muerto,
> busco el vivir que para amaros quiero.

> Siempre os quise, y amé, y amar espero
> hasta tener el monumento abierto;
> y estando el cuerpo allí difunto y yerto,
> sustentaré mi amor firme y entero.
> Y si de tanto amor no sois servida
> por vuestra condición desamorada,
> podrá mi triste muerte lastimaros.
> Y así vendréis a ser agradecida
> cuando ni vos podáis conmigo nada,
> ni yo pueda otra vez volver a amaros.   (D, p. 87)

I am in love and am dying of love; see what strange grief and disarray! Love has killed me and, being dead, I seek the life I need in order to love you. I always desired and loved you, and I hope to love you until my tomb lies open; and when my body there is dead and stiff, I shall preserve my love firm and entire. And if you are not obliged by such great love because of your unloving condition, my sad death may move you to pity. And thus you will come to feel gratitude when neither you may do anything with me, nor I return again to love you.

This kind of directness, and the purity of diction that goes with it, become increasingly rare in seventeenth-century poetry, though they reappear, as we shall see, in Villamediana, whose work I shall discuss in a later chapter (see pp. 208–12). All three of the poets I have so far referred to in this section, in fact – the Argensolas as well as Salinas – are writers who achieve a certain manner early in their careers which they are able to sustain without hesitation throughout the whole of their work. By contrast, the next two poets I want to consider, Carrillo and Espinosa, seem torn between styles – the essential mark of the 'transitional' writer – a situation which in the case of Espinosa is still further complicated by the move from secular to religious poetry.

Luis Carrillo de Sotomayor (1582/3–1610) is best known for his prose treatise, the *Libro de la erudición poética* (Book of Poetic Erudition) and for a single poem, the 'Fábula de Acis y Galatea' (1611), to which I have already referred (see above, p. 78). Again, the question of milieu is important: though Carrillo was born in Baena (Andalusia), his professional career as *cuatralbo* (commander of four galleys) in the Spanish fleet centred on two other places: Cartagena, where he came into contact with the group of Murcian writers under the critic Francisco de Cascales, and Puerto de Santa María (Cadiz), where he was friendly with the Conde de Niebla, the patron of Góngora and Espinosa and the dedicatee of the *Polifemo* and his own

'Fábula de Acis y Galatea'. It is this professional experience, moreover, which accounts for the vivid sea imagery of some of his finest poems – the ballad 'A la caza de unas galeotas turquesas' (In Pursuit of Some Turkish Galleys) or the sonnet 'A una ausencia, partiéndose en galeras' (To an Absence, on Leaving with the Galleys):

> Usurpa ufano ya el tirano viento
> a las velas los senos extendidos.
> ¡Adiós, playas, ya os pierdo! ¡Adiós erguidos
> montes a quien venció mi pensamiento!
> Ya es mar también el uno y el otro asiento
> en mis ojos, de lágrimas ceñidos,
> por perderos, oh montes, más perdidos;
> tal pierdo, triste tal, así tal siento.
> Ya esconde el ancho mar, en sí orgulloso,
> las frentes de los cerros levantados,
> en sus soberbias olas caudaloso.
> Así divide ausencia mis cuidados;
> mas no podrá jamás, oh dueño hermoso,
> de ti, mis pensamientos abrasados. (AC, p. 54)[30]

The tyrant wind now proudly usurps the swelling bosoms of the sails. Farewell, beaches, now I am losing you! Farewell, high mountains which my thought conquered! Now the twin seats of my eyes, ringed with tears, are likewise sea, from losing you, o mountains, still more lost: such is my love, such my sadness, thus so do I feel. Now the wide sea, proud in itself, hides from view the brows of the lofty peaks, mighty in its proud waves. Thus absence divides my cares; but it can never, o fair mistress [divide] my burning thoughts from you.

The verbal refinement of such a poem clearly owes a good deal to Herrera, though the theme of absence is very much Carrillo's own. Though it is difficult to speak with any finality of a poet who died while still in his twenties – Dámaso Alonso, for instance, describes him as a potentially major poet whose career ended just short of maturity[31] – there is no doubt that Carrillo's love poetry lies at the centre of his work. Yet even here one can detect a movement from the re-working of Petrarchan and Herreran situations towards an almost obsessive concern with mortality as a solution to the deceptions of love. Thus the recently discovered *décimas* to the artist Pedro de Ragis[32] – for the most part an elaborate set of instructions for painting the portrait of a much-admired woman – end with a bleak version of the *carpe diem* theme:

> Mi intento, señora, ha sido
> en pintar esta deidad,
> sacar a luz la beldad
> increíble que has tenido;
> antes que al tiempo el olvido
> suceda y al sol la helada:
> antes que a tu edad dorada
> la de plata encubra y seque
> un accidente y te trueque,
> de cielo que eres en nada.   (AC, p. 189)

My intention, lady, has been, in painting this deity, to bring to light the incredible beauty which has been yours; before oblivion succeeds time and frost the sun: before the Age of Silver overtakes your Golden Age and an accident withers and changes you from the heaven you are into nothing.

All these poems show a poet of considerable range, writing well within the limits of late sixteenth-century verse. And the same is true, by and large, of Carrillo's most ambitious poem, the 'Fábula de Acis y Galatea'; here, despite certain coincidences of vocabulary and the occasional complexity of the syntax, the general effect is much closer to sixteenth-century models than to Góngora's later, and much more original, reworking of the same subject, and the texture of the verse, more often than not, recalls the more direct technique of Lope or Barahona de Soto:

> 'Los premios del amor nos incitaban,
> la soledad y sombras persuadían,
> y el ver cómo las vides se abrazaban
> con los hermosos chopos y se asían;
> también dos tortolillas nos mostraban
> en besos dulces cuánto se querían:
> todo era, en fin, Amor, que Amor triunfaba
> hasta en la yerba que en el prado estaba...'
>   (lines 96–103; AC, p. 168)

'The rewards of love encouraged us, solitude and the shadows persuaded [us], and the sight of the vines embracing and clinging to the lovely poplars; likewise two turtle-doves showed us, by their sweet kisses, how much they loved one another: everything, in short, was Love, for Love triumphed even in the grass which grew in the meadow...'

Even in a relatively sustained poem like this, however, there are signs of stylistic uncertainty, and in some of the shorter poems the syntax occasionally breaks down, as if Carrillo were attempting effects beyond his powers of verbal control. Thus in his poetic practice he seems divided between a taste for clarity and simplicity and a wish to write 'difficult' poetry for the few. And something of the same conflict appears, at a more theoretical level, in the *Libro de la erudición poética*: on the surface, an apology for 'learned difficulty', yet also – perhaps influenced here by Cascales – a plea for clarity and the avoidance of unnecessary obscurity. As his most recent editor points out, the *Libro*, however much it may have helped to confirm Góngora in his own procedures, is neither the revolutionary manifesto it has sometimes been taken to be, nor simply a projection of Carrillo's own temperament,[33] but rather an attempt to come to terms with certain contemporary tendencies which at the time of writing he was unable to reconcile in his own work.

A similar kind of stylistic indecision can be seen in the work of Pedro de Espinosa (1578–1650), though here, as I have already suggested, the question of style also involves differences of subject-matter. Something of Espinosa's attitude to the poetry of the time can be inferred from his anthology, *Primera parte de flores de poetas ilustres de España* (First Part of the Flowers of Illustrious Poets of Spain; 1605),[34] which includes his own early work, together with that of other members of the Antequera group – Luis Martín de la Plaza, Agustín de Tejada – alongside poems by Lope, Góngora and the twenty-five-year-old Quevedo. The prominence of Góngora and the inclusion of Quevedo, soon to be recognized as the leading poet of the next generation, suggest a wish to identify himself with what is most 'modern' in contemporary poetry, an aim which is confirmed by his own poetic practice. Thus his two most ambitious early poems, the 'Fábula de Genil' (Fable of the [River] Genil) and 'A la navegación de San Raimundo' (On the Voyage of St Raymond), build on the descriptive manner of Herrera (see above, p. 26) to create a kind of writing in which any suggestion of an external reality is absorbed into the brilliant texture of the language:

> Colunas más hermosas que valientes
> sustentan el gran techo cristalino;
> las paredes son piedras transparentes,
> cuyo valor del Ocidente vino;
> brotan por los cimientos claras fuentes,
> y con pie blando, en líquido camino,
> corren cubriendo con sus claras linfas
> las carnes blancas de las bellas ninfas.
> ('Fábula de Genil', lines 105–12; LE, p. 25)[35]

Columns more beautiful than strong support the great roof of crystal; the walls are transparent stones, whose value comes from the Occident; clear springs issue from the foundations and, on light feet, by a liquid path they flow, covering with their waters the white bodies of the lovely nymphs.

This comes from a description of the underwater palace of the river god; despite its echoes of earlier pastoral writing, the scene – like the fable itself – is purely imaginary: a wholly secular nature created through verbal artifice whose dazzling surfaces are themselves a source of wonder.

III

The nature described in Espinosa's later, religious, poems is very different from this. In 1606, one year after the publication of the *Flores*, he withdrew from society and, under the name of Pedro de Jesús, lived for several years as a hermit; later, in 1615, he became chaplain to the Conde de Niebla, the patron of Góngora and Carrillo, in whose household he remained for the rest of his career. The years 1606–15, in fact, mark a series of spiritual crises in Espinosa's life, and the most important poems of the period, the two 'Psalmos' (Psalms) and the 'Soledad de Pedro de Jesús' (Solitude of Pedro de Jesús), reflect something of this personal background.

What is interesting, as we shall see, is that at this time of crisis Espinosa was able to draw on a familiar tradition of devotional writing. At this point, however, it is worth recalling the various kinds of religious lyric available to a Spanish poet in the early years of the seventeenth century. Here we can make a rough distinction between the 'penitential' poem – more often than not in sonnet form, and occasionally making use of the Ignatian scheme of meditation (see above, p. 14) – and the less sophisticated type of *a lo divino* poem (see above, p. 12), largely dependent on simple, and often over-ingenious, conceits, as popularized by a writer like Ledesma. One notable exponent of the first type of poem is Bartolomé Leonardo de Argensola, whose best religious sonnets, like the one quoted in chapter 1 (see above, p. 15) tend to be written from the personal point of view of a repentant sinner.[36] There is a strong line here which runs from Bartolomé Leonardo to Lope de Vega and ultimately to Quevedo, whose religious poetry I shall discuss in the next chapter. As against this – though the two categories are by no means mutually exclusive – the more popular type of poetry, though often mediocre, finds its most artistically satisfying expression in the religious *villancicos* of Lope and Góngora and in the wonderfully inventive poems of Valdivielso, to which I shall turn in a moment.

Espinosa's religious poetry shows traces of both these modes,[37] though its true centre of gravity lies elsewhere: in the tradition of meditation on the creatures – the idea of the created world as the symbolic alphabet of God – which has its roots in medieval writers like Hugh of St Victor and St Bonaventure.[38] Thus the first of the two 'Psalmos' opens:

> Pregona el firmamento
> las obras de tus manos,
> y en mí escribiste un libro de tu sciencia.
> Tierra, mar, fuego, viento
> publican tu potencia,
> y todo cuanto veo
> me dice que te ame
> y que en tu amor me inflame;
> mas mayor que mi amor es mi deseo.
> Mejor que yo, Dios mío, lo conoces;
> sordo estoy a las voces
> que me dan tus sagradas maravillas
> llamándome, Señor, a tus amores...   (LE, pp. 112–13)

The firmament declares the works of your hands, and in me you have written a book of your knowledge. Earth, sea, fire and wind proclaim your power, and all that I see tells me to love you and to burn with love of you; but greater than my love is my desire. You know it, God, better than I; I am deaf to the voices which your sacred wonders offer me, calling me, Lord, to your love.

Both poems are concerned with the speaker's inability to respond adequately to the summons of the creatures; in this sense, they are poems of self-scrutiny, since they argue that, when the soul awakens to the knowledge of God, it is not through any special grace imposed from outside, but through a rediscovery of the self. Yet, paradoxically, though both poems – more especially the second – speak of loss and privation, Espinosa's attempt to imagine the power of the divine creation throws up natural images of extraordinary visual precision:

> ¿Quién te enseñó, mi Dios, a hacer flores
> y en una hoja de entretalles llena
> bordar lazos con cuatro o seis labores?
>   ('Psalmo' 1, lines 14–16; LE, p. 113)

Who taught you, God, to make flowers and, on a leaf filled with patterns, to embroider bows with four or six stitches?

Such images, of course, are not included for their sensuous appeal, but as examples of divine order. Yet, as Espinosa recognizes, though the creatures are the symbols of God, they do not *contain* him. It is this gap which he attempts to bridge, not altogether successfully, in the 'Soledad de Pedro de Jesús', written probably in 1611 or 1612. On the surface, this poem – addressed to the Conde de Niebla – is an invitation to renounce the vanities of court life for the virtues of a country retreat. Yet the overall effect is curiously disjointed: at one point, the progress of the poem is interrupted by a vision of Christ on the Cross, whose sufferings threaten to invalidate the pleasure of the natural scene. Immediately after this, Espinosa attempts to assimilate the figure of Christ into the pastoral imagery of the rest of the poem:

> Convierte ya la vista cudiciosa,
> en tiernas tibias lágrimas deshecho,
> a esta tabla de flores, que es hermosa;
> a las pías de Juno has contrahecho.
> Mira marchita la cerviz de rosa
> y, entre claveles, blanqueando el pecho
> de un mancebo que yace al aire frío,
> bellísimo a mis ojos, Cristo mío.
> Mira cárdeno lirio el rostro santo,
> y el tirio carmesí del lado abierto.
> ¿Grita el león y el hijo duerme tanto?...
>
> (lines 41–51; LE, pp. 129–30)

Now direct your eager sight, dissolved in warm, gentle tears, to this patch of flowers, for it is beautiful; it has imitated Juno's peacocks. See the rosy neck withered and, amid carnations, the white breast of a youth who lies in the cold air, most beautiful to my eyes, my Christ. See the divine face [now] a pale lily, and the Tyrian purple of his open side. Does the lion roar and the son sleep so soundly?

Beautiful as these lines are, they do not really save the poem from incoherence: if to a modern reader the central part of the description reads like an *a lo divino* version of the death of Adonis, this in itself suggests the extent to which the real agony of Christ which had at first seemed to disrupt the general tenor of the poem is now tending to recede into a world of myth. What has broken down, in fact, is the attempt – common to much seventeenth-century poetry – to combine the pastoral and the ascetic traditions. In the psalm which concludes the poem, the theme of the Crucifixion is once again presented in pastoral terms – the crown of thorns, significantly, is replaced by a garland of flowers – though the lines which follow

(337–8) – 'Sólo mi amor me pides, / y el amor no se paga sólo en rosas' (You ask only my love, and love is paid not only in roses; LE, p. 120) – again suggest the insufficiency of the creatures, and perhaps of the pastoral device as a whole.

Espinosa is not a poet whose work shows a steady development of meaning, and the best of his religious poems, like the 'Psalmos', may have been written for his own spiritual guidance rather than for their possible literary effect. At the same time, it would be wrong to think of them as private poems: the themes and images he selects for composition belong for the most part to ancient traditions and it is in the method of combining these that his originality consists. This ability to bring together different traditions, both literary and theological, is an important aspect of Counter-Reformation sensibility, and no account of the religious poetry of the period can afford to overlook the role of the Church itself in encouraging poetry as a form of worship. Or as Rengifo put it at the time:

> Who does not see the great use which the Church makes of poetry, even in our own tongue. What feast is there of Christmas, of the Holy Sacrament, of the Resurrection, of Our Lady the Virgin and the saints, which they do not seek to celebrate with songs and *villancicos* and, where men of letters are present on such occasions, they fail to produce such a quantity and variety of verses that the churches and cloisters are no less adorned by them than by the awnings and canopies that are hung there?[39]

Both the sense of audience this entails and the kind of synthesis which was possible in an essentially public kind of poetry are splendidly illustrated in the work of José de Valdivielso (1562?–1638), for many years a chaplain of Toledo Cathedral and a close friend of Lope de Vega. Though Valdivielso is now recognized as one of the finest religious dramatists before Calderón, his main achievement as a poet is as a writer of *poesía a lo divino*, notably in the *Romancero espiritual* (Spiritual Ballads), first published in 1612.[40] His own Note to the Reader makes his didactic intentions quite clear: 'I have used some of these verses as an instrument for the conversion of certain souls grown old in vices; being persuaded that, if many were to read them, some might be brought back to the fold' (A, p. 9). Though Valdivielso refers here to readers, it is clear that many of his compositions were intended for performance as well as for private meditation, and throughout the collection his powers of persuasion are constantly reinforced by his unfailing dramatic sense. It could also be argued that the distinction I made earlier between the 'penitential' and the 'popular' for once breaks down; as Aguirre rightly stresses, the *Romancero* as a whole has a distinctly penitential character – the tears of the repentant sinner are a recurring theme – and the 'popular' tone, for all its apparent spontaneity, involves a good deal of literary tact.

The peculiar synthesis which Valdivielso achieves is composed of many elements: folksongs and ballads, the courtly love of the *cancioneros*, emblem literature and the Bible, to name only the most obvious. Most of these can be related to medieval traditions, both popular and sophisticated; as has often been pointed out, the *Romancero* can be read as a spiritual *cancionero* in which Christ is the lover of the human soul:

> A vistas sale un galán
> muerto de amor por su dama,
> a quien trae desde una herida
> en su pecho atravesada...   (A, p. 147)

A young gallant comes into view, dying of love for his lady, whom by virtue of a wound he bears lodged in his breast.

Such verse makes frequent use of 'homely' comparisons, like the image of Christ as swimmer I referred to in chapter 1 (see above, p. 12). More often than not, however, these are used to form part of an allegory, or continuous metaphor, as in the brilliant description of a bullfight which begins: 'Porque está parida la Reyna, / corren toros y cañas juegan' (Because the Queen [i.e. the Virgin] has given birth, they are fighting bulls and wielding lances). Often, as here, the two levels of the allegory are brought together in a piece of word play; at one point, the two *cuadrillas* – the bullfighters and their assistants – one headed by Love, the other by Grace, separate:

> Los dos puestos se dividen,
> y con destreza gallarda,
> toman adargas y huevos
> llenos de olorosas aguas.
> Cañas no quieren tomar,
> por ver que con una caña
> tienen de hazer a su rey
> una burla muy pesada.   (lines 53–60; A, p. 228)

The two groups divide and with graceful skill they take up shields and balls filled with scented water. They have no wish to use lances, since with a lance people are to play a cruel joke on their king.

Thus the bullfighter's lance becomes the 'rod', or mock sceptre, which is placed in Christ's hand before the Crucifixion; a moment later, the devices on the 'shields' turn out to be familiar biblical images, all associated in medieval typology with the Virgin Mary: the dove with the olive branch, the rainbow of the Covenant, and so on; and finally the pomanders are made to suggest the 'oranges' of the popular *copla* 'Arrojome las naranjitas...' (She threw me oranges...), sung now by the angels who are observing the scene from heaven. A bare summary like this can hardly do justice to the verve, still less the economy, with which Valdivielso achieves his effect – two qualities which are notably absent from most other practitioners of *a lo divino* poetry. At the same time, however entertaining such poems may be – and this of course is part of Valdivielso's intention – the seriousness of the enterprise is never in doubt. In his more meditative poems, like the fine sequence on the Rosary (A, pp. 171–220), the spirit of popular religion is re-created in a language which is neither naive nor archaic. Like Espinosa, though in a very different kind of spiritual context, Valdivielso shows a remarkable openness to recent poetic innovations, not least to the poetry of Góngora.[41] And such openness, we may conclude, is the sign of a continuing tradition in which popular idiom and extreme sophistication are not felt to be incompatible – a pattern we shall find repeated in other seventeenth-century poets, from Quevedo to Sor Juana Inés de la Cruz.

CHAPTER 6

Francisco de Quevedo: the force of eloquence

I

The *Flores* of Espinosa (1605) includes eighteen poems by Francisco de Quevedo (1580–1645) – a high proportion for a poet at the beginning of his career, and a sure indication of Espinosa's taste for the new. Like Lope de Vega (and unlike Góngora), Quevedo was also a prolific writer in other genres: his two most famous prose works, the *Vida del Buscón* (Life of the Swindler; 1626) and the satirical fantasies of the *Sueños* (Visions; 1627) – both begun when he was still in his twenties – are among the masterpieces of the period, and the many volumes of didactic writings, on subjects ranging from statecraft to Stoic philosophy, are remarkable both for their erudition and for the unremitting seriousness of their moral arguments. Given the sheer size and variety of such an *oeuvre*, generalization seems especially hazardous; yet, as Claudio Guillén points out, there is a real sense in which Quevedo's work as a whole constitutes a body of 'writing' – an *écriture* – which deliberately cuts across conventional notions of genre as a means of liberating the powers of language itself.[1]

Where the poetry is concerned, this involves both Quevedo's attitude to his models and his trust in the strengths of traditional rhetoric. Such matters, moreover, are not solely literary: insofar as they affect the composition of particular poems, they also raise the whole question of the 'self' which is being projected through the medium of language, and of the reader's response, both emotional and intellectual, to the words he is made to re-enact. And as we shall see, to realize the full implications of this is to by-pass the kind of circular argument which draws autobiographical inferences from the poetry only to project them back on it in different forms.

If we turn to the biographical facts, on the other hand, the signs of a strong personality are very clear. What strikes one most forcibly, perhaps, is Quevedo's closeness to important public figures and events: his father was secretary to the Empress María of Austria and later to Queen Ana, wife of Philip II; in 1613, Quevedo himself went to Naples as private secretary to the Duque de Osuna, Viceroy of Sicily, and was entrusted with a number of crucial diplomatic missions. After Osuna's disgrace in 1621, Quevedo was banished from Court and for a time imprisoned; shortly afterwards, however, his fortunes rose again as a result of his good relations with the new favourite, Olivares (later to become one of his most powerful enemies). As John Elliott has shown, there is a curious kind of complementarity in the relationship between Quevedo and Olivares, as if each helped to make and unmake the other; both men seem driven by a combination of idealism and self-interest, and Olivares, for a time at least, appears to have shared Quevedo's version of Christian Stoicism.[2] By 1634, however (the date of his ill-advised marriage), Quevedo's criticisms of the style of Olivares's government, as well as his changing perception of Olivares himself, were becoming increasingly obvious, a process which eventually led to his three years' imprisonment (1639–43) for reasons which remain obscure, but which may have involved treasonable dealings with the French. Finally, after the fall of Olivares, Quevedo was released, broken in health, though he continued to write on his estate of La Torre de Juan Abad in the province of Ciudad Real and later at Villanueva de los Infantes, where he died.

Faced with the dramatic quality of such a career, critics have often been tempted to equate what is known of Quevedo himself with the powerful *persona* which seems to emerge from many of the poems. Certain satirical pieces, it is true, can be connected with actual events or with particular relationships; nevertheless, in most instances, the gap between poems and biography remains obstinately wide, and attempts to close it have more often than not tended to distort the nature of the poetry itself.[3] At the same time, if one looks beyond the more public aspects of Quevedo's biography to the kind of attitudes which might link the life to the writings, a particular cast of mind begins to appear which can best be described as 'conservative'. In social terms, this has to do with Quevedo's status as a 'precarious aristocrat' (Guillén's phrase),[4] as someone who is neither a professional scholar nor in the conventional sense of the word a courtier, and whose economic security is never assured. This may help to explain his contempt for the trades and professions – a frequent target of his satire – as well as his dislike of popular values and speech. At a more abstract level, it may also account for a kind of inverted patriotism in which the denunciation of popular evils is set against a vaguely imagined feudal past whose simple justice and purity of national intentions are the necessary antidote to a corrupt and over-sophisticated civilization.[5] And running through all this is the mistrust of change expressed in the opening pages of his *Marco Bruto* (Marcus Brutus; 1631):

The world was lost through wishing to be otherwise, and men are lost by wishing to be different from themselves. Novelty is so little satisfied with itself that inasmuch as it is displeased by that which has been, just so does it weary of that which is.[6]

Transposed into literary terms, it is this same suspicion of change, of running counter to what he takes to be the genius of the language, which informs Quevedo's attacks on *culteranismo* and to a lesser extent his strictures on the poetic vocabulary of Herrera.[7] The most obvious sign of this is his decision to edit the work of two sixteenth-century poets, the great religious writer Luis de León (1527–91) and the otherwise unknown Francisco de la Torre. His polemical intention is clear: both editions were published in 1631, four years after the death of Góngora, whose poems were already beginning to take on the status of a classic. And in the long letter to Olivares which serves as a prologue to the poems of Luis de León, he writes what amounts to a defence of older standards:

In the first part... the diction is lofty [*grande*], proper, beautiful and fluent; of such purity that it is neither disqualified by commonness nor made strange by what is inappropriate. His whole style, with studied majesty, is suited to the greatness of the matter [*sentencia*], which does not display itself ambitiously outside the body of the discourse, nor hide itself in darkness, or rather lose itself in the affected confusion of figures and in a flood of foreign words.[8]

Quevedo, of course, is not the only writer of the time to attack *gongorismo* in the interests of 'clarity'. Where he differs, say, from a minor poet like Jáuregui is in his consistent application of the principle of decorum, not just as a test of other poets' intentions, but as the basis of his own poetic practice at a time when other criteria were beginning to qualify the underlying assumptions of Renaissance poetics. Again, this suggests a conservative stance: an attempt to preserve the discriminating powers of traditional rhetoric in the face of competing kinds of persuasiveness, not least by an appeal to earlier models. Two points follow from this. One is that what has often been described as Quevedo's 'modernity' – the sense in which he appears to speak directly to a twentieth-century reader – may result, para-doxically, from just this archaizing tendency; the bare diction and violent imagery of some of the best-known sonnets at times seem to echo an early sixteenth-century poet like Boscán,[9] and their argumentative rhetoric, though entirely explicable in Renaissance terms, may owe something to the cruder, though no less insistent, logic of *cancionero* poetry. The other concerns Quevedo's relation to *conceptismo* and to the theory of wit which is usually assumed to lie behind it. Modern critics – as I myself did in chapter 2 (see above, pp. 57–9) – will often take a Quevedo poem in order to demonstrate the workings of the poetic conceit. Provided one confines oneself to the way language actually functions within a particular poem, this seems quite legitimate. To go on from this, however, to regard Quevedo as the supreme example of a *conceptista* poet within the terms defined by, say, Gracián, is to misrepresent the character of his own poetics. The fact that for Gracián the great exponent of the *concepto* is Góngora, not Quevedo, should put us on our guard. More specifi-cally, Gracián's attempt to give an aesthetic dimension to the *ingenio*,[10] or the Italian theorists' insistence on 'wonder' have no counterpart in Quevedo. Thus, as Paul Julian Smith has argued: 'The theorists' emphasis on the beautiful as the end of wit (as opposed to the 'truth' of dialectic) is quite alien to the more serious conception of poetics adopted by Quevedo...'[11] This 'more serious conception of poetics' does not, of course, exclude the use of *conceptos*, which at times may overlap quite strikingly with the theory of wit; what it *does* mean is that, from Quevedo's point of view, such verbal strategies need no special pleading, but can be justified entirely in terms of accepted rhetorical practice.

At one extreme, then, Quevedo rejects both *culto* vocabulary and the style that goes with it. At the other, as his comments on Luis de León make clear, he objects just as strongly to popular language:

Petronius Arbiter [the author of the *Satyricon*] expressed it better than anyone. One must avoid all base words and choose those which are remote from the common people, so that one may be able to say: I despise the profane crowd.[12]

Though this is a commonplace of neo-Aristotelian poetics, such dismissiveness may seem strange on the part of a writer whose satirical verse, like much of his prose, shows an absolute mastery of common idiom, from popular bawdy to the highly specialized slang (*germanía*) of the criminal underworld. The gap between theory and practice, however, may not be as great as it appears at first sight. Though Quevedo regards popular poetry, for instance, not only as bad, but as in some sense an offence to civilized discourse, he is nevertheless fascinated by the possibilities which the popular lexicon offers for parody and burlesque. At times, to be sure, it is hard to distinguish between imitation and genuine creation. What seems clear, on the other hand, is the effect of distancing he often achieves by ascribing such language, not to his own poetic *persona*, but to an invented character whose mode of speech forms part of the parody. Moreover, as we shall see in some of the poems I discuss in the next section, even where the controlling 'voice' of the poem is the poet's own, the presence of 'base' words, far from offending against decorum, creates the kind of 'diminishing' effect which is fully allowed for in Renaissance theory.

II

All this points to the astonishing power of verbal play which is the dominating feature of Quevedo's work. In his poetry, as in much of the prose, this play takes on many forms, most conspicuously in the large body of satirical verse which spans practically the whole of his career. Here, as with Góngora, 'satirical' can only be an approximate term; satire and burlesque are often virtually interchangeable, and both frequently involve what James Iffland terms the 'grotesque': 'the co-presence of laughter and something which is incompatible with laughter'.[13] As Iffland goes on to say, the sheer virtuosity of such writing should deter us from seeking any unifying intention or persistent frame of mind; time and again, the mercurial quality of Quevedo's imagination – his ability to seize on the slightest hint of an alternative meaning – creates the kind of verbal effect which seems to detach itself from the apparent subject of the poem. Thus in the self-mocking ballad which begins 'Parióme adrede mi madre...' (My mother gave birth to me on purpose...; B, p. 842),[14] the speaker describes his horoscope in a splendid series of *double-entendres*:

> Nací debajo de Libra,
> tan inclinado a las pesas,
> que todo mi amor le fundo
> en las madres vendederas...   (lines 17–20)

I was born under Libra, so inclined to weights that I base all my love on mothers who sell their daughters...

The train of associations is clear enough: Libra (the Scales) implies weights ('pesas'), which in turn suggest buying and selling; yet the women shopkeepers ('las madres vendederas') are also mothers who sell their daughters – a possibility one could hardly have predicted at the start. Elsewhere, as in one of the frequent descriptions of ugly women, 'Viejecita, arredro vayas...' (Get back, little old woman...; B, p. 977), the meaning may be more compressed:

> Cuantos a boca de noche
> aguardan sus enemigos,
> a la orilla de tus labios
> aciertan hora y camino...   (lines 57–60)

All those who wait for their enemies at nightfall on the edge of your lips have hit on the right place and the right road.

Here, as so often with Quevedo's use of popular expressions, the effect depends on taking a cliché literally: 'a boca de noche' usually means 'at nightfall'; its literal meaning, however, is 'at the mouth of night', so that, by an astonishing twist of the imagination, the woman's cavernous mouth becomes a haunt of robbers and assassins.

These two examples show not only the characteristic riddling quality of Quevedo's wit ('what is the connection between a sign of the zodiac and a woman who sells her daughter?') but also the way in which a poem may suddenly refer to a whole new range of experience – the worlds of commercialized sex and of criminals who wait for their victims at dusk – by picking up an apparently casual verbal hint. And often such allusions have a topical resonance which links them firmly to Quevedo's own society, as in the opening of one of his most famous *letrillas*, 'Poderoso caballero es don Dinero ...' (A powerful knight is Sir Money...; B, p. 734):

> Madre, yo al oro me humillo;
> él es mi amante y mi amado,

> pues, de puro enamorado,
> de contino anda amarillo;
> que pues, doblón o sencillo,
> hace todo cuanto quiero,
> *poderoso caballero*
> *es don Dinero.*
>
> 　Nace en las Indias honrado
> donde el mundo le acompaña;
> viene a morir en España,
> y es en Génova enterrado.
> Y pues quien le trae al lado
> es hermoso, aunque sea fiero,
> *poderoso caballero*
> *es don Dinero...*　　　　　　　　　　　　　(lines 1–16)

Mother, I bow to gold; he is my lover and my beloved, since, through sheer loving, he constantly looks pale; and since, whether doubloon or lesser coin, he does everything I want, *a powerful knight is Sir Money.* He is born honourably in the Indies, where the world waits on him; he comes to die in Spain and is buried in Genoa. And since he who has him at his side is handsome, though he be ugly, *a powerful knight is Sir Money.*

What gives this poem its irresistible driving force is the parody of the traditional girl's lament to her mother; the replacement of the conventional lover by the powerful figure of Money – also seen, of course, as a lover – gives rise to a series of statements whose key terms consciously function on two levels. Thus in the first stanza, gold is 'pale' (literally, 'yellow') by nature and because this is the colour of lovesickness; and in the second stanza, what was at the time the usual itinerary of gold – from the Indies to Spain and thence to the vaults of the Genoese bankers – simultaneously suggests the life pattern of the 'honourable' suitor. (Notice, however, the further innuendo in line 10: great lords have large retinues, but people flock to the Indies in search of fortune.)

At this point, a question arises: granting the verbal brilliance of such poems, how seriously is Quevedo engaging with a reality outside the poetry? One possible answer is suggested by Claudio Guillén: despite its frequent vehemence, there is no sense, he argues, that Quevedo's satirical writing is aimed at reforming, or replacing, existing attitudes or social structures. What militates against this is the kind of conservatism we have already seen in other connections: not so much the wish to keep things as they are, as the feeling that no fundamental change is really possible – an attitude borne out by the pessimism of much of his other writing. So, from this point of view, Quevedo's obsessive verbal inventiveness becomes a way of manipulating – of defacing – a reality from which there is no escape, a supreme example, in Guillén's words, of the 'exasperation to which the most sombre conservative disposition may lead'.[15]

This is an attractive thesis, though, like most attempts to define Quevedo's satire as a whole, it fits certain poems better than others, where the energy of the writing often seems to come more from pleasure in its own skill than from any deeper psychological urgings. It would be wrong, nevertheless, to regard Quevedo's satirical poetry as mainly a matter of verbal play: satire, almost by definition, has a serious ethical function, a power of indictment which creates its effects through the precise handling of rhetoric. Such effects, moreover, are sometimes all the more powerful when achieved by indirection and insinuation; thus in many of Quevedo's poems, verbal dexterity does not so much replace ideological purpose as channel it in unexpected ways. Consider, for instance, the well-known sonnet originally entitled 'A un nariz' (To a Nose; B, p. 562):[16]

> Érase un hombre a una nariz pegado,
> érase una nariz superlativa,
> érase una alquitara medio viva,
> érase un peje espada mal barbado;
> > era un reloj de sol mal encarado,
> érase un elefante boca arriba,
> érase una nariz sayón y escriba,
> un Ovidio Nasón mal narigado.
> > Érase el espolón de una galera,
> érase una pirámide de Egito,
> los doce tribus de narices era;
> > érase un naricísimo infinito,
> muchísimo nariz, nariz tan fiera,
> que en la cara de Anás fuera delito.

There was once a man attached to a nose, there was once a superlative nose, there was once a crucible half alive, there was once a badly bearded swordfish; there was a badly adjusted sundial, there was once an elephant face upwards, there was once a scribe-and-executioner nose, an Ovidius Naso badly nosed. There was once the bowsprit of a galley, there was once a pyramid of Egypt, it was the twelve tribes of noses; there was once an infinite noses of noses [literally, 'nosiest'], a great quantity of nose, a nose so fierce that on the face of Annas it would have been a crime.

An 'innocent' reading of this poem would almost certainly dwell on the accumulation of ingenious metaphors, the series of fantastic hyperboles which seems increasingly to detach itself from any recognizable 'subject'. What we may fail to notice – though it is hard to imagine any seventeenth-century reader doing so – is that this is a strongly anti-Semitic poem, a fact which makes for an altogether different kind of reading. For anyone who knows the rest of Quevedo's work, there are a number of possible clues: the stereotype of the long-nosed Jew occurs frequently in his other writings; the 'executioner(s) and scribe(s)' are those responsible for the condemnation and death of Christ, the delegates, so to speak, of the 'twelve tribes' of Israel; similarly, Annas, whose name in Spanish provides an easy pun ('A-nás' = 'noseless'), was the father-in-law of Caiaphas, the high priest before whom Christ was brought to trial. Nevertheless, in a first reading the poem may seem curiously disjointed: the repeated verb 'érase' – the Spanish equivalent of 'once upon a time there was' – suggests the opening of a 'story' which never actually materializes, and the various Jewish allusions may appear no more than incidental effects of wit. Yet, as Maurice Molho has brilliantly demonstrated,[17] the poem does after all contain a 'story' – one which lends order to what might otherwise seem no more than a string of random ingenuities. The partially concealed event around which the poem is organized, and to which each item in the sequence points, is the rejection of Christ by the Jews, the crucial moment which divides the Old Dispensation from the New and at the same time establishes the Jew in his role of deicide. It is this 'primal scene' (Molho's term), never overtly present, which activates the potential Jewish references in the apparently neutral items of the series; the image of the sundial, for example, suggests not only a physical object but also the sense in which Judaism itself is 'badly orientated' vis-à-vis the Christian God. As for the 'story', it is as if the Genesis narrative – in particular, the progression from fish to animal to man – were being retold from an anti-Jewish point of view, as the prelude to the disastrous judgement of the Elders.[18] This concealed, though ultimately coherent, narrative, needless to say, places the verbal inventions of the poem in a different light, as vehicles of an aggressiveness whose power of ridicule is inseparable from its obliqueness of approach. Why Quevedo should have chosen to be oblique in just this way can only be a matter for speculation; if, as Molho suggests, there were both political and psychological reasons for avoiding a more direct form of attack, one can only feel that the strategy he adopted, whatever its cause, could in the end hardly be more lethal or more technically brilliant in its presentation of a 'displaced', though ultimately all-pervasive, subject.

Quevedo's anti-Semitism is not of course to be condoned, however much it may owe to tradition or to seventeenth-century perceptions of Christendom and its enemies. The literary roots of this particular poem, in fact, may go back to the *Greek Anthology*, where an epigram by Theodorus (xi, 198) runs: 'Hermocrates belongs to his nose, for if we were to say that the nose belongs to Hermocrates, we should be attributing the greater to the lesser.' This suggests a general feature of satirical writing which has often been remarked on: that, despite the various contemporary touches, the actual objects of satire vary little from one period to another. This is something we noticed earlier in connection with the Argensolas;[19] in Quevedo himself, though the emphases fall rather differently – no other seventeenth-century Spanish poet, for example, is so obsessively mysogynistic[20] – the range of types, from doctors and lawyers to deceived husbands and *nouveaux riches*, remains remarkably constant, as do the various kinds of vice they embody.

One reason for this is a common awareness of the existing classical tradition: the body of satirical verse most powerfully represented by Horace, Juvenal, Persius, Martial and the poets of the *Greek Anthology*. Quevedo's debt to such poets is often quite explicit: at times he refers directly to particular poems – the Second Satire of Persius, the Eleventh Satire of Juvenal – as supreme examples of their kind, and his first editor, González de Salas, often notes specific lines or phrases which Quevedo has imitated. What is crucial, however, is the way he uses such sources and the attitude to his models which this implies. Certain differences, to be sure, stand out immediately: as Mas is able to show,[21] the long satire on marriage which begins '¿Por qué mi musa descompuesta y bronca / despiertas, Polo...' (Why, Polo, do you awaken my harsh, discordant Muse...; B, p. 670) – supposedly an imitation of the Sixth Satire of Juvenal – owes less than a tenth of its lines to the original; where Juvenal's denunciation of marriage turns into a rambling catalogue of fashionable vices, Quevedo never loses sight of his central subject, whose particular target – the complaisant husband – has no counterpart in the Latin poem. Similarly with Martial, the chief model for Quevedo's anti-feminine satire, whose epigrammatic concision almost disappears in Quevedo's free translations of individual poems. Such obvious differences can easily distract one from the real nature of Quevedo's engagement with the classical satirists, in which questions of balance and poetic form matter less than the creation of specific kinds of discourse. In the case of Martial, as Lía Schwartz Lerner has recently shown,[22] this often entails an 'active re-reading' of the original text: time and again, Quevedo will take a particular word or rhetorical figure from the Latin and adapt it to his own purposes; alternatively, as in many of his poems addressed to old women – Martial's *vetulae* – he will expand certain features of the original while retaining just enough verbal similarities to enable one to identify the source. The degree of intertextuality this involves is likely to be lost on a modern reader; as Lerner argues, Quevedo repeatedly engages in what amounts to a dialogue with earlier satirical texts, not so much for their referential value, as for their power to generate new strategies of verbal representation in his own language.

The proof of Quevedo's skill in adapting such models lies in his ability to create the kind of tone one instinctively calls 'classical' and which, like that of the classical satirists themselves, can lend itself to a whole range of effects, from the elegantly ironic to the frankly scabrous.[23] Take, for instance, the following sonnet:

> Para comprar los hados más propicios,
> como si la deidad vendible era,
> con el toro mejor de la ribera
> ofreces cautelosos sacrificios.
>   Pides felicidades a tus vicios;
> para tu nave rica y usurera,
> viento tasado y onda lisonjera,
> mereciéndole al golfo precipicios.
>   Porque exceda a la cuenta tu tesoro,
> a tu ambición, no a Júpiter, engañas;
> que él cargó las montañas sobre el oro.
>   Y cuando l'ara en sangre humosa bañas,
> tú miras las entrañas de tu toro,
> y Dios está mirando tus entrañas.   (B, p. 62)

In order to buy the most propitious fates, as if deity were for sale, with the finest bull of these plains you offer cunning sacrifices. You beg happiness for your vices, for your rich, profiteering ship a steady wind and a favourable sea, when it deserves ocean chasms. So that your treasure may be past reckoning, you deceive, not Jupiter, but your own ambition; for it was he who raised mountains above gold. And when you drench the altar with smoking blood, you look into the entrails of your bull, while God is looking into your own.

Here the starting-point is almost certainly the opening of the Second Satire of Persius – 'Non tu prece poscis emaci, / quae nisi seductis nequeas committere divis…' (You never try to strike a bargain with heaven, asking the gods for things you would not dare mention except in private) – a passage which Quevedo reverts to more than once.[24] (The whole poem, in fact, can be seen as an expansion of the phrase 'prece…emaci': the idea of prayer as a bargain or transaction.) The first thirteen lines add up to what Lerner calls a 'reconstruction of pagan discourse',[25] a skilful refashioning of classical language and the kind of subject-matter that goes with it. The latter includes not only the details of what is evidently a Roman sacrifice, but also the characteristically Latin device of the anonymous addressee. The details of the second stanza, on the other hand, hover between two worlds: the reference to the merchant ship is perfectly explicable within the classical context, yet the combination of risky voyages and the exploitation of precious metals seems to edge the poem closer to the time of writing. The effect of the last line is more difficult to gauge. Despite the possible overtones just referred to, there is a continuity between the 'fates' of the opening line and the Jupiter who is responsible for the ordering of creation, just as the sequence of present tenses rules out any idea of a gap between the moment of speaking and an earlier time. The last line, however, changes all this: the perspective suddenly shifts, and the allusion to the Christian God creates the effect of distance which has so far been absent – one which firmly separates the speaker from the carefully reconstructed 'classical' discourse of the rest.

It is effects like these which prevent Quevedo's re-writing of classical satire from becoming mere pastiche. Something different occurs, however, when he engages with conventional images of the classical world, and more especially with earlier Renaissance versions of myths. Quevedo is not, of course, the only poet of the time to see the burlesque potential of such material; he is one of those writers, like Góngora and Lope, for whom parody is an almost obligatory exercise, a critical response to forms which are in danger of becoming over-rigid. Yet where Góngora, for example, explores the tragicomic possibilities of the mythological fable, Quevedo usually prefers an

openly disparaging form of parody,[26] as in the first of his two sonnets
on Daphne and Apollo:

> Bermejazo platero de las cumbres,
> a cuya luz se espulga la canalla,
> la ninfa Dafne, que se afufa y calla,
> si la quieres gozar, paga y no alumbres.
>   Si quieres ahorrar de pesadumbres,
> ojo del cielo, trata de compralla:
> en confites gastó Marte la malla,
> y la espada en pasteles y azumbres.
>   Volvióse en bolsa Júpiter severo;
> levantóse las faldas la doncella
> por recogerle en lluvia de dinero.
>   Astucia fue de alguna dueña estrella,
> que de estrella sin dueña no lo infiero:
> Febo, pues eres sol, sírvete de ella.   (B, p. 578)

Red-haired silversmith of the mountain tops, by whose light the rabble pick
their fleas; the nymph Daphne, who buggers off and is silent, if you want to
possess her, pay her and don't shine your light. If you want to spare yourself
headaches, eye of the sky, try to buy her; Mars sold his coat of mail for sweets
and his sword for pastries and jars of wine. Severe Jupiter turned himself into
a purse: the girl lifted her skirts to receive him in a shower of money. This
was the stratagem of some duenna-star, since I can't imagine it of a star
without a duenna: Phoebus, since you are a sun, make use of her.

The virtual untranslatability of such a poem points to its most
striking feature: the constant proliferation of meaning from which
scarcely a single word or phrase is exempt. The process, from start to
finish, is savagely reductive. The -*azo* suffix of 'Bermejazo' (*bermejo* = 'red') is both augmentative and pejorative: huge, but with a
suggestion of Jewishness (Judas traditionally has red hair); 'se afufa',
in the third line, is almost certainly a term from thieves' cant, in
which 'ninfa' is a common term for a prostitute. In the next stanza,
this descent into the criminal underworld is compounded by the
double meaning of 'ojo' ('eye', but also 'arsehole'), and by the
suggestion that Mars may have pawned his arms to provide a feast for
Venus. The story of Danae and Jupiter is similarly transformed:
where in the original myth the god descends from a cloud in a shower
of gold, he now becomes a purse scattering money into the lap of a
willing girl. (The equation money = semen means that her gesture
may be read in two ways: she 'lifts up her skirts' to catch the coins
and also as a preliminary to sex.) And this clears the way for the

conclusion of the last three lines: 'Such successful encounters could not have occurred without the help of a go-between – literally, a 'duenna-star' – since fate alone (another meaning of 'estrella') would not have sufficed; therefore, use her services yourself, since you are after all a 'sun' (i.e. master of the stars, but also a large gold coin). This by no means exhausts the possible meanings of the poem,[27] nor does it attempt to suggest the various echoes of Quevedo's other writings which an alert reader may catch. Two things, nevertheless, should be clear, and both are central to Quevedo's satirical writing as a whole. One is the sheer power of an imagination which works with such assurance in the mode of the grotesque, where the violence of the parody itself, as here, may prove stronger than the original parodic intention. The other, though hardly to be separated from this, is once again Quevedo's extraordinary verbal dexterity – in this instance, his ability to use popular language as a distorting lens while preserving the structures of formal rhetoric – which seems able to use virtually any theme as a pretext for its endless self-generating play.

III

In the first collected edition of Quevedo's verse, the poems are grouped under different 'Muses'; one muse (Thalia) for satire and another (Erato) for love poetry.[28] No seventeenth-century reader would have found this strange: according to the principle of decorum, different 'kinds' require a different approach from the writer, a fact which helps to explain why, questions of temperament apart, Quevedo is both a great love poet and the author of some of the most virulent anti-feminist satire in the language. Thus, rather than attempting to construct a 'personality' capable to combining such apparently contradictory attitudes, one should consider above all what is being said in each individual poem – not only the kind of ideas which are being presented, but also the nature of the speaker who is giving voice to them and the ways in which thought and emotion are impressed on the reader. To do otherwise is to risk serious misunderstanding; as Paul Julian Smith puts it in his fine study of the love poems: 'The emphasis on the writing subject at the expense of the text leads to anachronistic and misleading conclusions'[29] – the kind of conclusions which assert, against all the evidence, that Quevedo is in some sense a 'modern' poet, curiously at odds with his time.

As a way into some of the issues involved here, we might glance back at the sonnet 'En crespa tempestad del oro undoso...' (B, p. 496) which I quoted in chapter 2 (see above, pp. 57–9). There I discussed the poem mainly as an example of *conceptismo*, of the way a poetic conceit may work in practice. As Smith has shown, this involves a particularly dense handling of traditional rhetorical figures, so much so that one may easily overlook other, equally significant, features of the poem. To begin with, there is the question of intertextuality. Like many of Quevedo's poems, this one starts from a conventional *topos* – praise of a woman's hair – which in turn suggests certain basic Petrarchan equivalences or contrasts: hair–gold, fire–water. More specifically, as various critics have pointed out, there are close parallels between Quevedo's poem and one by the Italian poet Giambattista Marino (1569–1625) which begins 'Onde dorate, e l'onde eran capelli...' (Golden waves, and the waves are hairs...).[30] In the end, however, the differences are more notable than the similarities: in Marino's poem, there are no heroic or mythological examples; Quevedo, on the other hand, suppresses Marino's opening reference to the woman's comb – in the Italian, it is the comb, not the heart, which moves through the waves – and avoids the kind of trivializing which has Cupid making chains out of loose hairs. Thus Quevedo's poem is more argumentative, more generalized and above all more elevated in tone – something which reflects both on the speaker and on the woman he addresses. Moreover, if Marino, as is sometimes thought, reflects a new kind of sensibility – one found, a little later, in French *précieux* poetry – this makes Quevedo seem once again an archaizing poet. And Quevedo's relative austerity is emphasized from another direction: as Smith points out, the juxtaposition of Midas and Tantalus already occurs in Ovid (*Amores*, III, vii), in lines which Quevedo must have known; yet where Ovid's speaker almost invariably consummates his desires, such erotic pleasure is quite alien to Quevedo.[31]

Other features of the poem are already familiar from the satirical verse, in particular the sudden change of register brought about by the intrusion of the first-person singular ('que difuntas lloro'). The question of elevated tone, however, is especially pertinent to the love poetry, since it suggests a heroic quality in the speaker – the 'great lover' who associates himself with exceptional mythical figures – and a certain dignity in the addressee for whom such language is considered appropriate. This is not to say that the woman is idealized in the conventional Petrarchan manner: though physically present, she is also curiously absent – a depersonalized figure whose silence reflects the speaker's inability to communicate with her. This kind of one-sided relationship is also a commonplace of so-called courtly love poetry, a fact which raises once again the question of Quevedo's relationship with previous tradition. As I suggested earlier, there are several features – the idea of suffering through love, the state of 'having and not having' – which relate this poem to the ethos of courtly love, just as there are others – the sense of aspiration associated with Leander and Icarus – which could be thought of as neo-Platonic. Nevertheless, it would be a mistake to call this a 'courtly love poem', or even a 'neo-Platonic poem': however much Quevedo uses such ideas, they invariably form part of a unique and complex structure which escapes any simple classification.

What is true here on a small scale can be extended to Quevedo's love poetry as a whole. Though the basis of such poetry is inevitably Petrarchan, any attempt to extract a consistent ethical system from it seems misguided. Notions of courtly love no longer seem as central to his poems as they once did,[32] and efforts to shift the emphasis to neo-Platonism are scarcely more convincing.[33] The danger here lies, as so often, in taking ideas out of their context: though Quevedo frequently makes use of such concepts, more often than not they create the effect of different 'voices' which merge or conflict within the space of the poem. Take, for instance, the following sonnet:

> Mandóme, ¡ay Fabio¡, que la amase Flora,
> y que no la quisiese; y mi cuidado,
> obediente y confuso y mancillado,
> sin desearla, su belleza adora.
>   Lo que el humano afecto siente y llora,
> goza el entendimiento, amartelado
> del espíritu eterno, encarcelado
> en el claustro mortal que le atesora.
>   Amar es conocer virtud ardiente;
> querer es voluntad interesada,
> grosera y descortés caducamente.
>   El cuerpo es tierra, y lo será, y fue nada;
> de Dios procede a eternidad la mente;
> eterno amante soy de eterna amada.   (B, p. 359)

Alas, Fabio, Flora commanded me to love her and not to desire her; and my passion, obedient and confused and stained, without desiring her, adores her beauty. What human emotion feels and laments, the understanding enjoys, wooed by the eternal spirit, imprisoned in the mortal cloister which hoards it like a treasure. To love is to know an ardent virtue, to desire is a selfish act of will, perishably gross and discourteous. The body is earth, and will be so, and was nothing; from God the mind proceeds to eternity: I am the eternal lover of an eternal beloved.

Here, the basic contrast between two kinds of love ('querer'/ 'desear' = 'to desire physically'; 'amar' = 'to love spiritually or platonically') is a commonplace of neo-Platonic theory, and 'cuidado' (a stock word in courtly love vocabulary) suggests the idea of love as suffering which runs through the whole tradition. In Platonic terms, the first tercet can be read as simple definition, leading to the neat conclusion in the final line: 'eterno amante soy de eterna amada'. Yet, taken as a whole, the emotional effect the poem creates in the reader is very different. The '¡ay Fabio¡' of the first line sets the tone for the rest. The speaker's love obeys, but is 'confused and 'stained'; in theory, superior love of the understanding transcends the suffering of 'el humano afecto', yet the whole rhetorical strategy of the poem works against this. The key phrase here is 'amartelado del espíritu eterno': 'wooed', but also 'tormented' by the 'eternal spirit'. This emphasizes the conflict between body and mind, since the latter both 'woos' and 'is wooed by' God, and this summons to divine love is a torment to man while his understanding is still imprisoned in the body. Seen in terms of this conflict, the neo-Platonic references fall into place as one of the 'voices' of the poem, as if the speaker were saying: 'I know all about Platonic theory, which says that physical love is only a stage on the way to divine love. I know also that the body dies and the mind is eternal; therefore, if I am forced to love the woman with my mind, I am condemned to being an eternal lover.'

This question of 'voice' takes us back to the notion of a 'rhetorical self' which I referred to at an earlier stage (see above, p. 59). As we have just seen, conflicting 'voices' may emanate from the same speaker; alternatively, as in 'En crespa tempestad ...', the presence of mythological allusions may lend a heroic quality to the voice of the lover, whose case is made to seem equally exceptional. In either instance, it would be wrong to think in terms of a 'personality' 'expressing itself', a concept quite foreign to Renaissance theory. In Quevedo's love sonnets, the 'I' which speaks is always mediated – a 'voice' made up of other 'voices' which are woven together within the confines of the poem. This echo chamber effect is perhaps the most difficult feature of Quevedo's poetry for a modern reader to grasp, since it relies on what Smith calls the 'citational mode',[34] the ability to recognize allusions over a wide range of previous writing, both Renaissance and classical. The difficulty increases when such effects are least conspicuous, that is to say, where an intelligent seventeenth-century reader could be relied on to pick up the most casual of hints. Thus the apparently straightforward sonnet which begins:

> A fugitivas sombras doy abrazos;
> en los sueños se cansa el alma mía;
> paso luchando a solas noche y día
> con un trasgo que traigo entre mis brazos...   (B, p. 377)

I embrace fleeting shadows: my soul wearies itself in dreams; I spend night and day wrestling alone with a phantom I hold within my arms...

belongs to a long tradition of poems which describe the 'embracing of shadows', including Petrarch's own variant, 'Beato in sogno e di languir contento, / d'abbracciar l'ombre e seguir l'aura estiva...' (Blest in sleep and content to languish, to embrace shadows and follow the summer breeze; *Canzoniere*, 212). Petrarch's sonnet, though Quevedo had almost certainly read it, is hardly close enough to constitute a 'source'; the density of the later poem, on the other hand, lies partly in the suggestions of potent classical myths – Narcissus, Orpheus and Eurydice – which contemporary readers would have been able to elaborate from their own knowledge. For once, this is not a matter of imitation but of invoking parallel situations; and it is precisely here that the idea of 'voices' seems most apt, since it is not just Narcissus and Orpheus who impinge on the poem, but *Ovid's* Narcissus and *Virgil's* Orpheus.[35]

This 'I' which constitutes itself by drawing on the 'voices' of existing texts is also the 'I' which defines itself through its relationship to the woman it addresses. This relationship, as we have already seen, is one-sided: the self of these poems is their sole protagonist, and it is the eloquence of this self – its power of rhetorical persuasion – which enables the poem to take shape. Where Quevedo is concerned, we might press the sense of the 'rhetorical self' still further and claim that the depersonalized nature of the woman addressed is an essential part of the poem's rhetoric – in other words, that the argumentative strategies of the poem actually demand that the woman should remain an abstraction. We can see something of what this entails in the sonnet entitled 'Retrato de Lisi que traía en una sortija' (Portrait of Lisi which he [i.e. the speaker] wore in a ring):

> En breve cárcel traigo aprisionado,
> con toda su familia de oro ardiente,
> el cerco de la luz resplandeciente
> y grande imperio del Amor cerrado.
>   Traigo el campo que pacen estrellado
> las fieras altas de la piel luciente:
> y a escondidas del cielo y del Oriente,
> día de luz y parto mejorado.
>   Traigo todas las Indias en mi mano,
> perlas que, en un diamante, por rubíes,
> pronuncian con desdén sonoro yelo,
>   y razonan tal vez fuego tirano
> relámpagos de risa carmesíes,
> auroras, gala y presunción del cielo.   (B, p. 506)

In a tiny cell I bear captive, with all its family of burning gold, the circle of resplendent light and the vast empire of Love enclosed. I wear the starry field where the lofty beasts of gleaming skin graze; and concealed from the sky and the Orient, a day of light and better birth. I wear the whole Indies on my hand, pearls which, in a diamond, through rubies, scornfully utter sonorous ice, and speak at times a tyrannical fire, crimson lightning flashes of laughter, dawns, finery and the presumption of heaven.

As Gareth Walters remarks, this is another of those poems in which the opening stance gives way to something different, 'a shrinking away from what appears conventionally prescribed, whether ennoblement or celebration'.[36] What he has in mind is the shift in the speaker's attitude to the woman which takes place in the second quatrain, from implicit praise to the accusation of cruelty. At the same time, there is no question here of conflicting 'voices': the combination of praise and complaint is a regular feature of the Petrarchan sonnet, as is the *topos* of the portrait on which the whole poem is based. In Petrarch himself, the technique of enumerating the woman's physical characteristics entails a curious kind of fragmentation, in which any sense of the woman as a living presence is dissolved in the contemplation of particulars. In Quevedo's poem, this effect is heightened by the addition of a second *topos* – the ring – which brings with it notions of brevity ('en breve cárcel') and hence of concentration within a small space. Much of the poem's ingenuity comes from the way in which Quevedo works the two *topoi* together: the gold ring sets off the portrait as the woman's hair sets off her face, or as the sun is 'framed' by its own rays – and all of these, one might say, are enclosed by the 'tiny cell' of the poem itself.

The sensuous brilliance of the language, as has often been noticed, comes uncharacteristically close to Góngora,[37] though an image like 'relámpagos de risa carmesíes' (crimson lightning flashes of laughter) – often quoted as an example of Quevedo's 'modernity' – has much older roots, and already appears in slightly less concentrated forms in earlier poems by Quevedo himself. All this indicates that, as so often, Quevedo is revitalizing existing conventions and verbal forms by combining them in new ways. At the same time, the verbal richness is neither arbitrary nor superimposed: by assuming a reader capable of grasping its various subtleties, it both places the poem within the context of other poems which deal with the same *topoi* and reinforces the sense of difference which marks off Quevedo's own achievement. This, one might argue, is partly a matter of exclusion: by avoiding both the sensuality of Latin poetry and the trivializing detail of some of his Spanish and Italian contemporaries, he is deliberately re-creating a distinctly Petrarchan kind of lyric – one which he may well have felt to be under threat. And it is this self-denying, generalizing cast of the poem which ultimately determines the basic relationship: the central position of the protagonist – reinforced quite literally by the repeated 'traigo' – for whose discourse the woman is no more than a necessary point of focus, a depersonalized being who exists only as a function of the speaker's rhetoric.

This sonnet, like 'En crespa tempestad...', belongs to the sequence of seventy poems addressed to a single woman – 'Lisi' – whose real identity, if she ever had one, remains unknown. Quevedo's first editor, González de Salas, clearly thought that these poems were intended to form a *canzoniere*, though their actual arrangement in print, as he admits, is largely his own.[38] Though there is even less anecdotal material than is usual in such sequences – again, a sign of Quevedo's generalizing tendency – the presence of several anniversary sonnets seems consciously to invite comparison with Petrarch, as does the reference to Lisi's death in the final sonnet. There seems little point in trying to distinguish the Lisi poems from those addressed to other women – Aminta, Flora and others – except to note what is obvious: the increase in range compared with the shorter cycles and the presence of certain poems whose intensity is unequalled by any other writer of the period. The finest of these is entitled 'Amor constante más allá de la muerte' (Love Constant Beyond Death):

> Cerrar podrá mis ojos la postrera
> sombra que me llevare el blanco día,
> y podrá desatar esta alma mía
> hora a su afán ansioso lisonjera;
>   mas no, de esotra parte, en la ribera,
> dejará la memoria en donde ardía:
> nadar sabe mi llama la agua fría,
> y perder el respeto a ley severa.
>   Alma a quien todo un dios prisión ha sido,
> venas que humor a tanto fuego han dado,
> medulas que han gloriosamente ardido,
>   su cuerpo dejará, no su cuidado;
> serán ceniza, más tendrá sentido;
> polvo serán, mas polvo enamorado.   (B, p. 511)

The final shadow which will take away from me white day may close my eyes, and an hour indulgent to its anxious longing may set free this soul of mine; but it [i.e. the soul] will not, on the further shore, leave behind the memory in which it used to burn: my flame knows how to swim across the cold water and lose its respect for a harsh law. Soul for which no less than a god has been a prison, veins which have fed moisture to so great a fire, marrows which have gloriously burned, it will abandon its body, but not its love; they will be ash, but it will have feeling; they will be dust, but dust that is in love.

Here, the argumentative tone – 'Cerrar podrá ... podrá desatar ...' – is established from the beginning as a means of introducing the paradox of the second quatrain: the soul whose memory will cross the River Lethe, the 'flame' of love which its waters will not extinguish. In the tercets, however, the argument gives way to celebration: the uncertain future is replaced by a love which has already proved its constancy in the past.[39] The persuasiveness of the poem comes both from the power of its figurative language and from the appearance of logic. Yet this logic, as has often been pointed out, is fallacious: flames can't swim through water, any more than the soul can behave as if it were the body. These non-sequiturs, however, only add to the force of the poem; as Lorna Close puts it:

By means such as these Quevedo eloquently conveys the contradictions of the lover's state, where the power and the glory of the feeling can be measured by its seeming capacity to wrest momentary triumph over and *through* reason itself – a triumph whose poignancy is heightened rather than nullified by our simultaneous awareness that it falls into the category of *impossibilis* and is proof of vain delusion.[40]

Quevedo plays a number of variations on the 'ceniza amante' (loving ash) theme in the course of the Lisi poems. The theme itself is already present in Roman elegy, most specifically in Propertius;[41] once again, it is a 'classical' voice which speaks through Quevedo's poem: the blurring of the body–soul distinction runs counter to any neo-Platonic conception of love, just as the sense of immortality is divorced from any possible Christian context.[42] As we saw in a previous poem, these 'classical' echoes add to the poise of the speaker, whose reticent gravity determines the whole movement of the poem. And significantly, the woman, in this instance, is completely absent from the poem, as if the speaker were intent on defining himself solely in terms of a love whose godlike status is a measure of his own worth.

IV

The metaphysical implications of a poem like this go far beyond the limits of the conventional love sonnet, as if the subject-matter of love were being drawn more and more deeply into the meditation on human fragility which runs through the more strictly moral poems. Coming in what seems its most natural position almost two-thirds of the way through the sequence, 'Cerrar podrá...' represents a precarious kind of triumph whose claims are progressively undermined in the poems that follow. Thus in one of the later sonnets, 'En los claustros del alma la herida / yace callada...' (In the cloisters of the soul the wound lies silent; B, p. 520), the 'ceniza amante' image appears as the sign of a love which has already burnt itself out *before* death:

> Bebe el ardor hidrópica mi vida,
> que ya, ceniza amante y macilenta,
> cadáver del incendio hermoso, ostenta
> su luz en humo y noche fallecida...

My life, mad with thirst, drinks the fire which now, soiled enamoured ash, the corpse of a beautiful conflagration, displays its light expired in smoke and night...

and the poem ends on a note of confusion and horror:

> A los suspiros di la voz del canto,
> la confusión inunda l'alma mía,
> mi corazón es reino del espanto.

I surrendered the voice of song to sighs, confusion floods my soul: my heart is the realm of terror.

This ultimate questioning of the value of love itself is partly what makes the Lisi cycle so compelling, and the voice which speaks through a poem like this is scarcely to be distinguished from that in which Quevedo reflects on the human condition in general. Here again, it is sometimes difficult to separate one kind of poem from another: though satire and burlesque, as we have seen, also involve questions of morality, the moral and religious poems I shall be discussing in this section belong to a more 'serious' mode, in which the vocabulary, and occasionally the themes, of the love poetry tend to reappear in quite different contexts. One unifying factor here is the Neostoicism, or Christian version of Stoicism, which Quevedo seems to have adopted as his personal philosophy at a relatively early stage of his career. As Henry Ettinghausen has shown,[43] Quevedo's continuing dialogue with Seneca and other Stoic philosophers leads him into contradictions of which he scarcely seems aware. Nevertheless, both the possibility of associating Stoic imperturbability with Christian fortitude and the relevance of Stoic attitudes to his own critique of contemporary society provide some of the most powerful themes of his own writing, not least the Senecan equation of life with death which returns almost obsessively in both the poetry and the prose.[44]

One of his most famous sonnets is virtually an adaptation of Seneca:

> Miré los muros de la patria mía,
> si un tiempo fuertes, ya desmoronados,
> de la carrera de la edad cansados,
> por quien caduca ya su valentía.
> Salíme al campo, vi que el sol bebía
> los arroyos del yelo desatados,
> y del monte quejosos los ganados,
> que con sombras hurtó su luz al día.
> Entré en mi casa: vi que, amancillada,
> de anciana habitación era despojos;
> mi báculo, más corvo y menos fuerte.
> Vencida de la edad sentí mi espada,
> y no hallé cosa en que poner los ojos
> que no fuese recuerdo de la muerte.   (B, p. 32)

I beheld the walls of my native place, if once strong, now dilapidated, weary with the passage of time, through which their bravery now fails. I went out into the fields, I saw that the sun was drinking up the streams released from the ice, and that the cattle were complaining of the mountain which stole the light of day with its shadows. I went into my house; I saw that, stained, it was the remnants of an ancient habitation; my staff, more bent and less strong; I felt my sword overcome by age, and I found nothing on which to rest my eyes which was not a reminder of death.

'Patria' here has a distinctly Latin, if not Ovidian, ring to it: not so much 'native land' as 'birthplace' or 'ancestral home'.[45] The main source, however, is Seneca's Twelfth Letter to Lucilius, describing a visit to the author's country house, which begins: 'Wherever I turn, I see fresh evidence of my old age.'[46] It is usual, and natural enough, to read this sonnet as a reflection on time and decay, as a moral poem of a peculiarly 'classical' kind, in which the 'house' is both a real house and a metaphor for the human body. But supposing we were to think of it as a religious poem? An earlier, though not essentially different, version[47] appears in the sequence of 'Psalms' entitled *Heráclito cristiano y segunda arpa a imitación de David* (Christian Heraclitus and Second Harp in Imitation of David), written in 1613. At this time, or a little before it, Quevedo appears to have undergone what Ettinghausen calls an 'acute and prolonged crisis of conscience'.[48] The intention of the poems is penitential, as his note 'To the Reader' makes clear:

You who have heard what I have sung and what was dictated to me by appetite, passion or nature, hear now, with a purer ear, what true feeling and repentance for all the rest of my deeds impel me to say: for these things I lament since knowledge and conscience demand it, and I sang of those other matters since thus I was persuaded by my youth (B, p. 19).[49]

What is crucial, however, is that the twenty-eight poems of the *Heráclito cristiano* form a genuine sequence: though, as Walters points out, the note of resolution wavers from time to time – the lover and the moralist seem frequently in conflict – the last poem of all is both a renunciation of love and an act of dedication to God. Though in the circumstances it is hard to think of this as a definitive ending, the essential movement of the sequence is from the necessary destruction of the sinner's former self to the emergence of a new self through repentance. And read in its context, 'Miré los muros...' takes on a different, more strictly religious, meaning, in which the picture of time and decay is no longer absolute, but a description of the world as it must necessarily appear to the unregenerate soul.

This interpretation is reinforced by Quevedo's use of the Pauline concept of the 'new man',[50] as in the opening poem of the sequence:

> Un nuevo corazón, un hombre nuevo
> ha menester, Señor, la ánima mía;
> desnúdame de mí, que ser podría
> que a tu piedad pagase lo que debo.
> Dudosos pies por ciega noche llevo,
> que ya he llegado a aborrecer el día,
> y temo que hallaré la muerte fría
> envuelta en (bien que dulce) mortal cebo.
> Tu hacienda soy; tu imagen, Padre, he sido,
> y, si no es tu interés en mí, no creo
> que otra cosa defiende mi partido.
> Haz lo que pide verme cual me veo,
> no lo que pido yo: pues, de perdido,
> recato mi salud de mi deseo.   (B, p. 20)

My soul, Lord, requires a new heart, a new man: strip me of myself, that I may pay what I owe to your piety. I walk with stumbling feet through blind night, for now I have come to hate the day, and I fear that I shall find cold death wrapped in a mortal (though sweet-tasting) bait. I am your creature; I have been your image, Father, and, but for your interest in me, I think there is nothing else to defend my cause. Do what seeing me as I am demands, not what I myself demand: since, being lost, I conceal my salvation from my desire.

A poem like this has a good deal in common with those of Lope de Vega discussed in chapter 4 (see above, pp. 105–10), though the quality of the argument, as one might expect with Quevedo, is more subtle. As always with such poems, the reader – or at least the possible second reader – is God Himself, and it is to God that the persuasive forces of the poem are directed. The basic stratagem consists in shifting the emphasis from God the judge to God the advocate, in such a way that the sinner's weakness becomes a source of strength. The most obvious sign of this movement is the parallel shift from 'Lord' ('Señor') to 'Father'. In the opening lines, God is a creditor – someone to whom the speaker owes a debt; by the first tercet, however, He has become the one person capable of defending the sinner's cause. Two other features of the poem help to enforce this change. One is the series of commercial metaphors which runs from the payment of debts to ideas of property and interest. ('Tu hacienda', in line 9, is particularly telling here: literally, 'your creature', but also 'your property' – in other words, something one has a responsibility to administer.) The other is the way the speaker sustains and exploits the division between the 'old' man and the 'new' already established in the first line. This makes possible the paradox two lines later, where 'mí' equals 'my old self', and also underwrites the conflicting claims of the understanding and the senses at the end of the second quatrain. At the end of the poem, the division is re-stated, again in religious terms, in the contrast between 'salvation' and 'desire'. Yet just before this, something more subtle has taken place: the phrase 'tu imagen…he sido' (I was once your image) looks back for a moment to the original Creation, when Adam – the 'old' man – was made in the image of God. And the implication is surely clear: the redemption of the sinner – in St Paul's phrase, the 'putting on of the new man' – will involve nothing less than a new act of creation, a reversal of the original Fall of Adam.

Such openly religious poems, though often impressive, form only a small part of Quevedo's work.[51] More usually, his most serious reflections on human life occur in what Blecua calls the 'metaphysical' poems, of which there are several examples in the *Heráclito cristiano* itself. Here the sense of living speech recalls similar poems by Quevedo's English contemporary John Donne (1572–1631). Like Donne, he is a master of the arresting opening:

> ¡Cómo de entre mis manos te resbalas!
> ¡Oh, cómo te deslizas, edad mía!…   (B, p. 33)

How you slip from my hands! O age, how you slide away!…; or again:

> Ya formidable y espantoso suena
> dentro del corazón el postrer día;…   (B, p. 9)

Now fearful and terrible the final day sounds within my heart…

Even more characteristic of these poems is a quality which has sometimes been termed 'transparency': the sense that, though Quevedo's rhetorical skills are never in abeyance, his manner of deploying them is so natural as to seem inevitable. And occasionally his powers of verbal invention reshape the elements of the language itself in a way which goes beyond anything attempted by his contemporaries:

> '¡Ah de la vida!'…¿Nadie me responde?
> ¡Aquí de los antaños que he vivido!
> La Fortuna mis tiempos ha mordido;
> las Horas mi locura las esconde.

¡Que sin poder saber cómo ni adónde
la salud y la edad se hayan huído!
Falta la vida, asiste lo vivido,
y no hay calamidad que no me ronde.
    Ayer se fue, mañana no ha llegado;
hoy se está yendo sin parar un punto;
soy un fue, y un será, y un es cansado.
    En el hoy y mañana y ayer, junto
pañales y mortaja, y he quedado
presentes sucesiones de difunto.   (B, p. 4)

'Hello there, life!'…No one replies? Here with you, past years that I have lived! Fortune has gnawed away my time; my folly hides the Hours. That without being able to know how or whither, health and years have flown away! Life is absent, what has been lived is present, and there is no calamity which does not haunt me. Yesterday is gone; tomorrow has not arrived; today is going without a moment's pause; I am a 'was', and a 'will be' and a weary 'is'. In my today, tomorrow and yesterday, I join together swaddling clothes and shroud, and I remain the present successions of a dead man.

Here, the colloquial tone is established in the opening words: ''¡Ah de la vida!'' builds on the common phrase '¡Ah de la casa!' (Is there anyone in?) – the cry of a traveller arriving at a house, but now twisted, so that the 'house' is the speaker's own life, whose emptiness echoes only with his own voice. The implied metaphor extends into the second line. 'Aquí de…' is a phrase normally used to summon assistance: what are being summoned here, however, are 'los antaños' – a plural noun made out of the adverb 'antaño' (last year; in former times). Again, the verbal twist reinforces the general sense: to recall one's past life is like calling for servants or followers in a deserted house. This estrangement of the speaker from his own life, so vividly dramatized in the opening lines, is encapsulated in the astonishing paradox of verse 7; here, the apparent contrast between 'falta' (is lacking) and 'asiste' (is present) is an illusion: if 'life' is absent, the past ('lo vivido') which is 'present' to the speaker has itself already been defined as an absence, so that being and non-being are ultimately indistinguishable. From this point onwards, the emphasis shifts from space to time: in the first tercet, both syntax and punctuation reinforce the disjunction of past, present and future, as if the present moment were simply a transition from one absence to another. What is remarkable here is the way this sense of dislocation is carried into the sentence itself: 'se está yendo' (is going away) is already an unusual form of the verb 'ir' (to go), and this verbal deviation is compounded by the extraordinary eleventh line, where the three tenses of the verb 'to be' are wrenched into defining nouns. This triple self-definition – the speaker is past, present and future *simultaneously* – firmly sweeps aside any question of disjunction or continuity. Birth and death are emblematically joined as all tenses are telescoped into one, and the last line has the chilling precision, and also the Latinate sound, of a legal formula: if each moment – each 'present' – dies as another succeeds, then individual existence is a continuous series of deaths, in which life and death are ultimately synonymous.[52]

If one calls such a poem 'metaphysical', this is partly out of deference to literary history, partly because it embodies the kind of problems traditionally associated with metaphysics. Quevedo himself, however, would probably have found the term strange; as I have tried to suggest all along, he would have been much more likely to have explained both his aims and practice in the light of Renaissance theory, in particular the notion of 'eloquence' which Quintilian defines as 'the production and communication to the audience of all that the speaker has conceived in his mind'.[53] If the intensely verbal nature of his art and the persuasive power of its rhetoric are qualities which he felt it necessary to defend, this is both a measure of his trust in earlier tradition and the sign of an achievement which, for all its apparent 'modernity', can only be fully understood in the terms which he himself would have recognized.

CHAPTER 7

The literary epic

I

One kind of poetry has so far been left out of account: the literary epic. One reason for this is practical: the difficulty of dealing adequately with a genre whose chief examples run to many thousands of lines and, more often than not, are surrounded by an equally vast amount of critical debate. Another is the sense that Renaissance literary epic stands somewhat apart from the rest of the poetry of the time, both in the minds of contemporary readers and in the practice of the poets themselves – a notion that may help to explain, if not to excuse, the relative indifference of modern readers. Yet any suggestion that this is a peripheral genre is belied by Renaissance theory itself: with the possible exception of tragedy, epic is normally regarded as the highest kind of poetic writing, the most 'magnificent' and also the most comprehensive. Thus, as Scaliger puts it:

> In every sphere some one thing is fitting and preeminent, which may serve as a standard for the others; so that all the rest may be referred to it. So in the whole of poetry the epic genre, in which the nature and life and actions of heroes are recounted, seems to be chief. According to its pattern the remaining parts of poetry are directed...[1]

Such arguments for the centrality of epic are a commonplace of the time and derive essentially from the Renaissance reading of classical theory. If they make it clear that the epic is the genre to which every poet should aspire, they also raise the whole question of what sixteenth-century poets and theorists – often the same people – actually understood by 'epic' and how they conceived the actual writing of an epic poem. Here, the term 'literary epic' itself implies what, for modern readers at least, is a crucial division, between what is sometimes called 'primary epic' (Homer, *Beowulf*, the *Chanson de*

Roland, the *Poema de mío Cid*) and 'secondary epic' (Virgil's *Aeneid*, the *Pharsalia* of Lucan and the Renaissance epic itself). In terms of this distinction, 'primary epic' belongs to, or is at least related to, an oral tradition, with the special techniques this entails; 'secondary epic', on the other hand, though it may retain certain features of 'primary epic' – the Homeric simile, for instance – is essentially *written* epic, both more historically conscious and more explicit in its values. Such differences, however, can hardly have been so clear in the sixteenth century: the only 'primary epics' available to Renaissance writers were the *Odyssey* and the *Iliad* – more often read in Latin translation than in Greek, and with no sense of their oral origins. Certain distinctions *are* made, to be sure, as when Tasso – by far the most intelligent theorist of the time – claims that Virgil is superior to Homer because of his power of generalization;[2] nevertheless, there is a marked tendency to read Homer, and especially the *Iliad*, through the eyes of Virgil, as Tasso himself seems to do when he describes Homeric epic in general as a 'praise of virtue'.

Virgil, then, is the chief though, as we shall see in a moment, not the only model for Renaissance epic. As C. S. Lewis has pointed out, it is Virgil who brings to the epic the idea of a 'great subject', something which implies both historical perspective and a sense of national mission which goes beyond individual heroism.[3] Like other great writers, Virgil tends to be interpreted in accordance with the needs of a particular age: thus, where modern scholars frequently stress the ambivalence of the *Aeneid* – for example, what one recent critic calls 'the tension between patriotic optimism and private sorrow'[4] – Renaissance writers seize mainly on its 'public' qualities, in particular the extent to which it represents the 'making of a nation'. The relevance of this to sixteenth-century notions of empire building hardly needs to be stressed; what is more interesting is the kind of epic hero it presupposes and which reappears, with certain variations, in a great number of sixteenth- and seventeenth-century poems. One of the central facts, of course, about Aeneas is that he is a group hero, someone whose personal motives and desires must often be sacrificed for the common good. Hence the epithet *pius* which is constantly applied to him: the sense that he is spiritually responsible for those who share in his enterprise. Thus one arrives at the idea of a central figure who stands for something else, as Goffredo in Tasso's *Gerusalemme Liberata* (Jerusalem Freed; 1581) may be said to represent Christian chivalry. It is this sense of vocation in a national cause, expressed at the furthest stretch of the poetic imagination, which makes Virgil the supreme example for many later writers of epic, and at the same time suggests a development which Virgil himself could hardly have foreseen, namely the religious epic. As we shall see, the problem of adapting pagan epic to Christian themes is fraught with difficulties; nevertheless, in a very real sense the shift from literary epic to specifically religious epic is already prepared for by Virgil himself, as Lewis has rightly argued: 'If we are to have another epic it must go on from Virgil. Any return to the *merely* heroic... will now be an anachronism. The explicit religious subject for any future epic has been dictated by Virgil; it is the only further development left.'[5]

Not all Renaissance epics are religious epics, though most, as one would expect, have a strong Christian dimension. Nor is Virgil the only classical model: as Frank Pierce has shown, certain poems of Claudian invite a 'Christian' interpretation which could be exploited in religious poems;[6] more importantly, Lucan's *Pharsalia* – in some ways a deliberately non-Virgilian poem – suggested the possibility of writing an epic on comparatively recent events (in his case, the Civil War between Caesar and Pompey) and at the same time of dispensing altogether with supernatural machinery.[7] What complicates the situation I have just described, however, is something more fundamental: the existence alongside the Virgilian tradition of a very different kind of writing, often referred to as 'romantic' or 'chivalric' epic. Here, the two great examples are both Italian: Boiardo's *Orlando Innamorato* (Orlando in Love), left unfinished at his death in 1494, and Ariosto's continuation, the *Orlando Furioso* (The Madness of Orlando), first published in 1516 and added to in 1532. Boiardo's poem has been described as a 'brilliant but almost purely external spectacle of superhuman feats of valour, marvellous enchantments and frankly sensual loves, all informed by an unsubtle but rich humour'[8] – a courtly entertainment based, significantly, on popular tradition. Both facts are important: with Boiardo and Ariosto, the subject-matter of earlier French epic – specifically, the story of Charlemagne's invasion of Spain and his defeat at Roncesvalles – becomes part of the general stock of Renaissance poetry, though in the greatly modified form which Boiardo inherits from popular medieval tradition. What both Boiardo and Ariosto retain from this tradition is the sense of an active relationship between poet and audience: the right both to comment on the narrative and to manipulate the material for various kinds of literary effect. In

Ariosto's more sophisticated version, this amounts to the creation of a new kind of discourse: much of the formal interest of the poem comes from the calculated interruptions by which one story is replaced by another, only to be resumed at a later point – a feature regularly imitated by later writers – and the way this serves to control both poem and audience. This 'web-like' design, to use Ariosto's own phrase, produces what one critic has called 'a narrative that narrates itself being narrated'[9] – an infinitely expandable discourse which exists at several removes from any outside world. All this, of course, is very different from the relative impersonality of the classical epic, and the difference is compounded by the nature of the subject-matter itself. By choosing to centre his poem on the episode of Orlando's madness – Orlando (the Roland of the *Chanson de Roland*) becomes insanely jealous of Angelica's love for Medoro – Ariosto is building on the connection between literature and desire already present in Boiardo. One of the reasons why the poem can never be completely terminated is that desire itself, as Ariosto presents it, will never allow any sexual relationship to be successfully resolved. Thus Orlando's madness is only one particular manifestation of the inherent logic of desire; if, as Durling argues, the poem itself is no more than 'a lucid interval of mind in the rush of universal madness',[10] the author himself, as he appears in his text, makes no claim to be exempt from the general workings of desire and error. The great symbol of this in the poem is the forest – an image which recurs in many of Ariosto's imitators – where lovers lose themselves in their pursuit of illusory objects of desire: a 'forest of appearances' whose shifting nature reflects back on the complexities of the poem as a whole and on the ambiguous situation of the narrator himself.

Chivalric epic, as developed by Boiardo and Ariosto, is clearly a mixed kind of poetry, containing elements of classical epic, the *chanson de geste* and medieval courtly and popular romance. Half a century after Ariosto, Torquato Tasso (1544–95), the greatest theorist of the literary epic as well as one of its finest practitioners, compares the variety of the heroic poem to that of the universe itself:

Just so, I judge, the great poet...can form a poem in which, as in a little world, one may read here of armies assembling, here of battles on land and sea, here of conquests of cities, skirmishes and duels, here of jousts, here descriptions of hunger and thirst, here tempests, fires, prodigies, there of celestial and infernal councils, there seditions, there discord, wanderings, adventures, enchantments, deeds of cruelty, daring, courtesy, generosity, there the fortunes of love, now happy, now sad, now joyous, now pitiful. Yet the poem that contains so great a variety of matters none the less should be one...[11]

Apart from the reference to 'celestial and infernal councils' – a clear echo of classical epic – this might almost be a description of the *Orlando Furioso*. The last sentence, however, should give us pause: the whole passage, in fact, forms part of Tasso's contribution to a debate which had already been going on for some time in Italy concerning the unity or otherwise of Ariosto's poem. The question of unity versus multiplicity lies at the heart of Tasso's own theory and practice and is crucial to the discussion of the literary epic as a whole. Tasso's own solution is to distinguish between what he calls 'simple' and 'composite' unity, a strategy which expands the idea of unity itself, though not far enough to embrace what he regards as the 'confusion' of Ariosto's multiplicity. In this, as in other respects, Tasso, as has often been observed, is torn between the comparative freedom of Renaissance models and the demands of Counter-Reformation Catholicism.

As the *Gerusalemme Liberata* confirms, Tasso's imagination is deeply stirred by the subject-matter of romance; despite the impersonality of his narrative, which contrasts sharply with Ariosto's discursiveness, the world he creates is an intensely private one, shot through with the kind of tensions he attempts to resolve in his theorizing. From the latter it is clear that, for Tasso, a 'correct' epic must be both Virgilian and Christian; at the same time, he insists that epic and romance constitute a single genre, to be judged by identical standards, thus cutting through many of the intricacies of the contemporary debate. Other points follow from this: a) an epic must be 'truthful' and its subject, therefore, should be taken from Christian history; b) epic style should be 'magnificent', combining the 'simple gravity' of tragedy with the 'intricate loveliness' (*fiorita vaghezza*) of lyric; c) characters, both historical and fictional, should be open to allegorical interpretation; d) epic must also deal with the 'marvellous'. On this last point, Tasso writes: 'In my judgement, it is very necessary that any heroic poem should include the marvellous, that which goes beyond the usual action and even beyond human possibility, whether it be presented as the power of the gods as in the poems of the pagans, or as the power of angels, devils and magicians as in all modern poetry.'

What all this means in practice can best be seen in the *Gerusalemme* itself: here, the choice of subject – the First Crusade – is both historical and Christian, and at the same time goes back to something approaching the area of the earlier romances. Where it differs from the chivalric epic, however, is in its intense seriousness: more specifically, in the way it imposes a Virgilian manner on its romance material. Thus the traditional quest, with its possibilities of confusion and error, becomes a crusade for a definite, divinely sanctioned, end – one which embodies in a Christian form the Virgilian sense of mission. Among the various features of the poem which are to influence later epics, two seem especially important. One is the way in which Tasso incorporates the values of pagan epic within his own poem. Far from condemning pagan literature – something which his admiration for Virgil and Aristotle would scarcely have countenanced – he continues to regard it as a source of order and beauty only less adequate than the present Christian dispensation. And so with the theme of heroism: in the course of the poem, the classical world is invariably associated with the pagan point of view; the two great Muslim figures, Solimano and Argante, are both heroic and tragic, and their behaviour is clearly intended to arouse wonder and admiration in the reader. And this is the point; as a recent critic puts it: 'Their fate determines the boundaries of a classic heroic vision in Tasso's poem. He incorporates the poetry of ancient heroism into his epic as tragedy contained within the larger movement to salvation.'[12] The other feature takes us back to the question of unity and multiplicity and at the same time helps to confirm the Christian implications of the poem. The taking of Jerusalem by the Christians is both the aim of the action and the point of completion towards which the poem itself is striving. Because of man's fallen nature, however, the action can only be fulfilled as the result of divine intervention; in the course of the campaign, the Christian armies are continually deflected from their purpose by dissension and self-interest. Such episodes, to be sure, provide the poem with a good deal of its variety; what holds together such potentially disruptive material, however, is the sense in which each unit in the series represents an obstacle to be overcome in the long-term pursuit of victory. Thus for Tasso heroism becomes an inward quality: the real obstacles lie in human nature itself and can only be overcome by reason, self-mastery and faith, just as the final capture of Jerusalem represents both a literal triumph and the poem's own achievement in bringing order out of multiplicity.

The two finest examples of literary epic produced in the Peninsula – Camões's *Os Lusíadas* (The Lusiads; 1572) and Ercilla's *La Araucana* (1569–90) – both date from the last third of the sixteenth century. Camões's poem falls outside the scope of this study, though as Frank Pierce rightly insists, the fact that it is written in Portuguese by no means separates it from the rest of the Hispanic tradition and its influence was at least as great in Spain as in Portugal. Like Tasso, Camões takes Virgil as his principal model, but with some striking differences: though the Virgilian sense of mission is equally strong, the historical material of *Os Lusíadas* – the voyage of Vasco da Gama to India – has a much more direct bearing on the present and is combined very powerfully with the author's own experience. Again, though Da Gama himself takes the place of Aeneas in the poem, the true hero is a collective one: Portugal, or rather the 'sons of Lusus' to whom the title refers. And what is particularly important for the future of the literary epic is the combination of Virgilian and non-Virgilian elements: though Camões uses romance material in his poem, as in the Island of Love episode, this is never allowed to interfere with the moral purpose of the poem or to develop into the kind of fantasy world one finds in the *Gerusalemme Liberata*; similarly, if one bears in mind the increasing role of allegory in the later epic, the strategy by which Camões preserves the force of the pagan gods by making them into the instruments of divine providence creates what is perhaps the best solution of all to the problem of how to adapt the supernatural machinery of classical epic to a Christian context.[13]

On the face of it, Ercilla's *La Araucana* is a very different kind of poem: an epic account of the author's own experience as a soldier in the recent campaign against the Araucanian Indians of Chile. Though certain episodes are clearly modelled on the *Aeneid*, the poem avoids all references to the pagan or the supernatural and any sense of mission is severely qualified by the unheroic brutality of the events it records. In the course of the poem, one is made aware of the mental gulf which separates Ercilla – the last of the Renaissance soldier-poets – from the medieval attitudes of the *conquistadores* themselves, and also from the professional bureaucracy to which he is ultimately responsible. Significantly, the heroic dimension of the poem concerns, not the behaviour of the Spanish troops, but that of the Indians, whose efforts to 'redeem and maintain' their liberty – the phrase he uses in his preface – excite his deepest admiration. Most modern commentators, from the early nineteenth century onwards, have referred to the attractive personality of the poet-narrator; what has been less frequently observed, however, is the extent to which Ercilla's general mode of discourse relates to Ariosto. As Maxime Chevalier points out,[14] the opening lines of the *Araucana* –

> No las damas, amor, no gentilezas
> De caballeros canto enamorados,
> Ni las muestras, regalos y ternezas
> De amorosos afectos y cuidados...

I sing, not of ladies, passion or the fine deeds of knights in love, nor of the signs, the munificence, the tendernesses of loving affection and care...

– are in no sense intended as a criticism of Ariosto, but more as a way of taking up a stance towards a poet whom Ercilla regards as the 'new Virgil'. Thus for Ercilla, as for Tasso, there is no essential difference between romance epic and heroic epic. What Ercilla takes from Ariosto, on the other hand, is not so much romance material as what Chevalier calls his 'alert tone', a narrative voice which can comment on the action in ways which directly involve the reader, often with Ariosto's own sense of ironic distancing.

The popularity of the *Araucana*, which went into ten editions between 1590 and 1632 and was widely read in Spanish America, should make one reflect on the nature of the reading public for the literary epic. In Spain, the opportunity it gave for seeing national history in an epic perspective at a time of imperial expansion clearly accounts for a great part of its appeal, as does the fact that such poems were often linked to the fortunes and ancestry of particular aristocratic families, if not to those of the king himself. Moreover, the actual subject-matter of the epics is often reflected in other genres: historical writing, the ballad (both traditional and 'new'), lyric poetry and the theatre. (It is worth noting that most literary epics, unlike many shorter poems, were actually published in their authors' lifetimes.) One of the strongest reasons for their success, however, must have been their very 'seriousness', the fact that they were generally taken to represent the noblest of all genres. As Chevalier argues, everything points to the existence of a considerable number of educated people – by no means confined to the aristocracy – for whom the reading of epic verse must have seemed preferable to the mere entertainment value of prose fiction and the average lyric poetry of the time.[15] And one sign of this is the reaction of the poets themselves: the fact that for Góngora, Lope de Vega and a number of lesser poets writing around 1600, a poem like the *Araucana* could serve as a quarry for images and rhetorical figures which gradually came to form part of the general stock of seventeenth-century poetry.[16]

II

The examples of Ariosto and Tasso are crucial to the history of the Spanish literary epic, though, as we shall see, the influence of the *Orlando Furioso* had already begun to decline before 1600, to be replaced by imitations of Tasso or by the specifically religious epics I shall discuss in the final section.[17] One symptom of this change is the tendency to concentrate on single episodes from the *Orlando*, thus reducing the epic scope of the original and pushing it in the direction of romantic fantasy. The outstanding example here is Barahona de Soto's unfinished *Las lágrimas de Angélica* (The Tears of Angelica; 1586), a splendid piece of lyrical writing in narrative form, whose diction looks forward at times to the major poems of Góngora. Where Barahona at least preserves something of the moral seriousness of the epic, Lope de Vega's long poem on the same theme, *La hermosura de Angélica* (The Beauty of Angelica; 1602), represents a further stage of reduction, in which the loves of Angelica and Medoro are seen as a mere game, devoid of moral implications and completely closed off from reality.[18]

The one exception to this process is *El Bernardo*, the remarkable poem by Bernardo de Balbuena (1568–1627), published in 1624, though largely completed, it seems, by 1600. Though Balbuena was Spanish by birth, his poem was written in Mexico – further evidence of the close connection between the literary epic and the New World. The Bernardo of the title is Bernardo del Carpio, the legendary hero who is held to have defeated Charlemagne and his knights at the Battle of Roncesvalles which forms the climax of the poem. Thus the subject-matter is linked both to Spanish tradition – Bernardo del Carpio already figures in the medieval ballads and chronicles and in several earlier sixteenth-century narrative poems – and to the world of the *Orlando Furioso*, most of whose principal characters appear in the course of the poem.

Balbuena himself seems to have intended his poem as the culmination of the Boiardo–Ariosto tradition. Like Tasso, he sees the romance epic and the classical epic as a single genre, though his attempts to combine the two lead him into the kind of difficulties which Tasso himself is careful to avoid. To judge from his preface – the most intelligent theoretical statement of its kind in Spanish – Balbuena's intention seems to have been to express his romance material along classical lines. Thus the main characters are not only related to Ariosto, but also correspond to those of the *Iliad*: Bernardo and Roland/Orlando are modelled on Achilles and Hector, Ferraguto on Ajax, Morgante on Diomedes. And in the course of the poem, there are constant references, usually in the form of Homeric-type similes, to the world of Greek myth and legend. At the same time, Balbuena's attitude to 'truth' is very different from Tasso's: where Tasso insists on the need for a historical subject, he readily concedes the legendary nature of Bernardo's exploits and goes on to justify his procedure in terms of Aristotle's distinction between poetry and history: 'Thus it matters not for my work whether the traditions which I follow are certain or fabulous; for the less history they contain and the more plausible invention, the closer I shall have attained to the perfection I desire for it.' This already suggests what is true of the poem as a whole: that whatever his attempts to 'regularize' the romance epic by reference to classical models, Balbuena is too attached to his romance material to achieve anything like a true balance. Yet if it is difficult to remember the Homeric paradigm when one is actually reading the poem, the distance from Ariosto is equally obvious. Though Balbuena is closely indebted to Ariosto in his descriptions of war and chivalry – more so than in the love episodes – his tone, though occasionally capable of familiarity, is generally more serious, and the more epic passages of the poem are cast in a distinctly Virgilian high style. Moreover, as Frank Pierce has observed, there are times when the *Bernardo* comes close to the Christian epic, with its clear distinction between good and evil; where the romance tends to respect its Muslim protagonists, who are seen as part of a single world of chivalry, for Balbuena, as later for Lope de Vega, the division between Christian and infidel is clear-cut, with the good all on one side.[19]

These are not the only problems the poem raises: though it pays its tribute to divine providence, its supernatural machinery barely hangs together, and occasionally contradicts itself; moreover, despite a heavy insistence on mutability, there is a notable absence of any intellectual design which is actually realized within the poem. In a romance epic, one might argue, this is not necessarily a disadvantage: what matters, as in the *Orlando* itself, is the creation of a convincing world, not the fulfilment of an intellectual purpose. Yet this can scarcely apply to Balbuena, who goes out of his way to enforce a moral pattern on his poem in the form of allegorical commentary. Thus each of his twenty-four cantos concludes with a prose allegory: 'The Fates signify the effects and passions of the sensitive soul... Alcina, the appetite of love, Morgana, that of riches, Febosilla, that of fame...' (I), or again:

In Angelica, pursued by Venus and Alcina, who signifies the love of the senses, it is shown how, the flower of her youth now beginning to fade with time, it was inevitable that in those who beheld her, the delight she once gave should also fail, or in what way honour, signified by Angelica, is ever persecuted and soiled by sensuality... (XI).

Such allegorical treatment of the epic becomes increasingly common in the course of the sixteenth century, either in the form of glosses by other writers, as in the early commentaries on the *Orlando Furioso*, or of the author's own additions to his text, as with Tasso and Balbuena himself. At the same time, this allegorical dimension comes to be taken for granted by theorists; as López Pinciano puts it in his *Philosophia antigua poética* (1596): 'Epic has another soul within its soul, in such a way that what before was soul, that is to say the argument, is seen to be the body and matter beneath which is hidden that more perfect and essential soul, which is called allegory.' In his preface, Balbuena speaks of the 'hidden moral and allegory' of his poem as a means of persuading the reader to virtue, though nowhere does he define allegory precisely, and generally fails to distinguish moral symbolism from allegory proper. More seriously, the allegorical interpretations often fail to engage convincingly with the text; to read the adventures of Orimandro, Rinalso and Morgante as illustrating the operation of memory, understanding and will means discarding much of the richness and flexibility of the poem itself. Elsewhere, it is clear that Balbuena is using allegory as a way of rationalizing the fantastic; yet once again, as Frank Pierce has pointed out, the effect is either to overcomplicate what is basically simple or to simplify poetic fictions whose power lies precisely in their irreducibility.[20]

If Balbuena's allegorical commentaries, for all their seriousness, remain essentially marginal, this is partly because of the ability of the poem itself to resist such an approach. Seen as a whole, the *Bernardo* may seem to bear out the judgement of the eighteenth-century critic Juan Pablo Forner: 'a mine of poetry rather than a poem'. Yet despite obvious faults of construction – abrupt transitions, the fact that several of the main characters unaccountably disappear from the plot – the poem, read page by page, seldom fails to compel one's imagination and the quality of the verse is remarkably sustained. Like Ariosto, Balbuena gives full force to the traditional quest symbols of the forest and the sea – both actual places and the sites of strange encounters. In Balbuena, however, these are part of a much wider cosmic vision which, through skilful use of prophecies and magical voyages, can take in both Europe and the New World. What strikes one in all this is Balbuena's descriptive power, as in Bernardo's underwater journey (Book IX) or the episode of the magic mirror in Book XXI:

> Así en tan nueva perspectiva hecho,
> Que salir de su centro parecía
> Un movible escuadrón, que trecho a trecho
> Por el lustroso alinde se extendía;
> Y aunque en espacio de compás estrecho,
> Puesto en diámetros tales, que hacía
> En la más firme vista la figura
> De entera proporción y hermosura.
>
> Ahora el techo y distancias de la sala
> En tal aspecto y reflexión tuviese,
> Que cuanto en ella por adorno y gala
> El pincel puso, en su cristal se viese;
> O el arte alí a lo natural iguala,
> O con cercos su artífice fingiese
> Bullirse tras la clara vidriera
> Encantadas figuras de oro y cera...   (p. 360a)[21]

Thus it was constructed in such a novel perspective that from its centre there seemed to issue a moving squadron which at intervals stretched along its gleaming border; and though in the space of a narrow compass, placed in such diameters that to the most attentive gaze it offered a figure complete in its proportions and beauty. Now the roof and distances of the hall must have appeared reflected in such a way that everything the artist's brush had placed in it by way of ornament and decoration might be seen in its mirror; either art there is the equal of nature, or its creator, with his circles, must have made magic figures of gold and wax appear to move behind the clear glass...

Here, both the nature and the details of the description suggest something which is true of the poem as a whole: that Balbuena's fantasy world is also in many ways a world of artifice, a version of the supernatural in which the precision of the invention is balanced by a similar precision in the writing. Nevertheless, it would be wrong to praise the poem solely for its non-epic features. Though Balbuena has difficulty in combining the supernatural with his patriotic theme, the political dimensions of the poem – the rivalry between Spain and France – links an awareness of contemporary political relations to a sure sense of the national myth on which imperial claims continue to feed. This, at least, is genuine epic material, displayed at its best in the splendidly orchestrated account of the Battle of Roncesvalles which concludes the poem. And it is here, finally, that Balbuena achieves something of the 'magnificence' which Tasso finds in the Virgilian epic, as in his vision of the converging armies and the classical simile which introduces Morgante – the Ajax of the poem – as he goes to meet his death:

> Muévense entrambos campos, semejantes
> A dos tejidas selvas, cuyos pinos
> Son espigadas lanzas relumbrantes,
> Y las copadas hayas yelmos finos;
> Las ramas sus plumeros tremolantes,
> Donde hace el viento bellos remolinos,
> Y a las varias centellas del acero,
> En que el sol quiebra, se arde el bosque entero.
>
> ...
>
> Cual soberbio centauro que el monte Osa
> En veloz curso rompe y atraviesa,
> Y entero un pino da a la poderosa
> Mano, haciendo de él liviana empresa;
> Tiembla la alta montaña cavernosa,
> Y él, cual turbio raudal rota la presa,
> Hasta arrojarse en el vecino valle,
> Por cuanto al paso encuentra hace calle...   (p. 392a)

Both armies begin to move, like two dense forests whose pines are tall shining lances and whose spreading beeches are fine helmets; their branches trembling plumes, stirred by the wind in beautiful eddies, and with the various flashes of steel on which the sunlight breaks, the entire wood catches fire... Like a proud centaur which disturbs and crosses Mount Ossa in rapid flight and snatches up a whole pine tree in its powerful hand, making light of it; the tall, cavernous mountain trembles, and he, like the dense mass of water when a dam bursts, carves a passage through whatever stands in his way until he plunges into the nearby valley...

Such clear, unmetaphorical language must have seemed faintly archaic by 1624, the year in which the *Bernardo* was first published. Moreover, as Maxime Chevalier has demonstrated, the influence of Ariosto was by then a thing of the past: 'In 1624, no one believes any more in the epic value of the Ariosto-type narratives, and the greatest writers are no longer prepared to take them seriously.'[22] One sign of this is the appearance of the mock epic, a type of poem which I shall be discussing in the next section. In the meantime, however, the balance shifts decisively from Ariosto to Tasso – both to Tasso's own example and to his interpretation of Virgilian epic – as one can see from the most ambitious poem of the period, Lope de Vega's *La Jerusalén Conquistada* (Jerusalem Conquered; 1609).[23] As Lope explains in his preface, this vast poem – over 24,000 lines, divided into twenty Books – is intended as a continuation of the *Gerusalemme Liberata*,[24] an attempt, as we shall see in a moment, to move the subject-matter of the Italian poem on to Spanish ground.

There is no doubting the seriousness of Lope's intentions: the composition of the poem, by his own account, took him seven years, and he clearly regarded it as the most important work he had so far undertaken. This desire to present himself at all costs as a 'learned' writer accounts, unfortunately, for much of the ill-digested erudition of the preface and notes, as well as for the many obscure allusions in the text itself. One particular confusion concerns the actual subject-matter of the poem: the story of the Third Crusade (1187–92), the unsuccessful attempt by Richard Coeur-de-Lion and Philippe-Auguste of France to recapture Jerusalem from the forces of Saladin. It is here that Lope's patriotic intentions come into play: if Tasso had excluded Spain from his own epic, this must be rectified by imposing a strong Spanish presence on the new poem. Thus in his preface, Lope begins by claiming, on quite specious historical grounds, that Alfonso VII of Castile took an active part in the campaign, only to undercut his own argument by appealing to Aristotle's distinction between poetry and truth: 'And even if all this were far from the truth (as no Spaniard should believe), it is enough that Aristotle said: "It is not the function of the poet to relate what has happened, but what *may* happen – what is possible according to the law of probability or necessity".' This is the same argument which Balbuena

uses – much more convincingly – to justify his own departures from
'truth'; in Lope, however, it serves only to reveal his failure to reflect
seriously on the epic theory with which he attempts to impress his
readers.

Even if one grants Lope his poetic fiction, however, the poem
contains a number of glaring defects, most of which were pointed out
by early critics. Thus Quintana, writing in 1833 in what is still one of
the most perceptive essays on the literary epic,[25] remarks not only on
the frequent opacity and pretentiousness of the language – a natural
reaction on the part of an essentially neoclassical critic – but also on
the failure to create characters of genuine epic stature and on the way
in which the constant interruptions and digressions detract from the
main plot. The title itself, in fact, belies the reader's expectations:
Jerusalem is never 'conquered'; before the end of the poem, the
Christian leaders disperse in pursuit of their own interests and the last
four Books – included perhaps to match the twenty cantos of the
Gerusalemme Liberata – move away from the central subject to take in
the captivity of the English king and the sexual misdemeanours of
Alfonso VIII. Again, the significance of the poem's subtitle, 'epopeya
trágica' (tragic epic) is never made clear: at times it seems to refer to
the fact that Jerusalem is in the hands of the Saracens, though
towards the end it may point to the actual failure of the Christian
enterprise. The comparison with Tasso is especially revealing: though
Lope appears to have modelled certain characters and situations on
the *Gerusalemme*, his poem has nothing of Tasso's inward quality, and
the various authorial interventions scarcely affect the extrovert
nature of the whole.

All this might incline one to dismiss the *Jerusalén Conquistada* as an
aberration on the part of a writer of admittedly enormous poetic
talent. Though one cannot excuse the faults of the poem by turning
them into 'Baroque' virtues, as Entrambasaguas notoriously tries to
do,[26] there are nevertheless many points at which one is made aware
of Lope's real strengths, both as poet and narrator. Often this is a
matter of language, as when Richard Coeur-de-Lion is seen fording
a river on horseback:

> Pero Ricardo con la dura espuela
> Hiere al bridón, y en el cristal rompido,
> Parece que discurre por la tela,
> En esferas de espuma sumergido...
>
> (Book VIII, stanza 5; I, p. 310)

But Richard, with his hard spur, strikes the horse's snaffle and, in the broken crystal [i.e. the water], he seems to travel along the surface, submerged in globes of foam...

or again, in the sudden image which fixes the appearance of the Christian armies to their enemies:

> De tanta roja Cruz viene compuesto,
> Que al Persa, que los muros coronaba,
> Parece al descubrir las armas solas
> Trigo de Abril listado de amapolas.
>
> (Book IX, stanza 76; I, p. 372)

It [i.e. the Christian army] is composed of so many Red Crosses that to the Persian on top of the wall it seems, as he sights the arms alone, like corn in April streaked with poppies.

These, to be sure, are small-scale effects; nevertheless, the general effectiveness of Lope's similes suggests what is true of much longer sections of the poem: that a great deal of the best writing occurs in the course of digressions, most notably in the various examples of ekphrasis – the verbal description of a real or imaginary work of art – and in the descriptions of arms and chivalresque display, where Lope is able to draw on the strengths of the traditional ballads. Such passages, like the description of the Temple of Jerusalem (Book IV) or the impressive account of Saladin's treasures (Book XV), are among the great setpieces of the poem, and the technique they represent is a constant feature of epic writing from Homer onwards. Even so, not all the best qualities of the *Jerusalén Conquistada* are to be found in its incidentals; as Lapesa points out,[27] Lope's writing is often at its best in potentially dramatic situations, as in the scene where the arrogant Pacheco sits down in the presence of Saladin (Book XV) or in the romantic adventures of Ismenia – a blend of Tasso's Erminia and Clorinda – whose unrequited passion for the Spanish king leads her to disguise herself as a Christian knight. Above all, perhaps, there is a compassion for human suffering in any form, as in the description of the plague which strikes the German army on its way to Palestine:

> Las calles que el ejército cubría.
> Y en tantas ocasiones se cerraban,
> De una y otra lucida compañía,
> Que el paso a los plebeyos ocupaban:
> Ya el azote del cielo descubría
> De suerte, que de lejos se miraban,

Como después que del granizo horrendo
Se van las densas balas deshaciendo.

Book v, stanza 127; I, p. 220)

The streets which the army filled and which on so many occasions had been packed with one and another shining company which blocked the way of civilians: now the scourge of heaven laid them bare so that, seen from a distance, it was as if thick hailstones were melting after a terrible storm.

Only a long quotation could show how the graphic quality of such writing is made to convey the sense of horrified sympathy which runs through the entire episode. And, though by this stage the poem has abandoned any serious pretensions to epic, the dignity of Saladin's final speech on his deathbed (Book xx) shows for one last time the kind of generosity which so frequently surfaces at the more human moments of the poem – a fitting ending, one may think, for a different kind of narrative and an implicit denial of the stark polarities which Lope had imposed on himself by his choice of the epic form.

III

Like other kinds of serious poem, the epic easily lends itself to parody and burlesque. Mock epic – a term which covers a number of possibilities – is almost as ancient as epic itself, and some of its earliest examples – the pseudo-Homeric *Batracomiomachia*, or War of the Mice and the Frogs, and *Culex* (The Gnat), long thought to be a work of Virgil's – were well known to Spanish writers of the period. Whether the latter would have thought of such productions as 'mock epic' or simply as burlesque is another matter, though their belief that the two great creators of serious epic were also writers of parody must have helped to certify their own attempts in this direction. Thus José de Villaviciosa (1589–1658) dedicates his poem *La Mosquea* (The Flies) to his patron by invoking the example of Virgil himself: ' I confess that my gift is a humble one, and that it is boldness on my part to one who deserves the works of Virgil, no less; but I would not have been so bold had he himself not encouraged me with his *Culex*, which [like the *Aeneid*] he offered to Caesar Augustus...'. Villaviciosa's poem in twelve cantos, loosely derived from a macaronic Latin poem by Teofilo Folengo (1491–1544), describes, with many Virgilian touches, the war between the flies and the ants which ends in the former's defeat. Despite its excessive length, the *Mosquea* is a work of

considerable accomplishment, a poem which continually demonstrates its author's familiarity with the techniques and imagery of
serious epic. Several episodes, in fact, like the description of the cave
of the winds in Canto v, would scarcely be out of place in a poem like
the *Bernardo* – a fact which points to the close dependence of the
burlesque epic on its more ambitious counterparts. In their context,
however, such passages serve mainly as an ironic background to the
miniature world of action which provides the central narrative: a
scaled-down version of epic conflict, described with ingenious
precision, from which any trace of genuine epic feeling is deliberately
excluded.[28]

Villaviciosa's gently humorous treatment of the epic manner shows
no sign that the epic itself is in decline. At the other extreme,
Quevedo's one contribution to the mock epic, the unfinished *Poema
heroico de las necedades y locuras de Orlando el Enamorado* (Heroic Poem of
the Stupidities and Follies of Orlando in Love) seems bent on
annihilating the whole tradition of romantic epic which derives from
Boiardo. This 'pitiless caricature', as Chevalier calls it,[29] sets its tone
in the opening lines:

> Canto los disparates, las locuras,
> los furores de Orlando enamorado,
> cuando el seso y razón le dejó a escuras
> el dios enjerto en diablo y en pecado;
> y las desaventuradas aventuras
> de Ferragut, guerrero endemoniado;
> los embustes de Angélica y su amante,
> niña buscona y doncellita andante.
>
> (Canto I, 1–8; p. 1333)[30]

I sing of the follies, the mad deeds, the furies of Orlando in love, when the
god grafted to the devil and sin left his sense and reason in the dark; and the
unfortunate fortunes of Ferragut, that warrior possessed by a demon; the
tricks of Angelica and her lover, that swindling girl and damsel errant.

Yet what is truly disconcerting about the poem is the deliberate
mixture of styles: as in Góngora's *Píramo y Tisbe* (see above,
pp. 88–91), though on a much larger scale, passages of great beauty,
like the descriptions of Angelica, alternate with obscene word play
and the systematic deformation of standard epic formulae:

> Ya el madrugón del cielo amodorrido
> daba en el Occidente cabezadas,
> y pide el tocador, medio dormido,

> a Tetis, y un jergón y dos frazadas;
> el mundo está mandinga anochecido,
> de medio ojo las cumbres atapadas,
> cuando acabaron de sacar las suertes
> los paladines, regoldando muertes.
>
>   (Canto II, 41–8; p. 1362)

Now the great early riser of the slumbering heavens [i.e. the sun] was nodding his head in the west and, half asleep, was asking Thetis for his toilet things, a straw mattress and two blankets; the world is as dark as a Sudanese nigger, the mountain tops covered up to the eyes, when the paladins, belching death, finally draw lots.

The virtual untranslatability of such a passage points to something we have already seen in some of Quevedo's shorter poems (see above, pp. 164–5): the way in which his peculiar version of the grotesque often seems to be generated by the possibilities of language itself. Thus in the *Orlando*, the constant undermining of familiar characters and situations is achieved not only by manipulation of the narrative, but to an even greater extent by the sheer pressure of meaning which goes to create what is essentially a verbal universe. And, though it inevitably lacks the compression of his shorter poems, there is a good case for regarding the *Orlando* – even in its unfinished state a poem of over 1,700 lines – as Quevedo's most sustained exercise in a mode of writing whose verbal inventiveness is matched only by his satirical prose.

The last and finest of the seventeenth-century mock epics, Lope de Vega's *La Gatomaquia* (1634), is different again: not so much an epic parody as a brilliant fantasy which takes its points of reference from the romantic epic to create yet another, more light-hearted, version of a drama which runs through much of Lope's earlier work. This mock-epic account of love and war among cats – the *gatos* of the title – freely acknowledges its debt to the spurious poems of Homer and Virgil and effortlessly assimilates the kind of learned references which so overburden the *Jerusalén Conquistada*. Significantly, it was originally published as part of the *Rimas... de Tomé de Burguillos* (see above, pp. 118–20), with which it shares the mood of detached playfulness so characteristic of Lope's final phase. In *La Gatomaquia*, the playfulness is reflected in the choice of metre: not the *octavas* which are the standard vehicle of the literary epic, but the much more flexible *silva*, or free combination of eleven- and seven-syllable lines, rhyming for the most part in couplets:

Entre esta generosa ilustre gente
vino un gato valiente
de hocico agudo y de narices romo,
blanco de pecho y pies, negro de lomo,
que Micifuf tenía
por nombre, en gala, cola y gallardía
célebre en toda parte
por un Zapinarciso y Gatimarte.
Este, luego que vio la bella gata,
más reluciente que fregada plata,
tan perdido quedó, que noche y día
paseaba el tejado en que vivía
con pajes y lacayos de librea,
que nunca sirve mal quien bien desea;
y sucedióle bien, pues luego quiso,
¡oh gata ingrata!, a Micifuf Narciso,
dando a Marramaquiz celos y enojos.

(Silva I, 265–81; p. 92)[31]

Among this noble and illustrious people there came a valiant cat with sharp jaws and a Roman nose, white chest and paws, black back, Micifuf by name, for elegance, tail and gallantry famed in all parts as a Narcissus and Mars of cats. This creature, the moment he saw the lovely she-cat, more gleaming than polished silver, so lost his senses, that night and day he paced the roof where she lived with pages and lackeys in livery, for he who desires will never court badly; and things turned out well for him, since then – o ungrateful she-cat! – she fell in love with Narcissus-Micifuf, to the annoyance and jealousy of Marramaquiz.

Throughout the poem, Lope's delight in coining names ('Zapinarciso y Gatimarte') and his constant authorial comments ('que nunca sirve mal quien bien desea') form part of a self-reflexive parody which mocks at its own erudition and veers with consummate skill between different stylistic registers. Thus his cats not only read Ovid and quote Garcilaso – one poet-cat is referred to as a 'Gatilaso' – but perform actions which lend themselves to stylistic jokes:

Una perdiz con plumas
quiso tragarse, y no dejaba cosa
que no la deshiciese
por alta que estuviese;
trepaba la lustrosa
reluciente espetera
derribando sartenes y asadores;
y con estas demencias y furores
en una de fregar cayó caldera

(trasposición se llama esta figura)
de agua acabada de quitar del fuego,
de que salió pelado.　　　　　　(Silva IV, 356–67; p. 165)

He tried to swallow an unplucked partridge and left nothing undisturbed, however high up it was; he climbed the shiny polished spit, knocking down frying pans and skewers; and in his madness and fury, into a tub he fell for washing dishes – this figure is called 'transposition' – just filled with boiling water, whence he emerged half-skinned.

This passage comes from the description of Marramaquiz's 'madness', when, like Orlando, he is faced with a rival lover. Yet, despite the many references to Ariosto in the poem, there is no sense that he is satirizing his original, and the direct thrust of his narrative deliberately avoids the complexities of the romantic quest story. What satire the poem contains, in fact, is directed, not at literary models, but at Lope's own society. This is the truth behind Inez Macdonald's remark that, in *La Gatomaquia*, Lope has invented 'a small world... exactly parallel to, but different from, our own'.[32] Though his reflections on self-importance in human affairs have lost none of their relevance, the 'world' his poem most resembles is that of *La Dorotea* (see above, pp. 115–18), his most mature and detailed vision of the middle-class society of his own time. Thus, despite the superficial parallels with Ariosto, the central triangle of his poem – Marramaquiz–Zapaquilda–Micifuf – can be seen as the final transposition of the essential relationships – Don Fernando–Dorotea–Don Bela – of the prose dialogue. As we have seen, *La Dorotea* itself builds on a personal situation which had continued to obsess Lope for most of his writing career, but which he is now able to regard with the detachment of a lifetime's experience. In *La Gatomaquia*, one might argue, Lope goes one step further: in replacing human society by a world of cats, he not only creates a wonderfully inventive poem, but at the same time raises what had begun as a painful personal episode to a level of good-humoured serenity which is one of the triumphs of his art.

IV

By 1634, the date of *La Gatomaquia*, the period of the major Spanish literary epics is over, though epic poems of one sort and another continue to be written well into the eighteenth century. As we have just seen, both Lope and Quevedo, in their different ways, bear witness to the decline of the romantic epic as a serious form. As against this, however, Tasso's version of Christian epic retains its authority, though, as Frank Pierce suggests, it may have reached Spain too late to bring about any genuinely imaginative re-creation.[33] What is more, the Christian epic itself, as Judith Kates· points out, is a precarious kind of writing:

'Epic', by definition, implied the pagan culture of Greece and Rome and the humanist response to those cultures. It also assumed an enlargement of the human, an intense energizing of the life of this mortal earth. 'Christian' implied an opposing perception and response to experience more pre-occupied with the paradox of life after death and ways of bringing mortal life into conformity with it. Christian values and ideals changed the way people read epic poetry and what they expected of it.[34]

If there is one kind of poem which largely escapes this kind of tension, it is the religious epic proper: the poem which takes its subject-matter directly from the Scriptures or dramatizes the type of spiritual progress one finds in the lives of saints. It is, of course, hardly surprising that the religious epic should take root in Counter-Reformation Spain; what is more striking is the range and quality of the best work it produced, even where this implies a certain dilution of the actual concept of epic. One can see what is at stake here by comparing the two outstanding poems of the period based on the lives of saints: Lope de Vega's *Isidro* (1599), which describes the life of Isidore, the patron saint of Madrid, and José de Valdivielso's *Vida, Excelencias y Muerte del Glorioso Patriarca...San Joseph* (Life, Excellencies and Death of the Glorious Patriarch... St Joseph; 1604).

Lope's poem is one of his finest performances: an affectionate tribute to a local saint with whom he fells himself profoundly identified. Though it is not without its traces of erudition, the *Isidro* is essentially a popular poem on a popular subject. As in many of his plays, Lope's instinctive sympathy for traditional ballad material and common rituals and beliefs gives great conviction to the writing, an impression which is reinforced by the easy rhythms of the *quintilla*:

> La tiniebla que le ofusca
> va tentando, como ciego,
> llega al frío hogar, y luego
> entre la ceniza busca
> si hay reliquias del fuego.
>
> En fin, un tizón halló,
> y algunas pajas juntó
> sobre el extremo quemado,

> y, el rostro de viento hinchado,
> soplando, resplandeció.
>
> Enciende Isidro, y de presto
> huye la sombra y se extiende;
> él con la mano defiende
> la luz que afirma en el puesto,
> donde vestirse pretende.
>
> Cúbrese un capote viejo,
> sin cuidado y sin espejo,
> y anda a vueltas la oración,
> que orar en toda ocasión
> es del apóstol consejo. (Canto v; pp. 412b–413a)[35]

He finds his way through the darkness which confuses him, he reaches the cold hearth and searches among the ashes to see if there is any fire left. At last he found a half-burnt stick and placed some straws over the burnt end and, swelling his cheeks, he blew and it burst into flame. Isidore lights the fire and immediately the shadows flee and lengthen; with his hand he protects the light which he sets in its place, where he tries to dress. He puts on an old cloak, carelessly and without a mirror, praying all the time, since to pray on every occasion is the apostle's advice.

Here and elsewhere, the rapidity of the octosyllabic lines and the use of familiar imagery add movement and vividness to a basically simple narrative. What gives the poem a certain 'epic' quality, on the other hand, is the way in which this central theme at certain moments is made to open on wider perspectives, as in the vision of the Holy Land at the end of the fourth Canto or the allegorical descriptions of the Cave of Envy (Canto ii) and the Palace of Deceit (Canto vii).

Whether this is enough to qualify the *Isidro* as an epic poem is another matter: though it is clearly more than the versified life of a saint, its virtues lie in a different direction from the 'majesty' which Tasso and others claimed for the epic. Much the same could be said, despite obvious differences, of the *Vida...de San Joseph*. Here, to be sure, the resemblance to epic is more marked: the use of *octavas*, the actual scale of the composition – twenty-four cantos, amounting to over 15,000 lines – and the presence of allegorical machinery at least suggest the scope of Valdivielso's intentions. At the same time, it is hard to disagree with the opinion of the poem's nineteenth-century editor, Cayetano Rosell, that this is not so much an epic poem as a religious narrative cast in heroic form. Where Rosell goes wrong, however – partly through his failure to understand the nature of seventeenth-century rhetoric – is in condemning the poem for its

'artificiality' and 'bad taste'. On the contrary, to anyone familiar
with the literary epic as a whole, Valdivielso's poem is likely to seem
exemplary, both for the relative directness of its narrative style and
for the precision of its language:

> Envuelta en el precioso rebociño
> Viste el turón peludo, felpa y martas,
> Trayendo la estufilla como a niño
> Entre las joyas de las ricas sartas;
> Al hombro cuelga el delicado armiño,
> Que de su rostro cubre menguas hartas,
> Siempre escondida del contrario fiero
> Con más ropas que trae un pregonero.
>
> (Canto XXI; p. 190a)[36]

Wrapped in the precious cloak, she [i.e. the Virgin Mary] is clothed in thick
furs, plush and sable, carrying the tiny brazier like a child among the rich
strings of jewels. The delicate ermine hangs over her shoulders, covering the
various misgivings of her face, always hidden from hostile beasts with more
clothes than a towncrier wears.

A passage like this, from the description of the journey to Bethlehem,
draws on the same kind of popular strengths one finds in the *Isidro*.
Again, as in Lope's poem, there is an attempt to place the central
narrative within an allegorical framework, as well as a Lucanesque
taste for violence in episodes like the Massacre of the Innocents
(Canto XIX). Where Rosell sees 'bad taste', however, a modern reader
is more likely to admire the skill with which Valdivielso, as in his
shorter poems (see above, pp. 149–51), incorporates images and
simple conceits from the popular theology of his time, as when he
describes the carpenter Joseph's premonition of the Crucifixion:

> Si hace el oficial santo alguna cama,
> De la cruz se le acuerda, en que deshecho
> Ha de morir el que le sirve y ama,
> A su Esposa sacando de su pecho;
> Si alguna mesa labra, en Dios se inflama,
> Y un horno regalado de amor hecho,
> La del altar contempla en que su amado
> Hará el amor de amor dulce bocado. (Canto XXII; p. 232a)

If the holy craftsman makes a bed, it reminds him of the Cross on which He
who serves and loves him will die shattered, breaking his Spouse's heart; if
he works on a table, he burns in God and, now become a pleasant furnace
of love, he beholds the table of the altar on which his Beloved will make love
into a sweet mouthful of love.

The popularity of the *Vida... de San Joseph* – thirty editions before 1700 – points to a taste which later was lost, but which can now be seen to extend to other, more distinguished examples of seventeenth-century religious poetry. Yet if such poems relate only tangentially to epic, the same is not true of those which directly confront the figure of Christ – the one true epic hero, as Milton knew, in an essentially religious age. Even a poet as sceptical of the secular epic as Quevedo could write a serious short epic – the *Poema heroico a Cristo resucitado* (Heroic Poem to Christ Resurrected; before 1621) – on the Harrowing of Hell: a splendidly sustained poem of 800 lines, which elaborates with great resourcefulness the theme of the epic hell inherited from Tasso.[37] And with Hojeda's *La Cristiada* (The Christiad; 1611) – the one great masterpiece of its kind in Spanish – the long religious poem enters on a dimension which for once can be genuinely described as 'epic'.

Again, one notes the connection with the New World: Diego de Hojeda (1571?–1615), though born in Seville, emigrated at an early age to Peru, where he spent the rest of his life as a member of the Dominican Order. His twelve-canto poem, which describes the Passion of Christ from the Last Supper to the Crucifixion, is a consciously literary enterprise, drawing on Homer, Virgil, Tasso and the *Christias* (1535) of the Renaissance Latin poet Girolamo Vida (1485–1566). (It is also clear that much of his theology reflects earlier Dominican writing, from Aquinas to Luis de Granada and Alonso de Cabrera.) In terms of more immediate models, as Frank Pierce has argued, it is possible to trace a sequence which runs from the *De partu virginis* (On the Birth of the Virgin; 1526) of Sannazaro through Vida to Hojeda himself; yet one of the remarkable things about the poem is the skill with which Hojeda incorporates his various models into a single dramatic whole. This is especially true of his most complex piece of imitation, the description of Hell in the fourth Book, where he builds partly on Vida and Tasso to create a genuinely Christian hell in which Vida's monsters and Tasso's invented supernatural are replaced by the pagan gods themselves.[38] Thus, by a single bold stroke, the question of the supernatural which had proved so troublesome in earlier Christian epic is resolved by a simple decision to remain within the limits prescribed by Christian theology.

This decisiveness is characteristic of the poem as a whole. Unlike earlier writers of literary epic, Hojeda avoids the proliferation of multiple episodes and keeps his allegorical figures within a strictly

Christian context, as in the description of Christ's prayer mounting to
Heaven which opens the second Book:

> Dijo; y estas gravísimas razones
> Tomó en su mano la virtud suave
> Que almas consagra, limpia corazones,
> Y los retretes de la gloria sabe,
> La Oración, reina ilustre de oraciones,
> Que del pecho de Dios tiene la llave;
> Y dejando el penoso escuro suelo,
> Caminó al despejado alegre cielo.
>
> Con prestas alas, que al ligero viento,
> Al fuego volador, al rayo agudo,
> A la voz clara, al vivo pensamiento
> Deja atrás, va rasgando el aire mudo:
> Llega al sutil y espléndido elemento
> Que al cielo sirve de fogoso escudo,
> Y como en otro ardor más abrasada,
> Rompe, sin ser de su calor tocada.
>
> De allí se parte con veloz denuedo
> Al cuerpo de los orbes rutilante;
> Que ni le pone su grandeza miedo,
> Ni le muda el bellísimo semblante;
> Que ya más de una vez con rostro ledo,
> Con frente osada y ánimo constante,
> Despreciando la más excelsa nube,
> Al tribunal subió que agora sube.
>
> Estaban los magníficos porteros
> De la casa a la gloria consagrada,
> Que con intelectivos pies ligeros
> Voltean la gran máquina estrellada;
> Estaban, como espíritus guerreros,
> Para guardar la celestial entrada
> Puestos a punto, y viendo que subía,
> A su consorte cada cual decía...   (p. 411b)[39]

He spoke; and the gentle virtue which consecrates souls, cleanses hearts and
knows the hidden places of glory, Prayer, the illustrious queen of prayers,
who holds the key to God's breast, took these most solemn words into her
hands; and leaving the dark sorrowful earth, made her way to clear, happy
Heaven. On swift wings, which leave behind the light wind, the flying fire,
the keen ray, the clear voice, the living thought, she rends the silent air; she
reaches the subtle and splendid element which serves Heaven as a fiery
shield, and, as if burning more fiercely with a different ardour, she breaks
through it, untouched by its heat. From there she departs with bold speed

for the gleaming body of the spheres; for she is not afraid of its grandeur, nor does she flinch at its most beautiful countenance; since already more than once, with happy face, with daring brow and constant spirit, scorning the loftiest cloud, she has risen to the throne to which she now rises. The magnificent doorkeepers of the house sacred to glory were there, who on light, intellectual feet fly round the great starry machine; they were there, like warrior spirits, prepared to guard the heavenly entry, and seeing her mount up, each said to his companion...

A passage like this, with its high proportion of run-on lines, suggests something of the urgency which makes itself felt at many of the finest moments of the poem. Elsewhere, this urgency is compounded by a distinctive kind of authorial intervention, one which not only comments on the plot but involves the speaker directly in the moral and theological context of what he is describing. Like Valdivielso, Hojeda draws on all the resources of the preacher's art; as Frank Pierce puts it: 'He thickens the texture of his narrative by frequent appeals to the reader's wonder, compassion and anger, he berates mankind for its callousness in refusing to recognize the meaning of Christ's mission, and throughout he addresses God and his Hero.'[40] What adds conviction to all this is the author's sense of his own sinfulness:

> Por los pecados ¡oh mi Dios! del mundo
> Y por mis culpas, Hombre verdadero,
> Con gran consejo y con saber profundo
> Os dejó vuestro Padre en mal tan fiero;
> Y en él yo mi derecho ilustre fundo
> A todo el bien; que todo el bien espero
> Por ese mal de pena tan terrible
> Que sufrís, Hombre y Dios por mi pasible.
>
> (Book XII; p. 497a)

For the sins, o my God! of the world, and for my own errors, o true Man, with great counsel and deep wisdom your Father left you in so fierce a plight; and on Him I base my illustrious right to all that is good; for I hope for all good through that evil of such terrible pain which you suffer, Man and God who suffer for me.

Taken out of its context, this may seem no more than a piece of rhetorical strategy; coming where it does, however, as the climax to a moving account of the Crucifixion, it not only emphasizes the dramatic nature of the occasion but points to the very genuine struggle between good and evil which runs through the entire poem. Like Milton's Satan, Hojeda's Lucifer is a formidable adversary whose intelligence makes the ultimate victory of Christ all the more impressive. Yet even here the poem avoids any easy triumphalism; it ends quietly, not with the Resurrection but with the Entombment, on a note of distinctly human compassion:

> Llegando allí con reverente aspeto,
> Manos humildes y almas temerosas,
> Y lágrimas nacidas de respeto
> Y compasión suaves y copiosas;
> A Dios, que a muerte quiso estar sujeto,
> Entre dos enterraron blancas losas:
> Y cuando estos misterios acabaron,
> Tristes en el sepulcro le dejaron. (Book XII; p. 501b)

Coming to that place with reverent mien, with humble hands and fearful souls, and gentle, copious tears full of respect and compassion, they buried God, who wished to be subject to death, between two white stones; and when they had performed these mysteries, they left Him sadly in the tomb.

CHAPTER 8

Plenitude and decline: from Villamediana to the second half of the century

I

To move back from the literary epic to the shorter verse forms is to become aware, once again, of the immense amount of poetic activity going on in what seems at first sight a situation of quite bewildering complexity. One fact, however, stands out: where most of the poets I discussed in chapter 5 achieved their characteristic styles in the first decade of the seventeenth century or even earlier, the ones I now want to consider nearly all produced their best work in the half century or so following the appearance of Góngora's major poems, the *Polifemo* and the *Soledades*, in 1612–13. Whatever other factors come into play, this, clearly, is the great stylistic divide: from this point on, the example of Góngora, however much resisted in some quarters, becomes inescapable, and leaves its mark on a great deal of later poetry, both good and bad, until well into the eighteenth century. At the same time, as we shall see, other forces are at work: various regional groupings and affinities, the persistence of the literary academies, the new role of the court as patron of the arts and – more nebulous, though no less real – the growing sense of national crisis which is felt at every level of society, and which is inevitably reflected in the poetry of the time.

One sign of change, as I have already mentioned (see above, p. 140), is the appearance of a new kind of courtier poet, most notably represented by the Conde de Salinas and his slightly later successors, the Conde de Villamediana (1582–1622) and Antonio Hurtado de Mendoza (1586–1644). Like Salinas, whom he imitates in his early poetry, Villamediana became an important figure at the court of Philip III, though he was eventually banished from Madrid for his satires against political rivals. (The accession of Philip IV in 1621 promised to further his career; less than a year later, however, he was murdered by an unknown assassin, for reasons which remain obscure.) Villamediana's earliest poems are unmistakably Petrarchan, in a mode already familiar from Salinas: a combination of the intimate tone of Garcilaso and Camões and the less personal abstractions of *cancionero* verse. Nevertheless, he is one of the few poets of his generation to have recognized the true originality of Góngora *before* the appearance of the major poems; as his most recent editor, J. M. Rozas, points out, what Villamediana is attempting in the best of his early sonnets is a Gongoresque re-working of Petrarchism – 'un petrarquismo desde Góngora'[1] – in which verbal poise seems an essential part of the content. At the same time, the 'voice' he creates for such poems is very different from Góngora's – more reticent, yet urgently concerned with the emotional situation it is presenting:

> Tarde es, Amor, ya tarde y peligroso
> para emprender ahora que mis quejas
> hallen justa piedad en las orejas
> que concluyó el desdén más riguroso.
>
> Porque a tantos avisos no es forzoso
> idolatrar los hierros de unas rejas,
> ni juntar así nueva a penas viejas
> permite el tiempo a un ánimo dudoso.
>
> Tus cadenas, Amor, tus hierros duros
> mejor en mí parecen forcejados
> que peligrosamente obedecidos;
>
> bienes dudosos, males son seguros,
> y los desdenes más solicitados
> avisos con escrúpulo admitidos.   (R, p. 95)

It is late, Love, already late and dangerous to attempt to find just pity for my complaints in ears which the most rigorous disdain has closed. Since with so many warnings it is not necessary to worship the iron bars of a window, nor does time allow a doubtful spirit thus to add a new grief to old. Your chains, Love, your hard fetters seem now in me resisted, rather than dangerously obeyed; doubtful benefits are certain evils, and the most coveted disdains are warnings punctually admitted.

Here, only the occasional Latinism, like 'concluyó' (= 'closed') and 'escrúpulo', might make one think of Góngora; for the rest, the skilful manipulation of Petrarchan contrasts and the complete lack of anecdote are common features of Italianate love poetry from Garcilaso onwards. Ultimately, of course, it is this absence of explanation which deepens the mood of the poem and pushes it towards the final sense of disillusionment. In the meantime, however, there is not only the ominous sense of time running out, but also a whole interior drama, in which notions of compulsion and free will are played off against one another. As the insistence on words like 'aviso' (warning), 'desdén' (scorn) and 'peligroso' (dangerous) suggests, this is partly a matter of verbal echoes and repetitions, an effect which makes for the extraordinary compactness of the poem, and more especially for the moral weight of the ending. If this is a reticent poem, it is also clear that the reticence hints at powerful feelings – feelings which are both evoked and kept in place, one might argue, by the discipline of writing in a strict form. Moreover, as in other love poems of the period, feeling is virtually inseparable from thought: both come together, not just in the words of the poem, but in the sense of an actual 'voice' which controls these. Villamediana, in other words, is not so much writing a confession as creating a 'voice' which can be used to explain and, if possible, define a certain state of mind. Thus, if part of the apparent simplicity of the poem comes from the sequence of bare statements – 'es' (is) ... 'Porque no es' (Because it is not) ... 'son' (are) – what they convey, above all, is the sense of someone *judging* his own experience and at the same time suggesting the urgency of his present situation. The thoughtfulness mostly lies in the judging; yet any detachment this might imply is offset by the way in which judgement is absorbed into the general feeling of the poem. Both judgement and feeling, that is to say, come from the same source and, because this source is under pressure, the two things unite in a single line of force.[2]

As Luis Rosales makes clear, Villamediana is a courtier-poet, not simply because he is writing in a courtly milieu, but also because he believes in certain traditional courtly virtues which he feels to be under threat.[3] Thus, as he goes on to argue, poetry, for Villamediana, is never a self-sufficient art, but more a form of conduct, an attitude which helps to explain his amateur stance as a poet and what seems like the deliberate unmodishness of his most personal writing. Hence also the impression he gives of being a witness, both to his own passions and to the more general temper of the age, as in the devastating late sonnet which begins:

> Debe tan poco al tiempo el que ha nacido
> en la estéril region de nuestros años,
> que premiada la culpa y los engaños,
> el mérito se encoge escarnecido...   (R, p. 309)

He who was born in the barren region of our age owes so little to time, since [now that] guilt and deceits are rewarded, merit shrinks under mockery...

Such contemplative poems are a distillation of the savage personal satire directed at many of the leading figures of the time – an essentially new kind of poetry virtually invented by Villamediana. Where previous satirical writing had mostly confined itself to types, Villamediana spares no one, from the king down, as in the opening lines of his poem on the fall of the Duque de Lerma:

> Ya ha despertado el león
> que durmió como cordero,
> y al son del bramido fiero
> se asustó todo ladrón... (R, p. 283)

Now the lion [i.e. the king] who slept like a lamb has woken up, and every thief is scared by the sound of his fierce roaring...

This kind of verse, with its deliberate crudities, may seem poles apart from the rest of Villamediana's poetry. In practice, however, the political invective and the finely balanced sonnets are two sides of the same coin: the wish to denounce at all costs a state of affairs in which genuine courtly and aristocratic values are steadily losing ground in the prevailing atmosphere of complacency and corruption.

Villamediana's most ambitious single poem, however, is different again from those I have so far discussed. The *Fábula de Faetón* (Fable of Phaethon; 1617), which runs to over 1,800 lines, is beyond question the finest poem of its kind after the *Polifemo*: a mythological fable based largely on Ovid, though structured along the lines of Marino's *Adone*.[4] One fairly characteristic passage (from the description of Phaethon's death) may suggest something of the skill with which Villamediana employs Góngora's grand manner for his own purposes:

> Como la exhalación de nube opaca
> previene al campo formidable trueno,
> cuando la luz la parte etérea saca
> y busca el aire en su región sereno,
> que porción menos densa en parte flaca
> aborta el fuego del preñado seno,
> y en cándido farol celeste trompa
> ígnea compele a que impelida rompa,
>
> tal va cayendo del mayor planeta
> teñido el hijo en el humor sangriento,

y condolida la mortal saeta
errar quisiera el golpe y el intento.
Admiraron los orbes el cometa
que ni tierra exhaló ni formó viento,
lastimoso prodigio, pero bello,
bello rostro alumbró con su cabello.

(lines 1601–16; R, pp. 259–60)

Just as the exhalation of a dark cloud prepares the countryside for a terrible peal of thunder, when the light puts on its ethereal aspect and seeks the region of the calm air, since a less dense portion coinciding with a weak part cuts short the fire from the pregnant womb and compels the fiery blast from heaven to break into a pure beacon of light, so his son [i.e. Phaethon] falls bloodstained from the greatest planet [i.e. the Sun], and the mortal arrow, in pity, would prefer both stroke and purpose to fail. The spheres see with amazement the comet which was neither exhaled by the earth nor formed by the wind, a pitiful, though fair, wonder which lit up its lovely face with its hair.

Only a full reading of the *Faetón*, however, could bring out what Cossío calls the 'living quality' of the poem. This is partly a matter of Villamediana's obvious pleasure in re-creating the world of classical fantasy and in the opportunities this gives for rich sensuous effects. More importantly, though, it has to do with Villamediana's personal involvement in a poem which at first sight may seem no more than a superb piece of verbal artifice. Thus his choice of myth – the story of Phaethon's glorious, though fatal, attempt to drive the horses of the sun – scarcely seems fortuitous. Though it would be a romantic oversimplification to suggest that Villamediana identifies himself with the figure of Phaethon, there is a real sense in which his treatment of the myth re-enacts a pattern which runs through much of his other work. Unlike the more conventional versions of the story, in which Phaethon's temerity is justifiably punished, the *Faetón* avoids any kind of obvious moral. Instead, the final destruction of the central figure amounts to a 'heroic suicide' (Rozas's phrase), a fate which he tragically foresees and which he accepts, honourably and responsibly, in full awareness of the inevitable outcome, as though the attempt itself were its own justification.

Villamediana's poise and integrity, like his comparative indifference to literary fashion, are exceptional among the poets of his generation. Nevertheless, certain features of his work – the studied nonchalance of the amateur writer, the liking for traditional metres and for a kind of *conceptismo* which owes more to *cancionero* poetry than to contemporary models – are common to much of the poetry written at the court of Philip IV. The most striking example here is Antonio Hurtado de Mendoza, who, from the early 1620s to his death in 1644, served, in Gareth Davies's phrase, as 'sounding board for palace events',[5] with something like the status of unofficial poet laureate. This immediately suggests the social dimension of his verse. Though his satirical bite may sometimes remind one of Quevedo, Mendoza has none of Villamediana's subversiveness. His love poetry, for instance, though not without its moments of introspection, is for the most part a version of *poésie galante*, a courtly game which recognizes, and deliberately exploits, its own idealism. The rules of the game tend to produce their own dialectic, which often reads like a sophisticated re-working of *cancionero* verse:

> Lisi, pues ya no he de verte,
> muera yo de mi tristeza,
> que morir de tu belleza
> no lo merece mi muerte...   (BC, II, p. 93)[6]

Lisi, since now I am not to see you, may I die of my sadness, for my death does not deserve to die of your beauty...

or again, in the opening lines of a sonnet:

> Ojos del bien de amor, ricos y avaros,
> si os miro no os turbéis, que si pudiera
> dejaros de mirar, no os ofendiera,
> que no me cuesta poco el enojaros...   (BC, III, p. 217)

Eyes of love's treasure, rich and miserly: if I look at you, do not be distressed, for if I could cease to look, I would not offend you, since to annoy you costs me not a little...

It is partly Mendoza's skill in using *conceptos* which earns him a place of honour in Gracián's *Agudeza y arte de ingenio* (see above, pp. 60–3). His attitude to Góngora, on the other hand – 'a divine genius imitated by a hundred idiots' – is correspondingly guarded; despite his own use of *culto* diction – most notably in the *Vida de Nuestra Señora*, his long poem on the life of the Virgin – Mendoza consistently aligns himself with the defenders of clarity and more than once praises the line of poetry which runs from Garcilaso to Esquilache and Lope de Vega. How far this was a question of temperament and how far a part of the need to communicate with a courtly audience remains a matter for speculation; what is certain is that, within the limitations imposed by his public, Mendoza remains constantly alert to the poetic possibilities of his subject. Though the subjects themselves are often banal, his extraordinary rhythmical sense and his ability to create surprising metaphors go beyond mere verbal dexterity, as in these lines on a fountain:

> Penacho de sol, que en suma
> siembra en desperdicio leve
> de átomos de plata y nieve
> cada rayo y cada pluma.
> Cuyas garzotas tempranas
> se rizan de las más bellas
> lágrimas que llora en ellas
> la envidia de las mañanas.
> Mintiendo a lo natural
> parece que desde el suelo
> sus estrellas cierne el cielo
> en harina de cristal.
> Cándidas fraguas y bellas
> sin duda que el centro aloja
> que en buen aire el viento arroja
> nevadas tantas centellas.
> Desde los pardos confines
> del abismo al cielo sube
> y en flamante airosa nube
> polvos nieva de jazmines.   (BC, II, pp. 226–7)

Plume of sunlight, which, in sum, scatters in a light squandering of silver and snow each ray and each feather. Whose early crests curl with the loveliest tears which the envy of the mornings weeps on them. Deceiving nature, it is as if, from the ground, the sky were sifting its stars in a flour of crystal. Without doubt the centre contains white, beautiful forges, since the wind [i.e. of the bellows] casts into good air so many snowy sparks. It mounts skywards from the dark limits of the abyss and in a splendid, graceful cloud it snows powdered jasmine.

Though Mendoza's ultimate justification as a court poet lies in having created a pastoral myth in which his contemporaries could see an idealized version of their own lives,[7] the fragile vision of a passage like this – a fragility which is enacted verbally in the restless attempt to find the right metaphor for an object which literally dissolves before the eyes – suggests an ambivalence on Mendoza's part – a reluctance to be taken in by his own art – which hints at unsuspected depths of imagination. This, one might argue, is the finest of all

Mendoza's subtleties; as his best critic, Gareth Davies, points out, he is aware that, in a sense, the game of love may only serve to mark the absence of real love:

in Mendoza's world of enchanted feeling, the disenchantment may at any moment happen: the protestation of loyalty may only succeed in suggesting the possibility of disloyalty, the desire to immortalize may only hasten the approach of time's winged chariot. This double standard, that both asserts and destroys, is an essential part of Mendoza's originality, and of the reader's reaction to him.[8]

The ideals and practices taken for granted by Mendoza and other court poets were partly embodied in a prose work, the *Amante cortesano* (The Courtly Lover; 1627), by Gabriel de Bocángel (1603–58), modelled on Castiglione, but possibly with a real-life setting. Bocángel is the other outstanding court poet of the period: though neither a *grand seigneur* like Villamediana nor a member of the minor nobility like Mendoza – his father had been a doctor to Philip III – he secured the patronage of Philip IV's brother, the Cardinal Infante don Fernando, early in his career, and in his later years seems to have identified himself quite naturally with the severer atmosphere of a court by now visibly in decline. Like Mendoza, Bocángel was closely associated with the most famous literary academy of the 1620s and 30s, the Academia de Madrid, at which most of his early poems were directed. Significantly, however, he breaks with the amateur tradition of his social superiors to the extent of publishing his poems in his own lifetime; his first book, *Rimas y prosas* (Verse and Prose), which included the long poem on Hero and Leander, appeared in 1627, to be followed ten years later by his principal collection, *La lira de las musas* (The Lyre of the Muses; 1637). Though he seems to have avoided literary controversy, the fact that his chief mentors were Góngora and Jáuregui[9] suggests that, like other poets of his generation, he was aiming somewhere between the extremes of the plain style and the full complexity of Góngora's major poems. His own definition of good poetry bears this out; after identifying sophisticated poetry (*poesía culta*) with the 'grand style', he adds: 'For what counts in poetry is the structure of the words, the ability to combine great elegance with the utmost clarity, this last being even more important than the first.' In practice, Bocángel makes full use of Góngora's characteristic vocabulary and turns of syntax while deliberately avoiding any sense of obscurity. Thus, like Jáuregui himself, he shows that poetry can be both sophisticated and accessible, a combination, as his most recent editor, Trevor Dadson, puts it, of '*culto* clarity and elegance with the wit and sententiousness of *conceptismo*'.[10]

This emphasis on the *concepto* immediately links Bocángel to Villamediana, Mendoza and other courtly poets. Lines like:

> Partís, Anfrisa, de mí
> sin que yo parta de vos;
> ya veré que somos dos,
> que hasta agora no lo vi...   (D, p. 204)

You are leaving me, Anfrisa, though I do not leave you; and I shall see we are two, which until now I did not see...

clearly represent something in the nature of a group style, a common signature announcing an accepted mode of writing. Bocángel's true distinction, however, lies elsewhere: in his love poems and moral sonnets, in his re-working of a courtly form like the pastoral ballad, and in his one remarkable contribution to the mythological fable. Where the love poetry is concerned, it now seems clear that his love sonnets, though few in number, amount to a brief *canzoniere* in the Petrarchan manner. Like other such sequences, they move through most of the stages of a particular relationship. What strikes one most about them, however, is their general air of detachment. In Villamediana, as we saw, one sometimes has the sense of a writer who is judging his passions as he re-creates them; Bocángel, too, often seems to speak as a witness, though with less depth of involvement, as in what may be the final poem of the sequence:

> *Oyendo en el mar, al anochecer, un clarín que tocaba un forzado*
>
> Ya falta el sol, que quieto el mar y el cielo
> niegan unidos la distante arena:
> un ave de metal el aire estrena,
> que vuela en voz cuanto se niega en vuelo.
> Hijo infeliz del africano suelo
> es, que, hurtado al rigor de la cadena,
> hoy música traición hace a su pena
> (si pena puede haber donde hay consuelo).
> Suene tu voz (menos que yo) forzado,
> pues tu clarín es sucesor del remo,
> y alternas el gemido con el canto.
> Mientras yo, al mar de Venus condenado,
> de un extremo de amor paso a otro extremo,
> y, porque alivia, aun se me niega el llanto.   (D, p. 151)

On Hearing at Sea, near Sunset, a Trumpet Played by a Galley-slave Now the sun goes down, for sea and sky at rest together deny the distant sands: a bird of metal breaks through the air, which flies in voice as much as it is denied in flight. It is an unhappy child of African soil who, escaped from the rigour of the chain, now commits musical treason on his sorrow (if sorrow there can be where there is consolation). Let your voice ring out, slave (though less so than I), since your trumpet has taken the place of the oar, and you vary your groans with song. While I, condemned to the sea of Venus, pass from one extreme of love to the other and, since it relieves, even lament is denied to me.

Here, the conventional *topos* of lover as galley-slave is carried to unusual lengths – so much so that the splendid evocation of the real-life prisoner almost takes over the entire poem. The ending, on the other hand, despite the clear allusion to Garcilaso in the twelfth line,[11] seems quite unemotional compared with the older poet, as if the speaker were simply 'placing' himself objectively, with one last twist of ingenuity, in terms of the controlling simile.

In Bocángel's moral sonnets, the combination of detachment and clarity of diction can sound like Quevedo at his most direct:

> Huye del sol el sol, y se deshace
> la vida a manos de la propia vida... (D, p. 259)

The sun flees from the sun, and life is undone at the hands of life itself...

or again, from a sonnet on a clock which is also a candlestick:

> ...El concertado impulso de los orbes
> es un reloj de sol, y al sol advierte
> que también es mortal lo que más dura. (D, p. 371)

The concerted motion of the spheres is a sundial, and warns the sun that what lasts longest is also mortal.

The stoicism which Bocángel displays in such poems is, of course, very much of its period, though no less powerful for that. At the same time – and here he is closer to Góngora than to Quevedo – this does not preclude delight in sensuous beauty or the kind of language that goes with it. One of his best-known images – 'Entre mil verdes puñales / un lirio azul se resiste' (Among a thousand daggers [blades of grass] a single blue lily remains intact; D, p. 213) – shows very well the combination of metaphor and conceit which is characteristic of the best courtly poetry of the 1620s and 30s. Appropriately enough, these lines occur in a pastoral ballad of a type already familiar from

Mendoza and much encouraged by the anthologies of the time. Yet here again, though Bocángel clearly accepts the world of illusion which is the *raison d'être* of such poetry, there are occasions when he seems prepared to break with the prevailing mode: to leave behind the world of pastoral and 'Manzanarian idyll' and to engage with his own feelings at a deeper and more personal level.

It would be a mistake, however, to think of Bocángel mainly as a creator of small-scale effects. His one mythological fable, the *Fábula de Leandro y Hero* (1627), though an early poem, shows a sense of structure and a capacity for sustained writing which can bear comparison with the finest examples of its kind: the *Polifemo*, the *Fábula de Faetón* and the *Orfeo* of Jáuregui, to whom it is dedicated. Both Bocángel's debt to Góngora and the strength of his own imagination are clear from his description of Leander swimming:

> Ágil se otorga al agua sosegada,
> y cuanta arroja el brazo, el pie la hereda;
> pavón cerúleo, deja dibujada
> ojosa espuma en cristalina rueda...
>
> (lines 569–72; D, p. 338)

Nimbly, he entrusts himself to the calm water and what his arms sweep aside, his feet inherit; a cerulean peacock, he leaves traced behind him a foam of eyes on a crystal fan...

or from the final passage on Leander's death:

> Cárdeno el joven, contrastado y laso,
> llevar se deja ya, más no se mueve;
> bebe la muerte en proceloso vaso,
> y bebe sed de vaso que no bebe
> de aquella ninfa que, al farol escaso,
> contra los vientos da socorro leve;
> aplica el manto y la nevada mano,
> mas la nieve a la luz se opone en vano.
>
> (lines 745–52; D, p. 344)

The youth, purple with bruises, tossed about and exhausted, now lets himself drift, but makes no movement; he drinks death from a stormy cup, and drinks thirst for a cup he does not drink, for that nymph who, beside the faint light, gives slight help against the winds; she applies her cloak and snowy hand, but the snow vainly opposes itself to the light.

Yet the real interest of the *Leandro y Hero*, as Dadson makes clear in his fine analysis of the poem, lies elsewhere: in the coherence of what is ultimately a tragic vision and in the way the passion of the two lovers is made to bear on a world which is morally opposed to their desires. Hence the theme of sacrifice which runs through the poem, from the opening ceremony in the temple to what Dadson describes as the 'sacrificial suicide' of the lovers themselves – a sacrifice necessary for the restoration of order, which sets the seal on the individual tragedy and confirms the exemplary nature of the poem as a whole.

Other mythological fables of the time, like the *Fragmentos de Adonis* of Pedro Soto de Rojas (1584–1658), probably written about 1629, are more concerned with stylistic display than with the conscious reinterpretation of a particular myth. The display, in this instance, is impressive, though compared with Bocángel or Villamediana, the sensuousness of the descriptions – often brilliant in themselves – seems deliberately cut off from the world of human emotions, and still more from any serious moral concerns. Though the poem owes almost everything to Góngora – the fact that it is written in *silvas* rather than in *octavas reales* immediately relates it to the *Soledades* – the softening of Góngora's own manner may partly derive from Marino, whose influence on Soto's early sonnets and madrigals is unmistakable. With Soto, however, one begins to see how the standard models of the period may be recombined to produce a quite distinctive kind of poetry – one which, at most, is only implicit in the models themselves. This is partly a matter of local affinities: though his early years as a writer took him frequently to Madrid, where he was a member of the Academia Salvaje (later the Academia de Madrid) and a friend of Góngora, Lope de Vega and Mendoza, most of Soto's life was spent as a priest in his native Granada, to which he finally retired in 1631. This clearly sets him apart from those writers who, after similar beginnings, went on to become important figures at court. Significantly, his first book of poems, *Desengaño de amor en rimas* (Disillusionment of Love in Rhyme; 1623), hints at a more general disappointment with court society as a whole and at a personal inability to play the game of patronage. Yet if, as Orozco Díaz argues, the *Desengaño* poems already lay the psychological foundations for Soto's later work,[12] only the break with Madrid could have provided the circumstances for his one real masterpiece, the *Paraíso cerrado para muchos, jardines abiertos para pocos* (Paradise Closed to Many, Gardens Open to Few; 1652).

This poetic meditation on a garden which itself was conceived as a poem and an object of contemplation is both an extreme justification of the *culterano* manner and an attempt to perpetuate the elaborate formal garden which Soto constructed over a period of many years at his house in the Albaicín – the old Moorish quarter of Granada. The garden itself is of a type especially associated with Granada: a *carmen*, or garden-retreat, of miniature proportions, and deliberately closed off from the outside world.[13] In Soto's version, this becomes a garden for initiates: a space filled with paths, statues, paintings, emblems and allegorical topiary through which one may progress in what amounts to a pilgrimage of learning. This aspect of the garden was not lost on Soto's contemporaries; his friend Bartolomé Ramón de Morales, for instance, remarks on its 'vegetative eloquence, the studiously arranged plants on whose green leaves one could read the truth of fables, its composition seeming more like that of a book than of a garden'.[14] This points directly to the most singular feature of the poem, to what Aurora Egido calls its 'double meaning' (*doble sentido*):[15] the sense in which a garden conceived as a book is transposed into a book which at the same time is a garden. The most literal part of the process is reflected in the actual structure of the poem: the fact that it is divided into seven sections or 'mansions' which follow one's actual itinerary through the garden. Other references, however, are kept to the necessary minimum; as in the *Soledades*, external objects are filtered through a complex network of metaphor and conceit, as in the description of a fountain representing a sea battle:

> La pertinaz galante artillería,
> con el humo de balas, que son perlas,
> moja las luces del amante día;
> y si la noche mereció cogerlas,
> morena, pero hermosa,
> con pabellón de aljófares reposa
> y, entre faroles de cristal luciente,
> todo plata respira combatiente.
>
> (lines 326–33; A, pp. 108–9)

The persistent, gallant artillery, with the smoke of bullets (which are pearls), moistens the lights of loving day; and if the night was worthy to gather them up, it rests, dark though beautiful, in a tent of dewdrops and, among lanterns of gleaming crystal, all breathes contending silver.

The extended military metaphor, with its skilful shift from 'pearls' (= waterdrops) as bullets to 'tent of pearls' (= dewdrops), is characteristic of the poem as a whole, in which the surprise effects of the garden itself are continually said to 'assault' (*asaltar*) the senses of the spectator:

> Verdes las calles, cándidos arqueros
> bravos soldados de jazmín florido,
> cupidillos de amor llenos de antojos,
> dulces rayos apuntan a los ojos,
> del olfato, y disparan al sentido. (lines 865–9; A, p. 130)

In the green alleys, white archers, brave soldiers of jasmine in bloom, tiny Cupids of love full of fancies, aim sweet rays at the eyes of scent [i.e. of the sense of smell] and fire at the senses.

Soto had clearly learnt such effects from Góngora, who is a major presence throughout the poem. It would be wrong, however, to see the *Paraíso* mainly as a pastiche of Góngora, however brilliant; as Orozco Díaz has pointed out,[16] it is possible to feel that Soto pursues the *culterano* manner more single-mindedly than his model – he has no interest, for example, in popular poetry – and that this particular kind of verbalization is in some way inseparable from his chosen subject. Moreover, Soto is an erudite poet in a sense that Góngora never is: the margins of the original edition are filled with references to the Bible and the Church Fathers, though it is only in the closing lines that the poem itself turns to direct praise of God. It is also erudite in a different way, in that it seems to take into account a whole verse tradition, from Horace to Espinosa, in which the natural creation is seen as a source of profitable leisure. No combination of these partial precedents, however, quite explains the peculiar nature of the *Paraíso*, least of all the way in which language itself is made to seem the ultimate distillation of the outside world. If it is generally classed as a descriptive poem – a relatively new kind of poem which, as we shall see, comes into prominence in the 1620s and 30s – this does little to suggest its true originality or the degree of verbal sophistication it represents at a time when few other poets are capable of taking the full measure of Góngora's mature art.[17]

II

If Soto de Rojas builds almost exclusively on Góngora's most serious manner, other poets, encouraged no doubt by the competitive atmosphere of the academies, are more concerned to exploit his mastery of the burlesque. Academy poetry, as we have seen in the case of Mendoza, is not always easy to distinguish from court poetry; nevertheless, it is clear that the academies led well-regulated lives of their own within which poets of relatively humble origin might make a successful career. One obvious example of this is Anastasio Pantaleón de Ribera (1600–29), whose brief writing life is centred almost entirely on the so-called Academia de Madrid. As a poet, Pantaleón is an unrepentant follower of Góngora – 'poeta soy gongorino' (I am a Gongoresque poet), he says at one point – though, as Kenneth Brown rightly points out, this is not simply a matter of stylistic influence, but also of a similar predisposition to wit and humour.[18] Though some of his best poems, like the sonnet to a painter friend which begins:

> Poca, Diego, soy tinta, bien que debe
> en esa tinta poca a tu pintura
> tanto espíritu docta mi figura,
> cuanto pudo admitir lámina breve... (B, p. 317)

I am a little pigment, Diego, though in that little pigment my learned figure owes to your painting as much spirit as a small surface could admit...

fall outside the limits of academy verse, his *Fábula de Alfeo y Aristarco* (Fable of Alpheus and Aristarchus) – clearly composed for a particular audience – is one of the earliest and most successful imitations of Góngora's own burlesque manner in the *Píramo y Tisbe* (see above, pp. 88–91). Pantaleón's malicious wit, evident in this and other poems, and his ability to play off the *culto* style against commonplace material seem an accurate index of academy taste in the late 1620s; at the same time, he was famous for his *vejámenes*, or festive satires on fellow writers, and for the infectious brilliance of his improvisations on set themes, as in the following lines on an earthquake:

> Válgame Dios ¡qué porrada
> had dado un campanario,
> y trayéndose consigo
> asido el sacristán a su badajo!
> ¡Zas, acullá dio en el suelo,
> la Torrecilla del Prado,
> y dicen que mató a uno
> que vendía turrón y letuario!
> ¡Jesús! ¡y qué guacharada
> que junto a Provincia ha dado

aquella fuente, y ha muerto
un millón de alguaciles y escribanos!
¡Fuego de Cristo, un soneto
de Roa se viene abajo,
que aquel montón de cascote
catorce versos es, de cal y canto!   (B, pp. 355–6)

Good grief, what a thump that belfry made, coming down with the sexton
hanging on to the clapper! Crash! Over there the Little Tower of the Prado
fell to the ground, and they say it killed someone who was selling sweetmeats
and simples! Jesus! What a noise that fountain beside the Law Courts made,
and it killed a million officers and clerks! By Christ! One of Roa's sonnets
[Gabriel de Roa, a fellow academician] is coming down, for that mountain
of rubble is fourteen lines of solid stone wall!

One of the few literary representations of the activities of an
academy occurs in Polo de Medina's *Academias del jardín* (Academies
of the Garden; 1631). Like Pantaleón, the Murcian poet Polo de
Medina (1603–76) was best known at the time as a writer of witty
light verse and burlesque mythological poems in the manner of
Góngora. The latter – *Apolo y Dafne* (Apollo and Daphne; 1634) and
the later *Pan y Siringa* (Pan and Syrinx; first published 1774) – are
certainly among the best of their kind; as in Góngora, the burlesque
exists alongside passages of genuine beauty, though the frequent
word play and the intellectual ingenuity of certain conceits also
suggest a careful reading of Quevedo. The fact that Polo can use
Góngora and Quevedo as simultaneous models points, one might
argue, to a gap between theory and practice which is characteristic of
the years around 1630. Though a work like the *Academias del jardín*
shows a distinctly anti-*culterano* bias – perhaps influenced by his
mentor Cascales – the best of Polo's poetry could hardly have existed
without the example of Góngora. As Cossío observes, Polo's
theoretical statements seem fragile and impersonal when set against
his actual poetic achievement.[19] Indeed, as he goes on to argue, there
is a good case for regarding Polo as one of the finest of the *culterano*
poets, one whose constant reference to Góngora himself, rather than
to any of his imitators, underwrites the vitality of his own poems.

Polo's elegant playfulness often takes the form of a commentary on
his own writing:

Era, en efeto, blanco y era breve...
¡oh, qué linda ocasión de decir *nieve*
si yo fuera poeta principiante!   (DP, p. 212)[20]

It [her foot] was, in short, white and small… oh! what a nice opportunity to say 'snow' [*nieve*, which rhymes with *breve*] if I were a poet just beginning!

Nevertheless, his masterly parodies of a certain *culto* style do not prevent him from writing his own versions of some of Góngora's most famous set pieces, as in the description of fireworks at a wedding:

> Del salitre animadas
> otras exhalaciones dan carreras
> que son en las esferas
> del cabello del sol hebras cortadas,
> para ensartar estrellas hilos de oro,
> errantes paralelos,
> renglones de la plana de los cielos…   (DP, p. 100)

Enlivened by saltpetre, other exhalations run their courses which, in the spheres, are locks cut from the sun's hair, to string stars on threads of gold, wandering parallels, lines [traced] on the flat surface of the heavens…

This comes from the 'Epitalamio' (Epithalamium), perhaps his most insistently *culterano* poem and one of the few which is linked to a particular occasion. What strikes one in most of his work, however, is the sense of a poet who writes mainly for his own pleasure; in all but his last poems, there is a notable absence of moralizing, even where one might most expect it, as in the splendid flower poems included in *Las academias del jardín*. And characteristically, one of his best longer poems, *Ocios de la soledad* (Pleasures of Solitude; 1633) is an eminently sociable poem, quite remote from any Horatian suggestions of spiritual retreat. In his final book however – *A Lelio. Gobierno moral* (To Lelio. On Moral Government; 1657), a series of prose discourses with linking sonnets – it is as if the seriousness of the subject (and perhaps thoughts of approaching age) had finally brought together the moral seriousness of both Góngora and Quevedo in a poetry whose clarity and dignity raise it far above the level of mere pastiche:

> *Contra un ciprés que lo abrasó un rayo*
>
> Es verdad; yo te vi, ciprés frondoso,
> estrechar de los vientos la campaña;
> yo vi ser la soberbia que te engaña
> aguja verde en Menfis oloroso.
>   Creíste que por grande y poderoso
> no te alcanzase de un dolor la saña;
> rodear sabe el mal; por senda extraña

vino el castigo en traje luminoso.
Rigor tu vanidad llama a esta furia.
Si no son los castigos impiedades,
no se quejen tus culpas tan a gritos.
Nunca lo que es razón ha sido injuria,
ni por más que atormenten sus verdades
han de saber quejarse los delitos.   (DP, p. 177)

Against a Cypress Tree Struck by Lightning It is true; I saw you, a leafy cypress, embrace the region of the winds; I saw the pride which deceives you was a green pyramid in a scented Memphis. You thought that, because you were great and powerful, the anger of an affliction would not touch you; evil goes roundabout; punishment, clothed in light, came by a strange path. Your vanity calls this fury harshness. If punishments are not impieties, your faults should not complain so loudly. Never has what is reason been an offence, nor, however much its truths torment, should misdeeds try to protest.

What make this poem particularly memorable are the splendid Gongoresque images – 'aguja verde en Menfis oloroso'... 'castigo en traje luminoso' – which reinforce the moral thrust of the argument. More than most other kinds of poem, this type of meditative sonnet continues to produce interesting variants well after the middle of the century. Even a much less imaginative poet like López de Zárate (1580–1658) can on occasion rise to effects of some distinction in this particular mode:

Átomos son al sol cuantas beldades
con presunción debida, siendo flores,
siendo caducos todos sus primores,
respiran, anhelando a eternidades.
    ¿La Rosa, cuándo? ¿Cuándo llegó a edades,
con todos sus fantásticos honores?
¿No son pompas, alientos, y colores,
rápidas, fugitivas brevedades?
    Tú de flor, y de rosa presumida,
mira, si te consigue algún seguro,
ser, en gracias, a todas preferida.
    Ni es reparo beldad, ni salud muro:
pues va, de no tener, a tener vida,
ser polvo iluminado, o polvo escuro.   (SD, II, p. 54)[21]

All those beauties which, with due presumption, since they are flowers, since all their graces are ephemeral, breathe and yearn for eternal life, are atoms in the sun. The rose, when, when did it grow old in years, with all its fantastic honours? Are bubbles, breaths, colours not swift, fleeting brevities? You, who pride yourself on being a flower and a rose, see whether being exalted in graces above all others grants you any security. Beauty is no remedy, nor health a wall; for the difference between not having life and having it is that between bright dust and dark dust.

Here, the last line, though fine in itself, cannot help but recall even finer lines by Góngora or Quevedo. Nevertheless, the way in which the initial dactyl ('Átomos') rushes one into the opening quatrain and the agitated repetition of the fifth line ('...cuándo? ¿Cuándo...?') give the poem a direct, spoken quality which adds conviction to an otherwise conventional subject.

This poem comes from a collection published in 1651. As the century advances, however, there are signs that even this relatively productive vein is beginning to run thin. Hence the slightly desperate ingenuity with which another minor poet and dramatist of the time, Salazar y Torres (1642–73?), writes a sonnet – first published in 1681 – which neatly reverses the sense of Zárate's poem, making the brief life of the rose a cause for celebration:

> Este ejemplo feliz de la hermosura
> que en purpúreos ardores resplandece,
> si a dar admiraciones amanece,
> a no dar escarmientos se apresura...[22]

This happy example of beauty which shines in purple ardour, if it is born to cause wonder, it hastens *not* to serve as a warning...

Both the poets I have just mentioned show symptoms of decline in their other work: López de Zárate spent many years writing and revising a long religious epic, *La invención de la Cruz* (The Discovery of the Cross; 1648), for which his talents were clearly unsuited; Salazar's most ambitious poem, the *Fábula de Adonis y Venus*, is a notorious example of *culteranismo* at its most decadent. 'Decadence' (though with certain qualifications) also seems the right word for a more important figure of the time, Francisco de Trillo y Figueroa (1618?–80?), whose main poetic activity falls between 1645 and the early 1660s. Though he came from Galicia, Trillo spent most of his life in Granada, where he was a close friend of Soto de Rojas, to whose *Paraíso* he wrote an appropriately erudite prose introduction. In the notes to the *Neapolisea* (1651) – his epic poem on Gonzalo de Córdoba (1453–1515), the hero of Spain's Italian wars – he defends the achievement of Góngora with great vigour and argues in no uncertain terms for the supremacy of the 'high' style. When one turns to his own poems, however, things are very different: the *Neapolisea* is a pretentious and largely undistinguished poem which serves mainly to show how anachronistic the literary epic had become by mid-century; as for his imitations of Góngora, these are for the most part confined to burlesque poems, many of them obscene and obsessively anti-feminist. Moreover, as Robert Jammes has conclusively demonstrated, Trillo goes in for plagiarism on a scale which is exceptional even for the seventeenth century, often adapting or expanding his originals with little care for verbal precision.[23] Nevertheless, Jammes's final verdict – 'Trillo n'est pas un poète; c'est un érudit' – seems too harsh. Though he has some merit as a historical writer, much of Trillo's 'erudition' – like Lope's in his preface to the *Jerusalén conquistada* (see above, p. 193) – is commonplace and ill-digested; on the other hand, there is no doubting his very genuine feeling for popular poetry – something which is becoming increasingly rare outside the theatre, and which he is occasionally able to put to good use in his own verse:

> ¡Válgame Dios, que los ánsares vuelan;
> válgame Dios, que saben volar!
>   Andando en el suelo
> vide un ánsar chico,
> y alzando su pico
> vino a mí de vuelo,
> diome un gran consuelo
> de verlo alear.
>   ¡Válgame Dios, que los ánsares vuelan;
> válgame Dios, que saben volar!   (GM, p. 125)[24]

Bless my soul, the geese are flying; bless my soul, how they can fly! I saw a little goose walking on the ground and, lifting its beak, it came flying to me; it gave me great comfort to see it stretch its wings. Bless my soul, etc.

The rest of this poem develops, with great delicacy and simplicity, into a love complaint of a thoroughly traditional kind. What is remarkable, however, in this and other poems, is Trillo's use of popular Galician–Portuguese forms and rhythms – here the so-called *versos de gaita gallega*[25] – which he handles with great skill. If, as Cossío claims, Trillo tends to remain at a certain distance from the other Granada poets of his time[26] – a temperamental difference which may account for the virulence of some of his anti-Andalusian satire – the positive side of this is his continuing ability to draw on a source of poetry encountered long before he became a professional poet and never, it would seem, completely forgotten.

Trillo is only one example of the general exhaustion which seems to overtake the entire *culterano* tradition towards the middle of the century: of the failure to create new kinds of poem and of the gradual coarsening of what once had been a brilliantly inventive style. Nevertheless, there are exceptions: most notably the descriptive poem, one example of which we have already seen in the *Paraíso* of Soto de Rojas.

Once again, the debt to Góngora is immense: though the *Soledades* are clearly much more than descriptive poetry, their relative lack of narrative plot seemed strange at the time and was frequently remarked on by hostile critics. Other poets, however, were quick to see the possibilities of Góngora's descriptive manner and to use it as the basis for entire poems. One of the earliest, and most extraordinary, of these is the 'Canción real a San Jerónimo en Siria' (Ode to St Jerome in Syria; 1619) of Adrián de Prado (fl. 1620), in which the desert landscape is made to take on a menacing life of its own through the imaginative use of organic imagery:

> Entre aquestos peñascos perezosos
> levanta la cabeza encenizada
> la cerviz recia de un pelado risco,
> de cuyos hombros toscos y nudosos
> pende la espalda hidrópica y tostada
> con dos costillas secas de un lentisco;
> y del pecho arenisco
> dos hiedras amarillas,
> también como costillas,
> que por entre los músculos y huecos
> van paseando aquellos miembros secos,
> pintando venas hasta las mejillas,
> las cuales con su máscara de piedra
> pasar no dejan la asombrada hiedra.   (lines 57–69)[27]

Among these sluggish peaks there raises its ashen head the stiff neck of a bald crag, from whose rough, knotted shoulders there hangs a tanned, dropsical shoulder with the two dry ribs of lentisk; and from the sandy chest, two yellow strands of ivy, also like ribs, which insinuate their dry limbs between the muscles and hollows, painting veins as far as the cheeks, which with their stone mask prevent the astonished ivy from going further.

This remarkable poem, the work of a virtually unknown writer, was included in one of the most important manuscript anthologies of the time, the so-called *Cancionero de 1628*. Part of the interest of this collection, compiled in Saragossa, lies in its strong Aragonese bias: more specifically, in its value as an index of the reception of *culteranismo* in Aragon. What is particularly striking is the difference between generations and the change in poetic criteria this implies, a situation neatly illustrated by the inclusion of the 'Canción a San Jerónimo' alongside Lupercio Leonardo de Argensola's much earlier descriptive poem on the gardens of Aranjuez, first published in 1589. This poem – one of Lupercio's finest – has all the classical virtues I discussed in an earlier chapter (see above, p. 135); nevertheless, as I suggested then, there are signs that by this time, or shortly afterwards, the poetry of both the Argensolas was coming to seem outmoded.[28] This, no doubt, is an oversimplification: the Argensolas continued to be read and imitated, in Aragon and elsewhere; one of their greatest admirers, the poet and classicist Esteban Manuel de Villegas (1589–1669), had followed their example in his imitations and adaptations of Horace, Anacreon and other elegiac poets,[29] and their characteristic didactic note recurs in much of the work of the younger Aragonese poets. On balance, however, the triumph of Góngora – and, to a lesser extent, of Quevedo – is as complete in Aragon as it is in other parts of the Peninsula, though with interesting local variations. In general terms, the Aragonese poets of the next few decades form not so much a 'school' as a compact group of writers with a common source in *culteranismo* and strong connections with poets elsewhere.[30] Bocángel, for example, knew and corresponded with a number of Aragonese poets and scholars, including Pellicer, the commentator of Góngora; the Madrid poet Cáncer y Velasco (d. 1655), originally from Barbastro, continued to take part in poetic competitions in his native Aragon, where he was noted for his skill in word play. (It is also a sign of contemporary taste that an edition of Villamediana's poems was published in Saragossa in 1629.)

As Aurora Egido makes clear in her detailed study of the Aragonese poets,[31] the two main areas of interest were the descriptive poem and the mythological fable. The latter, at least in its burlesque versions, owes as much to Quevedo as to Góngora, and shows few signs of originality. The descriptive poems of the period, however – most notably in the work of poets like Juan de Moncayo (c. 1600–post 1651) and the roughly contemporary Miguel de Dicastillo[32] – are more distinctive. Though their tendency to expansiveness involves a dilution of Góngora's more concentrated manner, their delight in artifice and their mastery of Gongorine syntax and vocabulary show a professionalism sustained, no doubt, by mutual example. For the most part, the scenes and places they describe – as in Dicastillo's fine poem on the Charterhouse of Saragossa – amount to what Egido calls a 'nature made out of texts',[33] a re-creation of other poems, and only rarely a matter of direct observation. With *culterano* poetry, it could hardly be otherwise: the refraction of the external world through the prism of metaphor and conceit is part of a whole style, as in Mateo de Aguirre's description of the town of Calatayud:

> Sus castillos de peñas fabricados
> contra el tiempo soldados
> valerosos de piedra,
> que ni la flor admiten ni la yedra.
> ...
> Sus edificios graves
> Palacios deleitosos, y suaves,
> que a Tempe en sus jardines
> forman con verdes y plateados fines
> donde el cristal en surtidores ata
> cabellos de oro, con listol de plata.[34]

Its castles made of rocks, brave soldiers of stone who resist time and admit neither flower nor ivy...Its solemn buildings, delightful, gentle palaces whose gardens create [a new] Tempe with green and silvery limits, where crystal binds golden hair into fountains with ribbons of silver.

Yet, more often than not – and this seems especially characteristic of the Aragonese poets – the *culto* vocabulary and diction are loaded with moral implications, as in the more consciously classical poetry of the Argensolas. In Lupercio's poem on Aranjuez, all the classical ingredients – the ideal landscape, the *locus amoenus*, the Horatian praise of simplicity – are present in a concentrated form; in the later Aragonese poets, this vision, though for stylistic reasons more diffuse, still retains its authority, just as the model itself, for all its apparent archaism, is never entirely lost to sight.

III

The influence of the Argensolas can also be seen in one of the best religious poets of the time, Jerónimo de San José (1587–1654), a member of the Order of Discalced Carmelites and an early biographer of San Juan de la Cruz. As a poet, Jerónimo de San José owes a great deal to his friendship with Bartolomé Leonardo; though he also composed a series of attractive *redondillas* on religious themes, reminiscent at times of the doctrinal ballads of San Juan, his best work tends to occur in his sonnets on biblical and moral texts, like his meditation on the Vulgate version of James, 4.15:

> *Vita Nostra Vapor ad Modicum Parens*
>
> Al trasmontar del sol, su luz dorada
> cogió de unos fantásticos bosquejos
> la tabla, y al matiz de sus reflejos,
> dejóla de colores varïada.
>   Aquí sobre morada cairelada
> arden las fimbras de oro en varios lejos,
> acullá reverbera en sus espejos
> la nube de los rayos retocada;
>   suben por otra parte, en penachera
> de oro, verde y azul, volantes puros,
> tornasolando visos y arreboles;
>   mas, ¡oh breve y fantástica quimera!,
> pónese el sol, y quedan luego oscuros
> los vaporcillos, que eran otros soles.

Our Life is a Vapour, that Appeareth for a Little Time As the sun went down, its golden light touched with fantastic outlines the panel [of the sky] and, with the tint of its reflection, left it in various colours. Here on a purple fringe, the golden borders burn in various effects of distance, there the cloud, touched by rays of light, vibrates in their mirrors; elsewhere pure flames rise in plumes of gold, green and blue, making the gleams of light and the flushed clouds iridescent; but, o brief, fantastic mirage! the sun sets and then the little vapours, which were other suns, remain dark.

Both Jerónimo de San José's concern for clarity and his Christian moralizing link him to the Argensolas; at the same time, as María del Pilar Palomo has noted,[35] there is an unusual sensibility at work here which goes beyond mere classical imitation and which expresses itself through a more contemporary poetic idiom. One might, in fact, argue that it is only the title which makes this a religious poem: that most of the energy of the poem itself goes into creating the sequence of rich colour effects which is scarcely interrupted by the quick moralizing touch – '¡oh breve y fantástica quimera!' – just before the end.

Similarly, in the following poem by Pedro de Quirós (1607?–67), entitled 'A una perla, alusión a la Virgen María' (To a Pearl,

Alluding to the Virgin Mary), the careful working-out of the allegory in the tercets scarcely matches the descriptive power of the first eight lines:

> Del cristalino piélago se atreve
> tal vez marina concha a la ribera,
> y el fulgor puro de la luz primera
> su sed, menor que su avaricia, bebe.
> De la preciosa perla apenas debe
> quedar fecunda el alba lisonjera
> cuando al mar se retira, porque fuera
> ve los rayos del sol manchar su nieve.
> En el mar de la Gracia, ¿quién no mira
> que eres ¡oh Virgen! tú la perla pura
> por cuya luz aun la del sol suspira?
> Mancha el sol de tu perla la blancura;
> mas que en ti no haya mancha, ¿a quién admira,
> si aun al sol presta rayos tu hermosura?

Sometimes from the crystal ocean a sea shell ventures to the shore, and the pure brilliance of the first light [i.e. dawn] quenches its thirst, which is less than its avarice. The flattering dawn must scarcely be made fruitful by the precious pearl when the latter draws back into the sea, since outside it, it sees the rays of the sun stain its snow. In the sea of Grace, who does not see that you, o Virgin, are the pure pearl for whose light even that of the sun yearns? The sun stains the whiteness of your pearl; but that there should be no stain in you, who should wonder, if your beauty lends its rays even to the sun?

Both these instances point to a certain gap between intention and achievement – one which may have more to do with the nature of the poetic idiom than with any specific failure of the imagination. On the one hand, a poem like Adrián de Prado's 'Canción a San Jerónimo', despite its religious subject, is only marginally, if at all, a religious poem. And on the other, it is noticeable how often religious feeling enters into poems which are not strictly religious, as in Soto de Rojas's *Paraíso*, which, as we have seen, only becomes a religious poem in its closing stanzas.

Such problems of definition, to be sure, scarcely affect the countless religious poems composed, often all too mechanically, for public competitions and other forms of celebration. Nevertheless, if such conventional poetry is 'religious' in only a superficial sense, there are exceptions which show that, even after 1650, it was possible to write genuine religious poetry of considerable stature. One could point, among other minor instances, to the *Elegías sacras* (Sacred Elegies) or paraphrases of the *Lamentations* of Jeremiah of the Conde de Rebolledo (1597–1676), an otherwise pedestrian, though not unintelligent, poet, whose work was to undergo something of a revival in the eighteenth century. The outstanding example here, however, is the late poem by Pedro Calderón de la Barca (1600–81), the greatest dramatist of his generation, usually referred to as *Psalle et Sile*.[36] This 525-line poem – a sequence of nine mutually dependent poems in different metres which comprise a single whole – amounts to a verse sermon or meditation in the Ignatian manner (see above, pp. 14–15) on the words 'Calla y reza' (Be silent and pray) which appear on the choir screen of Toledo Cathedral, of which Calderón was a chaplain from 1652 onwards. As E. M. Wilson observes, it is as if Góngora's phrase from the First *Soledad*, 'habla callando' (it speaks by silence; line 197) had taken on a religious meaning, as silence and song are reconciled in divine worship. The intellectual grasp which is evident throughout Calderón's dramatic work is equally clear in the poem – not just in the 'composition of place' and the systematic application of memory, understanding and will, but in the precision of individual thoughts:

> No tan de balde sirves que no sea
> logro tuyo lo que uno y otro gana;
> pues el soldado por tu paz pelea,
> y el labrador por tu sustento afana.
> Lo que hay de una tarea a otra tarea,
> mide, y verás: ¡cuánto es más soberana
> la de tratar y conversar al Cielo
> que arder al Sol y tiritar al hielo! (lines 486–93)

You [the Cathedral clergy] do not serve so vainly that what one or another gains is not a gain for you; for the soldier fights for your peace, and the labourer toils for your nourishment. Measure the difference between one task and another, and you will see: how much more sovereign is that of treating and conversing with Heaven than burning in the sun or shivering in the frost!

Calderón's few, distinguished, poems would be exceptional at any time.[37] A different kind of exception, however, owes more to contemporary conditions: the presence of a small but important group of Jewish exile poets – Antonio Henríquez Gómez (1600?–63), Miguel de Barrios (1635–1701) and João Pinto Delgado (c. 1585–post 1633) – whose work, despite various affinities, often moves on a different plane from that of their contemporaries in the Peninsula. All three were prolific writers: both Barrios and Henríquez Gómez wrote plays, and the latter is perhaps best known for his *El siglo pitagórico y vida de don Gregorio Guadaña* (Century of Pythagoras and Life of Don G. G.: Rouen, 1644), a verse satire on contemporary manners which includes the picaresque novel referred to in the title. As a religious poet, however, Henríquez Gómez is the least interesting of the three: though he occasionally expresses his emotions as an expatriate with great feeling and dignity, his longer biblical poems are often facile, and he seems to need the constraints of the sonnet form to achieve his best effects, as in the reflection on time which begins:

> Este que, exhalación sin consumirse,
> por los cuatro elementos se pasea,
> palestra es de mi marcial pelea,
> y campo que no espera dividirse...[38]

This which, an exhalation which is never consumed, wanders through the four elements, is the arena of my martial conflict and a battleground where there is no hope of division...

Like Henríquez Gómez, both Barrios and Pinto Delgado spent a considerable part of their lives in Jewish communities abroad: Rouen, Antwerp or (in all three cases) Amsterdam. Barrios, who for a time led a curious double life – Christian in Brussels, Jew in Amsterdam – writes with great directness of his rejection of Christianity in favour of Judaism. Many of his poems, like those in praise of the Torah, involve specifically Jewish subject-matter, though his penitential poems have many points of contact with Christian writers, notably with Góngora, Quevedo and Calderón, who are his chief literary models. His liking for *culto* diction is especially noticeable at moments of religious celebration; in a poem on a contemporary Jewish martyr, Raquel Núñez Fernández, burnt by the Inquisition in 1665, he describes the victim as 'de un ardor mariposa, / salamandra de otro ardor' (a butterfly to one kind of burning [i.e. faith], a salamander to another [the flames]) and ends his praise in the same way:

> Ilustras con arreboles
> los diáfanos pensiles,
> tan rosa con veinte abriles
> cuan aurora con dos soles:
> los celestes girasoles
> llevan tu sacra beldad

a la eterna Majestad,
viendo con el resplandor
que naciendo para flor,
espiras para deidad.   (S, p. 245)[39]

You adorn with blushing clouds the transparent hangings, as much a rose
with your twenty springs as a dawn with twin suns [i.e. your eyes]: the
heavenly sunflowers bear your sacred beauty to the eternal Majesty, seeing
from your splendour that, born to be a flower, you expire to become a deity.

In the penitential poems, on the other hand, such stylistic flourishes
disappear, partly because of the nature of the Hebrew religious texts
on which they are based. Thus in his paraphrase of part of the service
for Yom Kippur, or the Day of Atonement, Barrios comes convincingly close to the austere rhetoric of the original:

> Sobre los que nos juzgan eres Justo
> y anduvimos nosotros en lo injusto;
> ¿qué diremos delante de ti, ansiosos,
> sino que fuimos torpes y alevosos?
> Da, o Morador de célicas alturas,
> la maná del perdón a tus criaturas.
> Tú lo encubierto y descubierto sabes,
> en tu mano del mundo están las llaves,
> todo lo abarcas sabio y poderoso:
> perdona al pueblo misericordioso,
> líbranos de pecados y prisiones,
> por pedirte contritos nos perdones.   (S, p. 179)

Above those who judge us, you are the Just One and we ourselves walked in
injustice; what shall we anxiously say in your presence, except that we were
slothful and treacherous? Bestow, o Dweller in the heavenly heights, the
manna of forgiveness on your creatures. You know what is hidden and what
is revealed, in your hand are the keys of the world, wise and powerful, you
encompass all things: pardon the people in your mercy, release us from sins
and captivity, that, contrite, we may pray for your forgiveness.

It is this penitential tone which links Barrios most closely to the
third, and finest, of this group of poets, Pinto Delgado. Unlike Barrios
and Henríquez Gómez, Pinto probably never set foot in Spain: he
came from a family of Portuguese *converso* Jews who emigrated, first
to Flanders and later to Rouen, where he joined them in 1627 and
was for some years the intellectual and spiritual leader of the Jewish
community. (His later years are obscure, though he almost certainly
died in Amsterdam.) Most of his verse is contained in a single volume,

Poema de la Reina Ester, Lamentaciones del Profeta Jeremías, Historia de Rut y varias poesías (Poem of Queen Esther, Lamentation of the Prophet Jeremiah, Story of Ruth and Other Poems; Rouen, 1627). His most important work consists of the three long poems referred to in the title, each directly derived from parts of the Hebrew scriptures. As E. M. Wilson has pointed out,[40] the originality of these poems comes partly from their combination of Christian and rabbinical sources, and partly from the attempt to write a type of poetry acceptable to contemporary taste. As is clear from the description of the feast near the beginning of *Ester*, Pinto had clearly learnt from the *Soledades*:

> Ave no sulca el aire con su vuelo,
> ni exquisito animal la tierra cría,
> ni fruto ofrece el más templado cielo,
> ni suave licor la caña envía,
> que no sirva en despojo a su grandeza
> tributo alegre de abudante mesa.   (R, p. 7)[41]

No bird furrows the air with its flight, the earth breeds no exquisite animal, the most temperate sky offers no fruit, the cane provides no soft juice, but serves as spoil for his greatness, the happy tribute of an abundant table.

Where Pinto goes deeper than either of his Hispano-Jewish contemporaries, however, is in his use of midrash – the rabbinical tradition of biblical exegesis to which I referred a moment ago – and in the way he combines this with other scriptural texts in the course of re-telling a particular Old Testament story. This device of 'inventive paraphrase', as A. D. H. Fishlock calls it,[42] is intensified in the *Lamentaciones* – his finest poem – where the need to follow a previous narrative pattern no longer exists. The blend of intellectual vision and lyrical sensitivity which runs through the whole poem is unlike anything else in the religious verse of the time:

> Movida de su aflicción,
> sus manos levanta al cielo
> la miserable Sión,
> mas halla que su consuelo
> sus mismas lágrimas son.
> ...
>   Allí, por su grave yerro,
> que le exaspera su mal,
> entre el dolor y el destierro,
> se vuelve el cielo en metal,
> la tierra se vuelve en hierro.   (R, p. 191)

Moved by her affliction, wretched Zion raises her hands to heaven, but finds that her own tears are her consolation... There, through her grave error which increases her ills, between grief and exile, the sky turns to metal, the earth to iron.

Or again, inserting the story of Abraham and Isaac in the main text:

> El yugo de su rigor
> me echó, justamente, al cuello,
> para pensar en mi error,
> pues su piedad y favor
> (por mi mal) no pudo hacello.
>
> Al mozo que en su inocencia
> llevaba el peso, esperando
> sólo la mortal sentencia,
> la vida, humilde, olvidando,
> su vida fue su obediencia.
>
> Cuando el cuchillo aguardaba
> (el corazón vuelto al cielo)
> del padre, que le animaba,
> satisfecho de su celo
> el Ángel se lo estorbaba.
>
> Que el que, dichoso, camina
> al monte, aunque en el subir
> dificultad imagina,
> descansa y vuelve a vivir
> en la presencia divina.   (R, pp. 178–9)

He cast the yoke of his severity, justly, about my neck, that I might think on my error, since his pity and favour (to my cost) could not make me. For the youth who bore the burden in his innocence, expecting only the mortal sentence, humbly forgetting life, his life was his obedience. While (his face turned heavenwards) he awaits the knife of his father, who exhorts him, satisfied with his zeal, the Angel prevented it. For he who journeys happily to the mountain, though on the way up he imagines difficulty, rests and lives again in the divine presence.

The economy of such passages depends partly on the verse form – the five-line octosyllabic stanzas known as *quintillas*. At the same time, one is left wondering at the skill with which Pinto writes in a language which, for him, was almost certainly an adopted one – a language, however, which he uses to create a kind of poetry which, because of its debt to a different spiritual tradition, makes a memorable and unexpected addition to the central body of seventeenth-century religious verse.

CHAPTER 9

Sor Juana Inés de la Cruz: the end of a tradition

I

Though the best poetry of the second half of the century is by no means negligible, the general impression is one of diminished possibilities, reinforced by the absence of any major talent. As well as this, there is a growing sense of fragmentation and dispersal: several of the most interesting poets of the period, as we have seen, are exiles, and in Spain itself, the kind of cohesion represented by the literary academies of the first half of the century and by the patronage of cultured politicians like Olivares has been largely lost. All this seems to point to the decline of a whole poetic tradition, one which, despite its former greatness, now appears to be reaching inevitable extinction. Again, however, one must be careful not to oversimplify: if the Spanish poets of the time were unable to renew the tradition in any significant way, the sense in which this was still possible appears, with startling clarity, in the work of the last major poet of the century, the Mexican nun Sor Juana Inés de la Cruz (1648–95).

The fact that Sor Juana is also the first great poet of the New World is in itself an index of the cultural differences between Spain and its American possessions. Where literary tradition is concerned, the crucial point is that poetry, in Mexico and elsewhere, begins as an offshoot of Spanish Renaissance verse – so much so, that the earliest Mexican poets, like Francisco de Terrazas (1525?–1600?) and Miguel de Guevara (1585?–1646), are barely distinguishable from their European counterparts.[1] What strikes one in such poets is both their highly professional assimilation of Spanish models and their lack of personal response to a virtually unique geographical situation, a fact clearly visible in the epic writing of Balbuena (see above, pp. 188–93), whose descriptions of the New World owe more to fantasy and to European pastoral convention than to direct observation.

238

Nevertheless, certain differences stand out: the cultural stagnation of late seventeenth-century Spain is hardly reflected in the splendours of a vice-regal court sustained by a version of Jesuit humanism which sees Mexico–Tenochtitlan as an image of classical Rome – a strong factor in the curious cultural amalgam which underlies much of Sor Juana's work.

A large part of Sor Juana's life, in fact, was centred on this court; though her origins were obscure – she was the illegitimate daughter of a Spanish father and a Mexican mother – her precociousness was phenomenal: she was already known as a poet by the age of ten, and a few years later was taken to court, where she learned Latin and astonished leading writers and scholars by her intellectual gifts. In 1677, she entered the Order of Discalced Carmelites, probably to find peace for her studies and to avoid a conventional marriage, and two years later, after a serious illness, became a nun of the Hieronymite Order, which she remained for the rest of her life. Seen in their full context, such biographical details suggest a conscious intellectual strategy: the culture with which Sor Juana has to come to terms is an essentially learned one, much concerned with the more arcane reaches of neo-Platonism, and at the same time deeply orthodox in its attitude to intellectual speculation. The crucial factor, from her point of view, is that this is a masculine culture, one to which her only hope of access lay through the convent or the court. The co-presence of these two milieux is central to her writing career: as has often been noted, her decision to become a nun has more to do with her intellectual inclinations than with any strong sense of religious vocation, and her position as unofficial poet laureate served for most of her life as a protection against possible interference from her ecclesiastical superiors. And this situation is reflected in her poems, where her so-called 'masculinization' – her tendency to adopt the role of a male speaker or, occasionally, to deny her own sex – is to be explained, not in terms of biological necessity, but rather as a strategy or disguise which enables her to enter a sphere in which any intrusion can be seen as an act of transgression.

The kind of problems this involves appear most strikingly in those poems which deal with questions of human love. Whether or not these are based on real experience – or even what would count as 'experience' in this context – no longer seems crucial. What is more to the point is the type of situation Sor Juana creates in such poems and the way she responds to it. Though several of these poems, as we shall see, are both moving and accomplished in their own right, the majority belong to what Alan Trueblood has called the 'casuistry of love'[2] – poems which speak for opposing points of view and which contain a good deal of theorizing, which is not always applied to a particular situation. (Where a situation *does* emerge, it is generally straightforward, not to say schematic: the speaker loves A, who does not love her; at the same time, she is loved by B, whom she rejects.) The question is, quite simply, how are we to take such poems? Are they merely examples of Sor Juana's skill in arguing both sides of a case, or is she arguing with herself in a more responsible sense, as part of a constantly shifting dialectic? Read as a group, they may strike one rather as the poems for an unwritten pastoral novel; that is to say, in spite of their inconsistencies, they revolve around a limited number of central ideas which they debate from different, though related, points of view. Or, thinking of the artistic process behind the poems, one might put it another way: although their author is not committed permanently to a particular attitude, she has had at different times to imagine the circumstances in which any given one might be true. Sor Juana, of course, is not alone in this: the whole tradition of love poetry from the *cancioneros* onward shows similar inconsistencies which need only trouble us if we insist on relating them to personal experience, rather than to a developing literary convention. What Sor Juana's poems have in common, then, is a rational framework of thought which rests on certain traditional polarities: reason–passion, soul–body, intuition–logic. And these polarities are more often than not combined with more specific features of earlier love poetry, with concepts taken from neo-Platonism or the theory of courtly love, though here again it would be wrong to look for a complete exposition of any one set of ideas.

Thus, one could argue, the real unity of the poems comes from the sense of a strong personality which binds together a large number of heterogeneous elements – something in which the tone of voice which speaks through the verse is at least as important as the biographical facts. This is hard to demonstrate in detail, though some such explanation is needed to account for the contrast between the almost line-by-line derivativeness of many of her poems and the extraordinary freshness of the whole. This is not to deny her lapses: many passages, and occasionally whole poems, strike one as overingenious or at times merely arid; her best verse succeeds, on the other hand, precisely because her imagination is able to find new patterns in traditional clusters of thought without accepting them schematically.

Allowing, then, for conflicting points of view, how comprehensive is the range of attitudes Sor Juana presents? Here it is possible to detect a preference for certain types of situation rather than others. It is noticeable, for example, that even in the poems which emphasize the idea of mutual love, there is little idea of what such love might be like – the sense of a relationship which, for better or for worse, involves the whole process of living. Nor is there much evidence of the characteristic neo-Platonic progression from sexual love to spiritual love. Though the love of beauty is described in a number of poems, notably in those addressed to her vice-regal patroness the Condesa de Paredes, there is no suggestion that this may lead to the contemplation of God, just as, at the other extreme, there is no indication that the woman's reflected beauty may be legitimately possessed.

Such qualifications are not meant as a criticism, but are mainly an attempt to indicate the area in which Sor Juana's love poetry moves and the kind of central situations on which it is based. One of these is the notion of 'correspondence' (*correspondencia*) – 'relationship', whether positive or negative; another, less easy to define, is the tendency to think in terms of a spiritual love which does not appear to lead on to the love of God. This love is what she calls a 'love of the understanding' (*amor del entendimiento*) which resides in the soul and which scorns the senses. Moreover, this kind of love can transcend differences of sex in a way which seems very characteristic of Sor Juana. As she writes to the Condesa de Paredes:

> Ser mujer, ni estar ausente,
> no es de amarte impedimento;
> pues sabes tú, que las almas
> distancia ignoran y sexo. (19, lines 109–12)[3]

To be a woman, or to be absent, is no obstacle to loving you; for you know that souls ignore distance and sex.

Such statements are common in the poems addressed to friends, both male and female, where there is no reason to suppose that she is acting a role. Thus, if there *is* a 'scale' in Sor Juana's poems, it is not a 'spiritual ladder' in the neo-Platonic sense, but one which runs through the varieties of 'voluntary love' (*amor por elección*), from spiritual love between the sexes to the natural demands of kinship.

And at the back of all these possibilities is the idea of sexual neutrality which she expresses so forcibly in poem 48:

> Con que a mí no es bien mirado
> que como a mujer me miren,
> pues no soy mujer que a alguno
> de mujer pueda servirle;
>   y sólo sé que mi cuerpo,
> sin que a uno u otro se incline,
> es neutro, o abstracto, cuanto
> sólo el Alma deposite.   (lines 101–8)

So it is disrespectful to regard me as a woman who can serve any man as such; and I only know that my body, without inclining to one man or another, is neutral or abstract, insofar as it only houses the Soul.

Here, certainly, it is safe to assume that Sor Juana is speaking from the standpoint of her religious vocation, though the attitude she is expressing seems almost a logical consequence of the conduct she envisages in several of the love poems. It would be tempting to draw the connection tighter, were it not for the evidence of other poems which present emotional situations of some intensity. Yet significantly, the most serious of these relate either to absence or death, or, in the one notable exception (poem 163), to the failure of the loved one to return the speaker's love. Thus poem 76 – 'Si acaso, Fabio mío...' (If by chance, my Fabio) – is in many ways the finest, and most moving, of Sor Juana's love poems, not merely because of the situation itself. This is exceptional enough – the woman who speaks is dying in the arms of her lover – yet what strikes one most is the complete absence of rhetoric and the effect of tenderness this creates. This is not merely a question of restraint or the avoidance of sentimentality: the boldness of a metaphor like 'De tu rostro en el mío / haz, amoroso, estampa' (Imprint your face, lovingly, on mine) and a phrase like 'Unidas de las manos / las bien tejidas palmas' (The well-woven palms of our hands united) are more physical than anything else in Sor Juana's poems. But what controls such detail is the same voice which can contemplate death as an 'eternal night' and, a moment later, move wittily through a series of legal metaphors which issue with sudden appropriateness in the image of a pagan underworld:

> Dáme por prendas firmes
> de tu fe no violada,
> en tu pecho escrituras,

>   seguros en tu cara,
>   para que cuando baje
>   a las Estigias aguas,
>   tuyo el óbolo sea
>   para fletar la barca.   (lines 45–52)

Give me as firm tokens of your inviolate faith deeds in your breast, securities in your face, so that when I go down to the waters of the Styx, yours may be the obol which charters the boat.

It would be difficult to deny the sense of intimacy; yet one suspects that such a mood has been achieved precisely because of the imminence of death. At one point in the poem, the speaker says:

>   dáme el postrer abrazo
>   cuyas tiernas lazadas,
>   siendo unión de los cuerpos,
>   identifican almas.   (lines 25–8)

Give me the final embrace, whose tender bonds, in uniting our bodies, make our souls identical.

In other poems, the unity of souls is directly opposed to the idea of physical union. Here, there is no such opposition, but rather a telescoping of the two states, so that one is indistinguishable from the other. Thus, in this particular poem, there is a sense in which the physical union, such as it is, achieves a dignity which it is not allowed elsewhere simply because of the unrepeatable nature of the situation, as if the urgency of the request guaranteed the merging of body and soul.

These invented situations lead one to reflect on the part played by the imagination in Sor Juana's work. This is not merely a question of invention, but also, in certain poems, a possible means of dominating the experiences which she presents. One cannot fail to notice, for example, how many of her love poems are concerned with absence. In several of the more conventional pieces, a male speaker claims that the woman he loves, though physically absent, is present – and more powerfully so – to the 'eyes of the soul'. Though the idea is often no more than a convenient hyperbole, it is the emphasis itself which is important: the notion that imagined pleasures are actually superior to those which are literally experienced. One sees the significance of this when one turns to a much finer poem (165), the sonnet entitled

'Que contiene una fantasía contenta con amor decente' (Which Contains a Fantasy Satisfied with a Decorous Love):

> Detente, sombra de mi bien esquivo,
> imagen del hechizo que más quiero,
> bella ilusión por quien alegre muero,
> dulce ficción por quien penosa vivo.
> Si al imán de tus gracias, atractivo,
> sirve mi pecho de obediente acero,
> ¿para qué me enamoras lisonjero
> si has de burlarme luego fugitivo?
> Mas blasonar no puedes, satisfecho,
> de que triunfa de mí tu tiranía:
> que aunque dejas burlado el lazo estrecho
> que tu forma fantástica ceñía,
> poco importa burlar brazos y pecho
> si te labra prisión mi fantasía.

Stay, shadow of my elusive love, image of the spell I most adore, fair illusion for whom I gladly die, sweet fiction for whom I live in pain. If my breast serves as an obedient needle to the attractive magnet of your graces, why do you woo me with flattery if you then mock me by fleeing? But you cannot boast, in satisfaction, that your tyranny triumphs over me: for though you escape the tight noose which bound your fantastic form, it matters little if you escape my arms and breast if my imagination builds a prison for you.

As Carlos Blanco Aguinaga explains in his fine analysis of this poem,[4] its whole strategy consists in deceiving the expectations aroused in the opening quatrains. Just at the moment when it seems likely that the shadow of the elusive lover will finally escape her, the speaker quietly announces her victory in the last few lines. Absence here, in other words, has become crucial: it is no longer a temporary condition, though neither is it the total absence of death. Quite simply, it is a state which, because of the power of the imagination, has ceased to be a deprivation at all – the only state, moreover, in which the imagination is at liberty to exercise its powers to the full. At this level, it hardly seems to matter whether the situation is invented or not. Without exception, the men and women of Sor Juana's love poems are 'shadows' evolved by the imagination. As Ramón Xirau has observed: 'It is as if Sor Juana wished to distance the loved object in order to shape it more easily; as if she wished to hold it in recollection in order to preserve it more fully in the images of memory.'[5] Hence the importance, not only of absence, but of all the other devices and arguments by which her poems elude the tensions of a living relationship. In all the situations she presents, there are two ways of dominating experience, the one intellectual, the other emotional, though the second is never entirely divorced from the first. As has often been pointed out, her mind habitually works in terms of traditional dualities. Her intellect is such that it can argue for opposing points of view; it is emotionally, through her imagination, that she comes closest to achieving a synthesis of contraries, a precarious undertaking which can only succeed in the face of rational impossibility and which, when it fails, plunges straight into disillusionment.

Octavio Paz, in his monumental study of Sor Juana,[6] relates the figure of the absent lover to the absence of the poet's father in real life: to the possibility that, for Sor Juana, an illegitimate child, her father may only have existed as a kind of imaginary projection. This may be overingenious, yet Paz is surely right to insist on the complex undercurrents which run beneath what are often taken to be no more than intellectual exercises. Similarly, one welcomes the sureness of touch he brings to a very different kind of personal poem: those addressed to Sor Juana's two vice-regal patronesses, the Marquesa de Mancera and the Condesa de Paredes. Many of these remain within the bounds of conventional *galanterie*; others, however – more so in the case of the Condesa de Paredes – fall into a kind of erotic language which seems to strain beyond any notion of 'Platonic friendship', as in poem 61:

> Tránsito a los jardines de Venus,
> órgano es de marfil, en canora
> música, tu garganta, que en dulces
> éxtasis aun al viento aprisiona.
> Pámpanos de cristal y de nieve,
> cándidos tus dos brazos, provocan
> Tántalos, los deseos ayunos:
> míseros, sienten frutas y ondas.   (lines 37–44)

A passage to the gardens of Venus, your throat is an ivory organ which imprisons even the wind in sweet ecstasies with its harmonious music. Tendrils of crystal and snow, your two white arms provoke barren desires, like those of Tantalus: they long miserably for fruits and water.

Yet here, as Paz rightly observes, we must avoid the mistake of reading seventeenth-century verse through Romantic eyes: if, as he concedes, there is nothing else quite like these poems in Spanish, they contain little that cannot be explained in terms of the Petrarchan tradition or related to the vocabulary of neo-Platonic love. The genuineness of the feeling which informs this 'loving friendship', as Paz calls it, is unmistakable, yet what ultimately keeps Sor Juana's discourse within the limits of decorum is the separation of soul and body which she is careful to observe even in her most extravagant moments, and which confirms, rather than conflicts with, her claims to sexual neutrality.

II

Sor Juana's religious poetry divides conveniently into the public and the private – the latter, as we shall see, not entirely disconnected from her secular love poems. The public poetry consists of six sets of *villancicos*, or poems in popular metres, written for performance in the cathedrals of Mexico, Oaxaca and Puebla.[7] Apart from anything else, these poems are a splendid example of the intelligence and sympathy with which Sor Juana contributes to the spiritual life of her community; though she is writing in a long established tradition, the consistent verve and ingenuity of her invention, together with her genuine feeling for popular religion in a multi-racial society, go far beyond the range of any possible models. Perhaps their greatest quality – one which, unfortunately, often makes them virtually untranslatable – is the diversity of verbal registers which they draw on: dog Latin, the defective Spanish of Basque and Portuguese speakers, Negro *patois* and – most original of all – whole sequences in Nahuatl, with which Sor Juana is clearly familiar. In a sense, these are unclassifiable poems, whose effect is difficult to grasp when divorced from its musical and dramatic context: closer, perhaps, to opera libretti than to actual theatre, and punctuated by astonishing bursts of pure lyricism, as in the *estribillo*, or refrain, which ends a limpid paraphrase of the *Song of Songs* (221):

> ¡Al Monte, al Monte, a la Cumbre
> corred, volad, Zagales,
> que se nos va María por los aires!
> ¡Corred, corred, volad, aprisa, aprisa,
> que nos lleva robadas las almas y las vidas,
> y llevando en sí misma nuestra riqueza,
> nos deja sin tesoros el Aldea! (lines 49–55)

To the hills, to the hills, to the summit, run, shepherd boys, fly, Mary is ascending the skies! Run, run, fly, quickly, quickly, she is bearing away our lives and souls, carrying our riches in herself and leaving our village without treasures!

As Dario Puccini remarks, the *villancicos* frequently disrupt the conventional division between 'sacred' and 'profane'.[8] The same might be said of Sor Juana's other religious poems, where the subject of divine love is often inseparable from questions of human love. In divine love, predictably, all contraries are resolved; as she puts it in poem 56: 'Que amor que se tiene en Dios / es calidad sin opuestos' (For love which is placed in God is a quality without opposites). In Sor Juana's presentation of divine love, therefore, there are none of the contradictory attitudes one finds in her poems on secular love. What problems there are come from a different source: roughly speaking, there are tensions involved in achieving divine love, and these come from the weakness of human nature, more specifically from the tendency of the attitudes of human love to intervene. Hardly surprisingly, therefore, several of the religious poems contain contrasts, open or implicit, with human love, and these are all the sharper for being expressed in a common terminology.

Once again, the key concept is 'correspondence'. In poem 56, from which I have just quoted, Sor Juana speaks of the difficulty of achieving disinterestedness in a divine context. On the face of it, she has rejected all kinds of human love – 'amor bastardo ... de contrarios compuesto' (illegitimate love ... formed from contraries) – in favour of the one legitimate love, that of God. Problems arise, however, when her spiritual desires become overlaid with human expectations; her difficulty comes about because she wishes God to return her love, though she regards this as a human failing. The result is division:

> Tan precisa es la apetencia
> que a ser amados tenemos,
> que, aun sabiendo que no sirve,
> nunca dejarla sabemos.
>   Que corresponda a mi amor,
> nada añade; mas no puedo,
> por más que lo solicito,
> dejar yo de apetecerlo.   (lines 45–52)

So necessary is the desire we have to be loved that, even though we know it is useless, we can never abandon it. If He responds to my love, it adds nothing; but, however much I wish to, I cannot cease to desire it.

Méndez Plancarte slightly misinterprets these lines: the source of the speaker's grief is not 'the desire for the absolute security of God's correspondence',[9] but the fact that she is unable to rise above the desire for such 'correspondence'. It would be a mistake, therefore, to suppose that she were denying the existence of God's love for man; in view of the earlier lines in which human love is rejected, it seems that what she really fears is that the purity of her love for God will be harmed by an excessively human idea of 'correspondence'.

Despite the possible echo of St Teresa,[10] there is nothing especially 'mystical' about this poem and others like it. As in all Sor Juana's writings, divine love is equated with reason and virtue, never with less rational qualities; unreason, on the other hand, is part of the normal fabric of human life, just as it belongs to a certain kind of secular love. This helps to explain why the contemplation of God, in the strict sense of the term, seldom enters her work, even as an ideal. What one finds instead is the constant humility of someone for whom divine favours are granted without regard for merit and for whom any thought of a more direct relationship with God would seem arrogant. And this may lead us to reflect once again on the love poems: if this is Sor Juana's view of her relations with God, is it surprising that her poems should avoid the idea that, through human love, one may arise to the contemplation of divinity?

III

In all Sor Juana's religious writing, there is one major theme: divine love is rational, consequently, there can be no direct, intuitive knowledge of God. This is why, in her sacred poems, the idea of divine love is continually approached through comparisons with human love, which is partly known, though limited by various kinds of convention. In the end, the contradictions of the love poems seem to indicate – how consciously, one cannot say – that such partial knowledge is the most one can hope to achieve. What matters for Sor Juana is not so much knowledge in itself as the search for knowledge, a fact which is very evident in her one undoubted masterpiece, the *Primero sueño* (First Dream), a dream vision of the universe which dramatizes the failure of the human mind to grasp reality by intellectual means.

The best short summary of the poem, which runs to almost a thousand lines, is that given by her early biographer, Father Diego

Calleja: 'It being night, I fell asleep; I dreamed that I wished to understand once and for all all the things of which the universe is composed; I was unable to, even when they were divided according to categories, and I failed to comprehend a single individual. Disillusioned, I awoke with the new day.'[11] Though the possible sources of the *Primero sueño*, from the *Somnium Scipionis* to earlier Spanish poems, have been studied in great detail,[12] such resemblances as there are do little to explain the main thrust of Sor Juana's poem. About its language, there can be less doubt; the title of the original edition (1692) describes the poem as an 'imitation of Góngora', and the diction and vocabulary of Góngora's major poems are clearly central to the whole composition:

> Piramidal, funesta, de la tierra
> nacida sombra, al Cielo encaminaba
> de vanos obeliscos punta altiva,
> escalar pretendiendo las Estrellas;
> si bien sus luces bellas
> – exentas siempre, siempre rutilantes –
> la tenebrosa guerra
> que con negros vapores le intimaba
> la pavorosa sombra fugitiva
> burlaban tan distantes,
> que su atezado ceño
> al superior convexo aun no llegaba
> del orbe de la Diosa
> que tres veces hermosa
> con tres hermosos rostros ser ostenta,
> quedando sólo dueño
> del aire que empañaba
> con el aliento denso que exhalaba;
> y en la quietud contenta
> de imperio silencioso,
> sumisas sólo voces consentía
> de las nocturnas aves,
> tan obscuras, tan graves,
> que aun el silencio no se interrumpía.   (lines 1–24)

Pyramidal, funereal, a shadow born of earth was directing heavenwards the lofty point of vain obelisks, attempting to scale the stars; though their lovely lights – always free, always shimmering – so distantly evaded the dark war which the fearful, fugitive shadow declared on Heaven, that its blackened frown did not as yet reach to the upper convex of the sphere of the Goddess [i.e. the Moon] who shows herself thrice beautiful, with three fair faces, remaining master only of the air it clouded with the dense breath it exhaled; and content with the stillness of the silent empire, it consented only to the submissive cries of the night birds, so dark and heavy that the silence was not even broken.

What strikes one immediately in these opening lines is both the assurance with which Sor Juana takes over her model and the quite different uses to which she puts the techniques one normally associates with Góngora.[13] And as the poem develops, the differences between the *Soledades* and the *Primero sueño* become increasingly obvious – so much so that one hesitates to call the latter a 'Gongoresque poem' in anything but a superficial sense. Apart from anything else, the *Primero sueño* is a tightly constructed poem with carefully placed dramatic climaxes; moreover, where Góngora transforms a given reality by means of richly sensuous metaphor, Sor Juana attempts to describe a reality which is strictly invisible and can only be grasped through intellectual abstractions and geometrical figures.

Taken as a whole, the *Primero sueño* is a philosophical, rather than a religious, poem: God is referred to simply as the 'High Being' (*Alto Ser*) or the First Cause and never as a dynamic force in human affairs. Nevertheless, the real nature of Sor Juana's philosophical interests is not always easy to gauge, and attempts to restrict her intellectual activity to a conventional version of neo-Thomism or to see her as a predecessor of the eighteenth-century Enlightenment have tended to suppress some of the most characteristic features of her mental landscape. Here one comes back to the kind of cultural synthesis I referred to earlier: more specifically, to the tradition of occult philosophy, in which the 'secret wisdom' of the *Corpus hermeticum* – an important component of neo-Platonism from Ficino onwards – is combined with the Renaissance taste for emblems and the growing interest in hieroglyphs. As Paz clearly demonstrates, the kind of speculation this involves forms a strong counter-current within the limits of official religion: the syncretism of the Jesuits – as evident in the Far East as it was in New Spain – itself owed a good deal to the hermetic tradition, and it was a German Jesuit, Athanasius Kircher (1601–81), whose writings provided Sor Juana with one of her most fertile sources.

Kircher's attempt to create a Christian synthesis of world religions, carried on through many volumes of Latin prose, proposes an 'Egyptocentric' vision of universal history, in which the Egypt of the hermetic tradition becomes the prototype of Catholic Rome, as well as the spiritual ancestor of China, India and pre-Christian Mexico. A glance at the illustrations from Kircher reproduced in Paz's book – the attributes of Isis, the Pyramids of Cheops and Memphis, the Tower of Babel, the magic lantern that is referred to in the *Primero sueño* – is enough to convince one of his importance for Sor Juana. It is these potent images, and the arcane learning in which they are enshrined, which convey most vividly both the scope and the limitations of Sor Juana's mental horizon and bring one closer to the nature of the intellectual endeavour which gave rise to her most ambitious poem.

Hence the fascination and, at the same time, the relative unimportance of sources. If, as Paz claims, 'Something ends with this poem and something begins',[14] the reasons have to do, not so much with the sources themselves, as with the new context Sor Juana creates for them. What she brings to conclusion, in Paz's terms, is the ancient tradition of the 'voyage of the soul'; at the same time, as Paz goes on to explain, she breaks with the previous tradition in two important ways: first, whereas for earlier writers, from Macrobius to Kircher, the soul is invariably accompanied by a guide, in Sor Juana it is left to confront the universe without any mediating agent; secondly, and more crucially, what begins as a visionary poem ends in an apparent failure of vision, 'the account of a spiritual vision which ends in a non-vision'.[15]

Though the verbal texture of the poem is extremely dense, the various stages of the soul's progress are clearly marked, from the initial failure to grasp the universe through a single act of the intellect, to the more gradual, and equally unsuccessful, attempt to apply discursive knowledge by recourse to individual categories. What gives resonance to this abstract scheme, however, is the series of central images – sky, pyramid, spiral, echoes and reflections – which convey the mysterious nature of the cosmos or, as in the lines on the magic lantern, the intricacies of mental process itself:

> Y del cerebro, ya desocupado,
> las fantasmas huyeron,
> y – como de vapor leve formadas –
> en fácil humo, en viento convertidas,
> su forma resolvieron.
> Así linterna mágica, pintadas
> representa fingidas
> en la blanca pared varias figuras,

> de la sombra no menos ayudadas
> que de la luz: que en trémulos reflejos
> los competentes lejos
> guardando de la docta perspectiva,
> en sus ciertas mensuras
> de varias experiencias aprobadas,
> la sombra fugitiva,
> que en el mismo esplendor se desvanece,
> cuerpo finge formado,
> de todas dimensiones adornado,
> cuando aun ser superficie no merece.   (lines 868–87)

And from the brain, now unoccupied, the phantoms fled and – as if formed of light vapour – changed to easy smoke, to wind, their shapes dissolved. As a magic lantern casts on a white wall various coloured, imaginary figures, assisted by shade as much as by light: so, in quivering reflections maintaining the appropriate distances of learned perspective, confirmed in their true measurements by numerous experiments, the fleeting shadow which fades in the brilliant light simulates the form of a body, adorned with all its dimensions, though it does not deserve to be considered even a surface.

Nevertheless, though the overall structure of the poem is clear enough, it finally resists any attempt to force its exploratory movement into a neatly coherent pattern. This is not just a question of certain 'dark', or unresolved, areas – does Sor Juana ever distinguish clearly, for instance, between human knowledge and knowledge of the divine? – but also of the actual open-endedness of the poem as a whole. The ending itself, in fact, is ambivalent:

> Consiguió, al fin, la vista del Ocaso
> el fugitivo paso,
> y – en su mismo despeño recobrada
> esforzando el aliento en la rüina –
> en la mitad del globo que ha dejado
> en Sol desamparada,
> segunda vez rebelde determina
> mirarse coronada,
> mientras nuestro Hemisferio la dorada
> ilustraba del Sol madeja hermosa,
> que con luz judiciosa
> de orden distributivo, repartiendo
> a las cosas visibles sus colores
> iba, y restituyendo
> entera a los sentidos exteriores
> su operación, quedando a luz más cierta
> el Mundo iluminado, y yo despierta.   (lines 959–75)

At last, her [i.e. Night's] fleeing steps came within sight of the West, and, recovering herself even in her fall, gaining new courage from her very ruin, in that part of the globe which the Sun has left unprotected, she resolves, once more rebellious, to see herself crowned sovereign, while our Hemisphere was lit up by the fair golden locks of the Sun, who, with the judicious light of orderly distribution, was allotting visible things their colours and restoring their full function to the outer senses, leaving the World illumined with more certain light and myself awake.

At first sight, this may seem no more than a splendidly artificial description of reawakening at the start of a new day – characteristically, the protagonist only reveals her sex in the final syllable of the poem – and the eventual restoration of the bodily senses. At the same time, the process it describes is infinitely repeatable: as day breaks in one hemisphere, 'rebellious' night gathers her forces and retreats to the other, where similar dreams may be dreamed in their turn. Thus, if there is disillusionment in the ending, it is by no means final: though human reason comes up against its limits for the second time in the poem, the fact of defeat is combined with the sense of a process which, though interrupted, is not to be abandoned. And this lends a striking ambivalence to the figure of Phaethon who is introduced at a late stage in the poem: in one sense a 'pernicious example' (*pernicioso ejemplo*; line 864), but also an image of the soul whose search for knowledge, with all that it entails of rebelliousness and transgression, must always be repeated, even in the face of certain failure.[16]

IV

Though the *Primero sueño* cannot be accurately dated, it seems safe to assume that it was written some years before the crisis of 1693 which marks the final stage of Sor Juana's career. Although the process which finally silenced her as a writer is complex and at some points still unclear, it shows a steady convergence of her personal difficulties and external circumstances. To link the poem to these later events, as some critics have done, is profoundly mistaken. Though, as we have seen, it describes the defeat of reason, it never repudiates the intellect or abandons the search for knowledge. That such an attitude persisted is clear from the remarkable self-defence set out, with incomparable skill, in Sor Juana's prose masterpiece, the *Respuesta a Sor Filotea de la Cruz* (Reply to Sor Filotea de la Cruz; 1691). This has rightly come to be regarded as one of the greatest feminist documents in the language:[17] in it, Sor Juana not only gives a vivid account of her religious life but defends her desire for secular learning and the right of women to a serious education. And running through it, there are constant references to her own powers of speculation:

If I saw a figure, I at once fell to working out the relationship of its lines, measuring it with my mind and recasting it along different ones. Sometimes I would walk back and forth across the front of a sleeping-room of ours – a very large one – and observe how, though the lines of its two sides were parallel and its ceiling horizontal, one's vision made it appear as if the lines inclined toward each other and the ceiling were lower at the far end, from which I inferred that visual lines run straight but not parallel, tending rather toward a pyramidal figure. And I asked myself whether this could be the reason the ancients questioned whether the world was spherical or not. Because, although it appears to be, this could be an optical illusion, and show concavities where there might in fact be none.[18]

Yet what is significant here is Sor Juana's actual *need* to defend herself at a time when her reputation might have seemed unassailable. The facts surrounding the writing of the *Respuesta* are well established: her attack on a sermon by the Portuguese Jesuit Antonio de Vieira in an earlier prose piece, the *Carta atenagórica* (Athenagoric Letter); the role of the Bishop of Puebla (to whom the *Respuesta* was addressed and who was responsible for its publication); the withdrawal of Sor Juana's confessor, Núñez de Miranda, and the final intervention of the Archbishop of Mexico, Francisco de Aguiar y Seijas. Nevertheless, certain questions remain: why did Sor Juana go out of her way to attack a sermon already forty years old? Why did the Bishop of Puebla both encourage and reproach her? Why, finally, did she agree to dispose of her books and scientific instruments and to spend the rest of her life in strict penance?

It is here that Octavio Paz's account – by far the fullest to have appeared so far – connects, tentatively though all too plausibly, with external events. Firmly rejecting the idea of a 'conversion', dear to older critics, he carefully reconstructs a situation in which Sor Juana falls victim to a combination of ecclesiastical rivalry and public discord. Thus the *Carta atenagórica* is a veiled attack on Aguiar y Seijas, an admirer of Vieira, but also the rival of the Bishop of Puebla and a noted anti-feminist. And it was Aguiar who, after quelling the popular rising of 1692 – an anti-famine protest which left the current Viceroy virtually powerless – contributed most to the atmosphere of religious superstition and collective guilt which ensued. As Paz remarks, we shall never know whether Sor Juana shared in this general feeling of guilt, though her use of the Phaethon myth makes a clear connection between knowledge and punishment. What is certain, however, is that by this stage she was exposed as at no other time in her life – her last remaining protector, the Marqués de la Laguna, died in the same year – and that the pressures to which she was now being subjected must have appeared to question her entire creative enterprise. If Paz is right – and on present evidence it would be hard to make a stronger case – his reconstruction of Sor Juana's last years is both painful and moving. Above all, perhaps, it brings together, with stunning clarity, the main points of discord which determine her whole career: the rival claims of the literary and the religious life, the scandal of her sex in a male-orientated world, and her search for a kind of knowledge which lay beyond the bounds of orthodox religion.

Epilogue

The silencing of the last major poet of the seventeenth century might seem a natural, if melodramatic, endpoint for the book I have been trying to write. Nevertheless, literary periods are seldom as clear-cut as their historians would have us believe, and Sor Juana's own poetic achievement should warn us against easy generalizations. However much one allows for cultural differences, this achievement is clearly the work of a writer for whom the complementary tendencies of *culteranismo* and *conceptismo* are still a natural means of expression, a medium through which she is still able to exercise the full range of her intelligence. The contrast with the general mediocrity of late seventeenth-century peninsular verse could hardly be more striking: here, as we have seen, everything seems to point to the decline of a once major tradition which is no longer capable of prolonging itself. Whether or not this was inevitable is another question: given the increasing isolation of Spain from European culture and intellectual life, one might be inclined to think that it was. Yet, as against this, the example of Sor Juana suggests that, granted sufficient talent, it was still possible to build on this same tradition which might otherwise have seemed to be reaching exhaustion.

Clearly, then, there is no easy equation between the quality of seventeenth-century poetry and the fortunes of the country itself: though both Góngora and Quevedo suffered personally through social failure or political manoeuvering, the greatness of their poetic achievement remains unaffected; conversely, Philip IV and Olivares, for all their political shortcomings, were genuinely cultured people whose role as patrons of the arts was both decisive and beneficial. And just as seventeenth-century poets respond by creative imitation to earlier kinds of poetry, so certain seventeenth-century modes are prolonged into the next century, either to be assimilated or finally rejected. Góngora's mature manner, for instance, after being widely imitated in the early decades of the eighteenth century, was firmly condemned in the influential neoclassical *Poética* (Poetics; 1737) of Luzán, only to be fully valued again in modern times.[1] On the other hand, poets like Villegas, Rodrigo Caro and the Argensolas, whose 'classical' qualities could be seen as an anticipation of eighteenth-century neoclassicism, were frequently reprinted and proposed as viable models.

As it is, seventeenth-century Spanish poetry, as I hope to have shown, is far from static and at its best can embrace both continuity and change. Though it bears a certain family resemblance to that of other countries, its range and quality are matched only by English verse of the period. It seems no coincidence that, in both instances, a strong tradition of lyric and narrative verse goes hand in hand with an equally powerful tradition of popular drama, or that poetic practice should be underpinned by an equally subtle understanding of Renaissance poetics. Yet in the long run such comparisons are invidious, if only because we are dealing with poetry in different languages. From the confessional sonnets of Lope de Vega to the impersonal world of the *Soledades*, the triumph of seventeenth-century Spanish poetry is above all one of language, of a language which is being pressed to its extremes of flexibility and descriptive power. Seen in perspective, the all-inclusiveness of its finest products was perhaps by its very nature precarious, a unique combination of talent and circumstance whose excellence could be neither repeated nor prolonged. Yet the fact remains that, while it lasted, this tradition, with its unique blend of the popular and the sophisticated, made possible a body of writing which, in its variety and richness, is one of the most compelling achievements in European poetry.

Notes

PREFACE

1 Thomas M. Greene, *The Light in Troy: Imitation and Discovery in Renaissance Poetry* (New Haven and London, 1982), p. 293.
2 Henry Gifford, *Poetry in a Divided World* (Cambridge, 1986), p. 78.

I THE INHERITANCE

1 *Anotaciones*, in Antonio Gallego Morell, ed., *Garcilaso de la Vega y sus comentaristas* (Granada, 1966), p. 286.
2 C. Ricks, ed., *English Poetry and Prose, 1540–1674: Sphere History of Literature in the English Language* (London, 1986), p. 252.
3 Ramón Menéndez Pidal, *Romancero hispánico* (Madrid, 1953), II, p. 60.
4 The point was made with startling clarity by Antonio Rodríguez-Moñino some years ago when, merely by listing the first editions of the leading sixteenth- and seventeenth-century poets, he was able to demonstrate that the great majority, including writers of the stature of Garcilaso, Luis de León, Aldana, Góngora and Quevedo, died before the publication of their collected poems. See Antonio Rodríguez-Moñino, *Construcción crítica y realidad histórica en la poesía española de los siglos XVI y XVII* (Madrid, 1965), especially pp. 19–24.
5 J. H. Elliott, *Imperial Spain, 1469–1716* (London, 1963), p. 374.
6 For an interesting comparison between Madrid and other sixteenth-century European capitals, see Fernand Braudel, *The Mediterranean and the Mediterranean World in the Age of Philip II* (London, 1975 [1973]), p. 207.
7 See José Sánchez, *Academias literarias del Siglo de Oro* (Madrid, 1961), and Willard F. King, 'The Academies and Seventeenth-Century Spanish Literature', *PMLA*, 75 (1960), pp. 367–76. King points out that the academies may have acted as a stimulus to the compilation of several of the best poetic anthologies of the early seventeenth century, notably the *Primavera y flor de los mejores romances...* (Madrid, 1621) and the *Cancionero de 1628*, produced in Saragossa. For details of the rules of a typical academy, see J. M. Blecua, 'La academia poética del Conde de Fuensalida', in *Sobre poesía de la Edad de Oro (ensayos y notas eruditas)* (Madrid, 1970), pp. 203–8.

258

8 J. H. Elliott, 'Monarchy and Empire (1474–1700)', in P. E. Russell, ed., *Spain: a Companion to Spanish Studies* (London, 1973), p. 125.

9 Peter Burke, *Tradition and Innovation in Renaissance Italy* (London, 1974 [1971]), p. 14.

10 P. E. Russell, 'El Concilio de Trento y la literatura profana; reconsideración de una teoría', in *Temas de 'La Celestina'* (Barcelona, 1978), pp. 441–78.

11 John Crosbie, 'Amoral "a lo divino" Poetry in the Golden Age', *MLR*, 66 (1971), pp. 599–607. See also Crosbie's more recent study, *A lo divino Lyric Poetry: an Alternative View* (Durham, 1989), which provides a useful corrective to the theories of Dámaso Alonso and Wardropper.

12 *De los nombres de Cristo*, CC (Madrid, 1914–21), II, p. 231.

13 'Courtly love' is a translation of the phrase *amour courtois*, first used in the nineteenth century by the French medievalist Gaston Paris. The term employed by the troubadours themselves is *fin'amors*, which is sometimes contrasted with *fals'amors* or simply with *amors*. However, apart from the implication of superiority, *fin'amors* is notoriously difficult to define: sometimes it means no more than sincere or faithful love, and at others it shades into the love of God. Moreover, though it distinguishes true love from mere concupiscence, it is still by no means necessarily 'Platonic'. Peter Dronke, in his monumental study *Medieval Latin and the Rise of European Love-Lyric* (Oxford, 1965), uses the term 'courtly experience' to describe the kind of sensibility found in the poetry – both courtly and popular – of many languages, in some instances much earlier than the eleventh century. Though this in no way denies the distinctiveness of troubadour poetry as a particular *development* of this experience, it effectively disposes of the idea that such poetry represents an entirely new kind of emotion. On the dangers of an over-rigid approach to the question of courtly love, see Douglas Kelly, *Medieval Imagination: Rhetoric and the Poetry of Courtly Love* (Madison, 1978), p. xv: 'The expression *courtly love* has been misunderstood and misused, largely because of the laudable desire to clarify it by definition and identification of the rules peculiar to its art. In this we forget that love is more an idea than a concept, and that an art is a skill, not an etiquette or a book of manners.'

14 R. O. Jones, *A Literary History of Spain. The Golden Age: Prose and Poetry* (London, 1971), p. 30.

15 Pedro Salinas, *Jorge Manrique o tradición y originalidad* (Buenos Aires, 1947), p. 15.

16 Keith Whinnom, 'Hacia una interpretación y apreciación de las canciones del *Cancionero general* de 1511', *Fi*, 13 (1968–9), pp. 361–81. See especially the remark on p. 380: 'What can be said with almost total certainty is that the *cancionero* poets are more obsessed by physical desire and by the tempting possibility of its fulfilment than by the vague vision of semi-mystical Neoplatonic ideas.' For an excellent critical survey of recent views concerning the nature of courtly love and its relation to

fifteenth-century poetry, see Whinnom's introduction to his edition of Diego de San Pedro, *Cárcel de Amor*, CCa (Madrid, 1971), pp. 7–43, and his definitive study, *La poesía amatoria cancioneril en la época de los Reyes Católicos* (Durham, 1981).

17 See Leonard Forster, *The Icy Fire: Five Studies in European Petrarchism* (Cambridge, 1969), especially chapter 1.

18 Arguably, this 'self' is constructed in the process of writing, rather than present from the beginning, a procedure which is repeated in later Renaissance poetic sequences. See John Freccero, 'The Fig Tree and the Laurel: Petrarch's Poetics', in Patricia Parker and David Quint, ed., *Literary Theory/Renaissance Texts* (Baltimore and London, 1986), pp. 21–32: 'the lady celebrated by Petrarch is a brilliant surface, a pure signifier whose momentary exteriority to the poet serves as an Archimedean point from which he can create himself' (p. 30).

19 F. T. Prince, *The Italian Element in Milton's Verse* (Oxford, 1954), p. 5.

20 A. A. Parker, 'An Age of Gold: Expansion and Scholarship in Spain', in Denis Hay, ed., *The Age of the Renaissance* (London, 1967), p. 244.

21 See my analysis of Aldana's sonnet '¿Cuál es la causa, mi Damón...' (What is the cause, my Damon...?) in my article 'Thought and Feeling in Three Golden-Age Sonnets', *BHS*, 59 (1982), pp. 237–46.

22 Parker, in *The Philosophy of Love in Spanish Literature, 1480–1680* (Edinburgh, 1985), pp. 77–8, rightly stresses Ebreo's sense of the suffering experienced by the body in its search for a perfect union which, given the nature of sexual love, it can never achieve. For a more detailed account of Ebreo's theories and their relation to Renaissance Aristotelianism, see A. J. Smith, *The Metaphysics of Love* (Cambridge, 1985), pp. 196–204.

23 Parker, *The Philosophy of Love*, pp. 112–113.

24 Oreste Macrí, *Fernando de Herrera* (Madrid, 1959), pp. 384–5.

25 M. J. Woods, in his article 'Herrera's Voices', in F. W. Hodcroft et al., ed., *Medieval and Renaissance Studies on Spain and Portugal in Honour of P. E. Russell* (Oxford, 1981), pp. 121–32, comments interestingly on the self-reflexive nature of Herrera's poetry, and on the way in which apparent inconsistencies of 'voice', like the one I have just discussed, draw attention to his deliberately constructed role of 'poet'.

26 The model in this instance seems to have been the late Latin poet Claudian (c. 370–404). Compare the two passages from the Panegyric on the Sixth Consulship of Honorius which Herrera quotes and translates in the *Anotaciones*, pp. 320 and 413–14.

27 Macrí, *Fernando de Herrera*, p. 309.

28 Two other such poets are Luis Barahona de Soto (1548–95) and Vicente Espinel (1550–1624). Barahona's poetry is linguistically less adventurous than Herrera's, but his taste for descriptive detail and rich colour effects looks forward to poets like Espinosa and Soto de Rojas. His longest poem, *Las lágrimas de Angélica* (1586; The Tears of Angelica), though incomplete, remains the most remarkable of the sixteenth-century imitations of Ariosto. Espinel's handling of Italianate metres was

acclaimed by numerous writers of the following generation, including Lope de Vega. His one collection of poems, *Diversas rimas* (Miscellaneous Rhymes; 1591), includes a miniature *canzoniere* in the Petrarchan manner, but is most remarkable for its songs and verse-letters. The latter contain many passages which not only convey the quality of his own life, but look forward in their vividness to his later work of fiction, the semi-autobiographical novel *Marcos de Obregón* (1615).

29 Diego's remark is quoted by Vicente Gaos in his edition of the *Viaje del Parnaso*, CCa (Madrid, 1973), p. 22.

30 Luis de Camões (1524–79), the great Portuguese writer and author of the verse epic *Os Lusíadas* (The Lusiads), also composed a large number of shorter poems in Portuguese and Spanish. As a lyric poet in the Italianate manner, he was a talented follower of Garcilaso, whom he translated and imitated. His work was well known in Spain, and its effect can be seen in several outstanding poets of the following generation, notably Villamediana (1582–1622) and the Conde de Salinas (1564–1630).

31 *La Galatea*, ed. Schevill and Bonilla (Madrid, 1914), i, pp. 17–20. All page references are to this edition.

32 See the poem which begins 'Salid de lo hondo del pecho cuytado' (Come from the depths of the troubled soul), i, pp. 199–202.

33 At another point in the novel, Erastro speaks as follows: 'And since loveliness and beauty are a chief reason for persuading us to desire and enjoy them, he who loves truth must not regard such enjoyment as his final goal, but, however much beauty may instil in him such a desire, he must love it merely in order to achieve goodness, and must not be moved by any other consideration; and this, even in earthly things, may be called true and perfect love, and is worthy to be appreciated and rewarded, as we see the Creator of all things rewards openly and abundantly those who, unmoved by any consideration of fear, suffering or hope of glory, love, adore and serve him, simply in order to be good and to be worthy of being loved; and this is the last and greatest perfection which is contained in divine love' (i, pp. 194–5). J. B. Avalle-Arce, in his book *La novela pastoril española* (Madrid, 1959), p. 209, quotes this passage, and relates the last part of it to the sixteenth-century mystical tradition of the *spirituali*, common to both Spain and Italy. The same tradition lies behind the famous anonymous 'Soneto a Cristo crucificado' (Sonnet to Christ Crucified), which begins 'No me mueve Dios para quererte / el cielo que me tienes prometido...' (O God, it is not the heaven you have promised me which moves me to love you...).

34 Cervantes is, however, known to have composed ballads early in his career, but only one of these has so far been identified. On Cervantes's 'lost' *romances*, see E. L. Rivers, '"Viaje del Parnaso" y poesías sueltas', in J. B. Avalle-Arce and E. C. Riley, ed., *Suma cervantina* (London, 1973), p. 128.

35 The poem was published for the first time in 1863. The claim that it is a

nineteenth-century pastiche has now been refuted, though its authenticity is still not completely established. See Rivers, '"Viaje del
Parnaso"', pp. 125–6.

36 The satirical intention of the poem becomes even clearer in the light of
the scandal which surrounded the original episode. The ceremony of
dedication should have taken place on 24 November 1598, but was
interrupted by a dispute over the order of precedence between the
Tribunal of the Inquisition and the City Council of Seville, and was only
completed five weeks later. A contemporary anecdote relates how
Cervantes himself entered the Cathedral on the day before the final
ceremony and recited the sonnet in public. See Francisco Ayala, 'El
túmulo', in *Cervantes y Quevedo* (Barcelona, 1974), pp. 185–200.

37 Luis Cernuda, 'Cervantes, poeta', in *Poesía y literatura*, II (Barcelona,
1964), pp. 55–6.

2 THEORY AND PRACTICE

1 C. H. Sisson, *The Poetic Art: a Translation of Horace's Ars Poetica* (Cheadle,
1975), p. 9.

2 Michel Foucault, *Les mots et les choses* (Paris, 1966), chapter 2. (English
verson: *The Order of Things*, trans. Alan Sheridan, London and New
York, 1970.)

3 Rosemond Tuve, *Elizabethan and Metaphysical Imagery* (Chicago, 1947),
p. 396.

4 Tuve, *Elizabethan and Metaphysical Imagery*, p. 391.

5 Bernard Weinberg, *A History of Literary Criticism in the Italian Renaissance*,
2 vols. (Chicago, 1971), II, p. 801.

6 Weinberg, *A History of Literary Criticism*, II, p. 806.

7 Sisson, *The Poetic Art*, p. 50.

8 Tuve, *Elizabethan and Metaphysical Imagery*, p. 403.

9 Thomas M. Greene, *The Light in Troy: Imitation and Discovery in
Renaissance Poetry* (New Haven and London, 1982), p. 30.

10 Terence Cave, *The Cornucopian Text: Problems of Writing in the French
Renaissance* (Oxford, 1979), p. 76.

11 Herrera, *Respuesta a las observaciones del Prete Jacopín* (Seville, 1870),
pp. 84–5.

12 Compare also lines 105–16 of the same poem, which emphasize the
process by which the raw materials of nature (gold dust, leaves, natural
dyes) become the materials of art.

13 Edward William Tayler, *Nature and Art in Renaissance Literature* (New
York, 1964), p. 36.

14 Derek Attridge, *Peculiar Language: Literature as Difference from the
Renaissance to James Joyce* (London, 1988), pp. 17–45. The quotation is
from p. 30.

15 Attridge, *Peculiar Language*, p. 37.

16 The division into three styles goes back at least as far as Horace. Most
Renaissance theorists, beginning with Landino (1482), base their

discussions on *Ars poetica*, lines 86 etc. See Weinberg, *A History of Literary Criticism*, I, pp. 80–1.

17 P. N. Furbank, *Reflections on the Word 'Image'* (London, 1970), p. 13.

18 Compare Herrera, *Anotaciones*, p. 323: 'since poetry is a speaking picture, just as painting is silent poetry'.

19 The rhetorical figure *enargeia* (Latin *illustratio* or *evidentia*) is praised by Quintilian and later theorists for its power of vivid description or, in Herrera's phrase, its ability to 'present matter in words so that one seems to see it with one's eyes' (*Anotaciones*, p. 302). Strictly speaking, this desire for the fusion of language and concept can only be entertained at the cost of suppressing the artifice by which all poetic effects are achieved. The illusion of such a possibility, however, continues to haunt sixteenth- and seventeenth-century poetry and helps to account for some of its most striking verbal effects. The issues involved here, both for the writing and the reading of Golden Age poetry, are explored with great subtlety by Paul Julian Smith in his article 'The Rhetoric of Presence in Poets and Critics of Golden Age Lyric: Garcilaso, Herrera, Góngora', *MLN*, 100 (1985), pp. 223–46. As he points out in his conclusion, poetry is never immediate in the way that *enargeia* would presuppose, and verbal imitation always 'tends to displace its supposed object or original' (pp. 245–6). A revised and expanded version of this article appears in Smith's book, *Writing in the Margin: Spanish Literature of the Golden Age* (Oxford, 1988), pp. 43–77.

20 Where a modern reader can go wrong is in projecting the emotion conveyed by the poem back on to its source (i.e. the poet); what matters invariably in the poetry of this period is the emotional effect *on the reader*. See my discussion of the Quevedo sonnet in the next section, pp. 57–9.

21 Tuve, *Elizabethan and Metaphysical Imagery*, p. 121.

22 In the *Anotaciones*, Herrera describes Garcilaso's metaphors in precisely these terms. In his note on Sonnet II, lines 9–11, for instance, 'mis lágrimas han sido derramadas / donde la sequedad y la aspereza / dieron mal fruto dellas, y mi suerte' (My tears have been split where drought and wilderness brought forth bad fruit from them and from my fate), the word 'sequedad' (drought) is glossed as 'a metaphor (*traslación*) from agriculture' (p. 293).

23 For a lucid account of the limitations of the Aristotelian theory of metaphor, see Paul Ricoeur, 'The Metaphorical Process', *Critical Inquiry*, 5 (1978), pp. 143–59.

24 Terence Hawkes, *Metaphor* (London, 1972), p. 9.

25 For the doctrine of universal analogy and the poetics of correspondence, see J. A. Mazzeo, 'Modern Theories of Metaphysical Poetry', *MPh*, 50 (1952), pp. 88–96.

26 Julius Caesar Scaliger (1484–1558), the Italian humanist and physician, and author of the *Poetices libri septem* (1561). For an excellent account of Scaliger's views on poetry, see Weinberg, *A History of Literary Criticism*, II, pp. 743–50. The differences between Scaliger and Herrera are discussed by Andreina Bianchini in 'Fernando de Herrera's *Anotaciones*: a New

Look at his Sources and the Significance of his Poetics', *RF*, 88 (1976), pp. 27–42.

27 *Anotaciones*, pp. 399–400.

28 For a good discussion of the concept of *admiratio*, see E. C. Riley, *Cervantes's Theory of the Novel* (Oxford, 1962), pp. 88–94.

29 Bianchini, 'Fernando de Herrera's *Anotaciones*', pp. 29–30.

30 *Anotaciones*, pp. 294–5.

31 For an explanation of these two much-debated terms, see below, n. 37.

32 Bianchini, 'Fernando de Herrera's *Anotaciones*', p. 42.

33 For the more conventional theorists, from Sánchez de Lima to Jáuregui, see the excellent chapter by Antonio Vilanova in G. Díaz-Plaja, ed., *Historia general de las literaturas hispánicas*, III (Barcelona, 1953), pp. 567–692. The best anthology of primary sources on poetic theory in the period is A. Porqueras Mayo, ed., *La teoría poética en el Renacimiento y Manierismo españoles* (Barcelona, 1986–9), 2 vols.

34 See the discussion of the passage beginning 'Cubrió el sagrado Betis...' in chapter 1, p. 26.

35 P. E. Russell, in Russell, ed., *Spain: a Companion to Spanish Studies* (London, 1973), p. 315.

36 René Wellek, *Concepts of Criticism* (New Haven and London, 1963), p. 93.

37 It should be pointed out that the distinction between *culteranismo* and *conceptismo*, corresponding to two rival 'schools' of poets, is an invention of eighteenth-century neoclassical criticism, later endorsed by the influential late nineteenth-century critic and scholar Menéndez y Pelayo (1856–1912). In the early seventeenth century, as will shortly emerge, the lines of opposition were drawn rather differently; though Lope de Vega and others refer to *culteranismo* (sometimes as an abuse of genuine *culto* writing), the terms *conceptista* and *conceptismo* were unknown at the time, and there is nothing in contemporary theory to suggest that *cultismos* and *conceptos* were regarded as mutually exclusive. The terms themselves, if handled with care, still have a certain shorthand utility, though, as usual, a knowledge of traditional rhetoric brings one closer to actual poetic practice. For the history of *culteranismo* and *conceptismo* as critical concepts, see Andrée Collard, *Nueva poesía: conceptismo, culteranismo en la crítica española* (Madrid, 1967).

38 Luis de Góngora, *Obras completas*, ed. J. and I. Millé y Jiménez (Madrid, 1943), p. 796. (This edition is subsequently referred to as 'Millé'.)

39 For a full, and extremely skilful, analysis of the rhetoric of this sonnet, see Paul Julian Smith, *Writing in the Margin*, pp. 68–70. In particular, Smith points to the 'arrested motion' of the opening lines as an example of *enargeia*, and concludes: 'In its density, scope and compression the poem might be seen itself as a marvellous construct ("máquina"), which seeks to stay time and encompass the world with the brilliant materiality of its linguistic presence' (p. 69).

40 Castor and Pollux were the children of Leda: they were believed to

protect seafarers and were associated with the phenomenon known as St Elmo's Fire. In the context, 'otra mejor Leda' (another, better Leda) suggests the Virgin Mary; the image of lights playing around the sails of the 'ship' is based on the candles which burn on the *túmulo*.

41 Dámaso Alonso, 'Claridad y belleza de las *Soledades*', in *Estudios gongorinos* (Madrid, 1955), p. 72. As I shall try to show in the next chapter, it is also a way of 're-writing' the world, a process which is specifically referred to in the text of the *Soledades*.

42 For details of this and other attacks on Góngora, see Ana Martínez Arancón, *La batalla en torno a Góngora (selección de textos)* (Barcelona, 1978) and Collard, *Nueva poesía*, pp. 73–112. What emerges most clearly from Collard's account is that, although seventeenth-century Spanish writers do not think in terms of an opposition between *conceptismo* and *culteranismo*, they nevertheless show signs of an incipient division, since the taste for *conceptos* is felt to be part of national tradition in a way that *cultismos* are not.

43 There is a terminological difficulty here, since Spanish *concepto* translates both English 'concept' and 'conceit'. As Parker has pointed out, there are many instances in which *concepto* – like 'conceit' in Elizabethan English – means simply 'idea' ('"Concept" and "Conceit": an Aspect of Contemporary Literary History', *MLR*, 67 (1982), pp. xxi–xxxv). In view of the tendency to speak of wit as a 'sudden illumination', it is worth emphasizing the amount of time it often takes for the more subtle type of seventeenth-century conceit to reveal its full implications to the reader. The point is well made by A. K. G. Paterson in his article '"Sutileza de pensar" in a Quevedo sonnet', *MLN*, 81 (1966), pp. 131–42.

44 Helen Gardner, ed., *The Metaphysical Poets* (Harmondsworth, 1957), p. 21.

45 Emmanuele Tesauro, *Il cannochiale aristotelico* (The Aristotelian Looking Glass; 1654), Book III, quoted in S. L. Bethell, 'Gracián, Tesauro and the Nature of Metaphysical Wit', *The Northern Miscellany of Literary Criticism*, I (1953), p. 26. Reprinted in Frank Kermode, ed., *Discussions of John Donne* (Boston, 1962), pp. 136–49.

46 On the likely reaction of seventeenth-century readers to such writing, Peter Russell sensibly remarks: 'We must not be misled by all this talk about "concepts" to any false ideas about the strictly intellectual quality of *conceptista* writing. It appealed to subtle, alert minds amused and surprised by unexpected correlations of ideas, but its creativity was, in the last resort, concerned with stylistics, not with expanding in any significant way the frontiers of thought' (*Spain: a Companion to Spanish Studies*, p. 319). For 'stylistics', I would prefer to say 'rhetoric'.

47 A. A. Parker, 'La "agudeza" en algunos sonetos de Quevedo', *Estudios dedicados a Don Ramón Menéndez Pidal*, III (Madrid, 1952), pp. 345–60. A revised version of this important article appears in Gonzalo Sobejano, ed., *Francisco de Quevedo* (Madrid, 1978), pp. 44–57.

48 For a detailed account of the rhetoric of this sonnet, see Paul Julian Smith, *Quevedo on Parnassus: Allusive Context and Literary Theory in the Love-Lyric* (London, 1987), pp. 79–81.

49 Mazzeo, 'Modern Theories', p. 92.

50 This is a revised and expanded version of the *Arte de ingenio*, originally published in 1642. For the differences between the two books, see the preface by Evaristo Correa Calderón to his two-volume edition of the *Agudeza*, CCa (Madrid, 1958), I, pp. 16–19.

51 For the ambiguity of the *concepto*, see note 43, above.

52 A. A. Parker, *Luis de Góngora, 'Polyphemus and Galatea': a Study in the Interpretation of a Baroque Poem* (Edinburgh, 1977), p. 32. Parker skilfully relates his theory of knowledge to the philosophy of Nicholas of Cusa (1401–64). The latter's theory of the coincidence of opposites is central to the thought of Giordano Bruno (1548–1600), the chief exponent of the doctrine of universal analogy. For Bruno's significance in this context, see Mazzeo, 'Modern Theories', pp. 88–9.

53 *Agudeza*, I, p. 55.

54 M. J. Woods, in his article 'Gracián, Peregrini and the Theory of Topics', *MLR*, 63 (1968), pp. 854–63, describes the difference as follows: 'Unlike the topics, which summarized thought processes, the categories were regarded as belonging to the structure of the material world, and hence as having an ontological as well as a logical status' (p. 862).

55 *Agudeza*, I, p. 64.

56 T. E. May, 'An Interpretation of Gracián's *Agudeza y arte de ingenio*', *HR*, 16 (1948), p. 290.

57 In her essay 'Du baroque espagnol en général et de la "commutatio" gongorique en particulier', *Criticón*, 6 (1979), pp. 7–44, Elsa Dehennin refers to the relatively uncomplex nature of the conceits which Gracián chooses for illustration: 'Jamais Gracián ne se réfère à une *agudeza* excessive, à une correspondance qui réunirait des objets trop distants l'un de l'autre. D'instinct et comme si cela allait de soi, il maintient l'*ingenio* sous un certain contrôle du *juicio*' (p. 28). Though at one point he praises both the *Polifemo* and the *Soledades*, Gracián only quotes two fairly straightforward passages from the *Polifemo* and none from the other poem. Dehennin goes too far, however, in suggesting that Gracián deliberately chose to overlook the 'excès baroques' of Góngora's major poems, whose wit is entirely comprehensible within Gracián's own terms. What *is* striking, on the other hand, is the large number of examples which Gracián includes from poets who are not normally thought of as 'conceited' writers, like Garcilaso and the Argensolas. This reinforces the fact that the term *concepto*, in Gracián's usage, covers not only 'conceits' of the 'metaphysical' variety, but also the poet's original idea or 'conception' and the way this is worked out in the course of an entire poem.

58 Abad de Rute, *Examen del Antídoto* (c. 1615), in Miguel de Artigas, *Don Luis de Góngora: biografía y estudio crítico* (Madrid, 1925), p. 426.

59 Mazzeo, 'Modern Theories', p. 89.
60 Tuve, *Elizabethan and Metaphysical Imagery*, p. 22.

3 LUIS DE GÓNGORA: THE POETRY OF TRANSFORMATION

1 R. Foulché-Delbosc, ed., *Poesías completas*, 3 vols. (New York, 1921).
2 For evidence of this, see R. P. Calcraft's excellent study, *The Sonnets of Luis de Góngora* (Durham, 1980), pp. 26–32.
3 Compare the use of anadiplosis, or reiteration, to create a rhetorical climax in lines 13–17 of 'Servía en Orán al Rey...': 'las adargas avisaron / a las mudas atalayas, / las atalayas los fuegos, / los fuegos a las campanas; / y ellas al enamorado...' (the shields warned the silent watchtowers, the towers the beacons, the beacons the bells; and these the lover).
4 B. W. Wardropper, '"La más bella niña"', *SP*, 63 (1966), pp. 661–76. The quotation is from p. 676.
5 Robert Jammes, *Etudes sur l'oeuvre poétique de Don Luis Góngora y Argote* (Bordeaux, 1967), p. 128.
6 E. M. Wilson, 'On Góngora's *Angélica y Medoro*', *BHS*, 30 (1953), pp. 85–94. The phrase quoted occurs on p. 92.
7 See Ball's excellent article, 'Poetic Imitation in Góngora's *Romance de Angélica y Medoro*', *BHS*, 57 (1980), pp. 33–54, to which I am indebted for several of the points which follow.
8 Ball, 'Poetic Imitation', p. 35.
9 Here, as elsewhere, the town–country opposition involves a contrast between Madrid – always to some extent alien territory for Góngora – and Andalusia, for which he feels intense local pride.
10 For this aspect of the poem, see C. C. Smith, 'Serranas de Cuenca', in R. O. Jones, ed., *Studies in Spanish Literature of the Golden Age, presented to Edward M. Wilson* (London, 1973), pp. 283–95.
11 This point is well brought out by R. D. Calcraft in his article 'The Lover as Icarus: Góngora's "Qué de invidiosos montes levantados"', in S. Bacarisse and others, ed., *What's Past is Prologue: Essays in Honour of L. J. Woodward* (Edinburgh, 1984), pp. 10–16.
12 Antonio Vilanova, *Las fuentes y los temas del 'Polifemo' de Góngora*, 2 vols. (Madrid, 1957). Vilanova's exhaustive study of literary parallels, both classical and Renaissance, is a fascinating demonstration of what intertextuality can mean at this period, though, as Jammes has pointed out, he sometimes presses the possibility of imitation too far: 'Vilanova parle d'imitation, voire de contrefaçon, là où il serait plus juste dans la majorité des cas de parler de coincidence, ou, si l'on préfère, communauté de langage entre poètes de culture identique' (*Etudes sur l'oeuvre poétique*, p. 536, n. 6).
13 See Dámaso Alonso, *Góngora y el 'Polifemo'*, 9th edn, 3 vols. (Madrid, 1974), I, pp. 225–30; Jammes, *Etudes sur l'oeuvre poétique*, pp. 546–7.

14 M. J. Woods, *The Poet and the Natural World in the Age of Góngora* (Oxford, 1978), p. 151.

15 A. A. Parker, *Luis de Góngora, 'Polyphemus and Galatea': a Study in the Interpretation of a Baroque Poem* (Edinburgh, 1977), p. 77.

16 For a good discussion of this point, see Woods, *The Poet and the Natural World*, pp. 109–11.

17 Pellicer claims that Góngora wished to present the four Ages of Man: youth, adolescence, maturity and old age. According to Díaz de Rivas, however, the poem was to be organized round four kinds of landscape: fields, seashore, forests and desert.

18 Not all critics agree that the Second *Soledad* (or even the whole poem) is incomplete. John Beverley, in *Aspects of Góngora's 'Soledades'* (Amsterdam, 1980), p. 93, claims that Góngora may have found a way of telescoping what he originally conceived as a four-part poem into two. L. J. Woodward, in 'Two Images in the *Soledades* of Góngora', *MLN*, 76 (1961), pp. 773–85, argues very forcibly that the last forty-three lines of the Second *Soledad* are a deliberate *reprise* of two of the central images of the poem: walls and hunting. Both critics attempt to account for the increasing violence of the Second *Soledad*; in Woodward's interpretation, the poem ends abruptly, though not inconclusively, on the impressive image of the owl – associated, not with wisdom, but with Ascalaphon, the creature of Hades and betrayer of Persephone.

19 Maurice Molho, *Sémantique et poétique: à propos des Solitudes de Góngora* (Bordeaux, 1969), pp. 44–8.

20 Beverley, *Aspects*, p. 87.

21 See the comprehensive study by Antonio Vilanova, 'El peregrino de amor en las *Soledades* de Góngora', *Estudios dedicados a Don Ramón Menéndez Pidal*, III (Madrid, 1952), pp. 421–60.

22 Paul Julian Smith, 'Barthes, Góngora and Non-Sense', *PMLA*, 101 (1986), pp. 82–94, now expanded in *The Body Hispanic: Gender and Sexuality in Spanish and Spanish American Literature* (Oxford, 1989), pp. 44–68.

23 R. O. Jones, 'The Poetic Unity of the *Soledades* of Góngora', *BHS*, 31 (1954), pp. 189–204, especially p. 196.

24 These themes are stressed, respectively, by the following critics: T. R. Hart, 'The Pilgrim's Role in the First *Solitude*', *MLN*, 92 (1977), pp. 213–26; J. F. G. Gornall, 'Góngora's *Soledades*: "alabanza de aldea" without "menosprecio de corte"?', *BHS*, 59 (1982), pp. 21–5; B. W. Wardropper, 'The Complexity of the Simple in Góngora's *Soledad primera*', *JMRS*, 7 (1977), pp. 35–51.

25 Compare the comment by the Abad de Rute: 'For if one considers... the setting [*lugar*], it is clear that those places which are removed from the traffic and affairs of cities have ever been called thus, and have been thought of as solitudes [*soledades*], however much frequented and inhabited by people' (quoted Artigas, *Don Luis de Góngora*, p. 403).

26 For further discussion of this point, see Woods, *The Poet and the Natural World*, p. 156.

27 St Augustine, for example, refers to the world as a 'beautiful poem' (*City of God*, xi, xviii). For an absorbing account of this metaphor and its implications for recent literary theory, see Jesse M. Gellrich, *The Idea of the Book in the Middle Ages: Language Theory, Mythology, and Fiction* (Ithaca and London, 1985), especially chapter 1.

28 Compare Gracián: 'Without the intervention of art, the whole of nature is perverted' (*Criticón*, I, 13). Such a statement comes strikingly close to Jacques Derrida's notion of art as a 'supplement' to nature: 'nature without the book is somehow incomplete. If the whole of what *is* were really one with the whole of the inscription, it would be hard to see how they would make two: nature *and* the Bible, being and the book... That the sense of this coupling by the *is* should be one of fulfilment, a fulfilling productivity that comes not to repeat but to complete nature through writing, would mean that nature is somewhere incomplete, that it lacks something needed for it to be what it is, that it has to be supplemented' (*Dissemination*, trans. Barbara Johnson, London, 1981, pp. 52–3).

29 Andrés Sánchez Robayna, *Tres estudios sobre Góngora* (Barcelona, 1983), pp. 54–5. This brilliant essay ('Góngora y el texto del mundo') draws attention to a number of other relevant passages in the poem: the landscape which offers itself to the pilgrim is described as a 'map', or graphic representation (*Sol* I, line 194); birds in flight form letters on the 'clear parchment' (*papel diáfano*) of the sky (*Sol* I, lines 609–11); the pilgrim-lover, like Icarus, will leave the memory of his daring inscribed in the 'transparent annals of the wind' (*los anales diáfanos del viento*) (*Sol* II, lines 137–43).

30 Smith, 'Barthes, Góngora', p. 90.

31 Góngora's two splendid plays, *Las firmezas de Isabela* (The Constancy of Isabella) and *El Doctor Carlino*, also date from this period. For details of these, see Jammes, *Studies sur l'oeuvre poétique*, pp. 467–531, and also Jammes's excellent edition of *Las firmezas*, CCa (Madrid, 1984).

32 B. W. Ife, in *Dos versiones de Píramo y Tisbe: Jorge de Montemayor y Sánchez de Viana* (Exeter, 1974), points to the importance of the version of *Píramo y Tisbe* usually ascribed (though probably wrongly) to Montemayor (first published 1561) as a precedent for Góngora's own poem.

33 Compare lines 41–4 – 'En el interín nos digan / los mal formados rasguños / de los pinceles de un ganso / sus dos hermosos dibujos' (In the meantime let the ill-formed scratchings of goose quills describe their two fair forms) – where the degree of ironic detachment exceeds anything a writer in the 'base' style would normally attempt.

34 On this point, see David L. Garrison, 'The Linguistic Mixture of Góngora's "Fábula de Píramo y Tisbe"', *RON*, 20 (1979), pp. 108–13.

35 For example, when Pyramus looks for Thisbe after she has fled from the lion, the moon comes out to 'leer los testigos / del proceso ya concluso' (to read the evidence of the now completed suit) (lines 377–8); later, the sword with which Pyramus kills himself is described as a 'roasting spit' (*asador*) (line 478).

36 C. S. Lewis, *English Literature in the Sixteenth Century, excluding Drama* (Oxford, 1954), p. 541.

37 B. W. Ife, 'Some Preliminary Remarks to a Study of Góngora's "Fábula de Píramo y Tisbe"', privately printed (London, 1973), p. 19.

38 Ife, 'Some Preliminary Remarks', p. 5.

39 Compare, as one passage typical of many: 'Now, sir, I take up my pen rather than take up a rope to end all and to grant Your Mercy rest from my troubles' (letter of 11 July 1623 to his administrator, Cristóbal de Heredia; Millé, p. 935).

40 D. S. Carne-Ross, *Instaurations: Essays in and out of Literature, Pindar to Pound* (Berkeley, Los Angeles and London, 1979), p. 140.

41 Calcraft, *The Sonnets*, p. 110. Góngora's specifically religious verse, though small in quantity, is not as negligible as Jammes, for instance, suggests, and includes at least one fine sonnet, 'Pender de un leño, traspasado el pecho...' (To hang from a tree, your breast pierced...; Millé, 265).

4 LOPE DE VEGA: RE-WRITING A LIFE

1 Lope's most substantial collections of verse are: *Rimas* (1602; expanded in 1609); *Soliloquios* (1612; expanded in 1626); *Rimas sacras* (1614); *La Filomena* (1621); *La Circe* (1624); *Rimas...de Tomé de Burguillos* (1634); *La Vega del Parnaso* (published posthumously, 1637). Lope's early ballads appeared in numerous anthologies from 1583 onwards; over a hundred are included in the *Romancero general* of 1600, though some of these are of doubtful authenticity. Several of his prose works, like *La Arcadia* (1598), also include poems. My own texts are taken mainly from J. M. Blecua, ed., *Obras poéticas* I (Barcelona, 1969) (referred to as B), supplemented where necessary by Antonio Carreño, ed., *Poesía selecta* (Madrid, 1984) (referred to as C).

2 See 'A la muerte de Carlos Félix' (B, p. 485) and the Epistle to Dr Matías de Porras, lines 79–108 (B, p. 1237).

3 Mary Gaylord Randel, 'Proper Language and Language as Property; the Personal Poetics of Lope's *Rimas*', *MLN*, 101 (1986), pp. 220–46. The quotation comes from p. 224.

4 Emilio Orozco Díaz, *Lope y Góngora frente a frente* (Madrid, 1973), p. 45.

5 For an exceptionally clear account of these relationships and their literary consequences, see chapter 1 of Alan Trueblood's monumental study *Experience and Artistic Expression in Lope de Vega: the Making of 'La Dorotea'* (Cambridge, Mass., 1974), to which I am greatly indebted at this and other points.

6 Trueblood, *Experience and Artistic Expression*, p. 311.

7 This point is well made by Carreño, *Poesía selecta*, p. 56.

8 Carreño, *Poesía selecta*, p. 54. See also Carreño's detailed study of this poem in *Romancero lírico de Lope de Vega* (Madrid, 1979), pp. 158–70.

9 For the previous history of this poem, see Francisco Rico's preface to his edition of *El caballero de Olmedo* (Salamanca, 1970), pp. 23–42. Geoffrey

Hill's poem 'The Pentecost Castle' (*Collected Poems*, Harmondsworth, 1985, p. 137) opens with a fine paraphrase of these lines.

10 The texts of these last two poems are taken from Dámaso Alonso and J. M. Blecua, ed., *Antología de la poesía española: poesía de tipo tradicional* (Madrid, 1956), p. 198. The preface to this splendid anthology is still the best short account of Spanish popular poetry. The selection itself is supplemented by Margit Frenk Alatorre's equally fine *Lírica hispánica de tipo popular* (Mexico, 1966).

11 The 20 sonnets of the *Rimas* were first published in a volume which also included *Las lágrimas de Angélica* (The Tears of Angelica; see above, p. 73) and *La Dragontea*, Lope's epic poem on Francis Drake. They were reprinted separately, with additional poems, in 1604, and further expanded in 1609 by the addition of the famous *Arte nuevo de hacer comedias en este tiempo* (A New Art of Writing Plays in these Times).

12 'Conceptos esparcidos' clearly echoes the opening sonnet (*Rime* I) of Petrarch's *Canzoniere*: 'Voi ch'ascoltate in rime sparse...' (You who hear in scattered rhymes).

13 For the problem involved here, see chapter 1, n. 18.

14 Compare Petrarch, *Rime* III: 'era il giorno ch'al sol si scolorare / per la pietà del suo fattore i rai...' (It was the day when the sun's rays grew pale with grief for its Maker).

15 Randel, 'Proper Language', p. 224.

16 Compare Sonnet LXXX: 'Siento el error, no siento lo que digo; / a mí yo propio me parezco extraño; / pasan mis años, sin que llegue un año / que esté seguro yo de mí conmigo.' (I feel the error, I do not feel what I say; I seem a stranger to myself; my years go past, though no year comes when I might be certain of myself.)

17 See the excellent essay by F. Lázaro Carreter, 'Lope, poeta robado. Vida y arte en los sonetos de los mansos', in *Estilo barroco y personalidad creadora* (Madrid, 1977), pp. 149–67.

18 This sonnet, though closely associated with the others, is not included in the *Rimas*, but appears in a manuscript dating from 1593–1600. See Lázaro Carreter, 'Lope, poeta robado', p. 151, n. 4.

19 Lázaro ('Lope, poeta robado', pp. 162–4) gives an interesting account of the variants to this poem. In particular, the change from 'pastorcillo' (little shepherd) to 'mayoral' in the first line stresses the social differences between the speaker and the rival; the replacement of 'y su grosero paño' (and its/her coarse cloth) by 'de labrado estaño' (line 5) eliminates the incongruous reference to the woman and preserves the coherence of the pastoral fiction.

20 On this poem, see the article by E. George Erdman Jr, 'Lope de Vega's "De Absalón", a *laberinto de conceptos esparcidos*', *SP*, 65 (1968), pp. 753–67.

21 Two interesting articles have appeared on this poem: Leo Spitzer, 'Lope de Vega's "Al triunfo de Judit"', *MLN*, 69 (1954), pp. 1–11 and E. George Erdman Jr, 'The Source and Structure of Lope de Vega's *Al triunfo de Judit*', *HR*, 36 (1968), pp. 236–48.

272   *Notes to pages 104–118*

22 As Erdman points out, the fusion of the Old Testament story of Judith with the classical 'triumph' first occurs in Petrarch's *Trionfi*, whence it passes into the common stock of Renaissance poetry.

23 Compare the conclusion of a sonnet on a relic of St Lawrence: 'Ángeles, si la mesa le habéis puesto, / decilde que la carne coma aprisa, / que el más cristiano Rey espera un hueso.' (Angels, if you have laid the table, tell him to eat the meat quickly, for the most Christian King is awaiting a bone.)

24 Carreño, *Poesía selecta*, pp. 75–6.

25 Carreño, *Poesía selecta*, p. 36.

26 Both Lope and Gracián praise the famous lines by the Comendador Escrivá which appear in the *Cancionero general* of 1511: 'Ven muerte, tan escondida, / que no te sienta conmigo, / porque el gozo de contigo / no me torne a dar vida' (Death, come so secretly that I do not feel your presence, lest the pleasure of being with you bring me back to life). For Lope, this is a perfect example of a *concepto*; Gracián quotes the same four verses in Discourse XXIV of the *Agudeza y arte de ingenio* as a fine instance of paradox (I, p. 237).

27 The fullest account of Lope's part in the controversy is given in Orozco Díaz, *Lope y Góngora*, chapters 9–19. For the literary issues at stake, chapter 2 of Andrée Collard, *Nueva poesía* is especially valuable.

28 For a detailed, though at times overgenerous, discussion of these poems, see J. M. de Cossío, *Fábulas mitológicas en España* (Madrid, 1952), chapter 13. There is an excellent edition of *La Circe* by Charles V. Aubrun and Manuel Muñoz Cortés (Paris, 1962). (I leave Lope's attempts at the literary epic for a later chapter.)

29 For Lope's imitations of Góngora, see Dámaso Alonso, *Poesía española: ensayo de métodos y límites estilísticos* (Madrid, 1950), pp. 472–8 and Orozco Díaz, *Lope y Góngora*, pp. 335, 346 and 374. *La Circe* contains lines like 'es Venus de aquel mar, del sol estrella' (she is the Venus of that sea, the star of the sun) and 'desprecias el coral y pisas flores' (you scorn coral and tread on flowers). (Compare also the typical Góngora construction in the fourth line of the passage I quote below: 'mansas cristal y removidas nieve'.) As Dámaso Alonso points out, Lope is much less skilful than Góngora in his handling of hyperbaton, or displaced word-order.

30 Alonso, *Poesía española*, p. 489.

31 Trueblood, *Experience and Artistic Expression*, p. 195.

32 Trueblood, *Experience and Artistic Expression*, p. 201.

33 The general sense here is that Spain is impoverished compared with other nations. There is also an allusion to the copper currency (the *vellón*) which was introduced in 1599 as a desperate measure to stave off bankruptcy; by an edict of 1 August 1628, its value was halved.

34 Trueblood, *Experience and Artistic Expression*, pp. 587–8.

35 Trueblood, *Experience and Artistic Expression*, p. 600.

36 This is again a very miscellaneous collection, containing over 160 sonnets and a section of religious ballads and *villancicos*, as well as the

mock epic *La Gatomaquia*, which I shall discuss in a later chapter. Moreover, not all the sonnets are burlesque; in a number of them Burguillos writes 'de veras', i.e. 'seriously', as if in Lope's own voice.

37 Carreño, *Poesía selecta*, p. 399.

38 Andrés Sánchez Robayna, in his essay 'Petrarquismo y parodia (Góngora y Lope)', included in *Tres estudios sobre Góngora* (Barcelona, 1983), pp. 11–13, compares this sonnet with the early sonnet by Góngora, 'No destrozada nave en roca dura…', I quote in the previous chapter (see above, p. 67). He sees each poem as a simultaneous 'homage and profanation' – Octavio Paz's phrase – and argues very convincingly for a 'positive' notion of parody which actually enriches the tradition it demystifies.

39 Lope is fond of referring to 'natural art' (*arte natural*) and 'artificial nature' (*naturaleza artificiosa*). In Spanish poetry, the latter notion appears for the first time in Garcilaso (see above, p. 41); as has often been pointed out, this particular way of idealizing nature is ultimately neo-Platonic. See, for example, Ramón Menéndez Pidal, 'Lope de Vega, el *Arte Nuevo* y la *Nueva Biografía*', in *De Cervantes y Lope de Vega* (Buenos Aires, 1943), pp. 65–134.

40 Trueblood, *Experience and Artistic Expression*, p. 327.

5 BETWEEN TWO CENTURIES: FROM MEDRANO TO VALDIVIELSO

1 My texts are taken from Dámaso Alonso, ed., *Poesías* (Madrid, 1988) (referred to as DA). This is a scaled-down version of the splendid edition by Dámaso Alonso and Stephen Reckert, *Vida y obra de Medrano* II (Madrid, 1958), long out of print.

2 Dámaso Alonso, *Poesías*, p. 254.

3 The *lira* is the Spanish name for the five-line stanza which Garcilaso imitated from the Italian poet Bernardo Tasso (1493–1569) and used in his Fifth *Canción*, which begins 'Si de mi baja *lira*…' (If [the sound] of my humble lyre). It consists of a combination of eleven- and seven-syllable lines (7 + 11 + 7 + 7 + 11), rhyming AbAbB.

4 Compare the much wordier ending of Luis de León's version: 'Siempre será de mí Lálaje amada, / La del reír gracioso, / La del parlar muy más que miel sabroso' (Lalage will always be loved by me, she of the pleasant smile, she who speaks much more sweetly than honey).

5 The formation *mal* + adjective, spelt as a single word, is unusual in Spanish, though Medrano uses it frequently, probably by analogy with Italian *malsicuro* (insecure), etc. On this point, see Dámaso Alonso, *Vida y obra* I (Madrid, 1948), pp. 172–3.

6 Dámaso Alonso, *Vida y obra* I, p. 293.

7 As Dámaso Alonso points out (*Vida y obra* I, p. 181), Medrano's use of hyperbaton is more radical than that of any other poet writing before 1607, including Góngora – a sustained attempt, no doubt, to imitate the flexibility of classical Latin syntax.

8 Compare Dámaso Alonso's comment on this poem: 'Here we glimpse something like the beginnings of a new period in the artistic life of the poet: the period of full maturity, in which Medrano, now so certain of his independence that he does not even need to forego models in a show of self-sufficiency, uses the model as starting-point, retouching it slightly at one point or another, and using it as a springboard for fresh creation' (*Poesías*, p. 325).

9 See Stanko B. Vranich, ed., *Obra completa de Juan de Arguijo* (Madrid, 1985), p. 30. This edition (referred to as V) is an expanded version of Vranich's earlier edition – *Obra poética* (Madrid, 1971) – which prints the poems in a different order.

10 As Vranich explains (*Obra completa*, pp. 43–4), sometime between 1597 and 1603, Medina went over the text of sixty of the sonnets, suggesting numerous revisions, many of which Arguijo eventually adopted. Though there are interesting differences of criteria – Medina, though always extremely lucid, sometimes fails to see the particular aesthetic effect which Arguijo is trying to create – the detailed precision of such criticism is a fine example of the exacting standards which Herrera himself had done so much to establish.

11 Antonio Prieto, *La poesía española del siglo XVI* II (Madrid, 1987), p. 541.

12 Most of Rioja's poems are contained in a manuscript dated 1614 and the rest were probably written soon afterwards. There are two good recent editions: Gaetano Chiappini, ed., *Versos* (Florence, 1975) (bilingual Spanish–Italian text) and Begoña López Bueno, ed., *Poesía* (Madrid, 1984) (referred to as LB), from which my own texts are taken.

13 Chiappini, *Versos*, p. 87.

14 Quoted López Bueno, *Poesía*, pp. 45–6.

15 Chiappini, *Versos*, p. 134.

16 The five existing versions of this poem are reproduced in P. Blanco Suárez, ed., *Poetas de los siglos XVI y XVII* (Madrid, 1933). See also E. M. Wilson, 'Sobre la *Canción a las ruinas de Itálica* de Rodrigo Caro', *RFE*, 23 (1936), pp. 379–96 and Agustín del Campo, 'Problemas de la *Canción a Itálica*', *RFE*, 41 (1957), pp. 47–139.

17 Dámaso Alonso, *La 'Epístola moral a Fabio' de Andrés Fernández de Andrada* (Madrid, 1978).

18 Luis Cernuda, 'Tres poetas metafísicos', in *Prosa completa* (Barcelona, 1975), pp. 760–76. The phrase quoted occurs on p. 772.

19 The most accessible modern editions are those by J. M. Blecua: *Rimas* (Lupercio) (Madrid, 1972) and *Rimas* (Bartolomé), 2 vols. (Madrid, 1974) (referred to respectively as B, B, 1 and B, II).

20 The second stanza, with its use of the place name, is close to the opening of one of Horace's best-known Odes (I, ix): 'Vides ut alta stet nive candidum / Soracte...' (See how the snow lies deep on glittering Soracte).

21 Compare Horace, *Odes*, III, x, lines 2–4: '...me tamen asperas / porrectum ante foris obicere incolis / plorares Aquilonibus', which in

James Michie's version reads: '...you'd relent before / Letting me lie stretched out to shiver / In the blizzard before your hard hut-door' (*The Odes of Horace*, London, 1964, p. 173).

22 Marcus Valerius Martialis (c. AD 40–104), born at Bilbilis, near Saragossa, was regarded as an 'Aragonese' poet by the Argensolas and their contemporaries. Gracián – another Aragonese writer – frequently quotes him in the *Agudeza y arte de ingenio*, and refers to him at one point as the 'first-born of wit' (*el primogénito de la agudeza*) (I, p. 85).

23 The death of Margaret of Austria was commemorated by many poets of the time. Compare the sonnet by Góngora – one of three – quoted in chapter 2 (see above, pp. 54).

24 See Emilio Orozco Díaz, *Lope y Góngora frente a frente* (Madrid, 1973), pp. 347–53. Francisco de Borja y Aragón, Prince of Esquilache (1577–1658), a descendant of the Borgia family, was Viceroy of Peru from 1615 to 1621. He was a close friend of the Argensolas, and his own poetry, though much less distinctive, shares their concern with formal elegance and simplicity of diction. Lope includes one of Esquilache's eclogues in *La Circe* (1614) as an example of 'Castilian clarity' (B, pp. 1263–76).

25 Luis Rosales, *El sentimiento de desengaño en la poesía barroca* (Madrid, 1966), p. 194.

26 For Camões, see chapter 1, n. 30. There is a good account of the influence of Camões on sixteenth- and seventeenth-century Spanish poets in Rosales, *El sentimiento de desengaño*, pp. 134–205.

27 Gracián quotes Salinas twice in the *Agudeza y arte de ingenio* (I, p. 243 and II, p. 150), where he refers to him as 'the witty Conde de Salinas, ornament of knowledge and redeemer of the Spanish nobility'.

28 There is no complete edition of Salinas's poems. I quote from the excellent selection edited by Trevor J. Dadson, *Antología poética 1564–1630* (Madrid, 1985) (referred to as D).

29 Sidney, *Astrophil and Stella*, Sonnet 1 ('Loving in truth and fain in verse my love to show...').

30 I quote from Angélica Costa, ed., *Poesías completas* (Madrid, 1984) (referred to as AC). The earlier edition by Dámaso Alonso – *Poesías completas* (Madrid, 1936) – contains a fine preface, now reprinted in Alonso, *Estudios y ensayos gongorinos* (Madrid, 1955), pp. 395–412.

31 Dámaso Alonso, *Estudios*, p. 412.

32 This poem was printed for the first time by Emilio Orozco Díaz in his book *Amor, poesía y pintura en Carrillo y Sotomayor* (Granada, 1967), along with a detailed study of its nature and circumstances.

33 Angélica Costa, *Poesías completas*, pp. 31–2.

34 Juan Quirós de los Ríos and Francisco Rodríguez Marín, ed., *Primera parte...* (Seville, 1896). A Second Part, containing many of Espinosa's religious poems, was compiled by Juan Antonio Calderón, but remained in manuscript until 1896.

35 My texts are taken from Francisco López Estrada, ed., *Poesías completas* (Madrid, 1975) (referred to as LE).

36 Compare the fine sonnet on his recovery from a serious illness which begins 'Si un afecto, Señor, puedo ofrecerte...' (If, Lord, I can offer you a sign of love; B, I, p. 211).

37 The sonnet on Hell which begins 'Allí, negra región de la venganza...' (There, black region of vengeance; LE, p. 83) uses the Ignatian technique of 'composition of place' (see above, p. 14); at the other extreme, Espinosa occasionally uses popular devotional images, as in the example quoted in chapter 1 (see above, p. 14), where he describes God as the owner of a *Botillería*.

38 See my own article, 'Pedro de Espinosa and the Praise of Creation', *BHS*, 37 (1961), pp. 127–44.

39 Díaz Rengifo, *Arte poética española* (1592), quoted in J. M. Aguirre, *José de Valdivielso* (Toledo, 1965), pp. 68–9.

40 The first edition was expanded in 1618 and again in 1638. My quotations from the *Romancero espiritual* are taken from the excellent edition by J. M. Aguirre (Madrid, 1984). Referred to as A. Valdivielso's religious verse epic, the *Vida... de San Joseph* (Life of St Joseph), will be discussed in a later chapter.

41 Valdivielso contributed a laudatory sonnet to Salcedo Coronel's commentary on the *Soledades* (1636). For echoes of Góngora in his own verse, see Aguirre, *Romancero espiritual*, pp. xvii, 48 and 69.

6 FRANCISCO DE QUEVEDO: THE FORCE OF ELOQUENCE

1 Claudio Guillén, 'Quevedo y el concepto retórico de literatura', in *El primer Siglo de Oro: estudios sobre géneros y modelos* (Barcelona, 1988), p. 243.

2 J. H. Elliott, 'Quevedo and the Count-Duke of Olivares', in James Iffland, ed., *Quevedo in Perspective: Eleven Essays for the Quadricentennial* (Newark, Delaware, 1982), pp. 227–50.

3 The dating of much of Quevedo's poetry is very uncertain. James Crosby's fundamental study, 'Cronología de unos 300 poemas', in *En torno a Quevedo* (Madrid, 1967), pp. 95–177, provides reliable dates for nearly 300 poems – just under a third of Quevedo's total output. See also Roger Moore's more speculative account, *Towards a Chronology of Quevedo's Poetry* (New Brunswick, 1977).

4 Guillén, *El primer Siglo de Oro*, p. 235.

5 See, for example, the satirical verse-letter addressed to Olivares which begins 'No he de callar por más que con el dedo...' (I shall not keep silent, however much [you urge silence] with your finger): 'La robusta virtud era señora, / y sola dominaba al pueblo rudo; / edad, si mal hablada, vencedora...' (Robust virtue ruled, and alone dominated the rude people; an age, if rough-spoken, victorious; B, p. 142, lines 46–8).

6 Francisco de Quevedo, *Obras completas: prosa*, ed. L. Astrana Marín (subsequently referred to as *Prosa*) (Madrid, 1932), p. 589b.

7 For Quevedo's criticisms of Herrera, see Peter M. Komanecky, 'Quevedo's Notes on Herrera: the Involvement of Francisco de la Torre in the Controversy over Góngora', *BHS*, 52 (1975), pp. 122–33.

8 *Prosa*, p. 1482a.
9 Juan Boscán (1474?–1542) was a close friend of Garcilaso de la Vega and an earlier experimenter in Italianate metres and verse forms. His own poetry was deeply influenced by that of the great fifteenth-century Valencian poet Ausiàs March (1397–1459). Quevedo clearly knew Boscán's work – both poets have a sonnet which begins 'Cargado voy de mí…' (I go burdened with myself) – though the example of March may have reached him more directly, either through the Latin translation of his friend Vicente Mariner (1634) or in the better-known Spanish version of Jorge de Montemayor (1562). For some interesting parallels between Quevedo and March, see Lorna Close's excellent article, 'Petrarchism and the "Cancioneros" in Quevedo's Love Poetry: the Problem of Discrimination', *MLR*, 74 (1979), pp. 836–55.
10 See above, chapter 2, pp. 60–3.
11 Smith, *Quevedo on Parnassus*, p. 141.
12 *Prosa*, p. 1484b. The last phrase comes from Horace, *Odes*, iii, i.
13 James Iffland, *Quevedo and the Grotesque* (London, 1978), 2 vols. The quotation is taken from Philip Thomson, *The Grotesque* (London, 1972), p. 3.
14 The most scholarly edition of the poems is the one by José María Blecua: *Obra poética* (Madrid, 1969–71), 3 vols. My own references are to Blecua's more accessible one-volume edition, *Obras completas, I: poesía original* (Barcelona, 1963) (= B), a revised version of which appeared in 1968. James O. Crosby's anthology in the Cátedra series, *Poesía varia* (Madrid, 1981), is invaluable both for the accuracy of its texts and for the comprehensiveness of its notes.
15 Guillén, *El primer Siglo de Oro*, p. 264.
16 I reproduce the text as it appears in González de Salas's edition of 1648 (see below, n. 28). For later (and possibly spurious) versions of the second tercet, see Blecua, *Obras completas*, i, pp. lxx–lxxi. The noun 'nariz' (nose), though normally feminine, appears as masculine in the title, thus suggesting the man/nose identification on which the poem is based.
17 Maurice Molho, 'Una cosmogonía antisemita: "Érase un hombre a una nariz pegado", in James Iffland, *Quevedo in Perspective*, pp. 57–79.
18 Molho goes further than this and – in my opinion, overingeniously – sees the presence of two further symbolic configurations: one relating to Egypt (associated with the Pyramids, alchemy and sun worship), the other to Rome (Ovid, galleys), viewed as a civilization which distanced itself at the time from the events of the Trial and Crucifixion.
19 See above, chapter 5, pp. 137–8.
20 For an exhaustive and fascinating study of Quevedo's presentation of women, see Amédée Mas, *La Caricature de la Femme du Mariage et de l'Amour dans l'Oeuvre de Quevedo* (Paris, 1957). Mas, like other critics, attempts to explain Quevedo's mysogyny in biographical terms, an approach which inevitably leads to conflicting interpretations for which there is little basis in the poetry. There may well be some kind of

'emotional defence-mechanism' (Walters's phrase) at work which would also account for the distinctly anti-Petrarchan stance in some of the 'serious' love poems. From a more strictly literary point of view, Quevedo's obvious debt to the Roman satirists and to medieval anti-feminist writing can be taken as another sign of the conservatism to which I have already referred.

21 Mas, *La Caricature de la Femme*, pp. 84–9.

22 Lía Schwartz Lerner, 'De Marcial a Quevedo', in *Quevedo: discurso y representación* (Pamplona, 1986), pp. 133–57.

23 See Elias L. Rivers, *Quixotic Scriptures: Essays in the Textuality of Hispanic Literature* (Bloomington, Indiana, 1983), pp. 102–4 for a discussion of the sonnet which begins 'La voz del ojo que llamamos pedo' (That hole's voice we call a fart; B, p. 631) – a poem which is both scabrous and elegant, and ultimately very serious.

24 These lines from Persius are also quoted by A. A. Parker in 'La "agudeza" en algunos sonetos de Quevedo' (scc above, chapter 2, n. 47) in connection with the sonnet 'Con mudo incienso y grande ofrenda, ¡oh Licas!' (With mute incense and a great offering, oh Licas!; B, p. 106).

25 Lerner, *Quevedo: Discurso y representación*, p. 215.

26 I refer to Quevedo's mock epic *Las locuras de Orlando* (The Follies of Orlando) in the next chapter, pp. 197–8.

27 For a more comprehensive discussion of this sonnet, see César Nicolás, *Estrategias y lecturas: las anamorfosis de Quevedo* (Cáceres, 1986), pp. 28–50.

28 This edition, *El Parnaso español*, was prepared by Quevedo's friend, the humanist González de Salas. It is unfortunately incomplete, since it includes only six of the nine Muses; the remaining manuscripts were published in 1670 by Quevedo's nephew, Pedro de Aldrete, under the title *Las tres últimas Musas castellanas*.

29 Smith, *Quevedo on Parnassus*, p. 7.

30 Marino's sonnet is itself an imitation of Lope de Vega's 'Por las ondas del mar de unos cabellos...' (Through the sea waves of some tresses). See Dámaso Alonso, 'Lope despojado por Marino', *RFE*, 33 (1949), pp. 110–43 and 'Adjunta a Lope despojado por Marino', *RFE*, 33 (1949), pp. 165–8.

31 Smith, *Quevedo on Parnassus*, pp. 83–4.

32 The claims made by Otis H. Green in his influential monograph *Courtly Love in Quevedo* (Boulder, Colorado, 1952), have been righly attacked, notably by Mas, *La Caricature de la Femme*, pp. 300–6, and Close, 'Petrarchism and the "Cancioneros"', pp. 836–9.

33 This is a weakness of J. M. Pozuelo Yvancos's otherwise perceptive study *El lenguaje de la lírica amorosa de Quevedo* (Murcia, 1979).

34 Smith, *Quevedo on Parnassus*, p. 11.

35 For a fuller analysis of this sonnet, which comments interestingly on the differences between Quevedo and his Italian contemporaries, see Smith, *Quevedo on Parnassus*, pp. 155–60.

36 D. Gareth Walters, *Francisco de Quevedo, Love Poet* (Cardiff, 1985), p. 80.

37 Compare, for instance, the sonnet by Góngora (Millé, 357) entitled 'De una dama que, quitándose una sortija, se picó con un alfiler' (On a Lady who, in Removing a Jewel, Pricked Herself with a Pin), which begins: 'Prisión del nácar era articulado / de mi firmeza un émulo luciente, / un diamante, ingenïosamente / en oro también él aprisionado...' (A diamond shining imitator of my constancy, was the prison of the articulated pearl [i.e. finger] itself ingeniously imprisoned in gold).

38 In his recent edition of the Lisi cycle – *Poems to Lisi* (Exeter, 1988) – Gareth Walters presents a new ordering of the poems, based partly on *El Parnaso español* (see above, n. 28), but incorporating the fourteen sonnets first published in the much less reliable Aldrete edition of 1670. Though on present evidence no such arrangement can be definitive, Walters's examination of the stylistic similarities between certain otherwise unrelated poems and the kind of creative process these suggest is very convincing.

39 For more detailed analyses of this much-discussed poem, see, for example, Smith, *Quevedo on Parnassus*, pp. 171–5, Julián Olivares, *The Love Poetry of Francisco de Quevedo* (Cambridge, 1983), pp. 128–41, A. A. Parker, *The Philosophy of Love in Spanish Literature, 1480–1680* (Edinburgh, 1985), pp. 170–1, Carlos Blanco Aguinaga, '"Cerrar podrá mis ojos..."': tradición y originalidad', *Fi*, 8 (1962), pp. 57–78, and my own article, 'Quevedo and the Metaphysical Conceit', *BHS*, 35 (1958), pp. 211–22. (The last two items are included in Gonzalo Sobejano, ed., *Francisco de Quevedo*, Madrid, 1978, pp. 308–18 and 58–70 respectively.)

40 Close, 'Petrarchism and the "Cancioneros"', p. 854.

41 Compare the elegy by Propertius (II, xiiib) which begins 'Quando-cumque igitur nostros mors claudet ocellos...' (Whenever, therefore, death may close my eyes) and goes on: 'Non nihil ad verum conscia terra sapit' (line 28) (Earth is not entirely unconscious of truth).

42 The image of the flame swimming the waters of Hades has often been associated with the famous lines from Garcilaso's Dedication to his Third Eclogue: 'Mas con la lengua muerta y fría en la boca / pienso mover la voz a ti debida...' (But with my tongue dead and cold in my mouth I intend to raise the voice I owe to you) – both a Virgilian reminiscence and an allusion to the death of Orpheus.

43 Henry Ettinghausen, *Francisco de Quevedo and the Neostoic Movement* (Oxford, 1972).

44 Ettinghausen, *Francisco de Quevedo*, p. 74.

45 Compare Ovid, *Epistulae ex Ponto*, I, iii, lines 33–4: 'optat / fumum de patriis posse videre focis' (He would like to see the smoke of his native hearth), imitated by Joachim du Bellay (1522?–60), whom Quevedo had read. See the sonnet 'Heureux qui, comme Ulysse, a fait un beau voyage...' (Happy the man who, like Ulysses, has had a good journey), lines 5–8: 'Quand revoyray-je, hélas, de mon petit village / fumer sa cheminée, et en quelle saison / revoyray-je le clos de ma pauvre maison...' (When shall I see again, alas, the chimneys of my little village smoking, and in what season shall I see the garden of my humble house?)

46 Compare the similar passage from the *Sueño de Infierno* (Vision of Hell; 1608): 'On what do you turn your eyes, which does not remind you of death? Your clothes which wear out, the house which falls, the wall which grows old, and even your daily sleep reminds you of death and pictures it in itself' (*Prosa*, p. 155b).

47 See R. M. Price, 'A Note on the Sources and Structure of "Miré los muros de la patria mía"', *MLN*, 78 (1963), pp. 194–9 (included in Gonzalo Sobejano, ed., *Francisco de Quevedo* [see above, n. 39], pp. 319–25. Price gives good reasons for preferring the earlier text, though here I have used the better-known version.

48 Ettinghausen, *Francisco de Quevedo*, p. 15.

49 Compare the letter of 12 November 1612 to his friend Tomás Tamayo de Vargas: 'I... wicked and lustful, write of honest matters, and what I most regret is that these will lose their credit on my account and that the bad opinion which I have deserved will make men suspicious of my writings' (*Prosa*, p. 1366b).

50 See, for example, *Ephesians* 4.24: 'And that he put on the new man, which after God is created in righteousness and true holiness.' For a good discussion of this poem, see Ana María Snell, *Hacia el verbo: signos y transignificación en la poesía de Quevedo* (London, 1981), pp. 86–90.

51 I discuss Quevedo's unfinished religious epic *Poema heroico a Cristo resucitado* (Heroic Poem to Christ Resurrected) in the next chapter, p. 204. Quevedo also translated the first chapter of the *Lamentations of Jeremiah*, with commentaries and paraphrases in free verse, often of real poetic merit. The entire manuscript was published for the first time in the superb edition of E. M. Wilson and J. M. Blecua, *Lágrimas de Hieremías castellanas*, *RFE*, Anejo 55 (Madrid, 1953), which includes a long and fascinating introductory study.

52 The same idea is spelt out in a letter of 16 August 1635 to Manuel Serrano de Castillo: 'Today I am fifty-two years old, and in these years I reckon as many burials. My infancy died irrevocably; my childhood, my adolescence, my youth all died; now also my years of manhood have passed away. Then how may I call life an old age which is a grave, where I myself am the burial of five dead men whose lives I have lived?' (*Prosa*, p. 1532a).

53 Quoted by Tuve, *Elizabethan and Metaphysical Imagery*, pp. 32–3.

7 THE LITERARY EPIC

1 Quoted by Alistair Fowler, *Kinds of Literature: an Introduction to the Theory of Genres and Modes* (Oxford, 1982), p. 217.

2 On this point, see Weinberg, *A History of Literary Criticism*, II, p. 572.

3 C. S. Lewis, *A Preface to 'Paradise Lost'* (Oxford, 1942), p. 26.

4 R. D. Williams, 'The Poetic Intention of Virgil's *Aeneid*', in Charles Martindale, ed., *Virgil and his Influence* (Bristol, 1984), pp. 25–35. The quotation is from p. 28.

5 Lewis, *A Preface*, p. 39.

6 F. W. Pierce, 'The Poetic Hell in Hojeda's "La Cristiada": Imitation and Originality', in *Estudios dedicados a Don Ramón Menéndez Pidal*, IV (Madrid, 1953), pp. 469–508. See especially pp. 472–5.

7 On Lucan, see Hugh Lloyd-Jones, 'Roman Grand Guignol', *New York Review of Books*, 36 (18 January 1990), pp. 21–2.

8 Robert M. Durling, *The Figure of the Poet in Renaissance Epic* (Cambridge, Mass., 1965), p. 105.

9 Eugenio Donato, '"Per Selve e Boscherecci Labirinti": Desire and Narrative Structure in Ariosto's *Orlando Furioso*', in Parker and Quint, *Literary Theory*, pp. 33–62. The quotation comes from p. 58.

10 Durling, *The Figure of the Poet*, p. 176.

11 Torquato Tasso, *Discourses on the Heroic Poem*, trans. M. Cavalchini and I. Samuel (Oxford, 1973), p. 78.

12 Judith A. Kates, *Tasso and Milton: the Problem of Christian Epic* (London and Toronto, 1983), p. 80.

13 For Camões, see Frank Pierce's introduction to his excellent edition of *Os Lusíadas* (Oxford, 1973), pp. vii–xxxvii.

14 Maxime Chevalier, *L'Arioste en Espagne (1530–1650). Recherches sur l'influence du 'Roland furieux'* (Bordeaux, 1966), p. 149.

15 Maxime Chevalier, *Lecturas y lectores en la España de los siglos XVI–XVII* (Madrid, 1976), pp. 122–4.

16 See Antonio Vilanova's monumental study *Las fuentes y los temas del 'Polifemo' de Góngora*, RFE, Anejo 66, 2 vols. (Madrid, 1957), I, p. 46. The same is true of the poems by Valdivielso and Hojeda discussed in the final section of this chapter.

17 The first Spanish translations of the *Orlando Furioso* and the *Gerusalemme Liberata* date from 1549 and c. 1585 respectively.

18 For Góngora's parody of *La hermosura de Angélica* in his poem 'Angélica y Medoro', see above, p. 73.

19 On this point, see F. W. Pierce, 'L'allégorie poétique au XVIᵉ siècle: son évolution at son traitement par Bernardo de Balbuena', *BH*, 51 (1949), pp. 381–406 and 52 (1950), pp. 191–227, especially p. 214. The article contains an extensive discussion of the question of allegory which I touch on in the next paragraph.

20 See Pierce, 'L'allégorie poétique', pp. 205–6.

21 My text is taken from Cayetano Rosell, ed., *Poemas épicos*, I, *BAE*, XVII (Madrid, 1851; 1945 reprint), pp. 139–399. Page references are to this edition.

22 Chevalier, *L'Arioste*, p. 395.

23 As well as the *Isidro* and *La Gatomaquia*, which I discuss later in this chapter, Lope wrote two other epic poems, *La Dragontea* (1598), on Sir Francis Drake, and *Corona trágica* (The Tragic Crown; 1627), on Mary, Queen of Scots, neither of great literary merit. For a brief discussion of these poems, see Frank Pierce, *La poesía épica del Siglo de Oro*, 2nd edn (Madrid, 1968), pp. 298 and 303.

24 It is clear from the text that Lope knew both the *Gerusalemme Liberata* and its less successful revised version, the *Gerusalemme Conquistata* (1593).

25 Manuel José Quintana, 'Sobre la poesía épica castellana', in Quintana, *Obras completas, BAE*, XIX (Madrid, 1852; 1946 reprint), pp. 158–73.

26 See J. de Entrambasaguas, ed., *La Jerusalén Conquistada*, 3 vols. (Madrid, 1951–4), to which my page numbers refer, and Frank Pierce's fine review article, 'The Literary Epic and Lope's *Jerusalén Conquistada*', *BHS*, 33 (1956), pp. 93–8.

27 Rafael Lapesa, 'La *Jerusalén* del Tasso y la de Lope', in *De la Edad Media a nuestros días* (Madrid, 1967), pp. 264–85.

28 The text of *La Mosquea* is included in Cayetano Rosell, *Poemas épicos*, I, pp. 571–624. There is also a good modern edition by José María Balcells (Madrid, 1983).

29 Chevalier, *L'Arioste*, p. 396.

30 Text from Blecua, *Obras completas*, I, pp. 1333–84, to which page numbers refer.

31 References are to the excellent edition by Celina Sabor de Cortazar, CCa (Madrid, 1982).

32 Inez Macdonald, 'Lope de Vega's *Gatomaquia*', *Atlante*, 2 (1954), pp. 27–44.

33 See Pierce, *La poesía épica*, p. 318.

34 Kates, *Tasso and Milton*, p. 10.

35 Page references are to F. C. Sainz de Robles, ed., Lope de Vega, *Obras escogidas II: verso y prosa*, 4th edn (Madrid, 1964).

36 The text is included in Cayetano Rosell, ed., *Poemas épicos*, II, *BAE*, XXIX (Madrid, 1853; 1948 reprint), pp. 137–244. Page references are to this edition.

37 On the fortunes of the 'short epic', or *canto épico*, see Frank Pierce, 'The *canto épico* of the Seventeenth and Eighteenth Centuries', *HR*, 15 (1947), pp. 1–48.

38 On this point, see Pierce, 'The Poetic Hell', pp. 490–1.

39 The text is included in Cayetano Rosell, *Poemas épicos*, I, pp. 401–501, to which page numbers refer. There is a better, though less accessible, edition by Sister M. H. P. Corcoran (Washington, D.C., 1935). See also the excellent selection by Frank Pierce in the Anaya series (Salamanca, 1971).

40 Frank Pierce, 'Diego de Hojeda, Religious Poet', in *Homenaje al Prof. William L. Fichter* (Madrid, 1971), pp. 585–99. The quotation is from p. 589.

8 PLENITUDE AND DECLINE: FROM VILLAMEDIANA TO THE SECOND HALF OF THE CENTURY

1 J. M. Rozas, ed., *Obras*, CCa (Madrid, 1969) (referred to as R). Quotation from p. 27. Rozas has also published Villamediana's early poetry in *Cancionero de Méndez Britto: poesías inéditas del Conde de Villamediana* (Madrid, 1965).

2 For a fuller discussion of this poem in the context of other seventeenth-

century love poetry, see my article, 'Thought and Feeling in Three Golden Age Sonnets', *BHS*, 59 (1982), pp. 237–46.

3 Rosales, *El sentimiento del desengaño*, pp. 197–8.

4 As Rozas explains (*Obras*, p. 32), the full version of the *Adone* was not published until 1623, a year after Villamediana's death. However, a shorter version had been circulating in manuscript for some years previously, and Villamediana is likely to have seen this in the course of his stay in Italy (1611–15). Another of Villamediana's mythological fables, *La Europa*, is to all intents and purposes a translation from Marino.

5 Gareth A. Davies, *A Poet at Court: Antonio Hurtado de Mendoza (1586–1644)* (Oxford, 1971). The remark quoted occurs on p. 43.

6 My texts are taken from R. Benítez Claros, ed., *Obras*, 3 vols. (Madrid, 1948) (referred to as BC).

7 Mendoza is the chief exponent of what Davies calls the 'Manzanarian idyll', the type of pastoral associated with the Royal Palace on the banks of the Manzanares in Madrid. See Davies, *A Poet at Court*, pp. 94–5, 109–17.

8 Davies, *A Poet at Court*, p. 111.

9 Juan de Jáuregui (1583–1641), as we have already seen, was a major participant in the Góngora controversy (see above, p. 82). His own early poems (*Rimas*, 1618), written before the impact of Góngora, show him to have been an excellent minor poet in the Italianate manner, and his verse translation of Tasso's *Aminta* (1607) was justly admired by his contemporaries. His reservations concerning *culteranismo* did not prevent him from making extensive use of *cultismos* in his *Orfeo* (1624), one of the most brilliant and successful of the seventeenth-century imitations of Ovid. The text of the *Orfeo* is contained in Pablo Cabañas, *El mito de Orfeo en la literatura española* (Madrid, 1948).

10 Trevor J. Dadson, ed., *La lira de las musas* (Madrid, 1988) (referred to as D). Quotation from p. 48.

11 Compare Garcilaso, *Canción* v, lines 34–5: 'al remo condenado, / en la concha de Venus amarrado' (condemned to the oar, bound to Venus's shell).

12 Emilio Orozco Díaz, *Introducción a un poema barroco granadino. De las 'Soledades' gongorinas al 'Paraíso' de Soto de Rojas* (Granada, 1955), p. 9.

13 On the garden/poem as an expression of the Granadine spirit (*granadinismo*), see Orozco Díaz, *Introducción*, pp. 135–42. García Lorca's splendid lecture, 'En homenaje a Soto de Rojas' (*Obras completas*, 5th edn, Madrid, 1963, pp. 1531–37), first delivered in 1926, also emphasizes the characteristic taste for the miniature and the fragmentary.

14 Quoted by Orozco Díaz, *Introducción*, pp. 85–6.

15 Aurora Egido, ed., *Paraíso cerrado para muchos, jardines abiertos para pocos; los fragmentos de Adonis* (Madrid, 1981) (referred to as E). The phrase quoted occurs on p. 27.

16 Orozco Díaz, *Introducción*, pp. 65–6.

17 On the seventeenth-century garden poem in general, see J. M. Cohen's

chapter 'Gardens and Landscapes' in *The Baroque Lyric* (London, 1963), pp. 89–108, which compares the *Paraíso* interestingly with Marvell's 'Upon Appleton House' and with poems by Marino, Saint-Amant and Théophile de Viau.

18 Kenneth Brown, *Anastasio Pantaleón de Ribera (1600–29). Ingenioso miembro de la república literaria española* (Madrid, 1950), p. 135. Brown's excellent book also includes a scrupulous edition of Pantaleón's collected poems (referred to as B), from which my own texts are taken.

19 J. M. de Cossío, *Obras escogidas* (Madrid, 1931), p. 78.

20 My texts are taken from Francisco J. Díez de Revenga, ed., *Poesía; Hospital de incurables* (Madrid, 1987) (referred to as DR).

21 The text of the sonnet is taken from J. Simón Díaz, ed., *Obras varias*, 2 vols. (Madrid, 1947) (referred to as SD).

22 Text from *Cítara de Apolo, Primera parte* (Apollo's Zither, First Part; 1681). There is no modern edition. For a recent study of Salazar as poet and theatre writer, see Thomas O'Connor, 'Language, Irony and Death. The Poetry of Salazar y Torres', *RF*, 90 (1978), pp. 60–9.

23 Robert Jammes, 'L'imitation poétique chez Francisco de Trillo y Figueroa', *BH*, 58 (1956), pp. 457–81.

24 Text from A. Gallego Morell, ed., *Obras* (Madrid, 1951) (referred to as GM).

25 Here, the refrain is traditional, and appears in the *Romancero general*, no. 921. Both the dactylic rhythm and the parallelistic construction are typical of the Galician–Portuguese tradition. Trillo's skill here consists in matching the refrain with the slightly irregular, song-like, metre of the intervening stanzas.

26 J. M. de Cossío, *Fábulas mitológicas en España* (Madrid, 1952), p. 659.

27 Text from J. M. Blecua, ed., *Cancionero de 1628, RFE*, Anejo 32 (Madrid, 1945), pp. 207–19. Nothing is known of Adrián de Prado except that he was a member of the Hieronymite Order. The 'Canción a San Jerónimo' was first published in Seville in 1619; the *Cancionero de 1628* also includes a second, unfinished, *canción* which shows the same mastery of pictorial detail (*Cancionero*, pp. 29–35).

28 Compare the comment of the young Aragonese poet Juan Nadal on the posthumous publication of the Argensolas' collected poems in 1634: 'I shall be glad if the work of the Leonardos appears quickly and meets with the reception which its authors deserve, but since the poetry will not be in the present-day manner, I fear they will not please' (letter to Andrés de Ustarroz, August 1634).

29 Villegas's only volume of poetry, *Las eróticas o amatorias* (Erotic or Amatory Poems), was published in 1615. His mastery of the seven-syllable line and his experiments in quantitative verse are unique at this period, and his poetry was to prove a major influence on the eighteenth-century neoclassical writers. Though his formal skill is undeniable, the content of his poems is often trivial and repetitive and reveals a general softening of classical discipline. There is a modern edition of the *Eróticas*

by N. Alonso Cortés (Madrid, 1913). For an interesting reassessment, see Francisco Ynduráin, 'Villegas, revisión de su poesía', in *Relección de clásicos* (Madrid, 1969), pp. 39–52.

30 The presence of Gracián must also have encouraged the *conceptista* aspect of their work. In the *Agudeza* (see above, pp. 60–3), Gracián frequently quotes examples of *conceptos* from contemporary Aragonese poets, and it seems that he had a hand in choosing the poems for Josef Alfay's important anthology *Poesías varias de grandes ingenios españoles* (Saragossa, 1654). See J. M. Blecua's preface to his edition of Alfay (Saragossa, 1946), pp. ix–xv.

31 Aurora Egido, *La poesía aragonesa del siglo XVII (raíces culteranas)* (Saragossa, 1979).

32 Aurora Egido has edited the *Rimas* of Juan de Moncayo (Madrid, 1976) and Dicastillo's *Aula de Dios, Cartuja Real de Zaragoza* (Saragossa, 1978).

33 Egido, *La poesía aragonesa*, p. 211.

34 From *Navidades en Zaragoza, divididas en quatro noches* (Christmas in Saragossa, Divided into Four Nights; 1634), quoted by Egido, *La poesía aragonesa*, pp. 244–5.

35 María del Pilar Palomo, *La poesía de la Edad Barroca* (Madrid, 1975), p. 96.

36 See E. M. Wilson, 'A Key to Calderón's *Psalle et sile*', in Frank Pierce, ed., *Hispanic Studies in Honour of I. González Llubera* (Oxford, 1959), pp. 429–40. There is a good facsimile edition of *Psalle et sile* by L. Trevor Paravicino and J. de Entrambasaguas (Valencia, 1939).

37 A much earlier poem, the fine elegy on the death of Inés Zapata, is included in the *Cancionero de 1628* (see n. 27 above), pp. 618–20.

38 From *Academias morales de las musas* (Moral Academies of the Muses; 1642), p. 71. There is no modern edition, but a number of Henríquez Gómez's poems are included in *BAE*, XLII (Madrid, 1923), pp. 363–91.

39 Kenneth R. Scholberg's definitive study, *La poesía religiosa de Miguel de Barrios* (Ohio, 1962), contains a good selection of the religious poems (referred to as S), from which my texts are taken.

40 E. M. Wilson, 'La poesía de João Pinto Delgado', in *Entre las jarchas y Cernuda: constantes y variables en la poesía española* (Barcelona, 1977), pp. 223–44. (This article originally appeared in English in *Journal of Jewish Studies*, 1 (1949), pp. 131–43.)

41 My texts are taken from I. S. Révah, ed., *Poema de la Reina Ester* (Lisbon, 1954) (referred to as R).

42 A. D. H. Fishlock, 'The Shorter Poems of João Pinto Delgado', *BHS*, 31 (1954), pp. 127–40. The phrase in question occurs on p. 131.

9 SOR JUANA INÉS DE LA CRUZ: THE END OF A TRADITION

1 For examples of the work of these and other poets, see Octavio Paz, ed., *Anthologie de la poésie mexicaine* (Paris, 1952).

2 The phrase occurs on p. 4 of Trueblood's excellent bilingual selection,

A Sor Juana Anthology (Cambridge, Mass., and London, 1988). For further discussion, see my article 'Human and Divine Love in the Poetry of Sor Juana Inés de la Cruz', in R. O. Jones, ed., *Studies in Spanish Literature of the Golden Age Presented to E. M. Wilson* (London, 1973), on which I have drawn in this and the following sections.

3 My texts are taken from A. Méndez Plancarte, ed., *Obras completas*, 4 vols. (Mexico, 1951–7), to which the numbering of the poems corresponds. There is also an excellent edition of Sor Juana's first published collection, *Inundación castálida* (Flood from the Castalian Spring), by Georgina Sabat de Rivers (Madrid, CCa, 1982). This volume contains most of the shorter poems, though not the *Primero sueño*.

4 Carlos Blanco Aguinaga, 'Dos sonetos del siglo XVII: Amor-Locura en Quevedo y Sor Juana', *MLN*, 77 (1962), pp. 145–62.

5 Ramón Xirau, *Genio y figura de Sor Juana Inés de la Cruz* (Buenos Aires, 1967), p. 32.

6 Octavio Paz, *Sor Juana Inés de la Cruz o las trampas de la fe* (Barcelona, 1982), a work to which I am much indebted. There is now an English version, *Sor Juana, or, the Traps of Faith*, trans. Margaret Sayers Peden (Cambridge, Mass., and London, 1988).

7 For details of the performance of the *villancicos*, see Sabat de Rivers, *Inundación castálida*, pp. 54–63. There is also a good discussion of the *villancicos* in Dario Puccini, *Sor Juana Inés de la Cruz; studio d'ua personalità del Barocco messicano* (Rome, 1967), pp. 145–86.

8 Puccini, *Sor Juana Inés de la Cruz*, p. 148.

9 Méndez Plancarte, *Obras completas*, I, p. 452.

10 Méndez Plancarte, *Obras completas*, I, p. 453 points to the parallel with St Teresa's famous paradox, 'Que muero porque no muero' (I die since I do not die).

11 Quoted by Paz, *Sor Juana Inés de la Cruz*, p. 471.

12 For a comprehensive study of the possible sources, see Georgina Sabat de Rivers, *El 'Sueño' de Sor Juana Inés de la Cruz: tradiciones literarias y originalidad* (London, 1977), pp. 23–124.

13 This is borne out by Rosa Perelmuter Pérez's recent study of the poem's language, *Noche intelectual: la oscuridad idiomática en el 'Primero sueño'* (Mexico, 1982). Perelmuter's systematic exploration of Sor Juana's use of *cultismos* and hyperbaton shows conclusively how in matters of lexicon the poem is less indebted to Góngora than is usually assumed, and how its syntax, far from being a passive imitation, is genuinely creative in a way which is acknowledged by seventeenth-century poetic theory.

14 Paz, *Sor Juana Inés de la Cruz*, p. 482.

15 Paz, *Sor Juana Inés de la Cruz*, p. 482.

16 It is often assumed that the *Primero sueño* is so named by analogy with the *Soledad primera* of Góngora, though the word 'primero' here may have as much to do with the repeatable nature of the dream. The word, however, may have been added by the original editor; in the *Respuesta*, Sor Juana herself simply refers to the poem as *El sueño*.

17 For a lighter, though no less pointed, version of Sor Juana's feminist stance, see the famous poem (92) on male hypocrisy which begins: 'Hombres necios que acusáis / a la mujer sin razón, / sin ver que sois la ocasión / de lo mismo que culpáis: // si con ansia sin igual / solicitáis su desdén, / ¿por qué queréis que obren bien / si las incitáis al mal?...' (Foolish men who accuse women without reason, without seeing that you are the occasion for the very thing you blame: if with unequalled keenness you court their scorn, why do you want them to act well if you encourage them to be bad?)

18 Trueblood's anthology (see above, n. 2) includes the whole of the *Respuesta* in a good English version, from which my quotation is taken.

EPILOGUE

1 For the reputation of Góngora in the eighteenth century, see the important article by Nigel Glendinning, 'La fortuna de Góngora en el siglo xviii', *RFE*, 44 (1961), pp. 323–49.

Select bibliography

ANTHOLOGIES

Alatorre, Margit Frenk, ed. *Lírica hispánica de tipo popular*, Universidad Nacional Autónoma de México, 1966
Alonso, Dámaso and Blecua, J. M., ed. *Antología de la poesía española: poesía de tipo tradicional*, Madrid, Gredos, 1956
Blanco Suárez, P., ed. *Poetas de los siglos XVI y XVII*, Madrid, Junta para Ampliación de Estudios, 1933
Paz, Octavio, ed. *Anthologie de la poésie mexicaine*, Paris, UNESCO, 1952
Rivers, Elias L., ed. *Renaissance and Baroque Poetry of Spain* (with English prose translations), 3rd edn, Illinois, Waveland Press, 1988
Rosell, Cayetano, ed. *Poemas épicos* I, *BAE* XVII, Madrid, 1851 (1945 reprint); *Poemas épicos* II, *BAE* XXIX, Madrid, 1853 (1948 reprint)
Terry, Arthur, ed. *An Anthology of Spanish Poetry, 1500–1700*, Pt II (1580–1700), Oxford, Pergamon, 1968

EDITIONS USED IN THE TEXT

Alfay, Josef (compiler). *Poesías varias de grandes ingenios españoles*, ed. J. M. Blecua, Saragossa, Institución 'Fernando el Católico', 1946
Argensola, Bartolomé Leonardo de. *Rimas*, ed. J. M. Blecua, 2 vols., Madrid, Espasa-Calpe, CC, 1974
Argensola, Lupercio Leonardo de. *Rimas*, ed. J. M. Blecua, Madrid, Espasa-Calpe, CC, 1972
Arguijo, Juan de. *Obra poética*, ed. Stanko B. Vranich, Madrid, Castalia, CCa, 1971
    Obra completa, ed. Stanko B. Vranich, Madrid, Albatros/Hispanófila, 1985
Bocángel, Gabriel. *La lira de las musas*, ed. Trevor J. Dadson, Madrid, Cátedra, LH, 1988
Camões, Luis de. *Os Lusíadas*, ed. Frank Pierce, Oxford, Clarendon Press, 1973
Cancionero de 1628. Ed. J. M. Blecua, *RFE*, Anejo 32, Madrid, 1945
Carrillo y Sotomayor, Luis. *Poesías completas*, ed. Angélica Costa, Madrid, Cátedra, LH, 1984

Cruz, Sor Juana Inés de la. *Obras completas*, ed. A. Méndez Plancarte, 4 vols., Mexico, Fondo de Cultura Económica, 1951–7

Inundación castálida, ed. Georgina Sabat de Rivers, Madrid, Castalia, CCa, 1982

A Sor Juana Anthology, ed. Alan Trueblood, Cambridge, Mass. and London, Harvard University Press, 1988

Dicastillo, Miguel de. *Aula de Dios, Cartuja Real de Zaragoza...*, ed. Aurora Egido, Saragossa, Institución 'Fernando el Católico', 1978

Espinosa, Pedro de. *Poesías completas*, ed. F. López Estrada, Madrid, Espasa-Calpe, CC, 1975

Espinosa, Pedro de (compiler). *Primera parte de flores de poetas ilustres de España*, ed. Juan Quirós de los Ríos and Francisco Rodríguez Marín, Seville, Sociedad de Bibliófilos Andaluces, 1896

Góngora, Luis de. *Obras completas*, ed. R. Foulché-Delbosc, 3 vols., New York, Hispanic Society of North America, 1921

Obras completas, ed. J. and I. Millé y Jiménez, Madrid, Aguilar, 1943

Gracián, Baltasar. *Agudeza y arte de ingenio*, ed. E. Correa Calderón, 2 vols., Madrid, Castalia, CCa, 1969

Hojeda, Diego de. *La Cristiada*, ed. Sister M. H. P. Corcoran, Washington, D.C., Doctoral dissertation, 1935

La Cristiada, ed. Frank Pierce, Salamanca, Anaya, 1971

Hurtado de Mendoza, Antonio. *Obras*, ed. R. Benítez Claros, 3 vols., Madrid, CSIC, 1948

López de Zárate, Francisco. *Obras varias*, ed. J. Simón Díaz, 2 vols., Madrid, CSIC, 1947

Medrano, Francisco de. *Poesías*, ed. Dámaso Alonso, Madrid, Cátedra, LH, 1988

Moncayo, Juan de. *Rimas*, ed. Aurora Egido, Madrid, Espasa-Calpe, CC, 1976

Pinto Delgado, João. *Poema de la Reina Ester, Lamentaciones del Profeta Jeremías, Historia de Rut y varias poesías*, ed. I. S. Révah, Lisbon, Institut Français en Portugal, 1954

Polo de Medina, Jacinto. *Obras escogidas*, ed. J. M. Cossío, Madrid, Los Clásicos Olvidados, 1931

Poesía; Hospital de incurables, ed. Francisco J. Díez de Revenga, Madrid, Cátedra, LH, 1987

Quevedo, Francisco de. *Obra poética*, ed. J. M. Blecua, 3 vols., Madrid, Castalia, 1969–71

Obras completas I: poesía original, ed. J. M. Blecua, Barcelona, Planeta, 1963

Poesía varia, ed. James O. Crosby, Madrid, Cátedra, LH, 1981

Poems to Lisi, ed. D. Gareth Walters, University of Exeter Hispanic Texts, 1988

Lágrimas de Hieremias castellanas, ed. E. M. Wilson and J. M. Blecua, RFE, Anejo 55, Madrid, 1953

Obras completas: prosa, ed. L. Astrana Marín, Madrid, Aguilar, 1932

Rioja, Francisco de. *Versos*, ed. Gaetano Chiappini, Florence, D'Anna, 1975
   Poesía, ed. Begoña López Bueno, Madrid, Cátedra, LH, 1984
Salinas, Conde de. *Antología poética 1564–1630*, ed. Trevor J. Dadson,
   Madrid, Visor, 1985
Soto de Rojas, Pedro. *Paraíso cerrado para muchos, jardines abiertos para pocos; los
   fragmentos de Adonis*, ed. Aurora Egido, Madrid, Cátedra, LH, 1981
Tasso, Torquato. *Discourses on the Heroic Poem*, tr. M. Cavalchini and I.
   Samuel, Oxford University Press, 1973
Trillo y Figueroa, Francisco. *Obras*, ed. A. Gallego Morell, Madrid, CSIC,
   1951
Valdivielso, José de. *Romancero espiritual*, ed. J. M. Aguirre, Madrid, Espasa-
   Calpe, CC, 1984
Vega, Lope de. *Obras poéticas* I, ed. J. M. Blecua, Barcelona, Planeta, 1969
   Obras escogidas II: verso y prosa, ed. F. C. Sáinz de Robles, Madrid,
   Aguilar, 1964
   Poesía selecta, ed. Antonio Carreño, Madrid, Cátedra, LH, 1984
   La Circe, ed. Charles V. Aubrun and M. Muñoz Cortés, Paris, Centre de
   Recherches de l'Institut d'Etudes Hispaniques, 1962
Villegas, Esteban Manuel de. *Eróticas*, ed. N. Alonso Cortés, Madrid,
   Espasa-Calpe, CC, 1913
Villamediana, Conde de. *Obras*, ed. J. M. Rozas, Madrid, Castalia, CC,
   1969
   Cancionero de Mendes Britto: poesías inéditas, ed. J. M. Rozas, Madrid,
   CSIC, 1965

GENERAL STUDIES

Alonso, Dámaso. *Poesía española: ensayo de métodos y límites estilísticos*, Madrid,
   Gredos, 1950; 2nd ed, revised, 1952
Blecua, J. M. *Sobre poesía de la Edad de Oro (ensayos y notas eruditas)*, Madrid,
   Gredos, 1970
Braudel, Fernand. *The Mediterranean and the Mediterranean World in the Age of
   Philip II*, trans. Siân Reynolds, 2 vols., London, Fontana/Collins, 1975
   [1973]
Chevalier, Maxime. *L'Arioste en Espagne (1530–1650)*, Bordeaux, Féret, 1966
   Lecturas y lectores en la España de los siglos XVI–XVII, Madrid, Turner, 1976
Cohen, J. M. *The Baroque Lyric*, London, Hutchinson, 1963
Collard, Andrée, *Nueva poesía: conceptismo, culteranismo en la crítica española*,
   Madrid, Cátedra, 1967
Cossío, J. M. de. *Fábulas mitológicas en España*, Madrid, Espasa-Calpe, 1952
Crosbie, John. *A lo divino Lyric Poetry: an Alternative View*, University of
   Durham Modern Languages Series, 1989
Domínguez Ortiz, Antonio. *El antiguo régimen: los Reyes Católicos y los Austrias*,
   Madrid, Alianza, 1973
Elliott, J. H. *Imperial Spain, 1469–1716*, London, Arnold, 1963
   Spain and its World, 1500–1700, New Haven and London, Yale University
   Press, 1989

Guillén, Claudio. *El primer Siglo de Oro: estudios sobre géneros y modelos*, Barcelona, Crítica, 1988

Hatzfeld, Helmut. *Estudios sobre el Barroco*, Madrid, Gredos, 1964

Jones, R. O. *A Literary History of Spain: the Golden Age: Prose and Poetry*, London, Arnold, 1971

Kamen, Henry. *The Iron Century: Social Change in Europe, 1550–1660*, London. Weidenfeld and Nicolson, 1976, 1971

Lapesa, Rafael. *De la Edad Media a nuestros días*, Madrid, Gredos, 1967

Lázaro Carreter, F. *Estilo barroco y personalidad creadora*, Madrid, Cátedra, 1977

López Bueno, Begoña. *La poética cultista de Herrera a Góngora*, Seville, Alfar, 1987

Menéndez Pidal, Ramón. *De Cervantes a Lope de Vega*, Buenos Aires, Espasa-Calpe, Colección Austral, 1943

Romancero hispánico, 2 vols., Madrid, Espasa-Calpe, 1953

Orozco Díaz, Emilio. *Temas del barroco*, Universidad de Granada, 1947

Palomo, María del Pilar. *La poesía de la Edad Barroca*, Madrid, Sociedad General Española de Librería, Colección 'Temas', 1975

La poesía en la edad de oro (barroco), Madrid, Taurus, 1987

Parker, A. A. 'An Age of Gold: Expansion and Scholarship in Spain', in *The Age of the Renaissance*, ed. Denis Hay, London, Thames and Hudson, 1967, pp. 221–48

The Philosophy of Love in Spanish Literature, 1480–1680, Edinburgh University Press, 1985

Pierce, Frank. *La poesía épica del Siglo de Oro*, Madrid, Gredos, 2nd edn, 1968

Porqueras Mayo, A. *La teoría poética en el Renacimiento y el Manierismo españoles*, 2 vols., Barcelona, Puvill, 1986–9

Priesto, Antonio. *La poesía española del siglo XVI* II, Madrid, Cátedra, 1987

Quintana, Manuel José. 'Sobre la poesía épica castellana', in *Obras completas*, *BAE*, XIX, Madrid, 1852 (1946 reprint)

Rivers, Elias L. *Quixotic Scriptures: Essays in the Textuality of Hispanic Literature*, Bloomington, University of Indiana Press, 1983

Rodríguez-Moñino, Antonio. *Construcción crítica y realidad histórica en la poesía española de los siglos XVI y XVII*, Madrid, Castalia, 1965

Rosales, Luis. *El sentimiento de desengaño en la poesía barroca*, Madrid, Ediciones Cultura Hispánica, 1966

Russell, P. E. *Temas de 'La Celestina'*, Barcelona, Ariel, 1978

Russell, P. E., ed. *Spain: a Companion to Spanish Studies*, London, Methuen, 1973

Sánchez, José. *Academias literarias del Siglo de Oro*, Madrid, Gredos, 1961

Smith, Paul Julian. *Writing in the Margin: Spanish Literature of the Golden Age*, Oxford, Clarendon Press, 1988

The Body Hispanic: Gender and Sexuality in Spanish and Spanish American Literature, Oxford, Clarendon Press, 1989

Vilanova, Antonio, 'Preceptistas españoles de los siglos XVI y XVII', in

Historia general de las literaturas hispánicas III, ed. G. Díaz-Plaja, Barcelona, Barna, 1953, pp. 567–692

Wardropper, B. W. *Historia de la poesía lírica a lo divino en la cristiandad occidental*, Madrid, Revista de Occidente, 1958

Whinnom, Keith. *La poesía amatoria cancioneril en la época de los Reyes Católicos*, University of Durham Modern Languages Series, 1981

Wilson, E. M. *Entre las jarchas y Cernuda: constantes y variantes en la poesía española*, Barcelona, Ariel, 1977

Ynduráin, Francisco. *Relección de clásicos*, Madrid, Prensa Española, 1969

STUDIES OF INDIVIDUAL POETS

Aguirre, J. M. *José de Valdivielso*, Toledo, Diputación Provincial, 1965

Alonso, Dámaso. *Estudios y ensayos gongorinos*, Madrid, Gredos, 1955
La 'Epístola moral a Fabio' de Andrés Fernández de Andrada, Madrid, Gredos, 1978

Alonso, Dámaso and Reckert, Stephen. *Vida y obra de Medrano*, 2 vols., Madrid, CSIC, 1948 and 1958

Artigas, Miguel de. *Don Luis de Góngora y Argote: biografía y estudio crítico*, Madrid, Revista de Archivos, 1925

Beverley, John. *Aspects of Góngora's 'Soledades'*, Purdue University Monographs in Romance Languages, Amsterdam, Benjamins, 1980

Brown, Kenneth. *Anastasio Pantaleón de Ribera (1600–29). Ingenioso miembro de la República literaria española*, Madrid, Porrúa, 1980

Calcraft, R. P. *The Sonnets of Luis de Góngora*, University of Durham Modern Languages Series, 1980

Carreño, Antonio. *El romancero lírico de Lope de Vega*, Madrid, Gredos, 1979

Crosby, James O. *En torno a Quevedo*, Madrid, Castalia, 1967

Davies, Gareth A. *A Poet at Court: Antonio Hurtado de Mendoza (1586–1644)*, Oxford, Dolphin, 1971

Egido, Aurora. *La poesía aragonesa del siglo XVII (raíces culteranas)*, Saragossa, Institución 'Fernando el Católico', 1979

Ettinghausen, Henry. *Francisco de Quevedo and the Neostoic Movement*, Oxford University Press, 1972

Gallego Morell, A., ed. *Garcilaso y sus comentaristas*, Universidad de Granada, 1966

Green, Otis H. *Courtly Love in Quevedo*, Boulder, Colorado, University of Colorado Press, 1952

Heathcote, A. Antony. *Vicente Espinel*, Boston, Twayne, 1977

Herrera, Fernando de. *Respuesta a las observaciones del Prete Jacopín*, Seville, Sociedad de Bibliófilos Andaluces, 1870

Ife, B. W. *Dos versiones de Píramo y Tisbe*, University of Exeter Hispanic Texts, 1974

Iffland, James. *Quevedo and the Grotesque*, 2 vols., London, Tamesis, 1978

Iffland, James, ed. *Quevedo in Perspective: Eleven Essays for the Quadricentennial*, Newark, Delaware, Juan de la Cuesta, 1982

Jammes, Robert. *Études sur l'oeuvre poétique de Don Luis de Góngora y Argote*, Bordeaux, Féret, 1967

Kelley, Emilia N. *La poesía metafísica de Quevedo*, Madrid, Guadarrama, 1973

Lerner, Lía Schwartz. *Quevedo: discurso y representación*, Pamplona, Universidad de Navarra, 1986

Macrí, Oreste. *Fernando de Herrera*, Madrid, Gredos, 1959

Mas, Amédée. *La caricature de la femme du mariage et de l'amour dans l'oeuvre de Quevedo*, Paris, Ediciones Hispano-Americanas, 1957

Molho, Maurice. *Sémantique et poétique: à propos des Solitudes de Góngora*, Bordeaux, Ducros, 1969

Moore, Roger. *Towards a Chronology of Quevedo's Poetry*, New Brunswick, York Press, 1977

Nicolás, César. *Estrategias y lecturas: las anamorfosis de Quevedo*, *AEF*, Anejo 5, Cáceres, Universidad de Extremadura, 1986

Olivares, Julián. *The Love Poetry of Francisco de Quevedo*, Cambridge University Press, 1983

Orozco Díaz, Emilio. *Introducción a un poema barroco granadino. De las 'Soledades' gongorinas al 'Paraíso' de Soto de Rojas*, Universidad de Granada, 1953

Orozco Díaz, Emilio. *Amor, poesía y pintura en Carrillo y Sotomayor*, Universidad de Granada, 1963

Lope y Góngora frente a frente, Madrid, Gredos, 1973

Parker, A. A. *Luis de Góngora, 'Polyphemus and Galatea': a Study in the Interpretation of a Baroque Poem*, Edinburgh University Press, 1985

Paz, Octavio. *Sor Juana Inés de la Cruz o las trampas de la fe*, Barcelona, Seix Barral, 1982; English version, *Sor Juana, or, the Traps of Faith*, trans. Margaret Sayers Peden, Cambridge, Mass. and London, Harvard University Press, 1988

Perelmuter Pérez, Rosa. *Noche intelectual: la oscuridad intelectual en el 'Primero Sueño'*, Universidad Nacional Autónoma de México, 1982

Pozuelo Yvancos, J. M. *El lenguaje de la lírica amorosa de Quevedo*, Universidad de Murcia, 1979

Puccini, Dario. *Sor Juana Inés de la Cruz: studio d'una personalità del Barocco messicano*, Rome, Edizione dell'Ateneo, 1967

Sabat de Rivers, Georgina. *El 'Sueño' de Sor Juana Inés de la Cruz: tradiciones literarias y originalidad*, London, Tamesis, 1977

Sánchez Robayna, Andrés. *Tres estudios sobre Góngora*, Barcelona, Llibres del Mall, 1986

Scholberg, Kenneth R. *La poesía religiosa de Miguel de Barrios*, Ohio State University Press, 1962

Smith, Paul Julian. *Quevedo on Parnassus: Allusive Context and Literary Theory in the Love-Lyric*, MHRA Texts and Dissertations, vol. 25, London, MHRA, 1987

Snell, Ana María. *Hacia el verbo: signos y transignificación en la poesía de Quevedo*, London, Tamesis, 1981

Sobejano, Gonzalo, ed. *Francisco de Quevedo*, Madrid, Taurus, 1978

Trueblood, Alan. *Experience and Artistic Expression in Lope de Vega: the Making of 'La Dorotea'*, Cambridge, Mass., Harvard University Press, 1974

Vilanova, Antonio. *Las fuentes y los temas del 'Polifemo' de Góngora*, 2 vols., *RFE*, Anejo 66, 1957

Walters, D. Gareth. *Francisco de Quevedo, Love Poet*, Cardiff, University of Wales Press, 1985

Woods, M. J. *The Poet and the Natural World in the Age of Góngora*, Oxford University Press, 1978

Xirau, Ramón. *Genio y figura de Sor Juana Inés de la Cruz*, Editorial Universitaria de Buenos Aires, 1967

OTHER WORKS MENTIONED

Broadbent, J. B. *Poetic Love*, London, Chatto and Windus, 1964

Cave, Terence. *The Cornucopian Text: Problems of Writing in the French Renaissance*, Oxford, Clarendon Press, 1979

Dronke, Peter. *Medieval Latin and the Rise of European Love-Lyric*, 2 vols., Oxford, Clarendon Press, 1965

The Medieval Lyric, London, Hutchinson, 1968

Durling, Robert M. *The Figure of the Poet in Renaissance Epic*, Cambridge, Mass., Harvard University Press, 1965

Forster, Leonard. *The Icy Fire: Five Studies in European Petrarchism*, Cambridge University Press, 1969

Fowler, Alistair. *Conceited Thought*, Edinburgh University Press, 1975

Kinds of Literature: an Introduction to the Theory of Genres and Modes, Oxford, Clarendon Press, 1982

Furbank, P. N. *Reflections on the Word 'Image'*, London, Secker and Warburg, 1970

Gardner, Helen, ed. *The Metaphysical Poets*, Harmondsworth, Penguin, 1957

Greenblatt, Stephen. *Renaissance Self-Fashioning: from More to Shakespeare*, University of Chicago Press, 1980

Greene, Thomas M. *The Light in Troy: Imitation and Discovery in Renaissance Poetry*, New Haven and London, Yale University Press, 1982

Hawkes, Terence. *Metaphor*, London, Methuen, The Critical Idiom 25, 1972

Kates, Judith A. *Tasso and Milton: the Problem of Christian Epic*, Toronto and London, Bucknell University Press and Associated University Presses, 1983

Kelly, Douglas. *Medieval Imagination: Rhetoric and the Poetry of Courtly Love*, Madison, University of Wisconsin Press, 1978

Lewis, C. S. *The Allegory of Love*, Oxford University Press, 1936

Martz, Louis L. *The Poetry of Meditation: a Study of English Literature in the Seventeenth Century*, New Haven and London, Yale University Press, 1954; 2nd edn, 1962

Parker, Patricia and Quint, David, ed. *Literary Theory/Renaissance Texts*, Baltimore and London, The Johns Hopkins Press, 1986

Tayler, Edward W. *Nature and Art in Renaissance Literature*, New York, Columbia University Press, 1964

Topsfield, L. T. *The Troubadours and Love*, Cambridge University Press, 1975

Tuve, Rosemond. *Elizabethan and Metaphysical Imagery*, Chicago University Press, 1947

Vickers, Brian. *In Defence of Rhetoric*, Oxford, Clarendon Press, 1988

Weinberg, Bernard. *A History of Literary Criticism in the Italian Renaissance*, 2 vols., University of Chicago Press, 1961

Wellek, René. *Concepts of Criticism*, New Haven and London, Yale University Press, 1963

Index